DOMESDAY BOOK

Worcestershire

History from the Sources

DOMESDAY BOOK

A Survey of the Counties of England

LIBER DE WINTONIA

Compiled by direction of

KING WILLIAM I

Winchester
1086

DOMESDAY BOOK

General editor

JOHN MORRIS

16

Worcestershire

edited by

Frank and Caroline Thorn

from a draft translation prepared by

Elizabeth Whitelaw and Sara Wood

PHILLIMORE
Chichester
1982

1982

Published by

PHILLIMORE & CO. LTD.,
London and Chichester

Head Office: Shopwyke Hall,
Chichester, Sussex, England

ISBN 0 85033 161 7 (case)

ISBN 0 85033 161 5 (limp)

Printed in Great Britain by
Titus Wilson & Son Ltd.,
Kendal

WORCESTERSHIRE

History from the Sources
General Editor: John Morris

The series aims to publish history written directly from the sources for all interested readers, both specialists and others. The first priority is to publish important texts which should be widely available, but are not.

DOMESDAY BOOK

The contents, with the folio on which each county begins, are:

Domesday Book is termed *Liber de Wintonia* (The Book of Winchester) in column 332c

INTRODUCTION

The Domesday Survey

In 1066 Duke William of Normandy conquered England. He was crowned King, and most of the lands of the English nobility were soon granted to his followers. Domesday Book was compiled 20 years later. The Saxon Chronicle records that in 1085

> at Gloucester at midwinter ... the King had deep speech with his counsellors ... and sent men all over England to each shire ... to find out ... what or how much each landholder held ... in land and livestock, and what it was worth ... The returns were brought to him.[1]

William was thorough. One of his Counsellors reports that he also sent a second set of Commissioners 'to shires they did not know, where they were themselves unknown, to check their predecessors' survey, and report culprits to the King.'[2]

The information was collected at Winchester, corrected, abridged, chiefly by omission of livestock and the 1066 population, and fair-copied by one writer into a single volume. Norfolk, Suffolk and Essex were copied, by several writers, into a second volume, unabridged, which states that 'the Survey was made in 1086'. The surveys of Durham and Northumberland, and of several towns, including London, were not transcribed, and most of Cumberland and Westmorland, not yet in England, was not surveyed. The whole undertaking was completed at speed, in less than 12 months, though the fair-copying of the main volume may have taken a little longer. Both volumes are now preserved at the Public Record Office. Some versions of regional returns also survive. One of them, from Ely Abbey,[3] copies out the Commissioners' brief. They were to ask

> The name of the place. Who held it, before 1066, and now?
> How many *hides*?[4] How many ploughs, both those in lordship and the men's?
> How many villagers, cottagers and slaves, how many free men and Freemen?[5]
> How much woodland, meadow and pasture? How many mills and fishponds?
> How much has been added or taken away? What the total value was and is?
> How much each free man or Freeman had or has? All threefold, before 1066, when King William gave it, and now; and if more can be had than at present?

The Ely volume also describes the procedure. The Commissioners took evidence on oath 'from the Sheriff; from all the barons and their Frenchmen; and from the whole Hundred, the priests, the reeves and six villagers from each village'. It also names four Frenchmen and four Englishmen from each Hundred, who were sworn to verify the detail.

The King wanted to know what he had, and who held it. The Commissioners therefore listed lands in dispute, for Domesday Book was not only a tax-assessment. To the King's grandson, Bishop Henry of Winchester, its purpose was that every 'man should know his right and not usurp another's'; and because it was the final authoritative register of rightful possession 'the natives called it Domesday Book, by analogy

[1] Before he left England for the last time, late in 1086. [2] Robert Losinga, Bishop of Hereford 1079-1095 (see *E.H.R.* 22, 1907, 74). [3] *Inquisitio Eliensis,* first paragraph. [4] A land unit, reckoned as 120 acres. [5] *Quot Sochemani.*

from the Day of Judgement'; that was why it was carefully arranged by Counties, and by landholders within Counties, 'numbered consecutively ... for easy reference'.[6]

Domesday Book describes Old English society under new management, in minute statistical detail. Foreign lords had taken over, but little else had yet changed. The chief landholders and those who held from them are named, and the rest of the population was counted. Most of them lived in villages, whose houses might be clustered together, or dispersed among their fields. Villages were grouped in administrative districts called Hundreds, which formed regions within Shires, or Counties, which survive today with minor boundary changes; the recent deformation of some ancient county identities is here disregarded, as are various short-lived modern changes. The local assemblies, though overshadowed by lords great and small, gave men a voice, which the Commissioners heeded. Very many holdings were described by the Norman term *manerium* (manor), greatly varied in size and structure, from tiny farmsteads to vast holdings; and many lords exercised their own jurisdiction and other rights, termed *soca*, whose meaning still eludes exact definition.

The Survey was unmatched in Europe for many centuries, the product of a sophisticated and experienced English administration, fully exploited by the Conqueror's commanding energy. But its unique assemblage of facts and figures has been hard to study, because the text has not been easily available, and abounds in technicalities. Investigation has therefore been chiefly confined to specialists; many questions cannot be tackled adequately without a cheap text and uniform translation available to a wider range of students, including local historians.

Previous Editions

The text has been printed once, in 1783, in an edition by Abraham Farley, probably of 1250 copies, at Government expense, said to have been £38,000; its preparation took 16 years. It was set in a specially designed type, here reproduced photographically, which was destroyed by fire in 1808. In 1811 and 1816 the Records Commissioners added an introduction, indices, and associated texts, edited by Sir Henry Ellis; and in 1861-1863 the Ordnance Survey issued zincograph facsimiles of the whole. Texts of individual counties have appeared since 1673, separate translations in the Victoria County Histories and elsewhere.

This Edition

Farley's text is used, because of its excellence, and because any worthy alternative would prove astronomically expensive. His text has been checked against the facsimile, and discrepancies observed have been verified against the manuscript, by the kindness of Miss Daphne Gifford of the Public Record Office. Farley's few errors are indicated in the notes.

[6] *Dialogus de Scaccario* 1,16.

The editor is responsible for the translation and lay-out. It aims at what the compiler would have written if his language had been modern English; though no translation can be exact, for even a simple word like 'free' nowadays means freedom from different restrictions. Bishop Henry emphasized that his grandfather preferred 'ordinary words'; the nearest ordinary modern English is therefore chosen whenever possible. Words that are now obsolete, or have changed their meaning, are avoided, but measurements have to be transliterated, since their extent is often unknown or arguable, and varied regionally. The terse inventory form of the original has been retained, as have the ambiguities of the Latin.

Modern English commands two main devices unknown to 11th century Latin, standardised punctuation and paragraphs; in the Latin, *ibi* ('there are') often does duty for a modern full stop, *et* ('and') for a comma or semi-colon. The entries normally answer the Commissioners' questions, arranged in five main groups, (i) the place and its holder, its hides, ploughs and lordship; (ii) people; (iii) resources; (iv) value; and (v) additional notes. The groups are usually given as separate paragraphs.

King William numbered chapters 'for easy reference', and sections within chapters are commonly marked, usually by initial capitals, often edged in red. They are here numbered. Maps, indices and an explanation of technical terms are also given. Later, it is hoped to publish analytical and explanatory volumes, and associated texts.

The editor is deeply indebted to the advice of many scholars, too numerous to name, and especially to the Public Record Office, and to the publisher's patience. The draft translations are the work of a team; they have been co-ordinated and corrected by the editor, and each has been checked by several people. It is therefore hoped that mistakes may be fewer than in versions published by single fallible individuals. But it would be Utopian to hope that the translation is altogether free from error; the editor would like to be informed of mistakes observed.

The maps are the work of Frank Thorn and Jim Hardy.

The preparation of this volume has been greatly assisted by a generous grant from the Leverhulme Trust Fund.

This support, originally given to the late Dr. J. R. Morris, has been kindly extended to his successors. At the time of Dr. Morris's death in June 1977, he had completed volumes 2, 3, 11, 12, 19, 23, 24. He had more or less finished the preparation of volumes 13, 14, 20, 28. These and subsequent volumes in the series were brought out under the supervision of John Dodgson and Alison Hawkins, who have endeavoured to follow, as far as possible, the editorial principles established by John Morris.

Conventions

★ refers to note on discrepancy between MS and Farley text

[ ] enclose words omitted in the MS ( ) enclose editorial explanation

WIRECESTRESCIRE.

172 a

IN CIVITATE WIRECESTRE HABEBAT REX EDW̄
hanc c̄suetudinē. Quando moneta uertebat: q̄sq; moneta
rius dabat . xx . solid ad lundoniā p cuneis monetæ accipiend.
Quando comitat geldabat: p . xv . hid se ciuitas adqetab.
De ead ciuitate habeb ipse rex . x . lib . 7 comes Eduin . VIII . lib.
Nullā aliā c̄suetudinē ibi rex capiebat: pter censū domoz
sicut unicuiq; ptinebat.

Modo hī Rex . W . in dn̄io . 7 partē regis 7 partē comitis.
Inde reddit uicecom . XXIII . lib 7 v . sol ad pensum . de ciuitate
7 de dn̄icis Maner regis redd . c . XXIII . lib . 7 IIII . sol ad pensū.
De comitatu ū redd . XVII . lib ad pensū.
7 adhuc redd . x . lib denarioz de . xx . in ora . aut accipitrem norresc.
7 adhuc . c . solid reginæ ad numerū . 7 xx ti . sol de . xx ti . in ora p sumario.
Hæ . XVII . libræ ad pensū . 7 XVI . lib ad numerū: sunt de placitis
comitat 7 Hundretis . 7 si inde n̄ accipit: de suo ppo reddit.
In ipso comitatu sunt . XII . hund . hoz . VII . ita sunt quieti
sic̄ scira dicit: qd uicecom nichil habet in eis . 7 idō sic̄ dicit
in firma multū pdit.
In hoc comitatu Siqs scienter fregerit pacē quā rex manu
sua dederit: vtlaghe iudicatur . Pacē ū regis quā uice
comes dat siqs sciens fregerit: c . solid emendabit.
Forestellū q fecerit: c . solid emd . Heinfarā q fecerit: c . solid.
Raptū qui fecerit: n̄ fit emendatio alia nisi de corpore iusticia.
Has forisfacturas hī rex in isto comitatu . excepta tra S petri
Westmonasterii . cui donauit rex . E . quicqd ibi habuit
ut comitatus dicit.

WORCESTERSHIRE

[C] [WORCESTERSHIRE CUSTOMS] 172 a

1 In the City of WORCESTER King Edward had this customary due: whenever the coinage was changed each moneyer gave 20s at London for receiving the dies for the coinage. Whenever the County paid tax the city settled for 15 hides. Also from this city the King used to have £10 himself and Earl Edwin £8. The King received no other customary due from it except for the dues on the houses as each was liable.

2 Now King William has in lordship both the King's part and the Earl's part. For these the Sheriff pays £23 5s by weight from the city, and from the King's lordship manors he pays £123 4s by weight. From the County he pays £17 by weight. He pays a further £10 of pence at 20 to the *ora*, or a Norwegian hawk, and a further 100s at face value to the Queen and 20s at 20 (pence) to the *ora* for a packhorse. These £17 by weight and £16 at face value are from the pleas of the County and from the Hundreds, and if he does not receive them from there he pays from his own resources.

3 In the County itself there are 12 Hundreds; 7 of them are exempt, as the Shire states, so that the Sheriff has nothing in them and therefore, as he states, he loses much in revenue.

4 In this County if anyone has knowingly broken the peace which the King has given with his hand, he is judged an outlaw. If anyone has knowingly broken the King's peace which the Sheriff gives, he will be fined 100s. A man who has committed highway robbery is fined 100s; a man who has committed housebreaking, 100s; a man who has committed rape pays no penalty other than corporal punishment. The King has these forfeitures from this County, with the exception of the land of St. Peter's, Westminster, to which King Edward granted whatever (rights) he had there, as the County states.

Quando rex in hostē ꝑgit:⁄ siq̃s edictu ei⁹ uocat⁹ remanserit. si ita liber hō est ut habeat socā suā 7 sacā. 7 cū tra sua possit ire quo uoluerit:⁄ de omi tra sua. ē in miscđia regis. Cui⁹cunq; ů alterius dn̄i liber homo si de hoste remanserit. & dn̄s ei⁹ ꝓ eo aliū hominē duxerit:⁄ XL. solid dn̄o suo qui uocat⁹ fuit emdabit. Qđ si ex toto nullus ꝓ eo abierit:⁄ ipse q̃dem dn̄o suo. XL. solid dabit. dn̄s autē ei⁹ totid solid regi emdabit.

HIC ANNOTANT TENENTES TERRĀ IN WIRECESTRE SCIRE.

.I. REX WILLELMVS.
.II. Æccła de Wirecestre.
.III. Ep̄s de Hereford.
.IIII. Æccła S dyonisii.
.V. Æccła de Couentreu.
.VI. Æccła de Cormelies.
.VII. Æccła de Glouuecestre.
.VIII Æccła de Westmonast.
.IX. Æccła de Persore.
.X. Eccła de Euesham.
.XI. Ep̄s Baiocensis.
.XII Æccła S Guthlaci.
.XIII Clerici de Wrehantone.
.XII. Comes Rogerius.
.XV. Radulfus de Todeni.
.XVI. Radulfus de Mortemer.
.XVII. Robertus de Stadford.
.XVIII. Rogerius de Laci.
.XIX. Osbernus filius Ricardi.
.XX. Gislebert⁹ filius Turoldi.
.XXI. Drogo filius ponz.
.XXII. Herald⁹ filius Radulfi.
.XXIII. Willelm⁹ filius Ansculfi.
.XXIIII Willelm⁹ filius Corbucion.
.XXV. Willelmus Goizenboded.
.XXVI. Vrso de Abetoth.
XXVII. Hugo Lasne.
.XXVIII Eldeue.

5 Whenever the King marches against the enemy, if anyone when called up by his proclamation has stayed behind, if he is a free man so that he has full jurisdiction and can go with his land where he would, he is at the King's mercy with all his land. But if a free man of any other lord has stayed away from the enemy and his lord has taken another man in his place, the man who was (first) called up will pay a 40s fine to his lord. But if no one at all has gone in his place, he will give 40s himself to his lord, and his lord will pay a fine of as many shillings to the King.

LIST OF LANDHOLDERS IN WORCESTERSHIRE

1 King William
2 Worcester Church
3 The Bishop of Hereford
4 St. Denis' Church
5 Coventry Church
6 Cormeilles Church
7 Gloucester Church
8 Westminster Church
9 Pershore Church
10 Evesham Church
11 The Bishop of Bayeux
12 St. Guthlac's Church
13 The Clergy of Wolverhampton
14 Earl Roger
15 Ralph of Tosny
16 Ralph of Mortimer
17 Robert of Stafford
18 Roger of Lacy
19 Osbern son of Richard
20 Gilbert son of Thorold
21 Drogo son of Poyntz
22 Harold son of Ralph
23 William son of Ansculf
24 William son of Corbucion
25 William Goizenboded
26 Urso of Abetot
27 Hugh Donkey
28 Aldeva

TERRA REGIS.

Rex. W. ten in dnio BREMESGRAVE. cu XVIII. berew.
Museleie. Nortune. Lindeorde. Warthuil. Witeurde.
Hundesfelde. Thessale. Weredeshale. Lea. Comble. Bericote.
Asseberga. Tothehel. Tuneslega. Focheberie. Suruehel.
Vdecote. Timbrehangre. Int oms simul cu m. sunt. xxx. hidæ.
Hoc m tenuit Eduin comes. T.R.E.
In dnio sunt m. II. car. 7 xx. uilli. 7 ppositus 7 bedellus cu pbro
7 quater xx 7 XII. bord. Int oms hnt. LXXVII. car.
Ibi. IX. serui. 7 I. ancilla. 7 III. molini. de. XIII. solid. 7 IIII. den.
Silua. VII. leuu lg. 7 IIII. leuu lat. 7 ibi. IIII. æiræ acci
pitru. Huic m ptin. XIII. salinæ in Wich. 7 III. salinarii.
reddtes de his salinis. CCC. mittas salis. qbz dabant T.R.E.
CCC. caretedes lignoz á custodibz siluæ. Ibi sunt. VI. plubi.
Ad hoc m ptinuit SVCHELEI Maner de. V. hid. T.R.E.
sed. W. comes inde abstulit 7 posuit in firma de Hereford.
Int totu. T.R.E. reddeb. XVIII. lib de firma.
Vrso uicecom reddid. XXIIII. lib ad peis. du habuit silua.

Ad hoc m ptinuit 7 ptinet GRASTONE. Ibi. III. hid 7 dim.
7 COCHESEI Ibi. II. hidæ 7 dim. 7 WILLINGEWIC. Ibi. II.
hidæ 7 III. uirg. 7 CELDVIC. Ibi. III. hidæ. Int tot XII.
hidæ una v min.
Has tras tenuer. v. teini Eduini com. Erniet. Aluuin Bric
tredus. Frane. Aluuold. nec poterant recede a dno manerii.
Modo ten has tras. IIII. milites de Vrsone uicecomite.
Roger. III. hid 7 dim. Vills. II. hid 7 dim. Walter. II. hid 7 III. virg.
Alured. III. hid.
In his tris sunt in dnio. v. car 7 dim. 7 un radchenistre
7 XXIX. bord. hntes. XI. car 7 dimid. Ibi. II. serui. 7 VI. bouarii.
7 I. car plus posset. ee. In Willingeuuic 7 Celduuic sunt. III.
leuuedes siluæ. sed in foresta posuit rex. In Wich. I. salina de. x. sol.
Int tot T.R.E. ualb. VI. lib 7 XIII. sol. Modo. C. sol int tot.

[1] LAND OF THE KING 172 b

[In CAME Hundred]

1a King William holds BROMSGROVE in lordship with 18 outliers: MOSELEY, (Kings) NORTON, 'LINDSWORTH', WYTHALL, WYTHWOOD, HOUNDSFIELD, 'TESSALL', REDNAL, LEA (Green), 'COMBLE', BURCOT, ASHBOROUGH, TUTNALL, 'TYNSALL', ROCKBURY, 'SHURVENHILL', WOODCOTE (Green), TIMBERHANGER. 30 hides between them, including the manor. Earl Edwin held this manor before 1066. Now in lordship 2 ploughs; A 162-

20 villagers, a reeve and a beadle with a priest and 92 smallholders; between them they have 77 ploughs. 9 male slaves, 1 female. 167

3 mills at 13s 4d; woodland 7 leagues long and 4 leagues wide; 4 hawks' eyries.

To this manor belong 13 salt-houses in Droitwich, and 3 salt-workers who pay 300 measures of salt from these salt-houses. Before 1066, 300 cartloads of timber were given them by the keepers of the woodland. 6 lead vats.

1b Before 1066 SUCKLEY, a manor of 5 hides, belonged to this manor, but Earl William took it away from here and placed it in the revenue of Hereford.

In total, it paid £18 in revenue before 1066. Urso the Sheriff paid £24 by weight, so long as he had the woodland.

1c To this manor belonged and belong GRAFTON, 3½ hides; COOKSEY (Green), 2½ hides; 'WILLINGWICK', 2 hides and 3 virgates; CHADWICK, 3 hides. In total, 12 hides, less 1 virgate.

Five thanes of Earl Edwin held these lands: Erngeat, Alwin, Brictred, Fran, Alfwold; they could not withdraw from the lord of the manor. Now four men-at-arms hold these lands from Urso the Sheriff: Roger, 3½ hides; William, 2½ hides; Walter, 2 hides and 3 virgates; Alfred, 3 hides. In these lands, in lordship 5½ ploughs;

1 riding-man and 29 smallholders who have 11½ ploughs. 2 slaves; 6 ploughmen; 1 more plough would be possible.

In 'WILLINGWICK' and CHADWICK are 3 leagues of woodland, but the King has put them in the Forest. In Droitwich 1 salt-house at 10s.

In total, value before 1066 £6 13s; now 100s, in total.

De tra eid m ten Wills . f . Ansculfi . III . virg jn Willingeuuic.
7 Balduin de eo . Vluuin tenuit tein com Eduini . Ibi . e un uills
cu dimid car . 7 una car 7 dim plus posset . ee . Valuit . v . sol . m . II . sol.

Rex . W . ten in dnio *CHIDEMINSTRE* . cu . XVI . Bereuuich.
Wenuertun . Trinpelei . Worcote . Frenesse 7 alia Frenesse . Bristi
tune . Harburgelei . Fastochesfelde . Gurbehale . Ribeford . 7 alia
Ribeford . Sudtone . Aldintone . Mettune . Teulesberge . Suduuale
In his tris simul cu m sunt . xx ti . hidæ . Hoc m fuit tot Wastu.
In dnio . e . I . car . 7 xx . uilli 7 xxx . bord cu . XVIII . car . 7 adhuc
. xx ti . car plus ibi possunt . ee . Ibi . II . serui . 7 IIII . ancillæ . 7 II . mo
lini de . XVI . solid . 7 II . salinæ de . xxx . solid . 7 piscaria de . c.
denar . Silua de . IIII . leuuis . In hoc m ten ppposit tra uni
Radchen . 7 ibi ht . I . car . 7 molin de . v . oris.
Ad hoc m ptin una dom in Wich . 7 alia in Wirecestre redd . x . den.
Tot m T.R.E . reddeb . XIIII . lib de firma . Modo . redd . x . lib.
7 IIII . solid ad peis. Silua hui m posuit rex in foresta.
De tra hui m ten Wills . I . hid . 7 tra uni Radchenistre.
7 ibi ht . I . uillm 7 VIII . bord . hntes . IIII . car 7 dimid . Val . XI . sol.
De ead tra ten Aiulf una v . Ibi . I . car . 7 II . serui . Val . II . sol.

In *WICH* habuit rex . E . dom . XI . 7 in . v . puteis . habeb rex . E.
sua parte . In . I . puteo Vpeuuic . LIIII . salinæ . 7 II . hocci redd . VI . sol.
7 VIII . den . In alio puteo Helperic . XVII . salinæ . In . III . puteo
MIDELWIC . XII . salinæ 7 . II . partes de uno hocco redd . VI . sol
7 VIII . den . In . v . aliis puteis . xv . salinæ.
De his omib3 habeb rex . E . de firma . LII . lib.

172 c

In ipsis puteis habeb Eduin com . LI . salina 7 dimid . 7 de hoccis
habeb . VI . solid 7 VIII . denar . Hoc tot reddeb de firma XXIIII . lib.
Modo ht rex . W . in dnio 7 qd rex . E . 7 qd com . E . habeb.
Inde redd uicecom . LXV . lib ad peis . 7 II . mittas salis du
silua habuit . Si eni silua non ht : nullo m ut dicit n redde potest.

1d Also of this manor's land William son of Ansculf holds 3 virgates in 'WILLINGWICK', and Baldwin from him. Wulfwin, a thane of Earl Edwin, held them.

1 villager with ½ plough; 1½ more ploughs would be possible.
The value was 5s; now 2s.

[In CRESSLAU Hundred]

2 King William holds KIDDERMINSTER in lordship, with 16 outliers: WANNERTON, TRIMPLEY, HURCOTT, FRANCHE, another FRANCHE, *BRISTITUNE*, HABBERLEY, *FASTOCHESFELDE*, WRIBBENHALL, RIBBESFORD, another RIBBESFORD, SUTTON, OLDINGTON, MITTON, *TEULESBERGE*, *SUDUUALE*. In these lands, including the manor, 20 hides.
The whole of this manor was waste. In lordship 1 plough;

20 villagers and 30 smallholders with 18 ploughs; a further 20 more ploughs possible. 2 male and 4 female slaves.

2 mills at 16s; 2 salt-houses at 30s; a fishery at 100d; woodland at 4 leagues.

In this manor the reeve holds the land of one riding-man; he has 1 plough and a mill at 5 *ora*.

To this manor belongs 1 house in Droitwich and another in Worcester which pay 10d.

The whole manor paid £14 in revenue before 1066; now it pays £10 4s by weight.

The King has placed the woodland of this manor in the Forest.
Of this manor's land William holds 1 hide and the land of one riding-man. He has 1 villager and 8 smallholders who have 4½ ploughs. Value 11s.

Also of this land Aiulf holds 1 virgate. 1 plough and 2 slaves there.
Value 2s.

[In CLENT Hundred]

3a In DROITWICH King Edward had 11 houses. King Edward had his share in 5 brine-pits. At one brine-pit, 'UPWICH', 54 salt-houses and 2 *hocci* which pay 6s 8d. At another brine-pit, HELPRIDGE, 17 salt-houses. At a third brine-pit, 'MIDDLEWICH', 12 salt-houses and 2 parts of 1 *hoccus* which pay 6s 8d. At 5 other brine-pits, 15 salt-houses.
From all these King Edward had £52 in revenue.

3b At these brine-pits Earl Edwin had 51½ salt-houses, and from 172 c
the *hocci* he had 6s 8d. The whole of this paid £24 in revenue.
Now King William has in lordship both what King Edward and what Earl Edwin had. From this the Sheriff paid £65 by weight and 2 measures of salt so long as he had the woodland; but if he does not have the woodland, he cannot pay this in any way, as he states.

De CHENEFARE: redđ. c. sol de. xx. in ora. H tra. ē in Stadfordscire. Similit ē 7 SVINESFORDE. De isto ϖ 7 aliis. II. qui sunt in Wirecestrescire. Hoc. ē Terdesberie de. IX. hiđ. 7 Clent de. IX. hiđ. de his. III. Man redđ uicecom. XV. lib den de. XX. in ora.

IN CAME HVND.

Rex. W. ten TERDEBERIE. Rex. E. tenuit. Ibi. IX. hidæ. In dnio. ē. I. car. 7 alia potest fieri. Ibi. II. uitti 7 XXVIII. bord cū. XII. car. In Wich sunt. VII. salinæ. 7 II. plūbi. 7 reddt XX. soliđ. 7 C. mittas salis.

Vicecom de Stadfordscire recip 7 reddit firmā hui ϖ in SVINESFORD. Idest. XI. lib denar de. XX. in ora.

IN CLENT HVND.

Rex. W. ten CLENT. Rex. E. tenuit. Ibi. IX. hidæ. In dnio. ē. I. car 7 dimiđ. 7 XII. uitt 7 III. bord cū. IX. car 7 dimiđ. Ibi. III. bouarii. 7 Siluæ. II. leuū.

Hui ϖ firma. IIII. lib. reddit in SVINESFORD In Stadfordscire.

In Wich. ē dimiđ hida. quæ ptin ad aulā de Glouuecestre.

.II. TERRA ÆCCLÆ DE WIRECESTRE.

ÆCCLA SCÆ MARIÆ DE WIRECESTRE. habet unū HVNDRET qđ uocat OSWALDESLAV.

In quo iacent. CCC. hidæ. De quib eps ipsius æcclæ a constitutione antiquoꝝ tēpoꝝ ht oms redditiones socharū. 7 oms ɔsuetudines inibi ptinentes ad dnicū uictū 7 regis seruitiū 7 suū. ita ut nullus uicecomes ullā ibi habere possit querelā. nec in aliq placito. nec in alia qualibet causa. Hoc attestat totus comitatus. Hæ pdictæ. CCC. hidæ fuer de ipso dnio æcclæ 7 siqđ de ipsis cuicunq; homini qlibet modo attributū uel prestitū fuisset ad seruiendū inde epo: ille qui eam terrā prestitā sibi tenebat. nullā omino ɔsuetudinē sibimet inde retinere poterat nisi p epm. neq; trā

4 From KINVER he pays 100s at 20 (pence) to the *ora*. This land is in Staffordshire. KINGSWINFORD likewise. From this manor and from another two which are in Worcestershire—that is TARDEBIGGE at 9 hides and CLENT at 9 hides—from these three manors the Sheriff pays £15 of pence at 20 to the *ora*.

In CAME Hundred

5 King William holds TARDEBIGGE. King Edward held it. 9 hides.
In lordship 1 plough; another possible.
2 villagers and 28 smallholders with 12 ploughs.
In Droitwich 7 salt-houses and 2 lead vats; they pay 20s and 100 measures of salt.
The Sheriff of Staffordshire receives and pays the revenue of this manor in Kingswinford, that is £11 of pence at 20 to the *ora*.

In CLENT Hundred

6 King William holds CLENT. King Edward held it. 9 hides.
In lordship 1½ ploughs;
12 villagers and 3 smallholders with 9½ ploughs. 3 ploughmen.
Woodland, 2 leagues.
The revenue of this manor, £4, is paid in Kingswinford in Staffordshire.

7 In DROITWICH, ½ hide, which belongs to the hall of Gloucester.

2 LAND OF THE CHURCH OF WORCESTER

1 St. Mary's Church of Worcester has one Hundred, which is called OSWALDSLOW, in which lie 300 hides. By an arrangement of ancient times the Bishop of this church has from them all the payments of the Jurisdictions, all customary dues there which belong to the supplies of the household, both the King's service and his own, so that no Sheriff can have any suit there, neither in any plea nor in any other case whatever. The whole County confirms this. The said 300 hides were (part) of the lordship itself of the church, and if any (part) of them was allotted or leased to any man, in whatever manner, to serve the Bishop therefrom, the man who held such land leased to him, could not keep back from it any customary due at all for himself, except through the Bishop, nor keep the land

retinere nisi usq; ad impletũ tẽpus qđ ipsi inter se
constituerant.7 nusquã cũ ea terra se uertere poterat.

172 d
In ipso HVND ten eps eidẽ æcclæ CHEMESEGÉ. Ibi. XXIIII.
hidæ geld. De his hid sunt. v. hidæ Wastæ.
In dñio sunt. II. car. 7 XV. uilli 7 XXVII. bord cũ. XVI. car
Ibi pbr 7 IIII. serui. 7 II. ancillæ. 7 XL. ac pti. Silua. I. lew lg.
7 dimid lew lat. In dñio sunt. XIII. hidæ.
T.R.E. ualb. XVI. lib. modo: VIII. lib.
De hoc ꝯ. ten Vrso uicec. III. BEREW de. VII. hid Mucenhil.
Stoltun. Vlfrintun. Ibi sunt. VII. car. 7 VII. uilli 7 VII. bord.
7 VII. serui. 7 XVI. ac pti. De his. III. tris reddebat firma. T.R.E.
qa de uictu sẽp fuer. Val. c. sol.
De ipso ꝯ ten Roger de Laci. II. hid ad Vlfrintun. 7 Aiulf
de eo. T.R.E. fuer in dñio. 7 Alric eas teneb etiã tpr regis. W.
7 reddeb inde oms ɔsuetudines firmæ sicuti reddeb antecessores
sui excepto rustico ope sic depcari poterat a pposito.
Ibi sunt. II. car cũ. I. uillo 7 II. serui. 7 molin de. XL. denar.
T.R.E. ualb. L. solid. Modo: XL. solid.
De eod ꝯ ten Walteri ponther. II. hid ad WIDINTVN. In dñio
fuer. T.R.E. Ailric tenuit ead ratione qua supdictas hidas.
In dñio sunt. II. car. 7 IIII. serui. 7 III. uilli 7 VII. bord cũ. IIII. car.
7 piscaria de. IIII. solid. 7 XII. ac pti. Silua. I. lew lg. 7 dim lat.
T.R.E. ualb. XXX. solid. modo. XL. solid.
In eod hd ten isd eps WICHE. Ibi. XV. hidæ geld. In dñio sunt
IIII. hidæ una v min. 7 ibi. IIII. car. 7 XII. uilli 7 XII. bord cũ
XII. car. 7 II. molini de. XII. solid. 7 II. piscarie de. VI. solid 7 VIII.
denar. 7 LX. ac pti. Silua. II. lew lg. 7 I. leuu lat.
T.R.E. 7 m uat. VIII. lib.

except until the completion of the time arranged between them; nor could he ever turn elsewhere with this land.

2 In this Hundred the Bishop of this church holds KEMPSEY. 172 d
24 hides which pay tax. Of these hides, 5 hides are waste.
In lordship 2 ploughs;
15 villagers and 27 smallholders with 16 ploughs. A priest;
4 male and 2 female slaves. A 84
Meadow, 40 acres; woodland 1 league long and ½ league wide.
In lordship 13 hides.
Value before 1066 £16; now £8.

3 Of this manor Urso the Sheriff holds 3 outliers at 7 hides:
MUCKNELL, STOULTON, WOLVERTON. 7 ploughs.
7 villagers, 7 smallholders and 7 slaves.
Meadow, 16 acres. A 85
Revenue was paid from these three lands before 1066,
because they were always for the supplies.
Value 100s.

4 Roger of Lacy holds 2 hides of this manor at WOLVERTON,
and Aiulf from him. Before 1066 they were in lordship.
Alric held them also in King William's time and paid
from them all the customary revenue dues, as his
predecessors had, except for rural work, on the terms
he could beg from the reeve. 2 ploughs, with
1 villager; 2 slaves. A 86
A mill at 40d.
Value before 1066, 50s; now 40s.

5 Walter Ponther holds 2 hides also of this manor at
WHITTINGTON. They were in lordship before 1066. Alric
held them in the same manner as the above hides.
In lordship 2 ploughs; 4 slaves; A 87
3 villagers and 7 smallholders with 4 ploughs.
A fishery at 4s; meadow, 12 acres; woodland 1 league
long and ½ wide.
Value before 1066, 30s; now 40s.

6 In the same Hundred the Bishop also holds WICK (Episcopi). 15 hides
which pay tax. In lordship 4 hides, less 1 virgate; 4 ploughs there;
12 villagers and 12 smallholders with 12 ploughs. A 88
2 mills at 12s; 2 fisheries at 6s 8d; meadow, 60 acres;
woodland 2 leagues long and 1 league wide.
Value before 1066 and now £8.

De hoc ϖ ten Vrso uicec .v. hid ad holte. Ailric tenuit sup dicta ratione. In dnio sunt .II. car.7 XII. uitti 7 XXIIII. bord cu .x. car.7 piscaria de.v. solid.7 in Wich .I. salina de .XIII. den. 7 XII. ac pti. Silua dimid lew lg.7 tntd lat. Ibi.e una haie.
Isd Vrso ten una hid ad Witlege.7 Walter de eo. In dnio.e una car.7 pbr 7 II. bord cu .I. car. Silua .III. qz lg.7 II. lat. Arnuin pbr tenuit redd æcclæ oms csuetud firmæ.7 I.sextar mellis. Val 7 ualuit .x. solid.
Isd Vrso ten .I. hid ad *CHECINWICHE*. 7 Walt de eo. In dnio sunt .II. car .7 VI. bord 7 IIII. serui. Vluuin tenuit reddes omem csuetud pposito firmæ. Silua dimid lew lg.7 dimid lat. T.R.E. ualb .xx. sol. Modo: xv. solid. ★
Isd Vrso ten .I. hid ad *CLOPTVNE*. In dnio.e .I. car 7 un bord. 7 VI. ac pti. Brictmar tenuit. reddes omia ut supdicti. T.R.E. ualb. xx. sol. Modo: xv. solid.
Isd Vrso ten .III. uirg ad *LAVRE*. Ibi ht in dnio .I. car .7 II. bord. Sauuin tenuit de dnio epi. Ibi .VI. ac pti. Valuit 7 ual .VII. solid. Ibid ht Vrso .I. virg de dnio epi. Val .VI. sol.
Isd Vrso ten .I. hid ad *GREMANHIL*.7 Godefrid de eo. Ibi .II. bord hnt .I. car. Eddid tenuit. reddes qd supdicti. Valuit 7 ual .VI. solid.
De eod ϖ ten Robt dispensator dimid hid ad *LAVRE*.7 ibi ht .I. car cu .I. bord.7 molin de .v. solid.7 VI. ac pti.7 XII. querc. Keneuuard tenuit. 7 deseruiebat sic eps uoleb. Valuit 7 ual .xx. solid.

7 Urso the Sheriff holds 5 hides of this manor at HOLT. Alric held them in the above manner. In lordship 2 ploughs;
12 villagers and 24 smallholders with 10 ploughs. A 89
A fishery at 5s; in Droitwich 1 salt-house at 13d;
meadow, 12 acres; woodland ½ league long and as wide.
1 hedged enclosure.
[Value . . .]

Urso also holds

8 at (Little) WITLEY, 1 hide. Walter holds from him. In lordship 1 plough;
A priest and 2 smallholders with 1 plough.
Woodland 3 furlongs long and 2 wide. A 90
Arnwin the priest held it, paying to the church all the customary revenue dues and 1 sester of honey.
The value is and was 10s.

9 at KENSWICK, 1 hide. Walter holds from him. In lordship 2 ploughs;
6 smallholders and 4 slaves. A 94
Wulfwin held it, paying every customary due to the revenue reeve.
Woodland ½ league long and ½ wide.
Value before 1066, 20s; now 15s.

10 at 'CLOPTON', 1 hide. In lordship 1 plough;
1 smallholder. A 91
Meadow, 6 acres.
Brictmer held it, paying everything like those above.
Value before 1066, 20s; now 15s.

11 at LAUGHERNE, 3 virgates. He has in lordship 1 plough;
2 smallholders. A 92; 95
Saewin held it from the Bishop's lordship.
Meadow, 6 acres.
The value was and is 7s.
Urso also has 1 virgate there from the Bishop's lordship.
Value 6s.

12 at GREENHILL, 1 hide. Godfrey holds from him.
2 smallholders have 1 plough. A 96
Edith held it, paying what those above (paid).
The value was and is 6s.

13 Robert the Bursar holds ½ hide also of this manor at LAUGHERNE. He has 1 plough, with
1 smallholder. A 93
A mill at 5s; meadow, 6 acres; 12 oaks.
Kenward held it, and gave service as the Bishop wished.
The value was and is 20s.

De ipso m̃ ten Osbñ.f.Ricardi.I.hid ad *Codrie*.7 ibi hr̃.I.car in dñio.7 VI.uill 7 IIII.bord cũ.IIII.car.7 molin de.V.solid. Ibi.XII.ac p̃ti.7 III.q̃z siluæ.Ricard tenuit ad seruitiũ qđ eps uoluit. Valeb 7 ual.XL.solid.

In eođ HVND ten isđ eps *Fledebirie*.Ibi.XL.hidæ geld. In dñio sunt.VII.hidæ.7 ibi.IX.car.7 pbr hñs dimid hid 7 XXIII.uitti 7 XVII.bord cũ.XIX.car. Ibi.XVI.serui.7 III. ancillæ.7 molin de.X.sol 7 XX stichs anguillarũ.7 L.ac p̃ti. Silua.II.lew lg.7 dimid lat.De q̃ hr̃ eps qcq̃d de ea exit.

173 a
in uenatione 7 melle.7 lignis ad salinas de Wich.7 IIII.sol. Valb.X.lib.Modo.IX lib.

De hoc m̃ ten eps de hereford.V.hid ad *Inteberge*.7 ibi hr̃ pbrm 7 VII.uittos cũ.IIII.car.7 pratũ bobz. Walter eps tenuit T.R.E.ad omẽ seruitiũ epi de Wirecestre. Valuit 7 ual.XXX.sol.

De ipso m̃ ten Vrso.V.hid ad *Abeleng*.7 ibi hr̃.II.car in dñio. 7 VII.uitt 7 I.bord 7 I.francig.cũ.VI.car.Ibi.IIII.serui 7 II.ancillæ. 7 p̃tũ Silua.II.q̃z lg.7 II.q̃z lat.Valuit 7 ual.IIII.lib. Godric tenuit seruiẽs inde epo ut poterat depcari.

Isđ Vrso ten.VII.hid ad *Biscopesleng*.7 Alured de eo.Ibi hr̃ in dñio.III.car 7 dimid.7 pbr 7 V.uitti 7 VII.bord cũ.V.car 7 dimid. Ibi.II.serui 7 II.ancillæ.7 molin de.IIII.solid.7 VI.ac p̃ti. Valuit.VI.lib.modo.VII.lib.Frane tenuit.V.hid faciẽs omẽ seruitiũ.7 eps habeb.II.hid in dñio.

De eođ m̃ ten Robt dispensator.V.hid ad *Pidele*.7 *More*. 7 *Hylle*.In dñio sunt.IIII.car.7 IIII.uitti 7 I.bord cũ.I.car. Ibi.III.serui.7 XXIIII.ac p̃ti. Valuit 7 ual.LX.solid. Keneuuard tenuit eo modo quo aliã supdictã.

14 Osbern son of Richard holds 1 hide of this manor at COTHERIDGE.
He has 1 plough in lordship;
6 villagers and 4 smallholders with 4 ploughs.
A mill at 5s. Meadow, 12 acres; woodland, 3 furlongs.
Richard held it for the service that the Bishop wished.
The value was and is 40s.

15 In the same Hundred the Bishop also holds FLADBURY. 40 hides which pay tax. In lordship 7 hides; 9 ploughs there;
A priest who has ½ hide; 23 villagers and 17 smallholders with 19 ploughs. 16 male and 3 female slaves. A 97
A mill at 10s; 20 sticks of eels; meadow, 50 acres; woodland 173 a
2 leagues long and ½ wide, from which the Bishop has whatever comes from it, in hunting and in honey and in timber for the salt-houses of Droitwich and 4s.
The value was £10; now £9.

16 The Bishop of Hereford holds 5 hides of this manor at INKBERROW. He has
a priest and 7 villagers with 4 ploughs.
Meadow for the oxen. A 99
Bishop Walter held it before 1066, for every service of the Bishop of Worcester.
The value was and is 30s.

17 Urso holds 5 hides of this manor at AB LENCH.
He has 2 ploughs in lordship;
7 villagers, 1 smallholder and 1 Frenchman with 6 ploughs. 4 male and 2 female slaves. A 98
Meadow . . .; woodland 2 furlongs long and 2 furlongs wide.
The value was and is £4.
Godric held it, serving the Bishop from it on the terms he could beg.

18 Urso also holds 7 hides at (Rous)LENCH, and Alfred from him. He has in lordship 3½ ploughs;
A priest, 5 villagers and 7 smallholders with 5½ ploughs. 2 male and 2 female slaves. A 100
A mill at 4s; meadow, 6 acres.
The value was £6; now £7.
Fran held 5 hides, performing every service, and the Bishop had 2 hides in lordship.

19 Robert the Bursar holds 5 hides also of this manor at (Wyre) PIDDLE, MOOR and HILL. In lordship 4 ploughs;
4 villagers and 1 smallholder with 1 plough. 3 slaves.
Meadow, 24 acres.
The value was and is 60s.
Kenward held it in the same way as the other above.

De ipso m̄ ten̄ Alric̄ archidiacon̄ . i . hid̄ ad *Bradelege* . 7 ibi hт̄ . i . car̄ in dn̄io . 7 iii . uitti 7 iii . bord̄ cū . i . car̄ 7 dim̄ . 7 un̄ seruus. Valuit 7 ual . xx . solid̄ . Eldred̄ archieps̄ præstitit suo p̄posito . T . R . E . 7 qdo uoluit iuste ei abstulit.

De eod̄ m̄ ten̄ Roger̄ de laci . x . hid̄ ad *Bisantvne* . 7 ii . franciḡ de eo . In dn̄io sunt . ii . car̄ . 7 pb̄r hn̄s dimid̄ hidā . 7 viii . uitti 7 ii . bord̄ cū . v . car̄ . Ibi . iiii . serui . 7 iiii . ancillæ . 7 molin̄ de . xii . denar̄ . 7 xx . ac̄ p̄ti . Valuit . xii . lib̄ . Modo : x . lib̄.

Quattuor lib̄i hōes teneb̄ de ep̄o T . R . E . reddtes om̄em socā 7 sacā 7 circset 7 sepultura 7 expeditiones . 7 nauigia . 7 placita ad p̄dictū hund̄ . 7 nc̄ faciunt similiter qui tenent.

In eod̄ *Hvnd* ten̄ isd̄ ep̄s *Breodvn* . Ibi . xxxv . hidæ geld̄ . In dn̄io sunt . x . hidæ . 7 ibi . iii . car̄ . 7 xxxiii . uitti 7 xiii . bord̄ cū . xx . car̄ . Ibi . vi . serui . 7 molin̄ de . vi . solid̄ 7 viii . den̄ . 7 qt̄ xx . ac̄ p̄ti . Silua . ii . lew̄ lḡ . 7 lew̄ 7 dimid̄ lat̄ . Inde hт̄ ep̄s . x . solid̄ . 7 qcqd inde exit in melle 7 uenatione 7 aliis reb; . T . R . E . ualb̄ . x . lib̄ . Modo : x . solid̄ minus.

Ad hoc m̄ iacent . iii . hidæ ad *Teotintvne* . 7 una hida ad *Mitvne* . 7 sunt de uictu monachoz . Ibi sunt in dn̄io . v . car̄ . 7 xii . uitti 7 vi . bord̄ . cū . ix . car̄ . Ibi . x . serui . 7 iii . ancillæ . 7 xl . ac̄ p̄ti . 7 ii . q̄z siluæ . Valuit 7 ual iiii . lib̄.

De hoc m̄ ten̄ Æilric̄ archidiac̄ . ii . hid̄ ad *Codestvne* . 7 ibi hт̄ . ii . car̄ . 7 pb̄rm 7 iiii . uitt . 7 vii . bord̄ cū . iii . car̄ . Valuit 7 ual . xxx . solid̄ . Hanc trā prestiterat Bricsteg ep̄s dodoni . s; Ældred̄ archieps̄ deratiocinauit eā c̄tra filiū ei̊ . T . R . W.

De ipso m̄ ten̄ Vrso . vii . hid̄ ad *Ridmerlege* 7 Witts de eo . ii . hid̄ ex istis . In dn̄io sunt . iiii . car̄ . 7 xxiii . uitti 7 ix . bord̄ cū . x . car̄ . Ibi . vi . serui . 7 ii . ancillæ . 7 molin̄ de . v . sol 7 viii . denar̄ . Silua . i . lew̄ lḡ . 7 dim̄ lat̄ . Valb̄ . viii . lib̄ . m̄ . x . sol min̄ . Azor 7 Goduin̄ tenuer̄ de ep̄o 7 deseruieb̄.

20 Archdeacon Alric holds 1 hide of this manor at BRADLEY (Green).
He has 1 plough in lordship;
3 villagers and 3 smallholders with 1½ ploughs; 1 slave. A 101
The value was and is 20s.
Archbishop Aldred leased it to his reeve before 1066; and took it away from him rightly, when he wished.

21 Roger of Lacy holds 10 hides also of this manor at BISHAMPTON,
and 2 Frenchmen from him. In lordship 2 ploughs; A 102
A priest who has ½ hide; 8 villagers and 2 smallholders with 5 ploughs. 4 male and 4 female slaves.
A mill at 12d; meadow, 20 acres.
The value was £12; now £10.
Four free men held it from the Bishop before 1066, paying full jurisdiction, Church tax, burial, military service by land and sea, and pleas to the said Hundred. The present holders do the same.

22 In the same Hundred the Bishop also holds BREDON. 35 hides which pay tax. In lordship 10 hides; 3 ploughs there;
33 villagers and 13 smallholders with 20 ploughs. 6 slaves.
A mill at 6s 8d; meadow, 80 acres; woodland 2 leagues long and 1½ leagues wide. The Bishop has from it 10s and whatever
comes from it in honey and hunting and other things. A 103
Value before 1066 £10; now 10s less.

23 In (the lands of) this manor lie 3 hides at TEDDINGTON and 1 hide at MITTON. They are for the monks' supplies.
In lordship 5 ploughs;
12 villagers and 6 smallholders with 9 ploughs. 10 male
and 3 female slaves. A 104
Meadow, 40 acres; woodland, 2 furlongs.
The value was and is £4.

24 Archdeacon Alric holds 2 hides of this manor at CUTSDEAN.
He has 2 ploughs and
a priest, 4 villagers and 7 smallholders with 3 ploughs.
The value was and is 30s.
Bishop Bricteah had leased this land to Doda. But Archbishop Aldred proved his right to it against his son after 1066.

25 Urso holds 7 hides of this manor at REDMARLEY (d'Abitot), and William 2 hides of them from him. In lordship
4 ploughs; A 105
23 villagers and 9 smallholders with 10 ploughs. 6 male and 2 female slaves.
A mill at 5s 8d; woodland 1 league long and ½ wide.
The value was £8; now 10s less.
Azor and Godwin held from the Bishop and gave service.

Isd Vrso ten . II . hid ad PEONEDOC . 7 ibi ht . II . car . 7 . III . bord . 7 III . seruos 7 I . ancill . Silua dimid lew lg . 7 dim lat . Valb . xxx . sol . m . IIII . sol min . Goduin tenuit ead ratione. supdicta

Isd Vrso ten . III . hid ad WASEBVRNE . 7 ibi ht . II . car . 7 v . uill 7 IIII . bord cu . II . car . Ibi . v . ac pti . Valb 7 ual XL . sol . Elmer tenuit . 7 pea monac fact . e . Eps u tra sua recepit.

Isd Vrso ten . IIII . hid ad WESTMONECOTE . 7 ibi ht . III . car . 7 . I uill . 7 II . bord cu . I . car . Ibi . XIIII . serui . 7 XII . ac pti . Valuit . L . solid . Modo LX . solid . Brictuin teneb . 7 inde epo seruieb sic depcari poterat.

173 b

De eod m ten Durand . II . hid ad NORTVNE . 7 ibi ht . I . car . 7 II . bord cu . I . car . 7 VI . acs pti . Valuit 7 ual . xx . solid . Leuuin tenuit . 7 inde radman epi fuit.

★ De ipso m tenuit de epo Brictric . f . Algar . I . hid . ad BISELEGE . 7 inde firmabat ipsu epm omi anno . 7 tam reddeb ad soca epi qcqd debebat ad seruitiu regis . Modo . e in manu regis . W . Vat 7 ualuit . XL . solid . Ibi sun xx . ac pti . 7 silua dimid lew lg . 7 III . qz lat.

In pdicto HVND ten isd eps RIPPEL . cu uno mebro VPTVN . Ibi . XXV . hidæ geld . De his sunt . XIII . in dnio . 7 ibi . IIII . car . 7 II . pbri hntes hid 7 dimid . cu . II . car . 7 XL . uill 7 XVI . bord . cu . XXX . VI . car . Ibi 7 una ancilla . VIII . serui . 7 molin . 7 XXX . ac pti . Silua dimid lew lg . 7 III . qz lat . In Malferna . De hac habeb mel 7 uenatione 7 qcqd exibat . 7 insup . x . solid . Modo . e in foresta . Pasnagiu u 7 igne 7 domoz emdatione inde accip eps . Valuit 7 ual . x . lib.

26 Urso also holds 2 hides at PENDOCK. He has 2 ploughs and
3 smallholders and 3 male slaves, 1 female.
Woodland ½ league long and ½ wide. A 106
The value was 30s; now 4s less.
Godwin held in the same manner as above.

27 Urso also holds 3 hides at (Little) WASHBOURNE. He has 2 ploughs;
5 villagers and 4 smallholders with 2 ploughs. A 107
Meadow, 5 acres.
The value was and is 40s.
Aelmer held it, and later became a monk; so the Bishop acquired his land.

28 Urso also holds 4 hides at WESTMANCOTE. He has 3 ploughs;
1 villager and 2 smallholders with 1 plough. 14 slaves.
Meadow, 12 acres. A 109
The value was 50s; now 60s.
Brictwin held them and served the Bishop from them on the terms he could beg.

29 Durand holds 2 hides also of this manor at (Bredons) NORTON. 173 b
He has 1 plough and
2 smallholders with 1 plough; A 108
meadow, 6 acres.
The value was and is 20s.
Leofwin held them and was a rider of the Bishop from there.

30 Brictric son of Algar held 1 hide of this manor from the Bishop at BUSHLEY. He paid revenue on it to the Bishop himself every year. Moreover, he paid to the Bishop's A 110
jurisdiction whatever he owed to the King's service. Now it is in King William's hands.
The value is and was 40s.
Meadow, 20 acres; woodland ½ league long and 3 furlongs wide.

31 In the said Hundred the Bishop also holds RIPPLE with 1 member, UPTON (on Severn). 25 hides which pay tax. Of these, 13 are in lordship; 4 ploughs there; A 111
2 priests who have 1½ hides with 2 ploughs; 40 villagers and 16 smallholders with 36 ploughs. 8 male slaves, 1 female.
A mill; meadow, 30 acres; woodland ½ league long and 3 furlongs wide, in Malvern (Chase). From this he had honey and hunting and whatever came from there and 10s in addition. Now it is in the Forest. The Bishop receives from it pasture dues, fire-wood and (timber) for repairing houses.
The value was and is £10.

De hoc m̄ ten̄ Ordric . I . hid̄ ad CRVBE . 7 ibi h̄t . III . car̄ . 7 III . uillos 7 V . bord̄ cū . III . car̄ . Ibi . XXIIII . ac̄ p̄ti . 7 III . q̄z silux. Valuit . XX . sol̄ . modo . XL . Godric̄ tenuit 7 de ep̄o deseruiuit. Eldred̄ arch̄ ab eo [iure] accep̄.

Ibid̄ ad CRVBE ten̄ Siuuard̄ . V . hid̄ . 7 ibi h̄t . I . car̄ . 7 VI . uill̄ 7 IIII . bord̄ cū . IIII . car̄ . Ibi . XII . ac̄ p̄ti . Silua . IIII . q̄z lḡ . 7 II . lat̄. Hanc t̄rā tenuit Sirof de ep̄o T . R . E . quó mortuo ded̄ ep̄s filiā ei cū hac t̄ra cuidā suo militi . qui 7 matrē pasceret 7 ep̄o inde seruiret. Valuit 7 ual̄ . XL . sol̄.

De ipso m̄ ten̄ Roger̄ de Laci . III . hid̄ ad HILCRVBE . 7 ibi h̄t . I . car̄ . 7 VIII . uill̄ 7 IIII . bord̄ cū . IIII . car̄ . Ibi XXX . ac̄ p̄ti . Silua dimid̄ lew̄ lḡ . 7 II . q̄z lat̄ . Valuit . III . lib̄ . m̄ . IIII . lib̄.

De eod̄ m̄ ten̄ Vrso . I . hid̄ ad HOLEFEST . 7 ibi h̄t . I . car̄ . 7 VII . bord̄ cū . I . car̄ . Ibi . V . ac̄ p̄ti . 7 II . q̄z silue. Valuit 7 ual̄ . XX . sol̄ . Duo p̄bri tenuer̄ de ep̄o.

De ipso m̄ habuit Radulf̄ de bernai . I . hid̄ ad CVHILLE. Ailric̄ tenuit T . R . E . 7 facieb̄ inde seruitiū ep̄i . Nc̄ . ē in manu regis . 7 ibi . VIII . ac̄ p̄ti . 7 II . q̄z siluæ. Valb̄ . XL . solid̄.

De eod̄ m̄ tenuit Brictric . f . Algar . I . hid̄ ad BVRGELEGE. eod̄ modo quo sup̄dictā . 7 ualb̄ . XV . solid̄ . Nc̄ . ē in manu regis.

In eod̄ HVND̄ ten̄ isd̄ ep̄s BLOCHELEI . Ibi . XXXVIII . hidæ geld̄. De his sunt in d̄nio . XXV . hid̄ 7 dimid̄ . 7 ibi . VII . car̄ . 7 p̄br hn̄s . I . hid̄ . 7 IIII . radmans hn̄tes . VI . hid̄ . 7 LX . III . uill̄ 7 XXV . bord̄ Int̄ om̄s hn̄t . LI . car̄ . Ibi . XIIII . serui . 7 XII . molini de . LII . solid̄ . III . den̄ min̄ . 7 XX IIII . ac̄ p̄ti . Silua dimid̄ lew̄ lḡ . 7 lat̄ . Valuit XVI . lib̄ . Modo : XX . lib̄.

32 Ordric holds 1 hide of this manor at CROOME. He has 3 ploughs and
3 villagers and 5 smallholders with 3 ploughs. A 112
Meadow, 24 acres; woodland, 3 furlongs.
The value was 20s; now 40[s].
Godric held it and gave service to the Bishop. Archbishop Aldred received it from him legally.

33 Siward holds 5 hides also at CROOME. He has 1 plough;
6 villagers and 4 smallholders with 4 ploughs. A 114
Meadow, 12 acres; woodland 4 furlongs long and 2 wide.
Sigref held this land from the Bishop before 1066.
When he died, the Bishop gave his daughter, with this land, to one of his men-at-arms, so that he might maintain (her) mother and serve the Bishop from it.
The value was and is 40s.

34 Roger of Lacy holds 3 hides of this manor at HILL CROOME. He has 1 plough;
8 villagers and 4 smallholders with 4 ploughs. A 113
Meadow, 30 acres; woodland ½ league long and 2 furlongs wide.
The value was £3; now £4.

35 Urso holds 1 hide also of this manor at HOLDFAST. He has 1 plough;
7 smallholders with 1 plough. A 115
Meadow, 5 acres; woodland, 2 furlongs.
The value was and is 20s.
Two priests held it from the Bishop.

36 Ralph of Bernay had 1 hide of this manor at QUEENHILL.
Alric held it before 1066 and performed the Bishop's service from it. Now it is in the King's hands.
Meadow, 8 acres; woodland, 2 furlongs. A 116
The value was 40s.

37 Brictric son of Algar held 1 hide also of this manor at BARLEY, in the same way as that above.
The value was 15s. Now it is in the King's hands.

38 In the same Hundred the Bishop also holds BLOCKLEY. 38 hides which pay tax. Of these, 25½ hides are in lordship; 7 ploughs there;
A priest who has 1 hide; 4 riders who have 6 hides; 63 villagers and 25 smallholders; between them they have 51 ploughs. 14 slaves. A 117; 120
12 mills at 52s, less 3d; meadow, 24 acres; woodland ½ league long and wide.
The value was £16; now £20.

De hoc ꝳ ten̄ Ricard̄ . II . hid̄ ad *DICFORD* . 7 ibi hT . I . car̄.
7 II . uilt . 7 I . bord̄ 7 II . seru̇ . cū . I . car̄ . Ibi . IIII . ac̄ p̄ti . Valuit
7 ual . xxx . solid̄ . Aluuard̄ tenuit . 7 seruitiū reddidit.

Ansgot ten̄ . I . hid̄ 7 dim̄ de ꝓpa tra uilloꝝ . 7 hT . I . car̄
cū . I . bord̄ . Ibi . III . ac̄ p̄ti . Val 7 ualuit . xv . solid̄.

Ad sup̄dictū ꝳ iacet . I . hida ad *IACVBE* . ꝑtin̄ ad uictū
monachoꝝ . Ibi sunt . II . car̄ . 7 IIII . uilt 7 II . bord̄ 7 IIII . serui.
cū . II . car̄ . H̄ app̄ciat̄ in capite ꝳ . Ibi . XII . ac̄ p̄ti.

Stefan̄ . f . fulchered ten̄ . III . hid̄ ad *EILESFORD* . 7 ibi hT
II . car̄ . 7 p̄brm 7 VI . uilt cū . V . car̄ . 7 IIII . seru̇ 7 I . ancill.
Ibi . XX . ac̄ p̄ti . Val 7 ualuit . III . lib̄.

Hereuuard̄ tenuit . V . hid̄ ad *EVNILADE* . Ibi sunt . II . car̄.
7 IX . uilt cū . III . car̄ . 7 I . seru̇ . 7 molin̄ fuit de . XXXII . den̄.
Val 7 ualuit . III . lib̄.

Has . II . t̄ras Eilesford 7 Eunilade . tenuit abb̄ de EVESHĀ.
de ep̄o de Wirecestre . quousq; ep̄s baiocs̄is de abbatia
accepit . 7 ipsæ t̄ræ fuer̄ de uictu monachoꝝ.

In eod̄ *HVND̄* ten̄ isd̄ ep̄s *REDINCTVN* . cū uno mēbro
TIDELMINTVN . Ibi . XXIII . hidæ geld̄ . Vna ex his . ē Wasta.
173 c
In dn̄io sunt . V . car̄ . 7 XLII . uilt 7 XXX . bord̄ . 7 p̄br hn̄s . I . hid̄.
7 I . radman . Int̄ om̄s hn̄t . XXIX . car̄ . Ibi . X . serui . 7 III . molini
de . XXXII . sol 7 VI . den̄ . Ibi . XXXVI . ac̄ p̄ti.
Valuit . X . lib̄ . Modo . XII . lib̄ 7 X . solid̄.

Ad *BLACHEWELLE* sunt . II . hidæ ꝑtin̄ ad uictū monachoꝝ.
In dn̄io sunt . III . car̄ . 7 X . uilti 7 VI . bord̄ . cū . IIII . car̄ . Ibi
VI . serui . 7 I . ancilla . 7 X . ac̄ p̄ti . Valuit 7 ual . L . solid̄.

39 Richard holds 2 hides of this manor at DITCHFORD. He has 1 plough;
2 villagers, 1 smallholder and 2 slaves with 1 plough. A 118
Meadow, 4 acres.
The value was and is 30s.
Alfward held it and rendered service.

40 Ansgot holds 1½ hides of the villagers' own land. He has 1 plough with
1 smallholder. A 119
Meadow, 3 acres.
The value is and was 15s.

41 At (Church) ICOMB 1 hide lies in (the lands of) the above manor; it belongs to the monks' supplies. 2 ploughs there.
4 villagers, 2 smallholders and 4 slaves with 2 ploughs.
It is assessed with the head of the manor.
Meadow, 12 acres.

42 Stephen son of Fulcred holds 3 hides at DAYLESFORD.
He has 2 ploughs and A 121
a priest; 6 villagers with 5 ploughs; 4 male slaves, 1 female.
Meadow, 20 acres.
The value is and was £3.

43 Hereward held 5 hides at EVENLODE. 2 ploughs.
9 villagers with 3 ploughs; 1 slave. A 122
There was a mill at 32d.
The value is and was £3.

44 The Abbey of Evesham held these two lands, DAYLESFORD and EVENLODE, from the Bishop of Worcester until the Bishop of Bayeux received them from the Abbey. These lands were for the monks' supplies.

45 In the same Hundred the Bishop also holds TREDINGTON with one member, TIDMINGTON. 23 hides which pay tax. 1 of these is waste. In lordship 5 ploughs; 173 c
42 villagers and 30 smallholders; a priest who has 1 hide; A 123
1 rider; between them they have 29 ploughs. 10 slaves.
3 mills at 32s 6d; meadow, 36 acres.
The value was £10; now £12 10s.

46 At BLACKWELL are 2 hides which belong to the monks' supplies.
In lordship 3 ploughs;
10 villagers and 6 smallholders with 4 ploughs. 6 male slaves, 1 female.
Meadow, 10 acres.
The value was and is 50s.

De eod ꝯ ten Gislebt.f.Turoldi.IIII.hid ad LONGEDVN.
Ibi ht.II.car.7 VIII.uilt 7 II.bord cu.IIII.car.Ibi.IIII.serui.
7 IIII.ancillæ.7 VIII.ac pti. Valuit.IIII.lib.Modo.III.lib.
Lefric pposit tenuit sic eps uoluit.

In eod HVND.ten isd eps.NORWICHE cu uno mebro
★ TIDBERTVN.Ibi.XXV hid. geld. Ex his sunt.III.hidæ 7 dimid
in dnio.7 ibi.IIII.car.7 ppposit hns.III.uirg.7 I.radman hns
III.uirg 7 XIII.uilt 7 XVIII.bord. Int oms hnt.XVIII.car.
Ibi.VIII.serui.7 III.molini de.L.solid.7 in Wic.I.salina
redd.C.mittas salis.p.C.caretedes lignoꝝ. De piscaria
IIII.solid. de pascuis.II.solid.Ibi.XL.ac pti.Silua.I.lew
lg.7 una lat. Ad ipsu ꝯ ptin in Wirecestre qt xx 7 x.
dom. De his ht eps in dnio.XLV.nil reddt nisi opus in
curia epi. Vrso ten.XXIIII.dom ex his.Osbn.f.Ricardi
VIII.Walter ponther.XI.Robt dispensator.I.
De burgo Wirecestre habuit eps T.R.E.tciu denariu.
7 modo ht cu rege 7 comite. Tc.VI.lib.Modo.VIII.lib.
Ad eund ꝯ ptin in Wich.III.dom.reddt.III.mittas salis.
7 de fabrica plubi.II.solid. Valuit.XIII.lib.Modo.XVI.lib
7 X.solid. In foro de Wirecestre ten Vrso de epo.XXV.
domos.7 reddt p annu.C.solid.

De eod ꝯ ten Vrso.V.hid ad HINDELEP 7 ALCRINTVN.
7 Godefrid de eo. In dnio sunt.II.car.7 pbr 7 III.uilt 7 IIII.
bord cu.II.car.Ibi.XXIIII.ac pti.Silua dimid lew lg.
7 dimid lat. Valuit XXX.sol.Modo.XX.solid.Silua.e in foresta.
Edric stirman tenuit 7 deseruiebat cu aliis seruitiis ad rege
7 epm ptinentib3.

Isd Vrso ten.I.hid 7 III.uirg ad WERMEDVN 7 ESTVN.
7 Robt de eo. Ibi ht.II.car.cu.II.seruis.7 XVI.ac pti ibi.
Silua.II.qꝝ lg.7 tntd lat.7 est in foresta.Val 7 ualuit
XVI.solid.H tra fuit 7 est de tra uilloꝝ.

47 Gilbert son of Thorold holds 4 hides also of this manor at LONGDON. He has 2 ploughs; A 124
8 villagers and 2 smallholders with 4 ploughs. 4 male and 4 female slaves.
Meadow, 8 acres.
The value was £4; now £3.
Leofric the reeve held as the Bishop wished.

48 In the same Hundred the Bishop also holds NORTHWICK with one member, TIBBERTON. 25 hides which pay tax. Of these, 3½ hides are in lordship; 4 ploughs there; A 125
A reeve who has 3 virgates; 1 rider who has 3 virgates; 13 villagers and 18 smallholders; between them they have 18 ploughs. 8 slaves.
3 mills at 50s; in Droitwich 1 salt-house which pays 100 measures of salt for 100 cartloads of timber; from the fishery 4s; from the pastures 2s. Meadow, 40 acres; woodland 1 league long and 1 wide.

49 To this manor belong 90 houses in WORCESTER. The Bishop has 45 of these in lordship; they pay nothing except work in the Bishop's court. Of these, Urso holds 24 houses, Osbern son of Richard 8, Walter Ponther 11, Robert the Bursar 1.
Before 1066 the Bishop had the third penny from the Borough of Worcester; now he has it with the King and the Earl.
[Value] then £6; now £8.

50 Also to this manor belong 3 houses in DROITWICH; they pay 3 measures of salt and 2s from the lead works.
The value was £13; now £16 10s.

51 In WORCESTER market place Urso holds 25 houses from the Bishop; they pay 100s a year.

52 Urso holds 5 hides also of this manor at HINDLIP and OFFERTON, and Godfrey from him. In lordship 2 ploughs;
a priest, 3 villagers and 4 smallholders with 2 ploughs. A 126;
Meadow, 24 acres; woodland ½ league long and ½ wide. 129
The value was 30s; now 20s.
The woodland is in the Forest.
Edric the Steersman held it and gave service, with other services belonging to the King and to the Bishop.

53 Urso also holds 1 hide and 3 virgates at WARNDON and (White Ladies) ASTON, and Robert from him. He has 2 ploughs, with 2 slaves. A 133
Meadow, 16 acres; woodland 2 furlongs long and as wide: it is in the Forest.
The value is and was 16s.
This land was and is (part) of the villagers' land.

Iſtd Vrſo teñ . I . hid ad *CVDELEI* . 7 ibi hт̃ . II . car̃ . 7 III . bord
7 II . ſeruos. Silua . ẽ de una q̃z . 7 eſt in foreſta . Valuit
7 uat . x . ſolid . Elfgiuæ moniat tenuit . ſic̃ depcari poterat.
De ipſo m̃ teñ Ordric . III . hid 7 . I . virgam. ad *ESTVN* . 7 ibi hт̃ . III . car̃.
7 v . uitt 7 IIII . bord cũ . IIII . car̃ . Valuit xx . ſot . Modo: xl . ſot.
H̃ terra fuit 7 eſt de dñio m̃ capitali.
Ordric teñ . I . hid ad *ODDVNCLEI* . 7 ibi hт̃ . I . car̃ . 7 I . uitt
7 III . bord cũ . I . car̃ . 7 ſalinã de . IIII . ſolid . 7 XII . ac̃s p̃ti.
Silua . II . q̃z lg̃ . 7 tntd lat̃ . 7 ẽ in foreſta . Turchil tenuit
7 inde ep̃o ſeruiuit.
Alric archidiac teñ . I . hid ad *HVDINTVNE* . 7 ibi hт̃ . II.
car̃ . 7 IIII . uitt 7 IIII . bord cũ . II . car̃ . Ibi moliñ reddeꝰ
. III . ſũmas annonæ . Silua de . III . ſolid . 7 ẽ in foreſta regis.
Vat 7 ualuit . xxx . ſolid . Vluric tenuit . ſic̃ ruſticus ſeruieꝰ.
De eod m̃ teñ Walter ponther . I . hid 7 dimid ad *WIDINTVN*
7 *RODELEAH* . 7 ibi hт̃ . I . car̃ . 7 VII . bord cũ . II . car̃ . 7 II . ſeru.
Ibi XVI . ac̃ p̃ti . 7 Silua ad ignẽ tant̃ . Valuit . xx . ſot . Modo . .
xxv . ſolid . Ailricus tenuit ſicut ſupiores.
Iſtd Walt teñ . III . hid ad *CIRCEHILLE* . 7 ibi hт̃ . II . car̃.
7 pbr̃m 7 III . uitt 7 III . bord cũ . III . car̃ . Ibi . III . ſerui.
7 moliñ de . IIII . ſolid . 7 III . ac̃ p̃ti . 7 II . q̃z ſiluæ . 7 ẽ in foreſta.
Valuit . L . ſolid . modo . XL . ſot . Azor tenuit . vt ſupdict̃.

173 d

Iſtd Walt teñ . III . hid ad *BRADECOTE* . 7 ibi hт̃ . I . car̃ . cũ . II . bord
7 II . ſeruis. Ibi . XVI . ac̃ p̃ti . Siluæ . II . q̃z . Valƀ . xxv . ſolid.
modo . xx . ſolid . Brictuuold pbr̃ tenuit 7 deſeruiuit ut ep̃s uoluit.
Silua . ẽ in foreſta regis.

54 Urso also holds 1 hide at CUDLEY. He has 2 ploughs and
3 smallholders and 2 slaves. A 134
Woodland at 1 furlong: it is in the Forest.
The value was and is 10s.
Aelfeva the nun held it on the terms she could beg.

55 Ordric holds 3 hides and 1 virgate of this manor at (White Ladies) ASTON. He has 3 ploughs; A 127
5 villagers and 4 smallholders with 4 ploughs.
The value was 20s; now 40s.
This land was and is (part) of the lordship of the head manor.

56 Ordric holds 1 hide at ODDINGLEY. He has 1 plough and
1 villager and 3 smallholders with 1 plough; A 128
a salt-house at 4s; meadow, 12 acres; woodland 2 furlongs long and as wide: it is in the Forest.
Thorkell held it and served the Bishop from it.
[Value . . .]

57 Archdeacon Alric holds 1 hide at HUDDINGTON. He has 2 ploughs;
4 villagers and 4 smallholders with 2 ploughs.
A mill which pays 3 packloads of corn; woodland at 3s: it is in the King's Forest.
The value is and was 30s.
Wulfric held it, serving as a countryman.

58 Walter Ponther holds 1½ hides also of this manor at WHITTINGTON and 'RADLEY'. He has 1 plough;
7 smallholders with 2 ploughs; 2 slaves.
Meadow, 16 acres; woodland only for fire-wood.
The value was 20s; now 25s.
Alric held it like those above.

59 Walter also holds 3 hides at CHURCHILL. He has 2 ploughs and
a priest, 3 villagers and 3 smallholders with 3 ploughs. 3 slaves.
A mill at 4s; meadow, 3 acres; woodland, 2 furlongs: it is in the Forest. A 130
The value was 50s; now 40s.
Azor held it like the above.

60 Walter also holds 3 hides at BREDICOT. He has 1 plough, with 173 d
2 smallholders and 2 slaves.
Meadow, 16 acres; woodland, 2 furlongs.
The value was 25s; now 20s. A 131
Brictwold the priest held it and gave service as the Bishop wished.
The woodland is in the King's Forest.

Herlebald ten̄ . I . hid̄ ad *PIRIAN* . 7 ibi hť . II . car̄ . 7 III . uilł
7 I . bord̄ 7 III . seruos . cū . I . car̄ . Ibi . X . ac̄ p̄ti . Silua . II . q̄z
lḡ . 7 una lat̄ . 7 est in foresta . Valuit . XXX . sol̄ . Modo : XX . sol̄ .
Godric tenuit ad uoluntatē epi .
In eod̄ *HVND* ten̄ ipsa æccła *OVREBERIE* . cū *PENEDOC* . Ibi
VI . hidæ geld̄ . In dn̄io sunt . III . car̄ . 7 XV . uilłi 7 VII . bord̄
cū . XI . car̄ . Ibi pb̄r hn̄s dimid̄ hidā 7 I . car̄ . Ibi . VI . serui 7 II .
ancillæ . 7 X . ac̄ p̄ti . 7 Silua . I . lew̄ lḡ . 7 I . lat̄ .
T . R . E . ualb̄ . VI . lib̄ . 7 m̄ similiter .
Ipsa æccła ten̄ *SECGESBARVE* . Ibi . IIII . hidæ geld̄ . In dn̄io
sunt . II . car̄ . 7 XI . uilłi 7 IIII . bord̄ cū . VII . car̄ . Ibi pb̄r hn̄s dim̄
hid̄ 7 dimid̄ car̄ . 7 IIII . serui . 7 una ancilla . 7 II . molini . de . X .
solid̄ . 7 VIII . ac̄ p̄ti . Valuit 7 ual̄ . III . lib̄ .
Dodd tenet 7 ē de uictu monachoz̄ . Eldred arch̄ diratiocinat̄ est
a Brictrico filio eius .
Ipsa æccła ten̄ *SCEPWESTVN* . Ibi . II . hidæ geld̄ . In dn̄io
sunt . II . car̄ . 7 XV . uilłi 7 V . bord̄ cū . VI . car̄ . Ibi . IIII . serui
7 una ancilla . 7 molin̄ de . X . solid̄ . 7 XVI . ac̄ p̄ti .
Valuit 7 ual̄ . L . solid̄ .
Ipsa æccła ten̄ *HERFERTHVN* cū *WIBVRGESTOKE* . Ibi
III . hidæ geld̄ . In dn̄io sunt . II . car̄ . 7 XII . uilłi 7 III . bord̄
cū . VI . car̄ . Ibi . IIII . serui . 7 una ancilla . 7 molend̄ de . X . sol̄ .
7 XXIIII . ac̄ p̄ti . Valuit 7 ual̄ . L . solid̄ .
Ipsa æccła ten̄ *GRIMANLEH* . Ibi . III . hidæ geld̄ . In dn̄io
sunt . III . car̄ . 7 XII . uilłi 7 XV . bord̄ cū . XV . car̄ . Ibi . VI . serui .
7 una ancilla . 7 molin̄ sine censu . 7 dimid̄ . piscaria redd̄
stiches anguilł . 7 VI . ac̄ p̄ti . Silua dimid̄ lew̄ lḡ 7 lat̄ .
Valuit 7 ual̄ . III . lib̄ .

61 Erlebald holds 1 hide at 'PERRY'. He has 2 ploughs and
3 villagers, 1 smallholder and 3 slaves with 1 plough.
Meadow, 10 acres; woodland 2 furlongs long and 1 wide:
it is in the Forest. A 132
The value was 30s; now 20s.
Godric held it at the Bishop's will.

62 In the same Hundred the Church itself holds OVERBURY with
PENDOCK. 6 hides which pay tax. In lordship 3 ploughs;
15 villagers and 7 smallholders with 11 ploughs. A 135
A priest who has ½ hide and 1 plough. 6 male and
2 female slaves.
Meadow, 10 acres; woodland 1 league long and 1 wide.
Value before 1066 £6; now the same.

63 The Church holds SEDGEBERROW itself. 4 hides which pay tax.
In lordship 2 ploughs; A 136
11 villagers and 4 smallholders with 7 ploughs.
A priest who has ½ hide and ½ plough. 4 male slaves,
1 female.
2 mills at 10s; meadow, 8 acres.
The value was and is £3.
Doda holds it; it is for the monks' supplies. Archbishop
Aldred had proved (their) right to it against his son Brictric.

64 The Church holds SHIPSTON (on Stour) itself. 2 hides
which pay tax. In lordship 2 ploughs;
15 villagers and 5 smallholders with 6 ploughs. 4 male
slaves, 1 female. A 137
A mill at 10s; meadow, 16 acres.
The value was and is 50s.

65 The Church itself holds HARVINGTON with *WIBURGESTOKE*.
3 hides which pay tax. In lordship 2 ploughs;
12 villagers and 3 smallholders with 6 ploughs. 4 male
slaves, 1 female. A 139
A mill at 10s; meadow, 24 acres.
The value was and is 50s.

66 The Church holds GRIMLEY itself. 3 hides which pay tax.
In lordship 3 ploughs;
12 villagers and 15 smallholders with 15 ploughs. 6 male
slaves, 1 female. A 138
A mill without dues; ½ fishery which pays . . . sticks of
eels; meadow, 6 acres; woodland ½ league long and wide.
The value was and is £3.

Vnā ex his . III . hid̄ ten̄ Rob̄t dispensator . 7 uocat̃ *CNIHTEWIC*.
7 ibi h̄t . I . car̄ . 7 VII . bord̄ cū . II . car̄ . 7 VI . ac̄s p̄ti . 7 siluā
II . q̄z lḡ 7 unā lat. Valuit 7 uat . XX . solid̄.
H̄ hida T . R . E . reddeb̄ in p̄dicto m̄ sacā 7 socā 7 om̄e regis
seruitiū . 7 est de dn̄ico uictu monachoz . sed præstita fuit
cuidā Edgidæ moniali . ut haberet 7 deseruiret q̄diu fr̄s
uoluissent 7 carere possent . Crescente ů c̄gregatione T . R . W.
reddidit . 7 ipsa adhuc uiuens inde . ē testis.
Ipsa æccła ten̄ *HALHEGAN* cū *BRADEWESHA*̄. Ibi
VII . hidæ geld̄. In dn̄io non . ē nisi . I . hida . 7 ibi . II . car̄ . 7 X.
uitti 7 XVI . bord̄ . cū . X . car̄ . Ibi . IIII . serui 7 II . ancillæ
7 molini . II . de . X . sol̄ . 7 piscaria de . XX . stich̄ anguillar̄.
7 XX . ac̄ p̄ti . 7 Silua . I . lew lḡ . 7 I . lat.
Ad hoc m̄ ptin̄ In Wich . X . dom̄ de . V . solid̄ . 7 Salina
redd̄ . L . mittas salis.
De hac t̃ra ten̄ . II . Radmanni . II . hid̄ . 7 ibi hn̄t . II . car.
T . R . E . ualeb̄ . C . solid̄ . 7 modo similiter.
De hoc m̄ ten̄ Walt de burh dimid̄ hidā jn *ERESBYRIE*.
7 ibi h̄t . I . car̄. Alric tenuit . 7 est de t̃ra uittoz. Vat . V . sol̄.
De ipso m̄ ten̄ Rogeri de laci . III . hid̄ 7 dimid̄ . ad *HIMELTVN*
7 *SPECLEA*. Himeltun fuit Wasta. Ibi sunt m̄ . II . uitti
7 II . bord̄ . cū . I . car̄ 7 dimid̄ . 7 VIII . ac̄ p̄ti . Silua dimid̄ lew
lḡ . 7 dimid̄ lat. Ad Speclea hn̄t . II . francig̃ . IIII . car.
7 VI . bord̄ cū . II . car̄. Ibi . XVI . ac̄ p̄ti . Siluæ . II . q̄rent.
Valuit 7 uat . L . solid̄. Hanc t̃rā tenuit Alric de dn̄ico
uictu monachoz . 7 inde faciebat seruitiū ad uoluntatē eoz.
174 a De eod̄ m̄ ten̄ Hugo grentemaisnil dimid̄ hid̄ ad *LAPPEWRTE* . 7 Balduin
de eo . 7 fuit 7 est de soca ep̄i. Ibi sunt . III . uitti 7 II . bord̄ . Ibi
pb̄r 7 un uenator. Hi hn̄t . I . car̄ 7 VI . boues. Silua . I . lewa
lḡ . 7 dimid̄ lat. Valuit 7 uat . XX . solid̄. De hac t̃ra p̄
singulos annos reddunt . VIII . den̄ ad æccłam de Wirecestre.
p̄ cirsette . 7 recognitione træ.

67 Robert the Bursar holds 1 of these 3 hides; it is called
KNIGHTWICK. He has 1 plough and A 140
7 smallholders with 2 ploughs;
meadow, 6 acres; woodland 2 furlongs long and 1 wide.
The value was and is 20s.
Before 1066 this hide paid full jurisdiction and every service of the King in the said manor. It is for the household supplies of the monks, but it was leased to a nun, Edith, to have and give service for as long as the brothers wished, and could do without it; but as their community grew after 1066, she gave it back. She is still alive and is herself the witness to this.

68 The Church itself holds HALLOW with BROADWAS. 7 hides which pay tax. It is not in lordship, except 1 hide; 2 ploughs there;
10 villagers and 16 smallholders with 10 ploughs. 4 male and 2 female slaves. A 141
2 mills at 10s; a fishery at 20 sticks of eels;
meadow, 20 acres; woodland 1 league long and 1 wide.
To this manor belong 10 houses in Droitwich at 5s
and a salt-house which pays 50 measures of salt.
2 riders hold 2 hides of this land; they have 2 ploughs.
Value before 1066, 100s; now the same.

69 Walter of 'Burgh' holds ½ hide of this manor in EASTBURY. A 142
He has 1 plough. Alric held it; it is (part) of the villagers' land.
Value 5s.

70 Roger of Lacy holds 3½ hides of this manor at HIMBLETON and SPETCHLEY. Himbleton was waste. Now there are
2 villagers and 2 smallholders with 1½ ploughs. A 143
Meadow, 8 acres; woodland ½ league long and ½ wide.
At Spetchley 2 Frenchmen have 4 ploughs;
6 smallholders with 2 ploughs.
Meadow, 16 acres; woodland, 2 furlongs.
The value was and is 50s.
Alric held this land for the household supplies of the monks and performed service from it at their will.

71 Hugh of Grandmesnil holds ½ hide also of this manor at LYPPARD, 174 a
and Baldwin from him. It was and is (part) of the Bishop's jurisdiction.
3 villagers and 2 smallholders. A priest and 1 hunter. They have 1 plough and 6 oxen. A 144
Woodland 1 league long and ½ wide.
The value was and is 20s.
From this land 8d is paid each year to the Church of Worcester for Church tax and acknowledgement of the land.

Ipſa æccła ten̄ *CROPETORN* cū̄ *NEOTHERETVNE*.
Ibi . L . hidæ. De his ſunt in dn̄io . XIIII . hidæ. 7 ibi . v . car̄.
7 pb̄r hn̄s dimid̄ hid̄ cū̄ . I . car̄. 7 XVIII . uiłłi 7 XII . bord̄
cū̄ . XI . car̄ . Ibi . x . ſerui . 7 IIII . ancillæ. 7 molin̄ de . x . ſolid̄.
7 xx . ſtiches anguillar̄. 7 xx . ac̄ p̄ti. 7 III . q̄rent̄ ſiluæ int̄ tot̄
Ibi ſunt Waſtæ . v . hidæ. Valuit . VII . lib̄ . m̄ . VI . lib̄.
De hoc m̄ ten̄ Rob̄t̄ diſpenſ̄. XI . hid̄. 7 ibi ht̄ . IX . car̄.
7 x . uiłł 7 XII . bord̄ . cū̄ . VII . car̄. Ibi eraṅt . VIII . ſerui . 7 II . ancillæ.
Vał̄b . VI . lib̄ . Modo . VII . lib̄. Keneuuard 7 Godric tenuer̄
7 deſeruieb̄ ſic̄ ab ep̄o dep̄cari poterant.
De ipſo m̄ ten̄ ab̄b̄ de Eueſhā̄ . v . hid̄ ad *HANTVNE*.
De q̄b; ep̄s de Wireceſtre T.R.E. tant̄modo geld̄ habuit
ad ſuū̄ hund̄. De reliq̄ tota . ē̄ q̄eta ad æccłam de Eueſhā̄
ut dic̄ comitatus.
De eod̄ m̄ ten̄ ab̄b̄ de *EVESHĀ* . IIII . hid̄ in *BENNICWORTE*.
7 ibid̄ ten̄ Vrſo uicecom̄ . VI . hid̄. 7 ibi ht̄ . II . car̄ . 7 XII.
uiłł. 7 II . bord̄ cū̄ . III . car̄ 7 dimid̄. Ibi . VI . ſerui 7 I . ancilla.
7 VI . ac̄ p̄ti. Vał̄b . LX . ſoł . modo . IIII . lib̄. 7 x . ſolid̄.
Azor tenuit. 7 ſeruieb̄ ut ep̄o placebat. *IN ESCH HVND̄*.
Ipſa æccła ten̄ *CLIVE* cū̄ *LENC*. Ibi . x . hidæ 7 dimidia.
In dn̄io ſunt . II . car̄. 7 pb̄r hn̄s . I . hid̄ 7 II . car̄. 7 IX . uiłłi 7 . v.
bord̄ . cū̄ . IIII . car̄ . 7 molin̄ redd̄ . I . ſextar̄ mellis. Ibi . IIII.
ſerui. 7 IIII . ancillæ. 7 xx . ac̄ p̄ti . Vał̄b . VII . lib̄ . m̄ . VI . lib̄.
De hac t̄ra ſunt waſtæ . II . hidæ una v̄ min̄.
Ipſa æccła ten̄ *FEPSETENATVN* . Ibi . VI . hidæ. Vna ex his n̄ geld̄.
Walter̄ ponther eā̄ ten̄. Aliæ . v . geldaṅt. 7 ibi ſunt . II . car̄.
7 IIII . uiłłi cū̄ . II . car̄. 7 IIII . ſerui. 7 VI . ac̄ p̄ti. Silua dim̄ lewa
lḡ. 7 una q̄z lat̄. 7 In Wich de ſalinis . x . ſolid̄. Vał̄b 7 uał . x . ſoł.

72 The Church itself holds CROPTHORNE with NETHERTON. 50 hides.
Of these, 14 hides are in lordship; 5 ploughs there;
A priest who has ½ hide with 1 plough; 18 villagers and 12 smallholders with 11 ploughs. 10 male and 4 female slaves. A 145
A mill at 10s; 20 sticks of eels; meadow, 20 acres; woodland, 3 furlongs in all.
5 hides are waste.
The value was £7; now £6.

73 Robert the Bursar holds 11 hides of this manor. He has 9 ploughs;
10 villagers and 12 smallholders with 7 ploughs. 8 male and 2 female slaves were there. A 146
The value was £6; now £7
Kenward and Godric held them and gave service on the terms they could beg from the Bishop.

74 The Abbot of Evesham holds 5 hides of this manor at HAMPTON. Before 1066 the Bishop of Worcester had from them only the tax for his Hundred. The other (obligations) are fully discharged at the Church of Evesham, as the County states.

75 The Abbot of Evesham holds 4 hides also of this manor in BENGEWORTH and there also Urso the Sheriff holds 6 hides.
He has 2 ploughs; A 147
12 villagers and 2 smallholders with 3½ ploughs. 6 male slaves, 1 female.
Meadow, 6 acres.
The value was 60s; now £4 10s.
Azor held them and served as it pleased the Bishop.

In ESCH Hundred

76 The Church itself holds CLEEVE (Prior) with (Atch) LENCH.
10½ hides. In lordship 2 ploughs;
A priest who has 1 hide and 2 ploughs; 9 villagers and 5 smallholders with 4 ploughs. A 7
A mill which pays 1 sester of honey. 4 male and 4 female slaves; meadow, 20 acres.
The value was £7; now £6.
2 hides, less 1 virgate, of this land are waste.

77 The Church holds PHEPSON itself. 6 hides. One of these does not pay tax; Walter Ponther holds it. The other 5 pay tax.
2 ploughs there.
4 villagers with 2 ploughs. 4 slaves.
Meadow, 6 acres; woodland ½ league long and 1 furlong wide; from the salt-houses in Droitwich, 10s.
The value was and is 10s.

Ad hoc ϖ ptin̄ . I Bereuuich CROHLEA . Ibi . v hidæ geld̄.
Laci Roger ten̄ . 7 Odo de eo . In dn̄io sunt . II . car̄ . 7 VII . uill̄i 7 III .
bord̄ . cū . IIII . car̄ . Ibi . IIII . serui . 7 una ancilla . 7 molin̄ de . II .
solid̄ . 7 Salina in Wich de . III . solid̄ . Ibi . XVI . ac̄ p̄ti . Silua
dimid̄ leuua lḡ . 7 una qz̄ lat̄ . H̄ est in foresta.
Simund tenuit . de dn̄io fuit . 7 inde reddeb̄ ep̄o om̄e ser
uitium | 7 geldum. 7 nusq̄ se cū hac t̄ra uertere poterat.
Val̄b . IIII . lib̄ . Modo . LXX . solid̄.
Ipsa æccl̄a ten̄ HAMBYRIE . Ibi . XIIII . hidæ geld̄ . In dn̄io
sunt . II . car̄ . 7 XVI . uill̄i 7 XVIII . bord̄ . 7 p̄b̄r 7 p̄positus.
Int̄ om̄s hn̄t . XXIIII . car̄ . Ibi . IIII . serui . 7 una ancilla . 7 XX ti .
ac̄ p̄ti . Silua . I . leuua lḡ . 7 dimid̄ lat̄ . sed in foresta . ē regis.
In Wich de salinis . C . V . mittas salis . Val̄b . VII . lib̄ . m̄ . VI . lib̄.
De hac t̄ra sunt . II . hidæ wastæ.
Vrso ten̄ de hac t̄ra dimid̄ hid̄ . 7 Radulf' de eo . Ibi h̄t . I . car̄.
Val̄b 7 ual . V . solid̄.
In om̄ib; his ϖ non possu͠t . ēe . plus carucæ quā dictū est.
Dicit uicecomitat' qd̄ de una quaq; hida t̄ræ libera uel
uillana quæ ad æccl̄am de Wirecestre p̄tinet . debet
ep̄s hab̄e in die festo S̄ Martini unā sūmā annonæ
de meliori quæ ibidē crescit . Qd̄ si dies ille n̄ reddita an
nona transierit: qui retinuit annonā reddet 7 undecies
p̄soluet . 7 insup̄ forisfacturā ep̄s accipiet . qualē de sua
terra habere debet.

IN CAME HVND̄.

174 b Ipsa æccl̄a ten̄ STOCHE cū . II . Bereuuich̄ ESTONE 7 BEDINDONE .
Ibi . X . hidæ . In dn̄io sunt . II . car̄ . 7 XIII . uill̄i 7 VII . bord̄ 7 p̄b̄r .
Int̄ om̄s hn̄t . XIIII . car̄ . Ibi . IIII . serui . 7 una ancilla . 7 II . molini
qui redd̄t . VII . oras . Silua . I . leuua 7 dimid̄ longa.
H̄ silua . ē in foresta . Val̄b . XL . solid̄ . Modo: C . solid̄.

78 To this manor belongs 1 outlier, CROWLE. 5 hides which pay tax. Roger (of) Lacy holds it, and Odo from him. In lordship 2 ploughs;
7 villagers and 3 smallholders with 4 ploughs. 4 male slaves, 1 female. A 10
A mill at 2s; in Droitwich a salt-house at 3s. Meadow, 16 acres; woodland ½ league long and 1 furlong wide: it is in the Forest.
Sigmund held it. It was (part) of the lordship (land) and from it he rendered the Bishop every service and tax. He could not turn anywhere with this land.
The value was £4; now 70s.

79 The Church holds HANBURY itself. 14 hides which pay tax. In lordship 2 ploughs;
16 villagers, 18 smallholders, a priest and a reeve; between them they have 24 ploughs. 4 male slaves, 1 female. A 8
Meadow, 20 acres; woodland 1 league long and ½ wide, but it is in the King's Forest; from the salt-houses in Droitwich, 105 measures of salt.
The value was £7; now £6.
2 hides of this land are waste.
Urso holds ½ hide of this land, and Ralph from him. He has 1 plough. The value was and is 5s.

80 In all these manors there cannot be more ploughs than is stated. The Shire states that from each and every hide of land, whether free or villagers', which belongs to the Church of Worcester, the Bishop should have at Martinmas one packload of corn of the better sort which grows there. But if that day has passed and the corn has not been handed over, whoever has kept it back shall hand over the corn, and shall pay elevenfold; and in addition the Bishop shall receive the forfeiture just as he should have from his land.

In CAME Hundred 174 b

81 The Church itself holds STOKE (Prior) with 2 outliers, ASTON (Fields) and 'BADDINGTON'. 10 hides. In lordship 2 ploughs;
13 villagers, 7 smallholders and a priest; between them they have 14 ploughs. 4 male slaves, 1 female.
2 mills which pay 7 *ora*; woodland 1½ leagues long: this woodland is in the Forest.
The value was 40s; now 100s.

Ipsa æccła ten̄ *Hverteberie*. *In Cresselav hvnd*.
cū .vi. Bereuū. Ibi .xx. hidæ .7 in dn̄io .iiii. car̄. 7 xxiiii.
uitti 7 iii. bord 7 pbr. Int̄ om̄s hn̄t .xxi. car̄. Ibi .xii. serui.
7 iii. ancille .7 ii. molini de .iiii. solid 7 x. sūmis annonæ.
Silua .i. leuua lḡ .7 dimid lat̄ .7 in Wich .v. dom̄ reddt
.v. mittas salis. T.R.E. ualb xvi. lib. modo .xiii. lib 7 x. sol.
Ipsa æccła ten̄ *Vlwardelei*. Ibi .v. hidæ.
In dn̄io sunt .ii. car̄ .7 iiii. uitt 7 v. bord cū .iiii. car̄.
Ibi pbr hn̄s dimid car̄ .7 un̄ lib hō hn̄s .i. hid .7 redd
ii. sextar̄ mett. Ibi .vi. int̄ seruos 7 ancillas .7 molinū
de .vi. solid. T.R.E. ualb .iiii. lib. modo .xxx. solid.
Ipsa æccła ten̄ *alvievecherche* .cū .iiii. *In Came hvnd*.
Bereuuich *Costone* .*Warstelle* .*Tonge* .*Ovretone*. In his cū m̄ sunt
xiii. hidæ. In dn̄io sunt .ii. car̄ .7 pbr 7 ppositꝰ 7 unꝰ Radchen̄.
7 xii. uitti 7 vii. bord. Int̄ om̄s hn̄t .xiiii. car̄. Int̄ seruos 7 ancitt
sunt .vii. 7 Siluæ .iiii. leuuedes. Inde rex tulit medietatē in suā
siluā. In Wich .viii. salinæ. Vna ex his redd .l. mittas sal.
aliæ .vii. reddt .lxx. mittas salis.
T.R.E. ualb .c. solid. 7 modo similiter. *In Dodintret hd*.
Sc̄a Maria ten̄ *Ardolvestone* 7 *Cnistetone*. de uictu monachoꝝ. rq
Duo m̄ sunt de .xv. hid. In dn̄io sunt .viii. car̄ .7 pbr 7 xv. uitt
7 x. bord cū .xv. car̄ .7 adhuc .iii. car̄ possent fieri. Ibi .xvii. serui.
7 molin̄ de .x. solid .7 piscaria .7 vi. ac̄ p̄ti. Silua dimid leuua lḡ.
7 iii. q̄ꝝ lat̄. Vat .viii. lib.

.III. Terra Epi De Hereford. *In Dodintret. hvnd*.
Eps de Hereford ten̄ de rege *Boclintvn*. Turchil te
nuit .7 poterat ire quo uoleb. Ibi .viii. hidæ geld. In dn̄io
sunt .ii. car̄ .7 ii. radmans .7 iiii. uitti 7 viii. bord cū .x. car̄.

In CRESSLAU Hundred

82 The Church itself holds HARTLEBURY with 6 outliers. 20 hides.
In lordship 4 ploughs;
24 villagers, 3 smallholders and a priest; between them they have 21 ploughs. 12 male and 3 female slaves.
2 mills at 4s and 10 packloads of corn; woodland 1 league long and ½ wide; 5 houses in Droitwich pay 5 measures of salt.
Value before 1066 £16; now £13 10s.

83 The Church holds WOLVERLEY itself. 5 hides. In lordship 2 ploughs;
4 villagers and 5 smallholders with 4 ploughs. A priest who has ½ plough. 1 free man who has 1 hide and pays 2 sesters of honey. 6 slaves, male and female.
A mill at 6s.
Value before 1066 £4; now 30s.

In CAME Hundred

84 The Church itself holds ALVECHURCH with 4 outliers, COFTON (Hackett), WAST HILLS, 'TONGE', *OVRETONE.* 13 hides in these, including the manor. In lordship 2 ploughs;
A priest, a reeve, 1 riding-man, 12 villagers and 7 smallholders; between them they have 14 ploughs; 7 slaves, male and female.
Woodland, 4 leagues; the King has taken half of it into his Wood. 8 salt-houses in Droitwich; one of these pays 50 measures of salt, the other 7 pay 70 measures of salt.
Value before 1066, 100s; now the same.

In DODDINGTREE Hundred

85 St. Mary's holds EARDISTON and KNIGHTON (on Teme) for the monks' supplies. The two manors are of 15 hides. . . . rq
In lordship 8 ploughs;
A priest, 15 villagers and 10 smallholders with 15 ploughs; a further 3 ploughs would be possible. 17 slaves.
A mill at 10s; a fishery; meadow, 6 acres; woodland ½ league long and 3 furlongs wide.
Value £8.

3 LAND OF THE BISHOP OF HEREFORD

In DODDINGTREE Hundred

1 The Bishop of Hereford holds BOCKLETON from the King. Thorkell held it; he could go where he would. 8 hides which pay tax. In lordship 2 ploughs;
2 riders, 4 villagers and 8 smallholders with 10 ploughs.

Ibi . xii . serui . Silua . i . lewa lḡ 7 dim̄ . 7 dimid lewa lata.
Valb . vi . lib . modo: iiii . lib . 7 ibi possunt . ee . plus . iiii . car.
Isd eps ten *Cver* . Walt eps tenuit . Ibi . ii . hidæ geld.
In dn̄io . ē . i . car̄ . 7 iii . bord . 7 iii . serui . Valb . xii . sol . m̄ x . solid.
Vrso ten de ep̄o . 7 . ii . car plus possunt ibi . ee. *In Esch hund.*
Isd eps ten *Inteberga* . Herald com tenuit iniuste . sed rex . W.
reddid Walterio ep̄o . q̄a de episcopatu erat . Ibi . xv . hidæ 7 dimid.
Ex his . x . hidæ geld . aliæ non . In dn̄io sunt . iiii . car̄ . 7 xv . uitti
7 xii . bord . cū . xiii . car . 7 adhuc . iiii . car̄ possent ibi fieri.
Ibi . iii . serui . 7 salina redd . xv . mittas salis . Silua . ii . lew
lḡ . 7 una leuua lat . de pasnag redd . c . porc.
T . R . E . uatb . xii . lib . 7 post: x . lib . Modo: xii . lib.

.IIII. ÆTERRA SC̄I DYONISII. *In Clent hd.*

Æccta S̄ Dyonisii ten . i . hidā in Wich . 7 ibi sunt . xviii . burḡses redđtes . iiii . solid . 7 vi . den . 7 una salina de . xx . den.

.V. ÆTERRA ÆCCL̄Æ DE COVENTREV. *In Clent hund.*

Æccta S̄ Marie de Couentreu ten *Salewarpe* . Ibi . i . hida in Wich . Vrso ten de abbe . 7 . H tra est in parco ei9 . 7 ipse hr̄ iiii . burḡses 7 vi . salinas in Wich . Valuit . xlv . sol . m̄ . xxxv . solid.

.VI. ÆTERRA ÆCCL̄Æ DE CORMELIIS. *In Dodintret hd.*

Æccta S̄ Mariæ de Cormeliis ten dimidiā hid in *Tametdeberie* . 7 geld. Ibi . ē pbr cū . i . car̄ . 7 val . v . solid . Witts com ded æcclæ.

12 slaves.
Woodland 1½ leagues long and ½ league wide.
The value was £6; now £4.
4 more ploughs possible.

2 The Bishop also holds KYRE. Bishop Walter held it.
2 hides which pay tax. In lordship 1 plough;
3 smallholders and 3 slaves.
The value was 12s; now 10s.
Urso holds it from the Bishop. 2 more ploughs possible.

In ESCH Hundred

3 The Bishop also holds INKBERROW. Earl Harold held it
wrongfully, but King William restored it to Bishop Walter
because it was the Bishopric's. 15½ hides. Of these, A 6
10 hides pay tax, the others do not. In lordship 4 ploughs;
15 villagers and 12 smallholders with 13 ploughs;
a further 4 ploughs would be possible. 3 slaves.
A salt-house which pays 15 measures of salt; woodland
2 leagues long and 1 league wide: it pays
100 pigs for pasture dues.
Value before 1066 £12; later £10; now £12.

4 LAND OF ST. DENIS' (CHURCH)

In CLENT Hundred

1 St. Denis' Church holds 1 hide in DROITWICH.
18 burgesses who pay 4s 6d.
A salt-house at 20d.
[Value . . .]

5 LAND OF THE CHURCH OF COVENTRY

In CLENT Hundred

1 St. Mary's Church of Coventry holds SALWARPE. 1 hide
in Droitwich. Urso holds from the Abbot. This land is in
his park. He has
4 burgesses and
6 salt-houses in Droitwich.
The value was 45s; now 35s.

6 LAND OF THE CHURCH OF CORMEILLES

In DODDINGTREE Hundred

1 St. Mary's Church of Cormeilles holds ½ hide in TENBURY
(Wells); it pays tax.
A priest with 1 plough.
Value 5s.
Earl William gave it to the church.

.VII. **TERRA ÆCCLÆ DE GLOWECESTRE.** *IN CLENT HVND.*

Æccla S PETRI de Glouuec ten dimid hid in *WICH*. 7 est in ead csuetudine qua .e 7 dimid hida regis quæ .e in *WICH*. ptin ad Glouuec.

174 c

.VIII. **TERRA SCI PETRI WESTMONASTERII.**

Eccla S PETRI WESTMONAST tenet *PERSORE*. Rex Eduuard tenuit hoc m. 7 eid ecclæ dedit ita qetu 7 liberu ab omi calunia. sicut ipse in suo dnio tenebat. Teste toto comitatu. Ibi. cc. hidæ. de his in psore sunt. II. hidæ. quæ nunqua geldau T.R.E. Ibi sunt in dnio. V. car. 7 X. uitti cu. VII. car. 7 XI. serui 7 una ancilla. Ibi. XXVIII. burgses reddt XXX. solid. 7 theloneu redd. XII. sol. Ibi. III. molini de. L. solid. 7 C. ac pti. Silua. II. lew lg. 7 III. qz lat. Eccla. I. na redd XVI. solid. Valet. XIIII. lib.

In hoc m qda francig ten terram Turchil stirmanni regis. E. 7 ht. I. car. 7 II. seru. 7 II. uitt cu. II. car.

In *WICHE*. sunt. VI. hidæ. Ibi. I. car in dnio. 7 IX. uitt 7 XXV. bord cu. XII. car. 7 un seru. 7 piscaria. Val. III. lib

De his. VI. hid ten Vrso. I. hid. 7 Gislebt dimid hid. Tor 7 Osuuard tenuer. Ibi. e. I. car. 7 II. bord. 7 II. serui. 7 I. ancilla. Val. XXV. solid.

In *PENDESHAM*. II. hidæ. 7 in dnio sunt. Ibi. II. car. 7 III. uitt 7 IX. bord cu. IIII. car. Ibi. IIII. serui. 7 XII. ac pti. Val. III. lib.

In *BERLINGEHA*. sunt. III. hidæ 7 I. virg. Ibi in dnio. II. car. 7 III. uitt 7 IIII. bord cu. IIII. car. 7 piscaria. 7 XX. ac pti. Valet. L. solid.

De hac tra ten Vrso. II. hid 7 una v. Aluric 7 Donning tenuer. Ibi sunt. II. car. 7 II. bord 7 IIII. serui. 7 X. ac pti. Valb. LX. sol. modo. XL. solid.

7 LAND OF THE CHURCH OF GLOUCESTER

In CLENT Hundred

1 St. Peter's Church of Gloucester holds ½ hide in DROITWICH, with the same customary dues as the King's ½ hide which is in Droitwich and which belongs to Gloucester.

8 LAND OF ST. PETER'S, WESTMINSTER 174 c

1 St. Peter's Church, Westminster, holds PERSHORE.
King Edward held this manor and gave it to this church as exempt and free from every claim, as he held it in his own A 33
lordship. The whole County bears witness to this. 200 hides. Of these, there are 2 hides in Pershore; they never paid tax before 1066. In lordship 5 ploughs;

10 villagers with 7 ploughs; 11 male slaves, 1 female.
28 burgesses pay 30s; a toll which pays 12s.
3 mills at 50s; meadow, 100 acres; woodland 2 leagues long and 3 furlongs wide; a church which pays 16s.

Value £14.

In this manor a Frenchman holds the land of Thorkell, King Edward's steersman. He has 1 plough, 2 slaves and 2 villagers with 2 ploughs.

2 In WICK there are 6 hides. 1 plough in lordship;
9 villagers and 25 smallholders with 12 ploughs; 1 slave.
A fishery. A 34;
Value £3. 46-47

Of these 6 hides Urso holds 1 hide, Gilbert ½ hide. Thor and Osward held them. 1 plough there.
2 smallholders and 2 male slaves, 1 female.
Value 25s.

3 In PENSHAM 2 hides. They are in lordship. 2 ploughs there.
3 villagers and 9 smallholders with 4 ploughs. 4 slaves. A 35
Meadow, 12 acres.
Value £3.

4 In BIRLINGHAM there are 3 hides and 1 virgate. In lordship 2 ploughs;
3 villagers and 4 smallholders with 4 ploughs.
A fishery; meadow, 20 acres. A 36; 48
Value 50s.

Urso holds 2 hides and 1 virgate of this land. Aelfric and Dunning held them. 2 ploughs there.
2 smallholders and 4 slaves.
Meadow, 10 acres.
The value was 60s; now 40s.

In BRICSTELMESTVNE . ſunt . x . hidæ. Ibi . x . uiłł 7 x . borđ cū . VI . caꝛ̃. 7 araɴ̃ 7 ſeminaɴ̃ . VI . acs de ꝓpio ſemine. Ibi xx . ac pti. Vał . xx . ſoliđ.

In DEPEFORDE . ſunt . x . hidæ. jnt ſiluā 7 planū. Ibi . VIII . uiłł 7 x . borđ cū . VI . caꝛ̃. 7 araɴ̃ . IIII . acs 7 ſeminaɴ̃ de ſuo ſemine. De hac tra hn̄t . II . francig . II . hiđ. 7 hn̄t . II . car. 7 IIII . bouar. Ibi . x . ac pti. Vał . L . ſoliđ. De iſta tra T.R.E. tenebat Alcot monac . I . hiđ. 7 faciebat ſeruitiū qđ ei pcipiebatur.

In AICHINTVNE ſunt . XVI . hidæ. De his ſunt in dn̄io . IX . hidæ. una v min. Ibi . II . car in dn̄io. 7 VI . uiłł 7 II . cot cū . II . caꝛ̃. Ibi . VI . colibti . redđ p ann . XI . ſoł 7 II . den. 7 araɴ̃ 7 ſeminaɴ̃ de ꝓpio ſemine . XII . acras . Ibi . IIII . ſerui. 7 una ancilla . Vał . c . ſoł. De hac tra ten Vrſo . IIII . hiđ . unā v min . Dunning tenuit. Ibi in dn̄io . II . caꝛ̃. 7 v . uiłł 7 VIII . borđ cū . III . caꝛ̃. Ibi . IIII . ſerui. 7 III . ancillæ. 7 moliñ de . x . soliđ. 7 XVI . acs pti. Vał . XL . ſoł.

De ipſa tra ten Turſtin. f. Rov . III . hiđ. Brictric tenuit. In dn̄io ſunt . II . caꝛ̃. 7 VII . uiłł 7 IIII . borđ cū . I . caꝛ̃ . Ibi . IIII. ſerui 7 III . ancillæ. 7 XVI . ac pti. Silua . II . qz lg. 7 tntđ lat. Vał . LX . ſoliđ . Hi duo Dunning 7 Brictric . ſecab in ptis dn̄i ſui. p conſuetudinē . unā diem.

In BEFORD ſunt . x . hidæ. Ex his in dn̄io ſunt . IIII . hidæ. Wills pbr ten de abbe. Ibi cū ſuis hōibz hť . I . car 7 dimiđ. 7 x . acs pti. Silua dimiđ lew lg. 7 III . qz lat. Valet . xx . ſoliđ.

De hac tra ten Vrſo . v . hiđ. Eduuard 7 Leuric tenueꝛ̃. Ibi hť . II . caꝛ̃. 7 II . uiłł 7 II . borđ cū . I . car . Ibi . IIII . ſerui. 7 II . ancillæ. 7 x . ac pti. Silua dimiđ lew lg. 7 III . qz lat. Vał . XXX . ſoł.

5 In BRICKLEHAMPTON there are 10 hides.
10 villagers and 10 smallholders with 6 ploughs; they plough and sow 6 acres with their own seed. A 37
Meadow, 20 acres.
Value 20s.

6 In DEFFORD there are 10 hides, both wood and open land.
8 villagers and 10 smallholders with 6 ploughs; they plough 4 acres and sow it with their seed. A 38
Of this land 2 Frenchmen have 2 hides; they have 2 ploughs and 4 ploughmen.
Meadow, 10 acres.
Value 50s.
Before 1066 Algot the monk held 1 hide of this land and performed the service that he was asked.

7 In ECKINGTON there are 16 hides. Of these, 9 hides, less 1 virgate, are in lordship. In lordship 2 ploughs; A 39;
6 villagers and 2 cottagers with 2 ploughs. 6 freedmen 49-50
who pay 11s 2d a year; they plough and sow 12 acres with their own seed. 4 male slaves, 1 female.
Value 100s.
Urso holds 4 hides, less 1 virgate, of this land. Dunning held them. In lordship 2 ploughs;
5 villagers and 8 smallholders with 3 ploughs. 4 male and 3 female slaves.
A mill at 10s; meadow, 16 acres.
Value 40s.
Thurstan son of Rolf holds 3 hides of this land. Brictric held them. In lordship 2 ploughs;
7 villagers and 4 smallholders with 1 plough. 4 male and 3 female slaves.
Meadow, 16 acres; woodland 2 furlongs long and as wide.
Value 60s.
These two, Dunning and Brictric, reaped for 1 day in their lord's meadows as a customary due.

8 In BESFORD there are 10 hides. Of these, 4 hides are in lordship. William the priest holds from the Abbot. With his men he has 1½ ploughs and A 40;
meadow, 10 acres; woodland ½ league long and 3 furlongs wide. 51-52
Value 20s.
Urso holds 5 hides of this land. Edward and Leofric held them. He has 2 ploughs;
2 villagers and 2 smallholders with 1 plough. 4 male and 2 female slaves.
Meadow, 10 acres; woodland ½ league long and 3 furlongs wide.
Value 30s.

De eađ tra ten Walt ponther . I . hiđ quæ nunq geldauit.
Wasta . ẽ 7 fuit . 7 tam ualƀ 7 uał . XVI . den

In *LONGEDVNE* . sunt . XXX . hidæ. Ex his sunt in dñio . XI . hidæ.
Ibi . III . car . 7 X . uilł 7 XVII . borđ cũ pƀro hñtes . VI . car.
Ibi . VI . serui 7 II . ancillæ . 7 XL . ac pti. Silua . III . lew lg.
7 II . lew lat. Vał . IX . liƀ.

De hac tra T.R.E. teneƀ . IX . libi hoẽs . XVIII . hiđ . 7 secabant
uno die in ptis dñi sui . 7 facieƀ seruitiũ sic eis pcipiebatur.
Elric . Reinbald . Eluuard . Brictric . Alfric . Godric (cloch.) 7 Godric . Aluui 7 Aluui (blac).
Qđ tenebanƭ int totũ . ualƀ . XI . liƀ 7 XI . solid.

174 d
De hac tra ten rex Witts . V . hiđ 7 III . uirg. Reinbald 7 Alfric
tenuer. In dñio sunt . III . car . 7 XII . uilł 7 XII . borđ cũ XIIII . car.
Ibi . VII . serui 7 III . ancillæ . 7 molin de . II . solid.

De eađ tra ten Drogo . f . ponzii . I . hiđ . Godric tenuit.
Ibi . ẽ . I . car . 7 II . bouarii . 7 VI . ac pti. Vał . XV . solid.

De eađ tra ten Vrso . V . hiđ . Quattuor ex supdictis tenuer.
Eluuar Brictric Aluui 7 Godric.
Ibi in dñio . V . car . 7 III . uilł . 7 IX . borđ cũ . III . car.
Ibi . VI (II). serui . 7 III . ancillæ. 7 XXVIII . ac pti. Silua . III . q̃z lg.
7 II . q̃z lat. Vał . LXX . solid.

De ipsa tra ten Witts . f . baderon . II . hiđ 7 dimiđ . Aluui tenuit.
Ibi hĩ . II . car . 7 IIII . uilł 7 V . borđ cũ . III . car. Vał . XL . solid.
Ibi . XII . ac pti.

De eađ tra ten Rog de laci . V . hiđ . Alric tenuit . In dñio nil hĩ.
Silua . ẽ . I . lew lg . 7 dimiđ lat. De eo ten . I . radman Lefric
unã hiđ 7 unã v . 7 ibi hĩ . I . car . 7 III . uilł 7 VIII . borđ . cũ . IIII.
car. Ibi . I . seru 7 III . ancillæ . 7 molin de . VIII . solid . 7 XII . ac pti.
Vał . XX . solid.

Also of this land Walter Ponther holds 1 hide which has never paid tax. It is and was waste, but the value was and is 16d.

9a In LONGDON there are 30 hides. Of these, 11 hides are in lordship. 3 ploughs there. A 41;
10 villagers and 17 smallholders, with a priest, who have 6 ploughs. 6 male and 2 female slaves. 53-61
Meadow, 40 acres; woodland 3 leagues long and 2 leagues wide.
Value £9.

9b Before 1066 nine free men held 18 hides of this land; they reaped for 1 day in their lord's meadows and performed service as they were asked: Alric, Reinbald, Alfward, Brictric, Aelfric, Godric Clock and Godric, Alfwy and Alfwy Black.
The value, in total, of what they held was £11 11s.

9c King William holds 5 hides and 3 virgates of this land. 174 d
Reinbald and Aelfric held them. In lordship 3 ploughs;
12 villagers and 12 smallholders with 14 ploughs. 7 male and 3 female slaves.
A mill at 2s.
[Value . . .]

9d Drogo son of Poyntz holds 1 hide also of this land. Godric held it. 1 plough there.
2 ploughmen.
Meadow, 6 acres.
Value 15s.

9e Urso holds 5 hides also of this land. Four of the above held them: Alfward, Brictric, Alfwy and Godric. In lordship 5 ploughs;
3 villagers and 9 smallholders with 3 ploughs. 8 male and 3 female slaves.
Meadow, 28 acres; woodland 3 furlongs long and 2 furlongs wide.
Value 70s.

9f William son of Baderon holds 2½ hides of this land. Alfwy held them. He has 2 ploughs;
4 villagers and 5 smallholders with 3 ploughs.
Value 40s.
Meadow, 12 acres.

9g Roger of Lacy holds 5 hides also of this land. Alric held them. He has nothing in lordship.
Woodland 1 league long and ½ wide.
A rider, Leofric, holds 1 hide and 1 virgate from him.
He has 1 plough;
3 villagers and 8 smallholders with 4 ploughs. 1 male and 3 female slaves.
A mill at 8s; meadow, 12 acres.
Value 20s.

In *POIWIC*. sunt. III. hidæ. Ibi in dn̄io. II. car. 7 XVI. uill 7 V. bord. cū. X. car. Ibi. IIII. serui. 7 I. ancilla. 7 III. buri colibti. reddt. III. sext mell. 7 XLV. denar. 7 un̄ molin̄ seruiens aulæ. Ibi. XX. ac p̄ti. 7 de quadā reddita. XXX. solid. Val. XX. lib.

Ibi un pbr hn̄s. I. car. 7 II. bouar 7. V. bord cū. II. car.

Ibi fuer̄. VIII. radmans. Ageluuard Eduuard Brictmer. Saulf. Aluuin. Godric Aluui. Ketelbert. hn̄tes int se. X. car̄. 7 plures bord. 7 seruos. cū. VII. car̄. Qd teneb ualb. C. solid.

Ipsi radmans secabant. I. na die in anno in p̄tis dn̄i. 7 om̄e seruitiū qd eis iubebat faciebant.

Vrso ten tras quas tenuer̄ Æluuard 7 Saulf 7 Brictmer 7 Aluuin. 7 ibi ht̄. VII. car̄. 7 XXII. bord 7 XIIII. seruos. Val tot̄. IX. lib. 7 V. sol.

Gisleb̄t. f. Turold ten qd tenuer̄ Aluui 7 Ketelbern. 7 ibi sunt in dn̄io. II. car̄. 7 VII. bord 7 III. serui. cū. I. car̄. 7 molin̄ de. XVI. denar. Val. XL. III. solid.

Walt ponther ten qd tenuit Godric. 7 ibi ht̄ dimid car. 7 un̄ uill 7 VI. bord 7 II. seru cū. II. car̄. Val. XXV. solid.

Quidā francig Artur ten qd tenuit Eduuard. 7 ibi ht̄. I. car.

In *SNODESBYRIE* sunt. XI. hidæ. De his sunt in dn̄io 7 II. bou. VII. hidæ| 7 una virg'. vna ex his| hidis nunq geld. Ibi sunt in dn̄io. II. car. 7 VI. uill 7 XVI. cot. 7 II. francig seruientes. Int̄ om̄s hn̄t. XI. car. Ibi. IIII. serui. 7 XX. ac p̄ti. Silua. I. lew lḡ. 7 tntd lat. Val. VII. lib 7 X. solid.

De hac tra ten Vrso. IIII. hid. unā v min. Aluuard tenuit. 7 p c̄suetud secab. I. die p̄ta dn̄i sui. 7 seruitia que iubebat facieb. Ibi. ē una car 7 dim. 7 V. cot 7 IIII. bouarii. cū. I. car 7 dimid. 7 VI. ac p̄ti. Silua. III. q̄z lḡ. 7 II. q̄z lat̄. Val. L. sol.

10a In POWICK there are 3 hides. In lordship 2 ploughs;
16 villagers and 5 smallholders with 10 ploughs. 4 male slaves, 1 female; 3 boors, freedmen, pay 3 sesters of honey and 45d. A 42; 62-67; 70
A mill which serves the hall. Meadow, 20 acres; from some payment, 30s.
Value £20.
A priest who has 1 plough; 2 ploughmen and 5 smallholders with 2 ploughs.
There were 8 riders: Aethelward, Edward, Brictmer, Saewulf, Alwin, Godric, Alfwy, Ketelbert, who had between them 10 ploughs and several smallholders and slaves with 7 ploughs. The value of what they held was 100s.
The riders reaped for 1 day a year in the lord's meadows and performed every service that was ordered them.

10b Urso holds the lands which Aethelward, Saewulf, Brictmer and Alwin held. He has 7 ploughs and
22 smallholders and 14 slaves.
Value of the whole £9 5s.

10c Gilbert son of Thorold holds what Alfwy and Ketelbern held. In lordship 2 ploughs;
7 smallholders and 3 slaves with 1 plough.
A mill at 16d.
Value 43s.

10d Walter Ponther holds what Godric held. He has ½ plough and
1 villager, 6 smallholders and 2 slaves with 2 ploughs.
Value 25s.

10e A Frenchman, Arthur, holds what Edward held. He has 1 plough and 2 ploughmen.
[Value . . .]

11 In (Upton) SNODSBURY there are 11 hides. Of these, 7 hides and 1 virgate are in lordship. 1 of these hides has never paid tax. In lordship 2 ploughs;
6 villagers, 16 cottagers and 2 Frenchmen who serve; between them they have 11 ploughs. 4 slaves. A 43; 68
Meadow, 20 acres; woodland 1 league long and as wide.
Value £7 10s.
Urso holds 4 hides, less 1 virgate, of this land. Alfward held it and as a customary due reaped his lord's meadows for 1 day and performed what services he was ordered. 1½ ploughs there.
5 cottagers and 4 ploughmen with 1½ ploughs.
Meadow, 6 acres; woodland 3 furlongs long and 2 furlongs wide.
Value 50s.

In *HVSENTRE*. sunt. VI. hidæ. Ibi. XI. uitti hnt. IIII. car.
7 redd p ann. c. caretedes lignoꝝ ad salinas de Wich.
Qui hanc trā custodit. hr de ea. I. hid. 7 ibi. I. car. 7 un uitt
7 VI. bord cū. II. car. Totū uat. XXX. solid.
In *WICH* fuer 7 sunt. IIII. furni. 7 reddeb T. R. E. p annū. LX.
solid 7 c. mittas salis. 7 XXXI. burgsis redd. XV. solid 7 VIII. den.
Ibi. II. pbri ten. I. hidā quæ nunq geldauit. 7 ē in dnio abbis.
7 Leuenot pbr. I. salinā redd. X. solid.
Totū hoc uat. c. solid 7 XII. solid 7 VIII. denar.
De decima regis de Wich. hr S Petrus. VIII. lib.
Witts. f. Corbuz. ten *DORMESTVN*. Waland tenuit. T. R. E.
Ibi. V. hidæ. 7 in dnio. II. car. 7 II. uitt 7 XIIII. bord cū. III. car.
Ibi. VI. serui 7 una ancilla. 7 III. ac pti. Silua dimid lew lg.
7 III. qz lat. De Witto ten Albt. II. hid. 7 ibi. hr. I. car. 7 un
uitt cū dim car. Ibi. II. serui. Predict Waland secabat prata
dni sui. 7 ome seruitiū qd iubebat facieb. Vat. IIII. lib 7 X. solid.
175 a
Vrso uicecom ten *PIDELET*. Toli. I. lib hō tenuit. Ibi. V. hidæ.
7 in dnio. II. car. 7 IIII. uitt 7 IIII. bord cū. III. car. Ibi. II. serui.
7 VIII. ac pti. Valb. XXX. solid. modo. LX. solid.
Toli supdict. seruieb de hac tra sic alii libi hoēs.
Ibi Isd Vrso ten *NEWENTVNE*. Tres libi hoēs tenuer. T. R. E.
x, hide Aluuard Saulf 7 Eluuard. In dnio sunt. IIII. car. 7 IIII. uitt
cū. II. car. Ibi. VIII. serui. 7 XII. ac pti. Silua. II. qz lg.
7 una qz lat. Valb. c. solid. modo. IIII. lib.
De his. X. hid ten Herbrand de Vrsone. III. hid 7 unā v.
7 ibi hr. II. car. 7 IIII. seruos 7 II. ancitt. 7 VI. acs pti. 7 II. cot.
Valb. LX. solid. modo. XL. solid. Qui has tras teneb. sic
alii libi hoēs seruiebant.

12 In (Martin) HUSSINGTREE there are 6 hides.
11 villagers have 4 ploughs and pay 100 cartloads of timber a year to the salt-houses of Droitwich. A 44
The man who has charge of this land has 1 hide of it, 1 plough there and
1 villager and 6 smallholders with 2 ploughs.
Value of the whole 30s.

13 In DROITWICH there were and are 4 furnaces; before 1066 they paid 60s a year and 100 measures of salt.
31 burgesses who pay 15s 8d. 2 priests hold 1 hide which A 45
has never paid tax; it is in the Abbot's lordship.
Leofnoth the priest (holds) 1 salt-house which pays 10s.
Value of the whole of this, 100s and 12s 8d.
St. Peter('s) has £8 from the King's tithe at Droitwich.

14 William son of Corbucion holds DORMSTON. Waland held it before 1066. 5 hides. In lordship 2 ploughs;
2 villagers and 14 smallholders with 3 ploughs. 6 male
slaves, 1 female. A 69; 71
Meadow, 3 acres; woodland ½ league long and 3 furlongs wide.
Albert holds 2 hides from William. He has 1 plough and
1 villager with ½ plough. 2 slaves.
The said Waland reaped his lord's meadows and performed every service that he was ordered.
Value £4 10s.

15 Urso the Sheriff holds (North) PIDDLE. Toli, a free man, 175 a
held it. 5 hides. In lordship 2 ploughs;
4 villagers and 4 smallholders with 3 ploughs. 2 slaves. A 72
Meadow, 8 acres.
The value was 30s; now 60s.
The above Toli served from this land like other free men.

16 Urso also holds NAUNTON (Beauchamp). Three free men, Alfward, Saewulf and Alfward, held it before 1066. 10 hides.
In lordship 4 ploughs; A 73
4 villagers with 2 ploughs. 8 slaves.
Meadow, 12 acres; woodland 2 furlongs long and 1 furlong wide.
The value was 100s; now £4.
Of these 10 hides Herbrand holds 3 hides and 1 virgate from Urso. He has 2 ploughs, 4 male and 2 female slaves and meadow, 6 acres; 2 cottagers.
The value was 60s; now 40s.
Those who held these lands served like other free men.

Isd Vrso ten GARSTVNE. Aluuin. I. lib hō tenuit. Ibi. II. hidæ. una v min. In dnio. ē una car. 7 III. bord 7 II. cot. 7 II. serui. 7 VI. ac pti. Valb XL. sol. Modo: XXX. solid. Qui hanc trā teneb. in pto. I. die secab. 7 alia seruitia facieb.

Isd Vrso ten PIDELET. Aluuin tenuit. Ibi. IIII. hidæ. Ex his una nunq geldau. In dnio sunt. II. car. 7 I. uilt 7 IIII. bord. 7 IIII. bouar. 7 I. ancilla. Int oms hnt. I. car. Valb. L. sol. modo: LX. sol.

WALTER ponther ten PERITVNE. Godric tenuit. Ibi. VI. hidæ. 7 in dnio. I. car. 7 III. uilt 7 X. bord cū. III. car 7 dimid. Ibi. IIII. serui. 7 VIII. ac pti. Silua. I. lew lḡ. 7 dimid lew lat. Valb. IIII. lib. Modo. L. sol.

Isd Walter ten GARSTVNE. Algar 7 Turchil tenuer. Ibi. VII. hidæ. 7 in dnio. III. car. 7 pbr 7 un francig 7 VI. uilti cū. V. car. Ibi. V. serui. 7 XII. ac pti. Silua dimid lew lḡ. 7 IIII. qz lat. Valb. IIII. lib. Modo. LXX. solid.

In PIPLINTVNE sunt. IIII. hidæ 7 dimid in dnio. 7 ibi un radman ten. III. uirg. 7 un francig ten trā uni uilti 7 un uilt 7 IIII. bord. jnt oms hnt. IIII. car. 7 ibi. II. cot reddt. III. sol.

In ead Bereuuiche tenuit Godric. III. hid 7 dimid. h dimid hida nunq geldauit. 7 Aluui tenuit. I. hid 7 unā v. h uirg nunq geldau. 7 alt Aluui tenuit. I. hidā. 7 Vluric tenuit. III. uirg. [una ex his n̄ geldauit T.R.E.] ipsi seruieb ut alii liberi homines.

Nc Walt ponther. ten trā Godric 7 Aluui. 7 ibi ht. I. car. 7 III. uilt 7 VI. bord cū. III. car. Ibi. IIII. serui. 7 X. ac pti. ⊙

Vrso uicecom ten hid quā alt Aluui teneb. Nil. ē ibi nisi. II. ac pti. 7 tam redd. c. den. ⊙ Qđ Walt ten: L. sol uat.

17 Urso also holds GRAFTON (Flyford). Alwin, a free man, held it.
2 hides, less 1 virgate. In lordship 1 plough;
3 smallholders, 2 cottagers and 2 slaves. A 74
Meadow, 6 acres.
The value was 40s; now 30s.
The man who held this land reaped for 1 day in the meadow and performed other services.

18 Urso also holds (North) PIDDLE. Alwin held it. 4 hides.
1 of these has never paid tax. In lordship 2 ploughs;
1 villager, 4 smallholders, 4 ploughmen and 1 female slave;
between them they have 1 plough. A 75
The value was 50s; now 60s.

19 Walter Ponther holds PIRTON. Godric held it. 6 hides.
In lordship 1 plough; A 76
3 villagers and 10 smallholders with 3½ ploughs. 4 slaves.
Meadow, 8 acres; woodland 1 league long and ½ league wide.
The value was £4; now 50s.

20 Walter also holds GRAFTON (Flyford). Algar and Thorkell
held it. 7 hides. In lordship 3 ploughs;
A priest, 1 Frenchman and 6 villagers with 5 ploughs. A 77
5 slaves.
Meadow, 12 acres; woodland ½ league long and 4 furlongs wide.
The value was £4; now 70s.

21 In PEOPLETON there are 4½ hides in lordship. 1 rider holds
3 virgates and 1 Frenchman holds the land of 1 villager.
1 villager and 4 smallholders; between them they have 4 A 78
ploughs. 2 cottagers pay 3s.
[Value . . .]

22 In the same outlier Godric held 3½ hides; the ½ hide has never paid tax. Alfwy held 1 hide and 1 virgate; this virgate has never paid tax. The other Alfwy held 1 hide. Wulfric held 3 virgates; 1 of these did not pay tax before 1066. They served like other free men.
Now Walter Ponther holds the land of Godric and Alfwy.
He has 1 plough;
3 villagers and 6 smallholders with 3 ploughs. 4 slaves.
Meadow, 10 acres. Ψ
Urso the Sheriff holds the hide which the other Alfwy held.
There is nothing there except 2 acres of meadow; however, it pays 100d.
Ψ Value of what Walter holds 50s.

GISLEBERT9. f. Turoldi ten CVBRINTVNE. Edric9 un9 lib hō tenuit. Ibi. IX. hidæ. 7 in dnio. I. car. 7 pbr 7 VII. uitti. 7 II. bord cū. IIII. car. Ibi. II. serui. 7 II. ancillæ. 7 XXX. ac pti. Ibi un9 francig ten. I. hid. 7 ibi ht. I. car. 7 II. seruos. 7 unā ancillā. Isd Edric9 facieb idem seruitiū qđ 7 alii libi hoēs. Valb. VI. lib. Modo. LXX. solid. Huic ptin una Bereuuicha de. X. hid. Vlf 7 Ansgot tenuer. 7 secab in pto dni. I. die in anno. 7 seruieb ut alii. Modo ten has. X. hid pdict9 Gisleb t9. 7 ht ibi. III. car in dnio. 7 XIIII. uitt 7 VI. bord cū. XI. car. Ibi. IIII. serui 7 una ancilla. 7 molin redd. XXX. sumas annonæ. 7 XXX. ac pti. Silua. I. lew lg. 7 tntd lat. Totū uatb. X. lib. modo: C. solid.

Vicecomes ten BROCTVNE. 7 Aiulf9 de eo. Bricsmar te nuit. Ibi. III. hidæ. 7 in dnio. ē. I. car. 7 dimid. 7 II. uitt 7 II. cot cū. I. car 7 dimid. Ibi. II. serui. 7 VI. ac pti. Valb. XL. sol. modo. XXX. solid. Bricsmar qui tenuit. seruieb sicut 7 alii.

IN WIRECESTRE SCIRE. ten Robt9 parler de Gislebto. f. Turoldi unū frustū træ 7 uocat Nadford. H tra n geldat. nec pgit ad hund. Ibi. ē pbr. sine car sine pecunia. Val. V. solid.

175 b

ALVERED9 de MERLEBERG ten STOCHE. Ibi. XV. hidæ. Isd ipse tenuit. XII. hid 7 unā v. T. R. E. Duo u Radmanni teneb . III. hid unā v min9. Aluuard 7 Vlfric9. Modo tot ht Aluredus. Ibi ht in dnio. III. car. 7 X. uitt 7 X. bord cū. V. car. 7 IIII. seru. pbr ht. I. car. Ibi. XX. ac pti. Silua. II. lew lg. 7 una lew lat. De hac tra ten. II. Radmanni. I. hid. 7 hnt ibi. II. car. 7 reddt. X. sol. De cad tra ten. II. hoēs Wills 7 Boselin9. II. hid 7 III. virg. 7 ibi hnt. II. car. 7 XI. bord cū. III. car. T. R. E. uatb int tot. XIII. lib. Modo: X. lib.

23 Gilbert son of Thorold holds COMBERTON. Edric, a free man, held it. 9 hides. In lordship 1 plough;
A priest, 7 villagers and 2 smallholders with 4 ploughs.
2 male and 2 female slaves. A 79-80
Meadow, 30 acres.
A Frenchman holds 1 hide. He has 1 plough, 2 male slaves, 1 female.
Edric also performed the same service as other free men.
The value was £6; now 70s.
To this (manor) belongs one outlier of 10 hides. Ulf and Ansgot held it and reaped for 1 day a year in the lord's meadow and served like the others. Now the said Gilbert holds these 10 hides. He has 3 ploughs in lordship;
14 villagers and 6 smallholders with 11 ploughs. 4 male slaves, 1 female.
A mill which pays 30 packloads of corn; meadow, 30 acres; woodland 1 league long and as wide.
The value of the whole was £10; now 100s.

24 The Sheriff holds BROUGHTON (Hackett), and Aiulf from him. Brictmer held it. 3 hides. In lordship 1½ ploughs;
2 villagers and 2 cottagers with 1½ ploughs. 2 slaves.
Meadow, 6 acres. A 81
The value was 40s; now 30s.
Brictmer who held it served like the others.

25 In Worcestershire Robert Parler holds from Gilbert son of Thorold a piece of land called NAFFORD. This land does not pay tax nor does it appear in the Hundred.
A priest without a plough or livestock.
Value 5s.

26a Alfred of Marlborough holds (Severn) STOKE. 15 hides. He 175 b
also held 12 hides and 1 virgate himself before 1066. Two riders, Alfward and Wulfric, held 3 hides, less 1 virgate. Now Alfred
holds the whole. He has in lordship 3 ploughs; A 17; 82
10 villagers and 10 smallholders with 5 ploughs; 4 slaves.
A priest has 1 plough.
Meadow, 20 acres; woodland 2 leagues long and 1 league wide.

26b Two riders hold 1 hide of this land; they have 2 ploughs and pay 10s.

26c Two men, William and Boselin, hold 2 hides and 3 virgates also of this land; they have 2 ploughs;
11 smallholders with 3 ploughs.
In total, value before 1066 £13; now £10.

VRSO teñ CVBRINTVNE. Ibi. II. hidæ. Azur tenuit. Ibi sunt IIII. uitti cū. II. car. Valb. x. solid. Modo: xx. solid.

OMS HÆ SVPDICTÆ TRÆ JACVERVNT 7 JACENT ad PSORE. Hoc Mⁿ T. R. E. reddebat qt xx. lib 7 III. 7 L. sextar mellis. cū omib; placitis francoꝝ hominū.

.IX. TERRA SČÆ MARIÆ DE PERSORE.

Eccta S MARIÆ De psore. tenuit 7 teñ ipsū Mⁿ PERSORE. Ibi. xxvi. hidæ geld. Ibi adjacent hæ Bereuuiche. Ciuintone. Edbritone. Wadberge. Broctune. Edbretintune. Wicha. Cūbritone. De supdictis .xxvi. hid. teñ modo Ipsa æccta. xxi. hid.
In dnio sunt. v. car. 7 xxiiii. uitti 7 viii. bord. cū xxii. car. Ibi. vii. serui. 7 moliñ de. iiii. solid. 7 ad pidele dimid moliñ de. x. solid 7 xx. stich anguil. Ibi. lx. ac pti. Silua. i. leuua lg. 7 dimid leuu lat. In Wich. i. salina. redd. xxx. mittas salis. .T.R.E. ualb. xiii. lib. modo. xii. lib.

De hac tra teñ Vrso. i. hid 7 dimid. 7 ibi ht. ii. car. 7 ii. uitt 7 iii. bord cū. i. car. Ibi. iiii. serui. 7 moliñ de. x. solid. Val. l. solid. Hanc trā tenuit Azor. 7 inde seruieb æcctæ. 7 p recognitione dabat in anno monachis unā firmā aut. xx. solid. 7 erat conuentio ut p mortē ei 7 uxoris suæ. rediret tra ad dniū æcctæ. Hic uiuebat die obit regis. E. 7 ita trā teneb. Postea ū uxore sua iā mortua: factus. ē Vtlagh.

De ead tra teñ isd Vrso. i. hid ad Broctune. 7 dicit qd. W. rex sibi eā ded. 7 inde debet æcctæ seruitiū reddere. Valb 7 ual. x. solid.

De ipsa tra teñ Robt dispens. iii. hid 7 dimid ad Wadberge. 7 ibi ht. ii. car. 7 ix. bord. 7 iiii. seruos. 7 parchū. Val. xl. sol. H tra fuit dnicoꝝ uittoꝝ. cū dimid hida q teñ un hō abbis.

7 Urso holds COMBERTON. 2 hides. Azor held it.
4 villagers with 2 ploughs. A 83
The value was 10s; now 20s.

8 All the above lands lay and lie in (the lands of) PERSHORE. Before 1066 this manor paid £83 and 50 sesters of honey, with all the pleas of freemen.

LAND OF ST. MARY'S OF PERSHORE

a St. Mary's Church of Pershore held and holds the manor of PERSHORE itself. 26 hides which pay tax. These outliers are attached to it: CHIVINGTON, ABBERTON, WADBOROUGH, (Drakes) BROUGHTON, ABBERTON, WICK, COMBERTON. Of the above 26 hides the church itself now holds 21 hides. In lordship 5 ploughs;
24 villagers and 8 smallholders with 22 ploughs. 7 slaves.
A mill at 4s; at (Wyre) Piddle ½ mill at 10s and 20 sticks A 148-156
of eels. Meadow, 60 acres; woodland 1 league long and ½ league wide. In Droitwich 1 salt-house which pays 30 measures of salt.
Value before 1066 £13; now £12.

b Urso holds 1½ hides of this land. He has 2 ploughs;
2 villagers and 3 smallholders with 1 plough. 4 slaves.
A mill at 10s.
Value 50s.

Azor held this land and served the church from it. In acknowledgement, he gave to the monks one revenue or 20s a year. There was an agreement that after his and his wife's death the land should return to the church's lordship. He was alive on the day of King Edward's death and held the land in this way. But later, when his wife was dead, he was made an outlaw.

c Urso also holds 1 hide of this land at (Drakes) BROUGHTON. He states that King William gave it to him and he has to render service to the church from it.
The value was and is 10s.

d Robert the Bursar holds 3½ hides of this land at WADBOROUGH. He has 2 ploughs and
9 smallholders and 4 slaves;
a park.
Value 40s.

This land, including ½ hide which a man of the Abbot holds, was (part) of the lordship villagers' (land).

In ead Wadbergæ.ē una hida træ.|In qua fuit uaccaria monachoꝝ. Hanc emit qdā Godricus teinus regis.E. uita triū hæredū.7 dabat in anno monachis.I.firmā p recognitione. Modo hт hanc trā tcius|heres. scilicet Vrso qui eā tenet. Post cuius mortē debet redire ad æcclam S MARIÆ.

Ipsa æccla ten *BEOLEGE*.cū uno mēbro *GERLEI*. Ibi.XXI.hida int planū 7 siluā. In dnio.ē.I.car.7 VIII.uitt 7 X.bord 7 unus Radman.cū.IX.car. Ibi silua.VI.lew lḡ.7 III.lew lat. 7 redd.XL.denar. Valб.VIII.libб.modo: C.solid.

Ipsa æccla ten *STVRE*. Ibi.XX.hidæ.7 in dnio.IIII.car.7 XXIIII. uitti 7 VIII.bord.cū.XI.car. Ibi.V.serui.7 II.molini de.XVII. solid 7 VI.denar. Ibi unus miles ten.II hid.7 II.radmans. Ibi.XX.ac pti. Valб.XII.libб.Modo: IX libб. Ħ tra geldat.

Ipsa æccla ten *BRADEWEIA*. Ibi.XXX.hidæ geld.in dnio ★ sunt.III.car.7 pбr 7 XLII.uitt cū.XX.car.Ibi.VIII.serui. Tot T.R.E.ualб.XII.libб 7 X.solid. Modo.XIIII.libб 7 X.solid.

175 c
De hac tra tenuit un libб hō T.R.E.II.hid 7 dim.7 emit de abбe Edmundo. Ħ tra erat de dnio. Nc sunt ibi.II.car in dnio abбis ad uictū. Valб 7 ual.XXX.sol.

Hanc trā reclamat Vrso de dono regis.7 dicit qđ ipse excābiauit eā contra abбem.ppt unū M qđ erat de dnio.

Ipsa æccla tenuit ad *LEGE*.III.hid geld. Ex his unā hid hт abб in dnio.7 ibi hт.II.car.7 XII.uitt 7 XXXII.bord cū.XXIX.car.Ibi.II.serui.7 II.molini de.X.sol 7 IX.den. 7 XXX.ac pti. Silua.III.lew lḡ.7 II.lew lat. T.R.E.ualб.XX.libб.modo: XVI.libб.

De hac pdicta trā tenuer.II.Radmans.I.hid 7 dimidiā. Modo ten Vrso uicecom.7 ibi hт.II.car.7 II.uitt 7 XI. bord 7 un francig. Int oms hnt.IIII.car. Ibi.II.serui. 7 molin de.IIII.solid. Vat.L.solid.

e In WADBOROUGH there is also 1 hide of land in which was the monks' cow pasturage. Godric, a thane of King Edward, bought it for the life-span of three heirs. He gave to the monks one revenue a year in acknowledgement. Now the third heir has this land, namely Urso who holds it. After his death it has to return to the Church of St. Mary.

The Church itself holds BEOLEY with one member, YARDLEY. 21 hides, both open land and wood. In lordship 1 plough;
 8 villagers, 10 smallholders and 1 rider with 9 ploughs. A 157
 Woodland 6 leagues long and 3 leagues wide; it pays 40d.
The value was £8; now 100s.

The Church holds ALDERMINSTER itself. 20 hides. In lordship 4 ploughs;
 24 villagers and 8 smallholders with 11 ploughs. 5 slaves.
 2 mills at 17s 6d. A 158
 1 man-at-arms holds 2 hides; 2 riders.
 Meadow, 20 acres.
The value was £12; now £9.
 This land pays tax.

The Church holds BROADWAY itself. 30 hides which pay tax. In lordship 3 ploughs;
 A priest and 42 villagers with 20 ploughs. 8 slaves. A 159-
Value of the whole before 1066 £12 10s; now £14 10s. 160
 A free man held 2½ hides of this land before 1066. He 175 c
bought them from Abbot Edmund. This land was (part) of the lordship (land). Now, 2 ploughs in the Abbot's lordship, for (his) supplies.
The value was and is 30s.
 Urso claims back this land as the King's gift. He states he exchanged it himself with the Abbot for one manor which was (part) of the lordship.

a The Church itself held at LEIGH 3 hides which pay tax. Of
these, the Abbot has 1 hide in lordship. He has 2 ploughs; A 161
 12 villagers and 32 smallholders with 29 ploughs. 2 slaves.
 2 mills at 10s 9d; meadow, 30 acres; woodland 3 leagues long and 2 leagues wide.
Value before 1066 £20; now £16.

b Of the said land two riders held 1½ hides. Now Urso the Sheriff holds them. He has 2 ploughs;
 2 villagers, 11 smallholders and 1 Frenchman; between them they have 4 ploughs. 2 slaves.
 A mill at 4s.
Value 50s.

Hui⁹ træ tcia hid ad Bradnesforde ten isd Vrso .7 ibi ht
in dnio . I . car .7 IX . bord cu . IIII . car .7 molin de . XX . solid.
Valet . IIII . lib. De hac hida dicit comitat⁹ . qd T.R.E.
fuit de æccla psorensi . 7 tam teneb ea abb de Euesham.
die obit⁹ regis . E. sed nesciunt quomodo . *IN* **DODINTREV** *HD.*

Ipsa æccla tenuit *MATMA*. Ibi . v . hidæ . sed non geld nisi . III.
Vna ex his . v . hid . iacet in Herefordscire in ***RADELAV*** *HD.*
Hanc ten . II . Radmans . Comitat⁹ de Wirecestre diratio
cinauit ea ad op⁹ S MARIE de psore .7 ptin ad supdictu M.
In hoc eod M sunt . II . car in dnio .7 VI . uill 7 XX . bord 7 I . fab.
cu . XII . car. Ibi molin de . XXX . denar. Valb . IX . lib . m: C . sol.
De hoc M ten Vrso . III . uirg .7 ibi ht . I . car .7 pbr 7 un⁹ uill
7 III . bord 7 ppósit⁹ . Int se hnt . III . car. Valet . XX . solid.
De ead tra ten Walt ponther una v . sed tota . e Wasta . Val . v . sol.

Dicit Comitat⁹ qd æccla de psore deb habere Circset de omib;
trecentis hid. scilicet de unaqq; hida ubi francus ho manet
una suma annonæ in die festo S Martini .7 si plures ht hid
sint liberæ .7 si dies ille fract⁹ fuerit: q retinuit annona psol
uet undecies . prius tam soluet qd debet .7 ipse abb de psore
habet forisfactura de suis . c . hid . quale habere debet de
sua tra . De aliis . cc . hid ht ipse abb suma 7 psolutione.
7 abb de Westmonast ht forisfactura . qa sua tra est.
7 abb de Euesha similit ht de sua tra ppa .7 oms alii similit
de suis terris.

TERRA ÆCCLÆ DE EVESHAM.

.X. **I**N EVESHAM uilla ubi sedet abbatia . sunt 7 fuer sep . III.
hidæ liberæ.

5c Urso also holds a third hide of this land at BRANSFORD.
He has 1 plough in lordship;
9 smallholders with 4 ploughs.
A mill at 20s.
Value £4.
Of this hide the County states that it was the Church of Pershore's before 1066; however, the Abbot of Evesham held it on the day of King Edward's death, but they do not know how.

In DODDINGTREE Hundred

6a The Church held MATHON itself. 5 hides, but it does not pay tax except for 3. 1 of these 5 hides lies in Herefordshire, in Radlow Hundred. Two riders hold it. The County of Worcester adjudged it for the use of St. Mary's of Pershore; it belongs to the above manor.

6b Also in this manor, 2 ploughs in lordship;
6 villagers, 20 smallholders and 1 smith with 12 ploughs.
A mill at 30d.
The value was £9; now 100s.

6c Urso holds 3 virgates of this manor. He has 1 plough.
A priest, 1 villager, 3 smallholders and a reeve; between them they have 3 ploughs.
Value 20s.
Walter Ponther holds 1 virgate also of this land, but the whole of it is waste. Value 5s.

7 The County states that the Church of Pershore should have Church tax from all the 300 hides; namely, from each and every hide where a freeman lives one packload of corn at Martinmas, and if he has more hides they should be free; and if that date should be missed the man who has kept back the corn shall pay for it elevenfold; however, first he shall pay what he owes.
The Abbot of Pershore himself has the forfeiture from his 100 hides just as he should have from his own land. From the other 200 hides the Abbot himself has (his) packload and payment in full. The Abbot of Westminster has the forfeiture because it is his land. The Abbot of Evesham has (it) likewise from his own land, and all the others likewise from their lands.

10 LAND OF THE CHURCH OF EVESHAM

[In FISHBOROUGH Hundred]

1 In the town of EVESHAM, where the Abbey is situated, there are and always were 3 free hides. . . .

Ibi sunt in dn̄io . III . car̄ . 7 XXVII . bord̄ seruientes curiæ.
7 hn̄t . IIII . car̄ . Ibi molin̄ de . XXX . solid̄ . 7 XX . ac̄ p̄ti.
De censu hominū ibi manentiū . XX . solid̄.
T.R.E. ualb̄ . LX . solid̄ . 7 post: IIII . lib̄ . Modo . CX . solid̄.
In *FISSESBERGE* hd̄ ht̄ æccl̄a de Euesham̄ . LXV . hid̄ . Ex his
XII . hidæ sunt liberæ. In illo *HVND* iacen̄t . XX . hidæ de
dodentreu . 7 XV . hidæ de Wircecestre . p̄ficiunt hundret.
Ipsa æccl̄a ten̄ *LENCHEWIC* . Ibi . ē . una hida libera.
7 sēp fuit . 7 In *NORTVNE* sunt . VII . hidæ.
In dn̄io sunt . V . car̄ . 7 XIII . uilli . 7 XI . bord̄ . 7 un̄ franciḡ.
Int̄ om̄s hn̄t . XI . car̄ . Ibi . X . serui . 7 II . molini de . XXII.
solid̄ 7 VI . denar̄ . 7 II . mill̄ anguill̄ . Ibi . XII . ac̄ p̄ti.
* T.R.E. ualb̄ . VII . lib̄. 7 post: CX . sol̄ . Modo: VII . lib̄.
In Oleberge sun̄t . XII . acræ t̄ræ . 7 ibi sun̄t . II . rustici porcarii.
7 Siluæ una leuuede. Val̄ . V . solid̄.
175 d
Ipsa æccl̄a ten̄ *OFFENHAM̄* . Ibi est . I . hida libera . 7 Ad *LITEL TVNE* sunt . VI . hidæ . 7 ad *BRATFORTVNE* . VI . hidæ.
In dn̄io sunt . III . car̄ . 7 XXV . uilli cū . VII . car̄ . 7 II . Radman.
7 II . franciḡ . quisq; eo₇ h̄t . I . car̄ . Ibi . XX . bord̄ 7 XX.
ac̄ p̄ti . 7 molin̄ de . XII . solid̄ 7 VI . den̄.
Ibi sun̄t boues ad . I . car̄ . sed petrā trahunt ad æccl̄am.
T.R.E. 7 post . ualb̄ . VIII . lib̄ . Modo . VI . lib̄ 7 X . solid̄.
Ad hoc Ⓜ iacet . I . Bereuuich . *ALDINTONE* . Ibi . I . hida
libera ad æcclam . 7 in dn̄io sun̄t II . car̄ . 7 V . bord̄ cu . I . car̄ . Ibi
. IIII . serui . 7 molin̄ de . V . solid̄. Valb̄ 7 ual̄ . XL . solid̄.
Ipsa eccl̄a ten̄ *WIQVENE* . Ibi sunt . III . hidæ liberæ.
7 ad *BRATFORTVNE* . VI . hidæ. In dn̄io sunt . IIII . car̄ . 7 XVI.
uilli 7 VII . bord̄ cū . X . car̄ . Ibi molin̄ de XL . den̄ . 7 X . ac̄ p̄ti.
Valb̄ 7 ualet . VI . lib̄.
Ipsa æccl̄a ten̄ *BADESEI* . Ibi T.R.E. fuer̄ . VI . hidæ 7 dimid̄.
In dn̄io sunt . II . car̄. 7 XII . uilli cu . VIII . car̄ . Ibi . IIII.
serui . 7 una uidua. Valb̄ . VI . lib̄ . modo . III . lib̄ . 7 X . solid̄.

In lordship 3 ploughs;
27 smallholders who serve the court; they have 4 ploughs.
A mill at 30s; meadow, 20 acres; from the dues of the men who live there, 20s. A 18
Value before 1066, 60s; later £4; now 110s.

2 In Fishborough Hundred the Church of Evesham has 65 hides. Of these, 12 hides are free. 20 hides of Doddingtree lie in that Hundred, and 15 hides of Worcester; they make up the Hundred.

3 The Church holds LENCHWICK itself. There is and always was 1 free hide. In NORTON there are 7 hides. In lordship 5 ploughs;
13 villagers, 11 smallholders and 1 Frenchman; between them they have 11 ploughs. 10 slaves. A 19-20
2 mills at 22s 6d and 2,000 eels. Meadow, 12 acres.
Value before 1066, £7; later 110s; now £7.

4 In OLDBERROW there are 12 acres of land.
2 countrymen, pigmen.
Woodland, 1 league.
Value 5s.

The Church itself holds 175 d

5 OFFENHAM. There is 1 free hide. At LITTLETON there are 6 hides; at BRETFORTON, 6 hides. In lordship 3 ploughs;
25 villagers with 7 ploughs; 2 riders and 2 Frenchmen; each of them has 1 plough. 20 smallholders. A 21-24
Meadow, 20 acres; a mill at 12s 6d. Oxen for 1 plough, but they draw stone to the church.
Value before 1066 and later, £8; now £6 10s.
One outlier, ALDINGTON, lies in (the lands of) this manor.
1 free hide for the church. In lordship 2 ploughs;
5 smallholders with 1 plough. 4 slaves.
A mill at 5s.
The value was and is 40s.

6 WICKHAMFORD. There are 3 free hides; at BRETFORTON, 6 hides. In lordship 4 ploughs;
16 villagers and 7 smallholders with 10 ploughs. A 25-26
A mill at 40d; meadow, 10 acres.
The value was and is £6.

7 BADSEY. Before 1066 there were 6½ hides. In lordship 2 ploughs; . . . A 32
12 villagers with 8 ploughs. 4 slaves; 1 widow.
The value was £6; now £3 10s.

Ipſa æccła teñ *LITELTVNE*. Ibi fueř. VII. hidæ T.R.E.
In dñio ſunt. II. caŕ. 7 XV. uitti 7 un francig cũ. II. uittis. Int oms hñt. VII. caŕ. Ibi. III. ſerui. 7 VIII. acre prati. Valƀ. IIII. liƀ 7 X. ſot. modo: LXX. ſolid.
Ipſa æccła teñ *HVNIBVRNE*. Ibi.. II. hidæ 7 dimid. T.R.E.
In dñio ſunt. IIII. caŕ. 7 pƀr 7 X. uitti 7 IIII. borđ cũ. IIII. caŕ.
Ibi. IIII. ſerui. Valƀ. III. liƀ. Modo: IIII. liƀ. Ibi. XI. ac pti.
Ipſa æccła teñ *AMBRESLEGE*. Hæc antiqt ꝑ. III. hiđ fuit liba.
ſic dñt cartæ de æccła. ſed T.R.E. fuit numerata ꝑ. XV. hiđ.
int ſiluã 7 planũ. 7 III. hidæ ex eis ſunt liberæ.
Ibi ſunt in dñio. V. caŕ. 7 XXX. uitti 7 XII. borđ. 7 II. pƀri. 7 II.
Radmanni. 7 X. bouarii. Int oms hñt. XX. caŕ. Ibi piſca
ria 7 dimid redđ. II. Mitt anguitt. 7 II. molini de. VIII. ſolid.
7 IIII. ac pti. Silua de. II. leuuedes. 7 In Wich. I. ſalina.
T.R.E. ualƀ 7 poſt: XVIII. liƀ. Modo: XVI. liƀ.
Ipſa æccła teñ *HANTVN*. Ibi. V. hidæ fueř. T.R.E. *IN OSWOLDESLAV HD*.
In dñio ſunt. III. caŕ. 7 XV. uitti 7 V. borđ. 7 un francig cũ. IIII.
borđ. Int oms hñt. VII. caŕ. Ibi. VIII. ſerui. 7 X. ac pti. 7 uinea
nouella ibi. 7 II. molini de. XX. ſolid. Valƀ. C. ſolid. modo: VI. liƀ.
Ipſa æccła teñ. IIII. hiđ ad *BENINGEORDE*. 7 V. hiđ teñ Vrſo.
Has. V. hiđ diratiocinauit Walt aƀƀ ad Ildebergã in. IIII. ſciris
corã epo baiocenſi 7 aliis baronib; regis.
Ibi ſunt. II. caŕ. 7 V. uitti 7 II. borđ cũ. II. caŕ. Ibi. VI. ſerui.
T.R.E. ualƀ. LX. ſolid. 7 poſt. L. ſot. Modo: LX. ſot. *IN ESCH HD*.
Ipſa æccła teñ *MORTVNE*. Ibi fueř. V. hidæ T.R.E. ſed ex eis
magna pars preſtita fuit foris. In dñio. ẽ una caŕ. 7 VII.
uitti 7 II. bouarii cũ. IIII. caŕ. Ibi. XV. ac pti. Silua. III. q̃z lg.
7 una q̃z lať. Valƀ 7 uał. XXX. ſolid. Rannulf teñ de aƀƀe.
Ipſa æccła teñ *ACHELENZ*. Ibi. IIII. hidæ 7 dimid. In dñio. ẽ
una caŕ. 7 III. uitti 7 IIII. borđ cũ. I. caŕ. Ibi. II. ſerui. 7 VI. ac ſiluæ.
T.R.E. ualƀ XXV. ſot. 7 poſt: XX. ſot. Modo: XV. ſolid.

8 LITTLETON. There were 7 hides before 1066. In lordship 2 ploughs;
15 villagers and 1 Frenchman with 2 villagers; A 27
between them they have 7 ploughs. 3 slaves.
Meadow, 8 acres.
The value was £4 10s; now 70s.

9 (Church) HONEYBOURNE. 2½ hides before 1066. In lordship 4 ploughs;
A priest, 10 villagers and 4 smallholders with 4 A 28
ploughs. 4 slaves.
The value was £3; now £4.
Meadow, 11 acres.

10 OMBERSLEY. In ancient times it was free at 3 hides, as the charters of the church state, but before 1066 it was counted as 15 hides, both wood and open land. 3 hides of these are A 29
free. In lordship 5 ploughs;
30 villagers, 12 smallholders, 2 priests, 2 riders and 10 ploughmen; between them they have 20 ploughs.
1½ fisheries which pay 2,000 eels; 2 mills at 8s; meadow, 4 acres; woodland at 2 leagues. In Droitwich 1 salt-house.
Value before 1066 and later £18; now £16.

in OSWALDSLOW Hundred

11 HAMPTON. There were 5 hides before 1066. In lordship 3 ploughs;
15 villagers, 5 smallholders and 1 Frenchman with 4 smallholders; between them they have 7 ploughs. 8 slaves. A 31
Meadow, 10 acres; a young vineyard there; 2 mills at 20s.
The value was 100s; now £6.

12 at BENGEWORTH, 4 hides, and Urso holds a fifth hide. Abbot Walter proved his right to these 5 hides at *Ildeberga* in four Shires in the presence of the Bishop of Bayeux and other barons of the King. 2 ploughs there. A 30
5 villagers and 2 smallholders with 2 ploughs. 6 slaves.
Value before 1066, 60s; later 50s; now 60s.

in ESCH Hundred

13 (Abbots) MORTON. There were 5 hides before 1066, but a great part of these had been leased elsewhere. In lordship 1 plough; A 13
7 villagers and 2 ploughmen with 4 ploughs.
Meadow, 15 acres; woodland 3 furlongs long and 1 furlong wide.
The value was and is 30s.
Ranulf holds from the Abbot.

14 ATCH LENCH. 4½ hides. In lordship 1 plough;
3 villagers and 4 smallholders with 1 plough. 2 slaves.
Woodland, 6 acres. A 12
Value before 1066, 25s; later 20s; now 15s.

Ipsa æccła teñ *BVINTVN*. Ibi .I. hida. 7 una car. 7 III. bord
7 III. ac̃ siluæ. Valuit xx. solid. 7 post. xv. sol. Modo: x. sol
Ipsa æccła teñ *CIRCELENZ*. Ibi fuer̃. IIII. hidæ T.R.E.
In dñio sunt. II. car̃. 7 pbr 7 III. uilli 7 II. bord. 7 IIII. bouarii.
7 un francig. Int oms hñt. III. car̃. Valuit 7 ual. xxx. solid.
In Ciuitate *WIRECESTRE*. hñ æccła de Euesh̃a
XXVIII. masuras. Ex his sunt. v. uuastæ. 7 aliæ reddt. xx. solid.

176 a

.XI. TERRA EPI BAIOCENSIS. *IN DODINTRET HD.*

Eps Baiocsis tenuit *ACTVNE*. 7 Vrso de eo. De æccła S MARIÆ
de Eueshã fuit. T.R.E. 7 postea Vrso recep de abbe
p excãbitione alteri træ. Modo teñ. de feudo epi baiocsis.
Ibi sunt. VI. hidæ. Ex his. III. geld. aliæ. III. ñ geld.
In dñio. VI. car. 7 un uills 7 IX. bord. cũ. IIII. car. Ibi. XII. serui.
T.R.E. ualb. LXX. sol. Modo: IIII. lib. *IN ESCH HVND.*
Isd eps teñ *LENCHE*. 7 Vrso de eo. Ibi. IIII. hidæ geld. Duas
ex his tenuer. II. teini. 7 alias. II. tenuit Ælueua qdã femina.
Hi poterañ ire quo uoleb. 7 p. III. m teneban.
In dñio sunt. II. car. 7 VI. uill. 7 II. bord. 7 IIII. serui. cũ. II.
car. 7 VIII. car plus possunt ibi. ee. Ibi silua redd. II. solid.
T.R.E. ualb. cx. sol. 7 post. xxx. sol. Modo: XLII. solid.
De hac tra. II. hid ded Gislebt. f. turoldi æcclæ de Eueshã.
p anima Willi comitis ccessu regis Willi. 7 pinde. e un mo
nachus in æccła positus. p aliis. II. hid ded. abb Eluui
unã mark auri. W. regi. 7 ipse p anima sua eand trã
æcclæ ccessit. teste Gislebto. f. Turoldi qui aurũ recep ad op regis.
De his. IIII. hid fuit ipsa æccła saisita multis annis. donec
eps baiocsis de æccła abstulit. 7 Vrsoni dedit.

15 BEVINGTON. 1 hide; 1 plough.
3 smallholders.
Woodland, 3 acres. A 14
The value was 20s; later 15s; now 10s.

16 CHURCH LENCH. There were 4 hides before 1066. In lordship 2 ploughs; A 11
A priest, 3 villagers, 2 smallholders, 4 ploughmen and 1 Frenchman; between them they have 3 ploughs.
The value was and is 30s.

17 In the city of WORCESTER the Church of Evesham has 28 dwellings. Of these, 5 are unoccupied and the others pay 20s.

11 LAND OF THE BISHOP OF BAYEUX 176 a

In DODDINGTREE Hundred

1 The Bishop of Bayeux held ACTON (Beauchamp), and Urso from him. It was (part) of (the lands of) St. Mary's Church of Evesham before 1066, and later Urso acquired it from the Abbot in exchange for another land. Now he holds from the Bishop of Bayeux' Holding. There are 6 hides. Of these, 3 pay tax; the other 3 do not pay tax. In lordship 6 ploughs;
1 villager and 9 smallholders with 4 ploughs. 12 slaves.
Value before 1066, 70s; now £4.

In ESCH Hundred

2 The Bishop also holds (Sheriffs) LENCH, and Urso from him. 4 hides which pay tax. Two thanes held 2 of these; Aelfeva, a woman, held the other 2. They could go where they would; they held them as 3 manors. In lordship 2 ploughs; A 4
6 villagers, 2 smallholders and 4 slaves with 2 ploughs; 8 more ploughs possible.
Woodland which pays 2s.
Value before 1066, 110s; later 30s; now 42s.

Gilbert son of Thorold gave 2 hides of this land to the Church of Evesham for the soul of Earl William, with King William's consent; accordingly, one monk was placed in the church. Abbot Alfwy gave 1 gold mark to King William for the other 2 hides. He assigned this land to the church for his (own) soul, as Gilbert son of Thorold, who collected the gold for the King's use, testifies.

The church itself had been in possession of these 4 hides for many years, until the Bishop of Bayeux took them from the church and gave them to Urso.

.XII. TERRA SC̄I GVTHLACI. *IN CLENT HVND.*

De S̄ GVLLACO ten̄ Nigell' medicus . I . hid̄ in *WICH*.

☞ Ibi sunt . IX . burḡses . reddtes . XXX . solid̄ de salinis 7 p omib; reb.

.XIII PRESBITERI de Wrehantune ten̄ *LVDELEIA*. Ibi . II . hidæ.
Ipsi tenuer̄ . T.R.E. Ibi hn̄t . II^os . uilt . 7 II . seru . 7 I . bord . cū . IIII . carucis. Val . XV . solid.

.XIIII. TERRA ROGERII COMITIS. *IN CLENT HVND.*

COMES ROGERIVS ten̄ de rege unū ɱ *HALĀ*. Ibi . X . hidæ. In dn̄io sunt . IIII . car . 7 XXXVI . uilti . 7 XVIII . bord . IIII . Radmans . 7 æccla cū . II . pb̄ris. Int̄ om̄s hn̄t . XLI . car 7 dimid . Ibi . VIII . serui 7 II . ancillæ.
De hac t̄ra ten̄ Rog̃ uenator . I . hid de comite . 7 dimid . 7 ibi ht̄ . I . car̄ . 7 VI . uilt 7 V . bord cū . V . car̄. Val . XXV . solid.
T.R.E. ualb hoc ɱ . XXIIII . lib . Modo: XV . lib . Oluuin' tenuit 7 habuit in Wich . salinā de . IIII . solid . 7 In Wirecest . I . domū de . XII . denar.
Isd̄ comes ten̄ *SALEWARPE* . 7 Urso de eo . Æluuin' cilt tenuit.
Ibi . V . hidæ. In dn̄io . ē una car̄ . 7 VI . uilt 7 V . bord . cū . VII . car̄. Ibi . III . serui . 7 III . ancillæ . 7 molin̄ de . X . solid . 7 V . salinæ de . LX . solid. Dimid leuua siluæ . 7 ibi parcus.
T.R.E. ualb . C . solid . modo . VI . lib . Ibi . II . car̄ plus possunt . ee.

.XV. TERRA RADVLFI DE TODENI. *IN DODINTREV HD.*

RADVLFVS de Todeni ten̄ *WERMESLAI*. Edwi 7 Ælnod tenuer̄ . p . II . ɱ . Ibi . II . hidæ geld . In dn̄io sunt . III . car . 7 II . Radman 7 . VIII . bord cū . VII . car . Ibi . VI . serui.
T.R.E. ualb . XL . solid . 7 post: XX . solid . Modo: IIII . lib.
Isd̄ Radulf' ten̄ *LINDE* . Æluuard tenuit tein' com Algari.
Ibi . II . hidæ geld . In dn̄io sunt . IIII . car . 7 XVI . bord 7 VI . bo uarii . cū . IIII . car . Ibi . II . serui.
T.R.E. ualb . XL . solid . 7 post: XX . sol . Modo: XVI . solid.

12 LAND OF ST. GUTHLAC'S

In CLENT Hundred

1 Nigel the doctor holds 1 hide in DROITWICH from St. Guthlac's.
9 burgesses who pay 30s from the salt-houses and for all else.

Ψ *12, 2 is added at the foot of col. 176a after 15, 3*

13 [LAND OF THE PRIESTS OF WOLVERHAMPTON]

[In CLENT Hundred]

1 The priests of Wolverhampton hold LUTLEY. 2 hides. They held them themselves before 1066. They have
2 villagers, 2 slaves and 1 smallholder with 4 ploughs.
Value 15s.

14 LAND OF EARL ROGER

In CLENT Hundred

1 Earl Roger holds one manor, HALESOWEN, from the King.
10 hides. ... In lordship 4 ploughs;
36 villagers, 18 smallholders, 4 riders and a church with 2 priests; between them they have 41½ ploughs. 8 male and 2 female slaves.
Roger Hunter holds 1½ hides of this land from the Earl; he has 1 plough.
6 villagers and 5 smallholders with 5 ploughs.
Value 25s.
Value of this manor before 1066 £24; now £15.
Wulfwin held it and had a salt-house at 4s in Droitwich and 1 house at 12d in Worcester.

2 The Earl also holds SALWARPE, and Urso from him.
Alwin Young held it. 5 hides. ... In lordship 1 plough;
6 villagers and 5 smallholders with 7 ploughs. 3 male and 3 female slaves.
A mill at 10s; 5 salt-houses at 60s; woodland, ½ league; a park there.
Value before 1066, 100s; now £6.
2 more ploughs possible.

15 LAND OF RALPH OF TOSNY

In DODDINGTREE Hundred

1 Ralph of Tosny holds WORSLEY. Edwy and Alnoth held it as 2 manors. 2 hides which pay tax. In lordship 3 ploughs;
2 riders and 8 smallholders with 7 ploughs. 6 slaves.
Value before 1066, 40s; later 20s; now £4.

2 Ralph also holds 'LINDON'. Aethelward, a thane of Earl Algar, held it. 2 hides which pay tax. In lordship 4 ploughs;
16 smallholders and 6 ploughmen with 4 ploughs. 2 slaves.
Value before 1066, 40s; later 20s; now 16s.

Isd Rad ten *HALAC*. Vlmer tenuit tein regis. E. Ibi. I. hida. geld. Ibi sunt. v. bord reddt. v. solid. Valb. IIII. solid. Duæ car possunt ibi. ee.

☞ Isd Nigelli ten *DVNCLENT*. 7 Vrso de eo. *IN CRESSELAV HD*. Ibi. III. hidæ. In dnio. e. I. car. 7 II. bord. 7 II. bouarii. 7 v. car posse ibi. ee. Valuit. xxv. solid. Modo: x. solid. Odo tenuit de S Gutlaco.

176 b

Isd Rad ten *ALVINTVNE*. Godric tenuit tein Algari comit. 7 poterat ire quo uoleb. Ibi. II. hidæ geld. In dnio sunt IIII. car. 7 pbr. 7 II. bord 7 II. radmans. cu. IIII. car. Ibi. VI. serui. 7 Silua. III leuu lg. 7 II. leuu lat. T.R.E. ualb. XL. solid. 7 post. xx. solid. Modo: LII. solid.

Isd Rad ten *MORE*. Grim tenuit. 7 potuit ire q uoluit. Ibi. I. hida geld. Ibi sunt. II. bord cu. I. car. 7 un lib ho cu. I. car. Valuit 7 ual. xx. sol. Ibi parua silua.

Isd Rad ten *BETVNE*. Edric 7 Leuui tenuer p. II. CO. 7 quó uoleb ire poterant. Ibi. III. hide 7 dimid geld. In dnio sunt. III. car. 7 IIII. uill 7 XIIII. bord 7 un rad man cu. XII. car. Ibi molin de. v. solid. T.R.E. ualb. LX. solid. 7 post. xxx. sol. Modo: IIII. lib. Rayner ten de Radulfo.

Isd Rad ten *MORE*. Leuenot tenuit 7 potuit ire q uoluit. Ibi. I. uirg geld. Ibi un uills cu. I. car. Silua dimid leuua lg. 7 III. qz lat. Valuit 7 ual. II. sol.

Isd Rad ten *EDBOLDELEGE*. Vlmer tenuit. 7 potuit ire quo uoluit. Ibi. II. hidæ 7 dimid geld. In dnio sunt. II. car. 7 XVIII. uill 7 VIII. bord 7 un francig 7 III. cot cu. XVII. car. Ibi pbr 7 un seruus. T.R.E. ualb. VII. lib. 7 post. IIII. lib. Modo: x. lib 7 x. sol.

3 Ralph also holds *HALAC.* Wulfmer, a thane of King Edward, held it. 1 hide which pays tax.
5 smallholders; they pay 5s.
The value was 4s.
2 ploughs possible.

Ψ *12, 2 is directed to its proper place by transposition signs*

In CRESSLAU Hundred

12, 2 Nigel also holds DUNCLENT, and Urso from him. 3 hides.
In lordship 1 plough;
2 smallholders and 2 ploughmen; 5 ploughs would be possible.
The value was 25s; now 10s.
Odo held it from St. Guthlac's.

Chapter 15 continued

Ralph also holds 176 b

4 ALTON. Godric, a thane of Earl Algar, held it; he could go where he would. 2 hides which pay tax. In lordship 4 ploughs;
A priest, 2 smallholders and 2 riders with 4 ploughs.
6 slaves.
Woodland 3 leagues long and 2 leagues wide.
Value before 1066, 40s; later 20s; now 52s.

5 ROCKMOOR. Grim held it; he could go where he would.
1 hide which pays tax.
2 smallholders with 1 plough. 1 free man with 1 plough.
The value was and is 20s.
A small wood.

6 BAYTON. Edric and Leofwin held it as 2 manors; they could go where they would. 3½ hides which pay tax. In lordship 3 ploughs;
4 villagers, 14 smallholders and 1 rider with 12 ploughs.
A mill at 5s.
Value before 1066, 60s; later 30s; now £4.
Rayner holds it from Ralph.

7 ROCKMOOR. Leofnoth held it; he could go where he would.
1 virgate which pays tax.
1 villager with 1 plough.
Woodland ½ league long and 3 furlongs wide.
The value was and is 2s.

8 ABBERLEY. Wulfmer held it; he could go where he would.
2½ hides which pay tax. In lordship 2 ploughs;
18 villagers, 8 smallholders, 1 Frenchman and 3 cottagers with 17 ploughs. A priest and a slave.
Value before 1066 £7; later £4; now £10 10s.

Isd Rad ten Eslei. 7 æccla S Taurini de eo. Ernesi te
nuit 7 potuit ire quo uoluit. Ibi. vi. hidæ geld. De his
ten S Taurin. iiii. hid. qetas 7 solutas ab omi csuetudine
quæ regi attinet. sic ipse. W. rex cceffit. qdo Rad ea sco ded.
Ibi in dnio sunt. ii. car. æccla 7 pbr. 7 xi. uill 7 iii. bord
7 un radman. Int oms hnt. xi. car. 7 dimid. Ibi. iii. serui.
7 ii. molini de. x. solid. Ad Wirecest. ii. burgses de. ii. solid.
Ad Wich. i. salina redd. xviii. mittas sal 7 lxiiii. den.
Silua. e nil redd. T.R.E. ualb hoc M. x. lib. 7 post 7 m. c. sol. Silua. i. lew lg. 7 dim lew lat.
Ibi ten Vrso. i. hid de Rad. 7 ht. iii. car in dnio. 7 iii. uill
7 xv. bord 7 ii. libos hoes cu. vii. car. Ibi. iiii. serui. 7 ii.
molini de. xx. solid. Valet. iii. lib 7 x. solid.

Ipse Rad ten Ridmerlege. Ibi. i. hida 7 dimid geld.
Vlmar 7 Vlchetel tenuer p. ii. M. 7 poterant ire quo uoleb.
In dnio. e. i. car. 7 xiiii. bord 7 i. fab cu. viii. car. Ibi
iiii. serui. T.R.E. ualb 7. xxx. solid. 7 post tntd. Modo: xl. sol.
Rad miles ten de Radulfo.

Isd Rad ten Celdeslai. 7 Walter de eo. Vlmar tenuit
7 potuit ire quo uoluit. Ibi. i. hida. In dnio sunt. ii. car. 7 ii. uilli
7 xiii. bord———cu. viii. car. Ibi. ii. serui. 7 piscaria
de. ii. solid. 7 xxx. ac pti. Silua dimid lew lg. 7 iii. qz lat.
T.R.E. ualb. l. solid. 7 post. xxx. sol. modo: l. solid.

Isd Rad ten Estha 7 Bestewde. 7 Herbt de eo. Edric tenuit
p. ii. M. Ibi. iii. hidæ In dnio sunt. ii. car. 7 pbr 7 v. uilli
7 viii. bord cu. v. car. Ibi. vi. serui. 7 un ho redd. xxxii. den.
7 molin de. vi. solid 7 viii. den. 7 lx. ac pti. Silua. ii. lew lg
7 una lew lat. T.R.E. ualb. iiii. lib 7 v. sol. 7 post: xlv. sol. m: iiii. lib.

Isd Rad ten Ælmeleia. 7 Walter de eo. In Cresselau hd.
Aluuold tenuit de Edded regina. Ibi. xi. hidæ. In dnio sunt. ii. car.

9 ASTLEY. St. Taurin's Church holds from him. Ernsy held it; he could go where he would. 6 hides which pay tax. Of these, St. Taurin('s) holds 4 hides exempt and freed from every customary due which belongs to the King, as King William himself consented when Ralph gave it to the Saint. In lordship 2 ploughs;

A church, a priest, 11 villagers, 3 smallholders and 1 rider; between them they have 11½ ploughs. 3 slaves.

2 mills at 10s. At Worcester 2 burgesses at 2s; at Droitwich 1 salt-house which pays 18 measures of salt and 64d. Woodland which pays nothing. Woodland 1 league long and ½ league wide.

Value of this manor before 1066, £10; later and now 100s.

Urso holds 1 hide from Ralph. He has 3 ploughs in lordship and 3 villagers, 15 smallholders and 2 free men with 7 ploughs. 4 slaves.

2 mills at 20s.

Value £3 10s.

10 Ralph holds REDMARLEY himself. 1½ hides which pay tax. Wulfmer and Ulfketel held it as 2 manors; they could go where they would. In lordship 1 plough;

14 smallholders and 1 smith with 8 ploughs. 4 slaves.

Value before 1066, 30s; later as much; now 40s.

Ralph, a man-at-arms, holds from Ralph.

Ralph also holds

11 SHELSLEY. Walter holds from him. Wulfmer held it; he could go where he would. 1 hide. In lordship 2 ploughs;

2 villagers and 13 smallholders with 8 ploughs. 2 slaves.

A fishery at 2s; meadow, 30 acres; woodland ½ league long and 3 furlongs wide.

Value before 1066, 50s; later 30s; now 50s.

12 EASTHAM and 'BASTWOOD'. Herbert holds from him. Edric held it as 2 manors. 3 hides. ... In lordship 2 ploughs;

A priest, 5 villagers and 8 smallholders with 5 ploughs. 6 slaves; a man who pays 32d.

A mill at 6s 8d; meadow, 60 acres; woodland 2 leagues long and 1 league wide.

Value before 1066 £4 5s; later 45s; now £4.

In CRESSLAU Hundred

13 ELMLEY (Lovett). Walter holds from him. Alfwold held it from Queen Edith. 11 hides. In lordship 2 ploughs;

7 pbr 7 XIIII . uilt 7 XV . bord cu . VIII . car . Ibi . III . molini reddt
c 7 IX . sol 7 IIII . den . 7 IIII . saline reddt . LXX . solid . 7 Ad Wich
v . dom de . XX , den . 7 ibi . VII . uitti reddt . III . solid .
Silua . I . leuu lg . 7 dimid lew lat .
T.R.E . ualuit . x . lib . Modo : xvi . lib .
Isd Rad ten in *WICH* . I . hid de . x . hid geldant . 7 Walter de eo .
t tra

176 c

.XVI **TERRA RADVLFI DE MORTEMER.** *IN DODINTRET HD.*

RADVLFVS de Mortemer ten de rege *SVDTVNE* . 7 un
miles ei de eo . Ælsi tenuit . 7 n poterat recedere a dno suo .
Ibi . I . hida. 7 in dnio . I . car . 7 I . fab 7 II . bord cu dimid
car . Ibi . III . serui . 7 III . qz siluæ . 7 una car plus posset ibi . ee .
Isd Rad ten *MAMELE* . Sauuold Valuit . xx . sol . m x . sol .
tenuit . 7 potuit ire quo uoluit . Ibi dimid hida geld .
In dnio . e . I . car . 7 III . uilt 7 VI . bord cu . IIII . car . Ibi . III . serui .
Silua dimid leuu lg . 7 III . qz lat . Valuit . xxx . sol . m . XL . sol .
Isd Rad ten *BROC* . Feche tenuit . 7 potuit ire quo uoluit .
Ibi dimid hida geld . In dnio . e car 7 dimid . 7 I . uilt 7 XI
bord cu . II . car 7 dimid . Ibi . IIII . serui . 7 dimid piscaria .
Siluæ . III . qrent . Valuit . x . sol . modo : xx . solid .
Isd Rad ten *COLINGVIC* . Sauuold tenuit 7 potuit ire quo
uoluit . Ibi . I . hida geld . Fili hui Sauuold ht ibi . I . car .
7 I . bord ibi . e . 7 II . serui . Valuit 7 ual . x . solid .

.XVII **TERRA ROBETI DE STATFORD.** *IN ESCH HVND.*

ROBERT de Stadford ten *MORTVNE* . Æluui tenuit .
Ibi . IIII . hidæ geld . Hic Eluui poterat ire quo uoleb . Ernold ten
de robto 7 ht . II . car in dnio . 7 VII . uilt 7 VI . bord cu . IIII .
car . Ibi . VI . serui . 7 un burgsis redd . x . sol . 7 salina
redd . II . sol . 7 VIII . mittas sal . Silua . I . leuu lg . 7 dimid
lat . T.R.E . uatb . IIII . lib . 7 post . xxx . sol . Modo : IIII . lib .

A priest, 14 villagers and 15 smallholders with 8 ploughs.
3 mills pay 109s 4d; 4 salt-houses pay 70s;
at Droitwich 5 houses at 20d. 7 villagers pay 3s.
Woodland 1 league long and ½ league wide.
Value before 1066 £10; now £16.

[in CLENT Hundred]

14 in DROITWICH 1 hide, or land, of the 10 hides which pay tax.
Walter holds from him.

16 LAND OF RALPH OF MORTIMER 176 c

In DODDINGTREE Hundred

1 Ralph of Mortimer holds SODINGTON from the King, and a man-at-arms of his from him. Alfsi held it; he could not withdraw from his lord. 1 hide. . . . In lordship 1 plough;
1 smith and 2 smallholders with ½ plough. 3 slaves.
Woodland, 3 furlongs. 1 more plough would be possible.
The value was 20s; now 10s.

2 Ralph also holds MAMBLE. Saewold held it; he could go where he would. ½ hide which pays tax. In lordship 1 plough;
3 villagers and 6 smallholders with 4 ploughs. 3 slaves.
Woodland ½ league long and 3 furlongs wide.
The value was 30s; now 40s.

3 Ralph also holds *BROC.* Feche held it; he could go where he would. ½ hide which pays tax. In lordship 1½ ploughs;
1 villager and 11 smallholders with 2½ ploughs. 4 slaves.
½ fishery; woodland, 3 furlongs.
The value was 10s; now 20s.

4 Ralph also holds CONNINGSWICK. Saewold held it; he could go where he would. 1 hide which pays tax. This Saewold's son has 1 plough.
1 smallholder; 2 slaves.
The value was and is 10s.

17 LAND OF ROBERT OF STAFFORD

In ESCH Hundred

1 Robert of Stafford holds MORTON (?Underhill). Alfwy held it.
4 hides which pay tax. This Alfwy could go where he would.
Arnold holds from Robert. He has 2 ploughs in lordship;
7 villagers and 6 smallholders with 4 ploughs. 6 slaves; A 3
1 burgess who pays 10s.
A salt-house which pays 2s and 8 measures of salt; woodland
1 league long and ½ wide.
Value before 1066 £4; later 30s; now £4.

I .XVII TERRA ROGERII DE LACI. *IN DODINTRET HD.*

ROGERIVS de Laci ten *STOTVNE*. Godric tenuit. 7 potuit ire quo uoluit. Ibi. III. hidæ geld. In dnio. I. car. 7 III. uilt 7 VI. bord. cu. III. car. 7 II adhuc possunt. ee. plus. Ibi. III. serui. 7 molin de. XX. sol. 7 III. qz siluæ. Valb T.R.E. L. solid. modo. LXX. solid.

Isd Rog ten *STANFORD*. Eddied regina tenuit. 7 Godric de ea. p. II. m. Ibi. II. hidæ 7 dim geld. Hugo ten de Rogerio. 7 ht ibi. I. car. 7 VII. uilt 7 II. bord. 7 IIII. car plus ibi possunt. ee. Silua dimid lew lg. 7 II. qz lat. T.R.E. ualb. L. solid. modo: XXX. solid. *IN ESCH HD.*

Isd Rog ten *SCELVES*. 7 Herman de eo. Aluui tenuit p. II. m. 7 poterat ire quo uoleb. Ibi. I. hida geld. In dnio. e. I. car. 7 II. bord 7 III. seruos. 7 IIII. salinas cu Silua de dimid leuu lg. 7 II. qz lat. redd LX. mittas salis. T.R.E. ualb. LX. solid. 7 post. XXX. sol. Modo: XV. sol. Silua missa. e in defenso.

Isd Rog ten *CHINTVNE*. Aluui 7 Eilaf 7 Tori tenuer p. III. m. Ibi. V. hidæ geld. Hi poterant ire quo uoleb. 7 habeb. I. haia

★ in qua capiebant feræ. Ibi sunt. II. car in dnio. 7 V. uilt 7 VII. bord cu. II. car. Ibi. II. serui. 7 Silua. I. lew lg. 7 II. qz lat. T.R.E. ualb. IIII. lib. 7 post 7 modo. L. solid. Duo milites ten de Rogerio.

In *MERLIE* ht Rogeri unu Radman. 7 redd ei. IIII. solid.

★ .XIX. TERRA OSBERNI FILII RICARDI. *IN DODINTRET HD.*

OSBERNVS fili Ricardi ten de rege *BERITVNE*. Ricard scrupe pat ei tenuit. Ibi. II. hidæ geld. In dnio sunt. II. car. 7 VIII. uilti 7 IIII. bord 7 fab 7 molinari. cu. IX. car. 7 una car plus posset ibi. ee. Ibi. IIII. serui. 7 IIII. ancillæ. 7 molin redd XXII. sumas Annonæ. 7 X. ac pti. Silua. I. lew lg. 7 dimid. 7 lat. I. leuua. Valuit 7 ual. XX. solid.

18 LAND OF ROGER OF LACY

In DODDINGTREE Hundred

1 Roger of Lacy holds STOCKTON (on Teme). Godric held it; he could go where he would. 3 hides which pay tax. In lordship 1 plough;
3 villagers and 6 smallholders with 3 ploughs; a further 2 more possible. 3 slaves.
A mill at 20s; woodland, 3 furlongs.
Value before 1066, 50s; now 70s.

2 Roger also holds STANFORD (on Teme). Queen Edith held it, and Godric from her, as 2 manors. 2½ hides which pay tax. Hugh holds from Roger. He has 1 plough;
7 villagers and 2 smallholders. 4 more ploughs possible.
Woodland ½ league long and 2 furlongs wide.
Value before 1066, 50s; now 30s.

In ESCH Hundred

3 Roger also holds SHELL, and Herman from him. Alfwy held it as 2 manors; he could go where he would. 1 hide which pays tax. In lordship 1 plough;
2 smallholders and 3 slaves; A 15
4 salt-houses with woodland at ½ league long and 2 furlongs wide; they pay 60 measures of salt.
Value before 1066, 60s; later 30s; now 15s.
The woodland has been put in an Enclosure.

4 Roger also holds KINGTON. Alfwy, Elaf and Thori held it as 3 manors. 5 hides which pay tax. They could go where they would. They had 1 hedged enclosure where wild animals were caught. In lordship 2 ploughs; A 16
5 villagers and 7 smallholders with 2 ploughs. 2 slaves.
Woodland 1 league long and 2 furlongs wide.
Value before 1066 £4; later and now 50s.
Two men-at-arms hold from Roger.

[In DODDINGTREE Hundred]

†5 In MARTLEY Roger has 1 rider who pays him 4s.

18, 6 is entered at the foot of col. 176c, interrupting 19, 2

19 LAND OF OSBERN SON OF RICHARD

In DODDINGTREE Hundred

1 Osbern son of Richard Scrope holds BERRINGTON from the King. His father Richard held it. 2 hides which pay tax. In lordship 2 ploughs;
8 villagers, 4 smallholders, a smith and a miller with 9 ploughs; 1 more plough would be possible. 4 male and 4 female slaves.
A mill which pays 22 packloads of corn; meadow, 10 acres; woodland 1½ leagues long and 1 league wide.
The value was and is 20s.

Isd Osbn ten TAMEDEBERIE. Pat ei tenuit. Ibi. III. hidæ geld. In dnio. e. I. car. 7 XIIII. int uill 7 bord cu. XII. car. 7 adhuc. II. car plus ibi possent. ee. Ibi. II. serui.

★ ☞ Isd Rog ten dimid hid. in Wich. Aluric mapesone tenuit. Ibi. XI. burgses. 7 I. salina 7 dimid. reddt XXX.II. mittas 7 dimid. Hoc m ptin suo m de Hereford.

176 d

Silua ibi. II. lew lg. 7 una leuua lat. Valuit. LX. sol. m. XL. sol.

Isd Osbn ten CLISTVNE. Rex. E. tenuit. Ibi. III. hidæ geld Robt de olgi ten de osbno. 7 ibi ht. III. car in dnio. 7 VI. uill 7 IIII. bord. 7 IIII. bouar. Int oms cu pbro hnt. VI. car. 7 adhuc V. car plus possen ibi. ee. Silua ibi. III. qz lg. 7 II. qz lat. T.R.E. 7 post. ualb. XX. sol. modo: XL. solid.

Isd Osbn ten CHVRE. Rex. E. tenuit. Ibi. III. hidæ geld. In dnio e. I. car. 7 V. uill 7 IIII. bord cu. VIII. car. Ibi. III. serui. T.R.E. 7 post 7 m: uat. XL. solid. Ibi molin redd. X. sumas frumti.

Isd Osbn ten STANFORD. Brictric tenuit tein Eddid reginæ. Ibi. I. hida 7 dimid geld. In dnio. e. I. car. 7 I. uill 7 I. bord cu. I. car. 7 adhuc. I. car posset. ee. Ibi. e. I. seruus. Valuit 7 uat. XX. solid.

Isd Osbn ten CALDESLEI. Simon tenuit tein comitis Eduini. 7 n potuit ab eo recede sine ei lictia. Ibi. I. hida geld. In dnio. e. I. car. 7 ppositus cu. III. uill 7 II. bord hnt. II. car. Ibi. III. serui 7 piscaria redd XVI. stiches anguill. Ibi. II. car plus possen. ee. T.R.E. ualb. XL. sol. 7 modo. XXX. solid.

Isd Osbn ten CVER. Pat ei tenuit. Ibi. I. hid geld. In dnio. e una car. 7 altera posset. ee. Ibi. II. bord 7 un Radman cu. I. car. Valuit. XV. sol. modo. X. sol. Herbt ten de osbno.

2 Osbern also holds TENBURY (Wells). His father held it.
3 hides which pay tax. In lordship 1 plough;
14 villagers and smallholders with 12 ploughs; a further 2 more ploughs would be possible. 2 slaves.

18, 6 interrupts 19, 2 and is directed to its proper place by transposition signs

[In CLENT Hundred]

†18,6 Roger also holds ½ hide in DROITWICH. Aelfric Mapson held it.
11 burgesses and
1½ salt-houses; they pay 32½ measures.
This manor belongs to his manor of Hereford.

19, 2 continued

Woodland 2 leagues long and 1 league wide. 176 d
The value was 60s; now 40s.

Osbern also holds

3 CLIFTON (on Teme). King Edward held it. 3 hides which pay tax. Robert d'Oilly holds from Osbern. He has 3 ploughs in lordship;
6 villagers, 4 smallholders and 4 ploughmen; between them, with a priest, they have 6 ploughs; a further 5 more ploughs would be possible.
Woodland 3 furlongs long and 2 furlongs wide.
Value before 1066 and later, 20s; now 40s.

4 KYRE. King Edward held it. 3 hides which pay tax. In lordship 1 plough;
5 villagers and 4 smallholders with 8 ploughs. 3 slaves.
Value before 1066, later and now, 40s.
A mill which pays 10 packloads of grain.

5 STANFORD (on Teme). Brictric, a thane of Queen Edith, held it.
1½ hides which pay tax. In lordship 1 plough;
1 villager and 1 smallholder with 1 plough; 1 further plough would be possible. 1 slave.
The value was and is 20s.

6 SHELSEY. Sigmund, a thane of Earl Edwin, held it; he could not withdraw from it without his permission. 1 hide which pays tax. In lordship 1 plough.
A reeve with 3 villagers and 2 smallholders have 2 ploughs. 3 slaves.
A fishery which pays 16 sticks of eels. 2 more ploughs would be possible.
Value before 1066, 40s; now 30s.

7 KYRE. His father held it. 1 hide which pays tax. In lordship 1 plough; a second would be possible.
2 smallholders and 1 rider with 1 plough.
The value was 15s; now 10s.
Herbert holds from Osbern.

Isd Osbn ten *HAME*. Ipse tenuit. Ibi. I. hida geld. In dnio. I. car.
7 VII. bord. cu. V. car. 7 una car plus posset. ee. Ibi. IIII. serui.
7 piscaria de. II. solid. 7 molin redd. XVI. sumas annonæ.
Valuit. XX. sol. Modo. XXX. solid.

Isd Osbn ten *SAPIE*. Ipse tenuit. Ibi. III. hidæ geld. In dnio
nisi. IX. animalia. 7 pbr 7 IX. uilt 7 IIII. bord cu XI. car. 7 III. car
plus ibi possent. ee. Ibi molin redd. VI. sumas annonæ.
Valuit. XLV. solid. Modo. XXX. solid.

Isd Osbn ten *CARLETVNE*. 7 Odo de eo. Pat ei tenuit. Ibi. I. hida
7 una v. geld. In dnio sunt. II. car. 7 II. uilt 7 II. bord cu. I. car 7 dimid.
7 III. car plus possunt ibi. ee. Ibi. VII. serui. Silua dimid leuu lg.
7 III. qz lat. Valuit. X. solid. Modo. V. solid.

Isd Osbn ten *EDEVENT*. Vlfac tenuit. 7 potuit ire quo uoluit.
Herbt ten de Osbno. Ibi. I. hida geld. 7 in dnio. I. car. 7 I. uilt 7 V.
bord cu. III. car. Ibi. II. serui. Valuit. XX. sol. modo. XXVIII. sol.

Isd Osbn ten *WICELBOLD*. Goduin comes tenuit.
Ibi. XI. hidæ. Ex his. IIII. hidæ erant a geldo qetæ. In dnio. e. I. car.
7 II. car plus possent. ee. 7 XIX. uilt 7 XXVII. bord cu XVIII. car.
Ibi. II. serui. 7 V. molini de. IIII. lib 7 VIII. solid. 7 XXVI. salinæ
reddt. IIII. lib 7 XII. solid. 7 XIII. burgses in Wich secantes. II. dieb
in Augusto 7 Marcio. 7 seruientes curiæ. Siluæ. I. leuuede.
T.R.E. 7 post. ualb. XIIII. lib. Modo: XV. lib.

Isd Osbn ten *ELMERIGE*. Ældiet tenuit. Ibi. VIII. hidæ. Ex his
. III. hidæ sunt a geldo qetæ. teste comitatu. Ibi sunt. VIII. uilli
7 XXVI. bord cu. X. car. 7 aliæ. X. car possent. ee. Ibi. I. seruus.
7 salina de. IIII. solid. 7 L. ac pti. Silua. I. leuu lg. 7 dimid lat.
T.R.E. ualb. C. solid. Modo: L. solid.

8 HOMME (Castle). He held it himself. 1 hide which pays tax. In lordship 1 plough;
7 smallholders with 5 ploughs; 1 more plough would be possible. 4 slaves.
A fishery at 2s; a mill which pays 16 packloads of corn.
The value was 20s; now 30s.

9 (Lower) SAPEY. He held it himself. 3 hides which pay tax. In lordship only 9 cattle.
A priest, 9 villagers and 4 smallholders with 11 ploughs; 3 more ploughs would be possible.
A mill pays 6 packloads of corn.
The value was 45s; now 30s.

10 CARTON. Odo holds from him. His father held it. 1 hide and 1 virgate which pay tax. In lordship 2 ploughs;
2 villagers and 2 smallholders with 1½ ploughs; 3 more ploughs possible. 7 slaves.
Woodland ½ league long and 3 furlongs wide.
The value was 10s; now 5s.

11 EDVIN (Loach). Wulfheah held it; he could go where he would. Herbert holds from Osbern. 1 hide which pays tax. In lordship 1 plough;
1 villager and 5 smallholders with 3 ploughs. 2 slaves.
The value was 20s; now 28s.

[in CLENT Hundred]

12 WYCHBOLD. Earl Godwin held it. . . . 11 hides. Of these, 4 hides were exempt from tax. In lordship 1 plough; 2 more ploughs would be possible.
19 villagers and 27 smallholders with 18 ploughs. 2 slaves.
5 mills at £4 8s; 26 salt-houses pay £4 12s. 13 burgesses in Droitwich who reap for 2 days in August and March and who serve the court. Woodland, 1 league.
Value before 1066 and later £14; now £15.

13 ELMBRIDGE. Aldgeat held it. 8 hides. Of these, 3 hides are exempt from tax, as the County testifies.
8 villagers and 26 smallholders with 10 ploughs; another 10 ploughs would be possible. 1 slave.
A salt-house at 4s; meadow, 50 acres; woodland 1 league long and ½ wide.
Value before 1066, 100s; now 50s.

IN ESCH HVND.

Isd Osbn ten *CROELAI*.7 Vrso de eo. Chetelbt tenuit 7 potuit ire quo uoluit. Ibi.v.hidæ geld. In dnio.e.i.car 7 dim.7 iii.bord 7 iii.cot

.XX. TERRA GISLEBTI FILII TVROLDI. *IN DODINTRET HD.*

GISLEBERTVS filius Turoldi ten de rege *DODEHA*. Celmar tenuit.7 potuit ire quo uoluit. Ibi.i.hida geld. In dnio.e.i.car. 7 iii.uilt 7 viii.bord 7 iiii.cot 7 i.molinari. Int oms hnt.vii.car. Ibi.ii.bouarii.7 molin de.xii.sol. Valuit.xx.sol. modo: xl.ii.sol.

Isd Gislebt ten *REDMERLEIE*. Sauuard tenuit.7 potuit ire quo uoluit. Ibi.i.hida 7 dimid. Radulf ten de Gislebto. 7 ht in dnio.i.car.7 xi.bord 7 un francig cu.iii.car.7 una car plus posset.ee. Ibi.ii.serui. Valuit.xxx.sol.7 post: xv. M: xxx.sol.

Isd Gislebt ten *HANLEGE*.7 Roger de eo. Eduui tenuit 7 potuit ire quo uoluit. Ibi.i.hida 7 dimid geld. In dnio sun.ii.car. cu dimid car.7 adhuc.iii.car possun ibi.ee. Ibi.iii.serui.7 un burgsis de.ii.sol. ★ 7 ii.salinæ de.vi.solid. Silua dimid leuua.ad.c.porc. Valuit.lx.sol. M xl.

177 a 7 xi.bord 7 un francig cu.iii.car.7 adhuc.iii.poss.ee. Ibi.ii.serui. T.R.E. uatb.lx.sol.7 post: xx.sol.m: xl.sol.

Isd Gislebt ten *HANLEGE*.7 Hugo de eo. Cheneuuard 7 Vlchete tenuer p.ii.m.7 poteran ire quo uolb. Ibi.iii.hidæ geld. In dnio sunt.ii.car.7 x.bord 7 un fab.7 un francig cu.iii.car.7 adhuc.v.car plus possen.ee. T.R.E.uatb.lxx.sol. Modo: l.solid.

Isd Gislebt ten *ALRETVNE*.7 Hugo de eo. Eduui 7 Eduuin tenuer p.ii.m 7 poteran ire quo uolebant. Ibi.i.hida 7 dimid geld. In dnio sunt.iii.car.7 ii.uilt 7 ii.bord cu.i.car. Ibi.ii.serui.7 ii.piscariæ reddt xl.stiches anguilt. Siluæ.ii.qz ent. T.R.E.uatb.xl.sol.7 post 7 modo: xxx.solid.

in ESCH Hundred

14 CROWLE. Urso holds from him. Ketelbert held it; he could go where he would. 5 hides which pay tax. In lordship 1½ ploughs;
3 smallholders and 2 cottagers Ψ

This entry is continued at the foot of col. 176d, interrupting 20, 3

20 LAND OF GILBERT SON OF THOROLD

In DODDINGTREE Hundred

1 Gilbert son of Thorold holds DODDENHAM from the King. Ceolmer held it; he could go where he would. 1 hide which pays tax. In lordship 1 plough;
3 villagers, 8 smallholders, 4 cottagers and 1 miller; between them they have 7 ploughs. 2 ploughmen.
A mill at 12s.
The value was 20s; now 42s.

2 Gilbert also holds REDMARLEY. Saeward held it; he could go where he would. 1½ hides. . . . Ralph holds from Gilbert. He has in lordship 1 plough and
11 smallholders and 1 Frenchman with 3 ploughs; 1 more plough would be possible. 2 slaves.
The value was 30s; later 15s; now 30s.

3 Gilbert also holds HANLEY, and Roger from him. Edwy held it; he could go where he would. 1½ hides which pay tax. In lordship 2 ploughs;

19, 14 continued, interrupting 20, 3 and directed to its proper place by transposition signs

Ψ 19,14 with ½ plough; a further 3 ploughs possible. 3 slaves; 1 burgess at 2s.
2 salt-houses at 6s; woodland ½ league for 100 pigs.
The value was 60s; now 40[s].

20, 3 continued

11 smallholders and 1 Frenchman with 3 ploughs; a further 3 possible. 2 slaves. 177 a
Value before 1066, 60s; later 20s; now 40s.

4 Gilbert also holds HANLEY, and Hugh from him. Kenward and Ulfketel held it as 2 manors; they could go where they would. 3 hides which pay tax. In lordship 2 ploughs;
10 smallholders, 1 smith and 1 Frenchman with 3 ploughs; a further 5 more ploughs would be possible.
Value before 1066, 70s; now 50s.

5 Gilbert also holds ORLETON, and Hugh from him. Edwy and Edwin held it as 2 manors; they could go where they would. 1½ hides which pay tax. In lordship 3 ploughs;
2 villagers and 2 smallholders with 1 plough. 2 slaves.
2 fisheries pay 40 sticks of eels; woodland, 2 furlongs.
Value before 1066, 40s; later and now 30s.

Isd Gislebt ten HADESORE.7 Walter gener ei de eo. Bricsmar tenuit tein regis.E.Ibi.II.hidæ In dnio sunt.II.car.7 II.uitt 7 VIII.bord 7 IIII.cotmanni cu.II.car.7 tcia posset.ee.ibi. Ibi.IIII.bouarii.7 VII.salinæ reddt.CXI.mittas salis. IN CLENT HVND.

T.R.E.ualb.LX.solid.Modo.XLV.solid.

.XXI. TERRA DROGONIS FILII PONZ. IN DODINTRET HD.

DROGO filius ponz ten de rege HOLIM. Vlmar tenuit 7 potuit ire quo uoluit. Ibi.I.hida geld.7 una car posset.ee.ibi. Wasta.e 7 uuasta fuit.T.R.E.ualb.V.solid.

Isd Drogo ten STILLEDVNE. Vlchet tenuit.7 n poterat discedere á dno suo Vlmaro.Ibi dimid hida geld.Tra.e II.car.Valuit.V.solid.Modo.e Wasta.

Isd Drogo ten GLESE. Vlmar tenuit 7 potuit ire quo uoluit. Ibi.I.hida geld. In dnio dimid car.7 I.uitt 7 III.bord cu.I.car.7 alia posset ibi.ee. Ibi molin de IIII.sot 7 VIII.denar. Valuit.XX.sot.Modo:X.solid.

Isd Drogo ten una v in MERLIE m regis.7 geldat. Ibi ht.I.Radman redd.VI.solid p annu.Ernuin tenuit.

.XXII TERRA HERALDI FILII RADVLFI COMIT.

HERALD fili com' Radulfi ten de rege.I.hida in WICH. 7 ibi ht.XX.burgses.cu.VII.salinis.reddt L.mittas salis. Valuit 7 ualet.XL.solid.

XXIII. TERRA WILLI FILII ANSCVLFI. IN CAME HVND.

WILLS filius Ansculfi ten de rege ESCELIE.7 Wibt de eo.Vluuin tenuit.Ibi ptin una Bereuuiche BERCHELAI.Int tot.IIII.hidæ. In dnio.e dimid car. 7 II.uitti 7 IX.bord cu.IIII.car.Nem.I.leuua lg. T.R.E.ualuit.C.sot.Modo:LX.solid.

Hoc m emit isd Wluuin T.R.E.de epo cestrensi ad ætate triu houm.Qui cu infirmat ad fine uitæ uenisset:

In CLENT Hundred

6 Gilbert also holds HADZOR, and Walter his son-in-law from him. Brictmer, a thane of King Edward, held it. 2 hides. In lordship 2 ploughs;
2 villagers, 8 smallholders and 4 cottage-men with 2 ploughs; a third would be possible. 4 ploughmen.
7 salt-houses pay 111 measures of salt.
Value before 1066, 60s; now 45s.

21 LAND OF DROGO SON OF POYNTZ

In DODDINGTREE Hundred

1 Drogo son of Poyntz holds HOLLIN from the King. Wulfmer held it; he could go where he would. 1 hide which pays tax. 1 plough would be possible. It is waste and was waste.
Value before 1066, 5s.

2 Drogo also holds STILDON. Ulfketel held it; he could not withdraw from his lord Wulfmer. ½ hide which pays tax. Land for 2 ploughs.
The value was 5s; now it is waste.

3 Drogo also holds GLASSHAMPTON. Wulfmer held it; he could go where he would. 1 hide which pays tax. In lordship ½ plough;
1 villager and 3 smallholders with 1 plough; another would be possible.
A mill at 4s 8d.
The value was 20s; now 10s.

4 Drogo also holds 1 virgate in MARTLEY, a manor of the King; it pays tax. He has 1 rider who pays 6s a year. Ernwin held it.

22 LAND OF HAROLD SON OF EARL RALPH

[In CLENT Hundred]

1 Harold son of Earl Ralph holds 1 hide in DROITWICH from the King. He has
20 burgesses with
7 salt-houses; they pay 50 measures of salt.
The value was and is 40s.

23 LAND OF WILLIAM SON OF ANSCULF

In CAME Hundred

1 William son of Ansculf holds SELLY (Oak) from the King, and Wibert from him. Wulfwin held it. One outlier, BARTLEY (Green), belongs there. In total, 4 hides. . . . In lordship ½ plough;
2 villagers and 9 smallholders with 4 ploughs.
A wood 1 league long.
Value before 1066, 100s; now 60s.

Wulfwin bought this manor before 1066 from the Bishop of Chester, for the lives of three men. When he was ailing and had come to the

uocato filio suo epo. Li. 7 uxore sua 7 pluribȝ amicis suis: dixit. Audite uos amici mei. Hanc trã quã ab æccla emi: uolo ut teneat uxor mea dũ uixerit. 7 post mortẽ eius: recipiat æccla de quá accepi. 7 qui inde abstu lerit: excõmunicat⁹ sit.

Hoc ita fuisse testificant meliores hões toti⁹ comitat⁹.

177 b

Isd Wills ten NORDFELD. Aluuold⁹ tenuit.
Ibi. VI. hide. In dñio. ẽ. I. car. 7 pbr 7 VII. uilli. 7 XVI. bord 7 VI. cotmanni cũ. XIII. car. 7 adhuc. V. car possent fieri. Ibi. II. serui. 7 I. ancilla. Silua dimid leuu lg. 7 III. qz lat. T.R.E. ualb. VIII. lib. Modo. C. solid.

Isd Wills ten FRANCHELIE. 7 Balduin⁹ de eo. Vluuin⁹ tenuit. Ibi. I. hida. In dñio. ẽ una car. Ibi. IX. bord cũ. V. car. 7 II. serui. Silua. I. leuu lg. 7 dimid lat. T.R.E. ualb. XL. sol. Modo. XXX. sol.

Isd. W. ten WELINGEWICHE. 7 Balduin⁹ de eo. Ibi. III. virg træ. Ibi. ẽ. un⁹ uill 7 I. bord cũ dimid car. Adhuc. II. car 7 dimid possent ibi. ee. Valuit. V. solid. Modo: III. solid.

Isd. W. ten ESCELIE. Tumi 7 Eleua tenuer. p. II. m̃. Robt⁹ ten de Willo. Ibi. I. hida. In dñio. ẽ. I. car. 7 III. uill 7 II. bord 7 II. bouar cũ. II. car. Siluæ. I. leuuede. T.R.E. ualb. XX. solid. Modo: XV. sol.

Isd. W. ten WERWELIE. 7 Alelm⁹ de eo. Æiluuard tenuit. Ibi dimid hida. In dñio. ẽ. I. car. 7 II. uill 7 VIII. bord. cũ. IIII. car 7 dimid. Ibi. II. serui. T.R.E. ualb. XVII. solid. Modo: X. solid.

Isd. W. ten CERCEHALLE. 7 Walter⁹ de eo. Wigar tenuit. Ibi. II. hidæ. In dñio. ẽ. I. car. 7 adhuc. V. car ibi possunt. ee. Valuit. LX. sol. Modo: VIII. sol.

end of his life, he summoned his son, the Bishop (of) Li(chfield?), his wife and many of his friends, and said: 'Hear me, my friends, I desire that my wife hold this land which I bought from the church so long as she lives, and that after her death the church from which I received it should accept it back. Let whoever shall take it away from it be excommunicated'. The more important men of the whole County testify that this was so.

William also holds 177 b

2 NORTHFIELD. Alfwold held it. 6 hides. . . . In lordship 1 plough;
A priest, 7 villagers, 16 smallholders and 6 cottage-men with 13 ploughs; a further 5 ploughs would be possible. 2 male slaves, 1 female. A 168
Woodland ½ league long and 3 furlongs wide.
Value before 1066 £8; now 100s.

3 FRANKLEY. Baldwin holds from him. Wulfwin held it. 1 hide. . . .
In lordship 1 plough;
9 smallholders with 5 ploughs. 2 slaves.
Woodland 1 league long and ½ wide.
Value before 1066, 40s; now 30s.

4 'WILLINGWICK'. Baldwin holds from him. 3 virgates of land. . . .
1 villager and 1 smallholder with ½ plough; a further 2½ ploughs would be possible.
The value was 5s; now 3s.

5 SELLY (Oak). Tumi and Aeleva held it as 2 manors. Robert holds from William. 1 hide. In lordship 1 plough;
3 villagers, 2 smallholders and 2 ploughmen with 2 ploughs.
Woodland, 1 league.
Value before 1066, 20s; now 15s.

[in CLENT Hundred]

6 WARLEY. Alfhelm holds from him. Aethelward held it. ½ hide. . . .
In lordship 1 plough;
2 villagers and 8 smallholders with 4½ ploughs. 2 slaves.
Value before 1066, 17s; now 10s.

7 CHURCHILL. Walter holds from him. Withgar held it. 2 hides. . . .
In lordship 1 plough; a further 5 ploughs possible.
The value was 60s; now 8s.

Ifd.W.ten BELLEM. Leuenot tenuit. tan regis. E. Ibi. III. hidæ. Robt ten de Witto. In dnio. e. I. car. 7 VII. uitt 7 IIII. bord cu. IIII. car. Ibi. II. ferui. 7 falina de. II. oris. Ibi. III. car plus poff. ee. Valuit. XXV. fol modo: XV. fol. Hoc ∞ tenuit Rad. f. Hubti plufquā. v. annis. fed. Witts filius Osbn iniufte ei abftulit. IN CLENT HVND.

Ifd. W. ten HAGELEIA. 7 Roger de eo. Godric tenuit tain regis. E. Ibi. v. hidæ 7 dimid. In dnio. e. I. car. 7 pbr 7 v. uitti 7 x. bord cu. v. car. 7 adhuc. VIII. car plus pof funt. ee. Ibi. II. ferui. Silua dimid lew lg. 7 III. q̄z lat. T.R.E. ualb. LX. folid. Modo. L. folid.

Ifd. W. ten DVDELEI. 7 ibi eft caftellu eius. Hoc ∞ tenuit Eduinus comes. Ibi. I. hida. In dnio. e. I. car. 7 III. uitt 7 x. bord 7 un faber. cu. x. car. Ibi. II. ferui. 7 II. leuued filuæ. T.R.E. ualb. IIII. lib. Modo: III. lib.

Ifd. W. ten SVINEFORDE. 7 Acard de eo. Vluuin tenuit. Ibi. III. hidæ. In dnio. e. I. car. 7 pbr 7 v. uitti 7 XI. bord. cu. VII. car. Ibi. II. ferui. 7 molin de. v. folid. Siluæ. I. leuued. T.R.E. ualb. VI. lib. Modo. III. lib.

Ifd. W. ten PEVEMORE. 7 Acard de eo. Turgar tenuit. Ibi. III. hidæ In dnio. e. I. car. 7 III. uitt 7 pbr 7 x. bord 7 III. cotman cu. v. car 7 dim. 7 adhuc car. III. poffunt ibi. ee. In Wirecestre. II. mafuræ de. II. fol. 7 una leuu filuulæ. T.R.E. ualb. IIII. lib. Modo. L. folid.

Ifd. W. ten CRADELEIE. 7 Pagan de eo. Wigar tenuit Ibi. I. hida. In dnio nichil. Ibi funt. IIII. uitt 7 XI. bord cu. VII. car. Valuit. XL. fol. Modo. XXIIII. folid.

Ifd. W. ten BELINTONES. in caftellaria fua. Elric 7 Holand tenuer p. II. ∞. Ibi. v. hidæ. Tra. e. v. car. Wasta fuit 7 eft. Ibi. IIII. q̄z filuæ. fed eft in forefta regis. prata hui ∞. ual. IIII. denar.

in CLENT Hundred

BELL (Hall). Leofnoth, a thane of King Edward, held it.
3 hides. . . . Robert holds from William. In lordship 1 plough;
7 villagers and 4 smallholders with 4 ploughs. 2 slaves.
A salt-house at 2 *ora*. 3 more ploughs possible.
The value was 25s; now 15s.
Ralph son of Hubert held this manor for more than 5 years, but William son of Osbern wrongfully took it from him.

HAGLEY. Roger holds from him. Godric, a thane of King Edward, held it. 5½ hides. In lordship 1 plough;
A priest, 5 villagers and 10 smallholders with 5 ploughs; a further 8 more ploughs possible. 2 slaves.
Woodland ½ league long and 3 furlongs wide.
Value before 1066, 60s; now 50s.

0 DUDLEY. His castle is there. Earl Edwin held this manor. 1 hide. . . .
In lordship 1 plough;
3 villagers, 10 smallholders and 1 smith with 10 ploughs. 2 slaves.
Woodland, 2 leagues.
Value before 1066 £4; now £3.

1 (Old) SWINFORD. Acard holds from him. Wulfwin held it. 3 hides. . . .
In lordship 1 plough;
A priest, 5 villagers and 11 smallholders with 7 ploughs. 2 slaves.
A mill at 5s; woodland, 1 league.
Value before 1066 £6; now £3.

2 PEDMORE. Acard holds from him. Thorgar held it. 3 hides. . . .
In lordship 1 plough;
3 villagers, a priest, 10 smallholders and 3 cottage-men with 5½ ploughs; a further 3 ploughs possible.
In Worcester 2 dwellings at 2s; a little wood, 1 league.
Value before 1066 £4; now 50s.

3 CRADLEY. Payne holds from him. Withgar held it. 1 hide. . . .
Nothing in lordship.
4 villagers and 11 smallholders with 7 ploughs.
The value was 40s; now 24s.

4 BELLINGTON, in his castlery. Alric and Holland held it as
2 manors. 5 hides. Land for 5 ploughs. It was and is waste.
Woodland, 4 furlongs, but it is in the King's Forest.
Value of the meadow of this manor, 4d.

177 b

.II.
.XXII. TERRA WILLI FILII CORBVCION *IN CLENT HD.*

WILLS filius Corbucion ten de rege *WITONE IN WICH.* Tuini tenuit. tain regis. E. Ibi. II. hidæ. In dnio sunt. II. car. 7 XVIII. bord. 7 pbr cu. I. car. Ibi. IIII. serui. 7 una ancilla. 7 In Wirecestre. I. burgsis de. II. solid. 7 Sa linæ tres reddt. LX. mittas salis. 7 partem de una salina de. X. mittis salis. Siluæ dimid leuuede.
Valuit 7 ualet. III. lib.

.XXV. TERRA WILLI GOIZENBODED. *IN CLENT HVND.*

WILLS Goizenboded ten *CELVESTVNE.* 7 Wills de eo. Ricard iuuenis tenuit T.R.E. Ibi. I. hida. 7 ibi sunt. IIII. bord cu. I. car. T.R.E. ualb. X. solid. modo: IIII. sol.

.XXVI. TERRA VRSON DE ABETOT. *IN DODINTRET HD.*

VRSO ten *COCHEHI.* 7 Herlebald de eo. Godric .I. lib hō te nuit. Ibi. II. hidæ 7 dimid geld. In dnio. e. una car. 7 II. bord. 7 II. car plus possunt ibi. ee. Ibi. II. serui. 7 un burgsem de. XVI. denar. 7 IIII. mittas salis. 7 III. q̃z siluæ lg. 7 II. q̃z lat.
T.R.E. ualb. LXX. solid. 7 post. XL. sol. Modo: L. solid.

Isd Vrso ten *OSMERLIE.* 7 Herlebold de eo. *IN CAME HD.* Aluuold tenuit. Ibi. I. hida. In dnio. e. I. car. 7 X. bord cu. III. car. Ibi. II. serui 7 II. ancillæ. In Wirecestre. una dom de. XVI. den. 7 in Wich. I. salina redd. XII. mittas salis. Nem dimid leuua.
Valuit. XX. sol. ual. XIII. solid.

Isd Vrso ten *COSTONE.* Leuiet 7 Aluric 7 Adelric te nuer p. III. m. Ibi. III. hidæ. Turold ten. II. as. 7 Walter una hid de Vrsone. In dnio sunt. II. car. 7 XI. bord 7 III. cotmani. cu. IIII. car. 7 adhuc. I. car plus potest. ee. Ibi molin seruiens aulæ uni eoz. Silua. III. q̃z lg. 7 una lat. sed. e in foresta regis.
T.R.E. ualb. XXXV. solid. Modo: XX. VII. solid.

4 LAND OF WILLIAM SON OF CORBUCION 177 c

In CLENT Hundred

William son of Corbucion holds WITTON in Droitwich from the King. Tuini, a thane of King Edward, held it. 2 hides.
In lordship 2 ploughs;
18 smallholders and a priest with 1 plough. 4 male slaves, 1 female; in Worcester 1 burgess at 2s.
3 salt-houses pay 60 measures of salt and a part of 1 salt-house at 10 measures of salt; woodland, ½ league.
The value was and is £3.

5 LAND OF WILLIAM GOIZENBODED

In CLENT Hundred

William Goizenboded holds CHAWSON, and William from him. Richard, a young man, held it before 1066. 1 hide.
4 smallholders with 1 plough. . . .
Value before 1066, 10s; now 4s.

6 LAND OF URSO OF ABETOT

In DODDINGTREE Hundred

Urso holds COOKHILL, and Erlebald from him. Godric, a free man, held it. 2½ hides which pay tax. In lordship 1 plough;
2 smallholders; 2 more ploughs possible. 2 slaves. A 5
(He has) 1 burgess at 16d, and 4 measures of salt. Woodland, 3 furlongs long and 2 furlongs wide.
Value before 1066, 70s; later 40s; now 50s.

Urso also holds

in CAME Hundred

'OSMERLEY'. Erlebald holds from him. Alfwold held it. 1 hide. In lordship 1 plough;
10 smallholders with 3 ploughs. 2 male and 2 female slaves.
In Worcester 1 house at 16d; in Droitwich 1 salt-house which pays 12 measures of salt; wood ½ league.
The value was 20s; value 13s.

COFTON (Hackett). Leofgeat, Aelfric and Aethelric held it as 3 manors. 3 hides. Thorold holds 2, and Walter 1 hide, from Urso.
In lordship 2 ploughs;
11 smallholders and 3 cottage-men with 4 ploughs; a further 1 more plough possible.
A mill which serves the hall of one of them; woodland 3 furlongs long and 1 wide, but it is in the King's Forest.
Value before 1066, 35s; now 27s.

177 c

Isd Vrso ten *BENESLEI*.7 Wills de eo. Leuric tenuit. de Eduino comite. Ibi. I. hida. In dnio.e. I. car.7 IIII. bord cu. III. car. Silua. I. leuu lg.7 dimid lat.
T.R.E. ualb. XXX. sol. Modo: XVI. solid.
Isd Vrso ten *VDECOTE*.7 Herlebald de eo. Wlsi tenuit. tain regis. E. Ibi. I. hida 7 dimid. Ibi. e un uills 7 II. bord cu. I. car. Silua dimid leuua. sed rex posuit in foresta.
T.R.E. ualb. X. solid. uat modo. V. solid. *IN CRESSELAV HD*
Isd Vrso ten *RVSSOCOC*.7 Hunulf de eo. Achil tenuit. Ibi. V. hidæ. In dnio. e una car 7 dimid. 7 XIII. uill 7 I. bord 7 III. cotmani cu. VI. car 7 dimid. Int seruos 7 ancillas. IIII. Salina de. V. oris. Siluæ: una leuua 7 dimid.
T.R.E. ualb. L. solid. Modo: XXX. solid.
Isd Vrso ten *STANES*. Tumi 7 Euchil tenuerunt p. II. M. Ibi. VI. hidæ. Herlebald ten de Vrsone. In dnio sunt. II. car.7 VII. uill 7 XV. bord cu. VI. car. Ibi. IIII. serui.7 molin de. III. oris.
T.R.E. ualb. XL. solid. Modo: XXX. solid.
Isd. Vrso ten *LVNVREDELE*.7 Wills de eo. Turbnus tenuit tain regis. E. Ibi. II. hidæ. In dnio sunt. II. car. 7 æccla 7 pbr 7 faber.7 IIII. uill 7 IIII. bord cu. IIII. car. Ibi molin de. IIII. solid.7 salina ad Wich de. IIII. sol.
T.R.E. ualb. XXX. solid. Modo: XL. solid.

177 d
Isd Vrso ten *HATETE*.7 Gunfrid de eo. Erniet 7 Eliet tenuer. p. II. M.7 poterant ire quo uoleb. Ibi. I. hida. In dnio. e. I. car.7 alia potest. ee. Ibi molin de. II. solid. 7 un bord nil habens.
T.R.E. ualb. XXX. solid. Modo: X. solid.

4 BENTLEY. William holds from him. Leofric held it from Earl Edwin.
1 hide. In lordship 1 plough.
4 smallholders with 3 ploughs.
Woodland 1 league long and ½ wide.
Value before 1066, 30s; now 16s.

5 WOODCOTE (Green). Erlebald holds from him. Wulfsi, a thane of King Edward, held it. 1½ hides.
1 villager and 2 smallholders with 1 plough.
Woodland ½ league, but the King has placed it in the Forest.
Value before 1066, 10s; value now 5s.

in CRESSLAU Hundred

6 RUSHOCK. Hunwulf holds from him. Aki held it. 5 hides.
In lordship 1½ ploughs;
13 villagers, 1 smallholder and 3 cottage-men with 6½ ploughs.
4 slaves, male and female.
A salt-house at 5 *ora*; woodland, 1½ leagues.
Value before 1066, 50s; now 30s.

7 STONE. Tumi and Alfkell held it as 2 manors. 6 hides.
Erlebald holds from Urso. In lordship 2 ploughs;
7 villagers and 15 smallholders with 6 ploughs. 4 slaves.
A mill at 3 *ora*.
Value before 1066, 40s; now 30s.

8 DOVERDALE. William holds from him. Thorbern, a thane of King Edward, held it. 2 hides. In lordship 2 ploughs;
A church, a priest, a smith, 4 villagers and 4 smallholders with 4 ploughs.
A mill at 4s; at Droitwich a salt-house at 4s.
Value before 1066, 30s; now 40s.

9 *HATETE*. Gunfrid holds from him. Erngeat and Alfgeat held 177 d
it as 2 manors; they could go where they would. 1 hide.
In lordship 1 plough; another possible.
A mill at 2s.
1 smallholder who has nothing.
Value before 1066, 30s; now 10s.

Isd Vrso ten *HAMTVNE*.7 Robt de eo. Aluuold tenuit.
Ibi.IIII.hidæ. In dnio.e una car.7 pbr 7 v.uitti 7 II.bord.
cu.IIII.car.7 adhuc.IIII.car possunt.ee.Ibi.VII.salinæ
reddt.XIIII.oras.Ibi.II.bouarii. Valuit.IIII.lib.M.III.lib.
Isd Vrso ten *HORTVNE*.7 Robt de eo. Aluric tenuit.
7 potuit ire quo uoluit.| Ibi.II.hidæ. In dnio sunt.II.car.7 IIII.bouarii
7 II.bord. Ibi parua silua. Ibi salina de XL.denar.
T.R.E. ualb.L.solid. Modo: XVIII.sol.
★ Isd Vrso ten *COCHESIE*.7 Herbrand 7 Witts de eo. Aluuin 7 Atilic
tenuer p.II.M.Ibi.II.hidæ. In dnio.e.I.car.7 III.bord.7 II.francig.
hntes int se.IIII.car.7 adhuc.I.car potest.ee.h tra ex multa
parte.e Wasta. Silua dimid leuua lg.7 III.qz lat.
T.R.E. ualb.XLV.solid.modo: XXVII.solid.
Isd Vrso ten *BROTVNE*. Godeua comitissa tenuit. Ibi.II.hidæ. In dnio
sunt.II.car.7 v.uitt 7 x.bord 7 æccta 7 pbr. Int oms hnt.VI.
car. Ibi.IIII.serui. In Wich.v.salinæ reddt.c.mittas salis.7 v.
oras. Siluæ.III.leuuedes.
T.R.E.ualb.IIII.lib.modo: IIII.lib 7 x.solid. *IN EOD HVND.*
Isd Vrso ten una hid qeta a geldo 7 ab omi csuetudine.
7 Robt ten de eo. Ibi.III.bord.nil hntes. Valuit 7 ual.III.sol.
Aluric tenuit. T.R.E.
Isd Vrso ten *VPTVNE*.7 Herlebald de eo. Aluuin abb de
euesha tenuit.7 in abbatia recte debet.ee. teste comitatu.
Ibi.III.hidæ. In dnio sunt.II.car.7 VII.uitt 7 XIII.bord
7 pbr cu.v.car. Ibi.IIII.serui.7 molin de.IIII.sol. In Wirecest
un burgsis de.II.sol. In Wich.III.salinæ reddt.XL.mitas sal.
Silua.III.qz lg.7 II.qz lat. Valb.LX.sol. Modo.L.sol.

in CLENT Hundred

0 HAMPTON (Lovett). Robert holds from him. Alfwold held it.
4 hides. In lordship 1 plough;
A priest, 5 villagers and 2 smallholders with 4 ploughs; a further 4 ploughs possible.
7 salt-houses pay 14 *ora*. 2 ploughmen.
The value was £4; now £3.

1 HORTON. Robert holds from him. Aelfric held it; he could go where he would. 2 hides. In lordship 2 ploughs;
4 ploughmen and 2 smallholders.
A small wood. A salt-house at 40d.
Value before 1066, 50s; now 18s.

2 COOKSEY (Green). Herbrand and William hold from him. Alwin and Atilic held it as 2 manors. 2 hides. In lordship 1 plough;
3 smallholders and 2 Frenchmen who have 4 ploughs between them; a further plough possible. Much of this land is waste.
Woodland ½ league long and 3 furlongs wide.
Value before 1066, 45s; now 27s.

3 BELBROUGHTON. Countess Godiva held it. 2 hides. In lordship 2 ploughs;
5 villagers, 10 smallholders, a church and a priest; between them they have 6 ploughs. 4 slaves.
In Droitwich 5 salt-houses pay 100 measures of salt and 5 *ora*; woodland, 3 leagues.
Value before 1066 £4; now £4 10s.

in the same Hundred

4 1 hide exempt from tax and from every customary due.
Robert holds from him.
3 smallholders who have nothing.
The value was and is 3s.
Aelfric held it before 1066.

15 UPTON (Warren). Erlebald holds from him. Abbot Alwin of Evesham held it; it ought rightly to be in the Abbey (lands), as the County testifies. 3 hides. . . . In lordship 2 ploughs;
7 villagers, 13 smallholders and a priest with 5 ploughs. 4 slaves.
A mill at 4s; in Worcester 1 burgess at 2s; in Droitwich 3 salt-houses pay 40 measures of salt; woodland 3 furlongs long and 2 furlongs wide.
The value was 60s; now 50s.

177 d

Isd Vrso ten *WITVNE*. in Wich. 7 Gunfrid de eo. Æccla de Eueshā tenuit. T.R.E. Ibi dimid hida. In dnio. ē. I. car. 7 II. serui 7 II. bord. 7 VII. burgses in Wich. 7 una salina 7 dimid redd. xxx. denar. Valuit. xx. solid. Modo. xv. sol. Hanc trā donauit qdā Vluiet eid æcclæ de Eueshā. 7 po suit donū sup altare qdo fili ei. Aluiet fact est ibi monachus. Hoc factū. ē qnto anno regni regis. E. Postea ů præstitit abb Æluuin hanc trā suo auunculo quādiu ipse hō uiueret. Qui postea mortuus fuit in bello Heraldi ctra norrenses. 7 æccla recep trā suā antequā rex. W. in anglia uenisset. 7 tenuit isd abb qdiu uixit. 7 etiā successor ei Walterius abb similit tenuit amplius quā. VII. annis.

Isd Vrso ten *HANTVNE*. Abb de Eueshā tenuit. T.R.E. Ibi. IIII. hidæ. Robt ten de Vrsone. In dnio. ē una car. 7 IIII. uitt 7 VI. bord cū. II. car. 7 adhuc. II. car possunt. ee. Ibi. II. serui. 7 molin de. xxx. solid. 7 salina redd. III. oras. T.R.E. uatb. IIII. lib. Modo: L. solid.

Hoc m emit abb eid æcclæ á qdā taino qui trā suā recte poterat uendere cui uellet. T.R.E. 7 emptū donauit æcclæ p unū textū positū sup altare. teste comitatu.

.XXVII. TERRA HVGONIS LASNE. *IN CAME HVND.*

HVGO asin ten de rege *TICHENAPLETREV*. 7 Witts de eo. Aluuold tenuit. Ibi. III. hidæ. In dnio sunt. II. car. 7 VIII. bord. 7 un francig cū. III. car. Ibi. IIII. bouarii 7 una ancilla. 7 XII. ac pti. In Wich salina. redd. xxx. mittas salis. T.R.E. uatb. XL. sol. modo: xxx. solid.

6 WITTON in Droitwich. Gunfrid holds from him. The Church of Evesham held it before 1066. ½ hide. In lordship 1 plough; 2 slaves;
2 smallholders; 7 burgesses in Droitwich.
1½ salt-houses which pay 30d.
The value was 20s; now 15s.

One Wulfgeat gave this land to the Church of Evesham. He placed his grant upon the altar when his son, Alfgeat, became a monk there. This was done in the fifth year of King Edward's reign. But later on Abbot Alwin leased this land to his (own) uncle for as long as the man should live. Later he died in Harold's war against the Norse and the church recovered its land, before King William came to England. The Abbot held it as long as he lived, and his successor, Abbot Walter, likewise held it for more than 7 years.

7 HAMPTON (Lovett). The Abbot of Evesham held it before 1066. 4 hides. Robert holds from Urso. In lordship 1 plough;
4 villagers and 6 smallholders with 2 ploughs; a further 2 ploughs possible. 2 slaves.
A mill at 30s; a salt-house which pays 3 *ora*.
Value before 1066 £4; now 50s.

The Abbot of this church bought this manor from a thane who before 1066 could rightly sell his land to whom he would. He gave his purchase to the church through a document placed upon the altar, as the County testifies.

27 **LAND OF HUGH DONKEY** C

In CAME Hundred

1 Hugh Donkey holds 'THICKENAPPLETREE' from the King, and William from him. Alfwold held it. 3 hides. . . . In lordship 2 ploughs;
8 smallholders and 1 Frenchman with 3 ploughs. 4 ploughmen; 1 female slave.
Meadow, 12 acres; in Droitwich a salt-house which pays 30 measures of salt.
Value before 1066, 40s; now 30s.

XXVI II EDDEVE qdā femina ten de rege *CEDESLAI*. *IN CRESSELAV HD*.
Ipsa tenuit T.R.E. Ibi . xxv . hidæ . cū . VIII . Bereuuiches . Ex his
.x . hidæ erant quietæ a geldo . teste comitatu.
In dnio sunt . III . car. 7 XXXIII . uitt 7 xx . bord 7 II . pbri cū
IIII . bord . Int oms hnt . xxv . car . Ibi . VIII . int seruos 7 ancillas.
7 III . molini redd . XII . sūmas annonæ. In Wirecestre . II . burgses
redd . XII . den. 7 In Wich . v . salinæ reddt . XXI . solid 7 IIII . den.
Ibi Silua de . II . leuuis. 7 alia silua de . I . leuua.
T.R.E. 7 modo . uat . XII . lib.

Wlmar tenuit *HILHAMATONE* . Ibi . I . uirg træ. 7 est Wasta.
T.R.E. uatb . XII . denar.

In *ESCH HVND* iacent . x . hidæ in *FECHEHA*. 7 III . hidæ in *HOLEWEI*.
7 Scriptæ sunt in breui de Hereford.

In *DODINTRET* hd iacent . XIII . hidæ de *MERTELAI*. 7 v . hidæ
de *SVCHELEI*. quæ hic placitant 7 geldant. 7 ad Hereford reddt
firmā suā. 7 sunt scriptæ in breue regis.

28 [LAND OF ?ALDEVA] 178 a

In CRESSLAU Hundred

1 Edeva, a woman, holds CHADDESLEY (Corbett) from the King; she held it herself before 1066. 25 hides with 8 outliers. Of these, 10 hides were exempt from tax, as the County testifies. In lordship 3 ploughs;

33 villagers, 20 smallholders and 2 priests with 4 smallholders; between them they have 25 ploughs. 8 slaves, male and female.

3 mills which pay 12 packloads of corn; in Worcester 2 burgesses who pay 12d; in Droitwich 5 salt-houses pay 21s 4d; woodland at 2 leagues; another woodland at 1 league.

Value before 1066 and now £12.

[X] [ADDENDUM]

[In DODDINGTREE Hundred]

1 Wulfmer held HILLHAMPTON. 1 virgate of land; it is waste. Value before 1066, 12d.

In ESCH Hundred

2 lie 10 hides in FECKENHAM and 3 hides in HOLLOW (Court). A 1-2
They are entered in the return for Hereford.

In DODDINGTREE Hundred

3 lie 13 hides of MARTLEY and 5 hides of SUCKLEY; they hold pleas and pay tax here. They pay their revenue to Hereford and are entered in the King's return.

HOLDINGS IN WORCESTERSHIRE IN 1086, ENTERED ELSEWHERE IN THE SURVEY

The Latin text for these entries will be found in the county volume concerned
(References to Evesham A appear in the right margin)

In the Herefordshire folios

1 LAND OF THE KING 179 c

E1 In DODDINGTREE Hundred 180 c

39 The King holds MARTLEY. Queen Edith held it. 10 hides and 1 virgate of land. In lordship 8 ploughs;
47 villagers, 16 smallholders and 2 riders with 43 ploughs.
A mill at 8s; 2 weirs pay 2,500 eels and 5 sticks.
A reeve and a beadle have 2 virgates of land and 2 ploughs.
In Worcester 3 houses which pay 12d.
The villagers and smallholders pay 12s for fish and timber.
This manor pays to Hereford £24 of pence at 20 to the *ora*, and 12s in gifts.

Earl William gave to St. Mary's of Cormeilles this manor's church with the land belonging to it and its tithe, and
2 villagers with 2 virgates of land.

The Earl himself gave Ralph of Bernay 2 riders; he put them outside this manor, with the land they held; they have 2 ploughs.

The Earl also gave Druward 1 virgate of land, which he still holds.

E2 In ASH Hundred

40 The King holds FECKENHAM. Five thanes held it from Earl Edwin; they could go where they wished with the land. Under them they had 4 men-at-arms, as free as they were themselves; between them there were 13 ploughs. 10 hides. In lordship 6 ploughs; A 1
30 villagers, 11 smallholders, a reeve, a beadle, a miller and a smith; between them they have 18 ploughs. 12 male and 5 female slaves. A rider holds ½ hide, 2 parts of ½ hide and 1 croft; he has 1 plough.
A mill at 2s; in Droitwich 4 salt-houses; the woodland of this manor has been put outside into the King's woodland, and ½ hide of land which Earl William gave to Jocelyn Hunter.
Earl William gave to St. Mary's Church this manor's tithe and church with a priest, and 2 virgates of land with 1 villager.
Walter of Lacy gave 1 hide out of the lordship land to one Hubert; he has ½ plough.

E3 41 The King holds HOLLOW (Court). Siward, a thane and kinsman of King Edward, held it. 3 hides. In lordship 3 ploughs;
4 villagers, 1 smallholder, a reeve and a beadle with 3 ploughs. 6 slaves, male and female. A 2
A park for wild animals, but it has been put outside the manor, with all the woodland; in Droitwich 4 salt-houses and 1 *hoch*; in Worcester 1 house which pays 2 plough-shares; another 2 houses which belong to Feckenham: they paid nothing and have been put outside (the manor).

These two manors pay to Hereford £18 of pence at 20 to the *ora*.

E4 In WORCESTERSHIRE 180 d

44 The King holds BUSHLEY. Brictric held it; he bought it from Leofing Bishop of Worcester for 3 gold marks; also a house in the City of Worcester which pays a silver mark a year; also a woodland 1 league long and as wide. He bought the whole of this and held it exempt, so that he did not serve any man for it. In this manor 1 hide. In lordship 2 ploughs;

4 villagers, 8 smallholders, a reeve and a beadle; between them they have 4 ploughs. 8 slaves, male and female; a cowman and a dairymaid. A forester holds ½ virgate of land.

In PULL (Court) there are 3 virgates of land which lay in (the lands of) Longdon, a manor of Earl Oda's. Earl William put this land in Bushley. 1 plough there. A man of the monks of Lyre holds 1 virgate of land.

Earl William put 2 foresters, one from Hanley (Castle), the other from Bushley, outside his manors to guard the woodlands.

E5 45 The King holds QUEENHILL. Aethelric, brother of Bishop Brictric, held it. 1 hide. In lordship 1 plough;

7 villagers and 3 smallholders with 4½ ploughs. 1 pigman, 2 ploughmen and a dairymaid.

The woodland has been put outside the manor.

Earl William gave to St. Mary's of Lyre this manor's tithe, with 1 villager who holds ½ virgate of land.

Herman holds 1 villager of this manor who has ½ virgate of land.

E6 46 The King holds ELDERSFIELD. Reinbald the Chancellor held it before 1066. Earl William exchanged it with him. 5 hides. In lordship 3 ploughs;

12 villagers and 13 smallholders with 11 ploughs. 5 slaves, male and female; 6 ploughmen.

A mill at 2s; woodland 2 leagues long and as wide: it has been put outside the manor.

Ansgot, Earl William's man, holds ½ virgate of land, Wulfgeat 1 hide of free land.

St. Mary's has 1 villager there who holds 1 virgate of land....

E7 47 The King holds SUCKLEY. Earl Edwin held it. 5 hides. In lordship 2 ploughs;

22 villagers and 24 smallholders with 27 ploughs. Another 10 impoverished smallholders.

A mill at 6s; a keeper of 12 beehives; the woodland has 5 leagues in both length and width; a fishery there.

In Worcester 1 burgess, but he pays nothing. A mill at 6s.

St. Mary's holds the tithe of this village, with 1 villager and ½ virgate of land.

Earl Roger gave ½ virgate of land in absolute freedom to one Richard.

These six manors pay to Hereford £50 in revenue and 25s in gifts.

In the Shropshire folios

4 LAND OF EARL ROGER 253 b

[In ALNOTHSTREE Hundred]

E8 1,5 The Earl holds MORVILLE himself with 18 outliers. King Edward held it. 12 hides. One of these outliers, CHAWSON, at 1 hide, is in Worcestershire...

ENTRIES REFERRING TO WORCESTER AND DROITWICH

WORCESTER
In the Herefordshire folios

2 LAND OF THE CHURCH OF HEREFORD 181 c

E9 32 In CODDINGTON ...
3 dwellings in Worcester belong to this manor; they pay 30d... 182 b

DROITWICH
In the Buckinghamshire folios

1 LAND OF THE KING 143 b

E10 3 M. (Princes) RISBOROUGH ... 143 c
In this manor there lie and lay (the dues of) a burgess of Oxford who pays 2s; further a salt worker of Droitwich pays ... packloads of salt...

In the Gloucestershire folios

1 LAND OF THE KING 162 d

E11 24 TEWKESBURY... 163 b
a salt-house at Droitwich which belongs to this manor...
a salt-house at Droitwich... 163 c

E12 27 STANWAY...
A salt-house at Droitwich...

E13 47 THORNBURY... 163 d
at Droitwich 40 sesters of salt or 20d...

E14 48 (Old) SODBURY...
1 virgate in Droitwich belongs to this manor; it paid 25 sesters of salt. Urso the Sheriff has so oppressed the men that now they cannot pay the salt.

18 LAND OF THE CHURCH OF EYNSHAM 166 b

E15 1 MICKLETON...
24 measures of salt from Droitwich...

50 LAND OF OSBERN GIFFARD 168 c

E16 1 ROCKHAMPTON...
a salt-house at Droitwich at 4 packloads of salt...

In the Herefordshire folios

1 LAND OF THE KING 179 c

E17 4 MARDEN...
from the salt-houses in Droitwich, 9 packloads of salt or 9d...

E18 7 (Much) MARCLE... 179 d
A woodland which pays 5s which are given to Droitwich for 60 measures of salt...

E19 8 CLEEVE... 180 a
25 measures of salt from Droitwich belonged there also then (before 1066)...

E20 10a LEOMINSTER...
woodland 6 leagues long and 3 leagues wide which pays 22s. From these, 5s are given in Droitwich for buying timber, and 30 measures of salt are had from there.

2 LAND OF THE CHURCH OF HEREFORD 181 c

E21 18 ULLINGSWICK... 181 d
part of a salt-house in Droitwich ...

E22 20 MORETON (Jeffries)...
1 salt-house in Droitwich...

E23 26 LEDBURY... 182 a
Part of a salt-house in Droitwich...

E24 27 EASTNOR...
part of a salt-house in Droitwich...

E25 28 'BAGBURROW'...
part of a salt-house in Droitwich...

E26 34 TUPSLEY... 182 b
a salt-house at Droitwich which pays 16 measures of salt...

29 LAND OF HUGH DONKEY 187 a

E27 11 WELLINGTON... 187 b
At Droitwich he has 17 measures of salt at 30d...

In the Oxfordshire folios

1 LAND OF THE KING 154 c

E28 6 BAMPTON...
from pig-pasturage, from the salt-houses of Droitwich, and from the men's other customary dues, £9 13s...

58 LAND OF RICHARD AND OTHERS OF THE KING'S OFFICERS 160 c

E29 4 (Great) ROLLRIGHT...
3 packloads of salt at Droitwich...

In the Shropshire folios

4 LAND OF EARL ROGER 253 b

E30 1,24 DONNINGTON... 253 d
in Droitwich 5 salt-houses which pay 20s...

E31 1,25 DITTON (Priors)...
In Droitwich 1 salt-house which pays 2s. ...

E32 11,4 CAYNHAM ... 256 d
4 packloads of salt from Droitwich ...

In the Warwickshire folios

28 LAND OF WILLIAM SON OF CORBUCION 243 a

E33 14 BINTON... 243 b
from Droitwich 3 packloads of salt...

35 LAND OF URSO OF ABETOT 243 d

E34 1 HILLBOROUGH...
a salt-house in Droitwich which pays 3s...

OUTLIERS OF THE GLOUCESTERSHIRE MANOR OF WESTBURY ON SEVERN

1 LAND OF THE KING 163 a

E35 11 In WESTBURY (on Severn) 30 hides...
Later 6 hides were taken from this manor in KYRE, and in CLIFTON (on Teme) 10 hides; in NEWENT and KINGSTONE 8 hides; in EDVIN (Loach) 1 hide. The Abbot of Cormeilles, Osbern and Williams sons of Richard, now hold these lands; however the Sheriff finds the whole revenue from the remainder. The men of the County state, however, that the fir-wood lay in Westbury in King Edward's revenue.

HOLDINGS OUTSIDE WORCESTERSHIRE IN 1086, LATER TRANSFERRED TO THE COUNTY

Noted here to complete the description of the modern county.
See Notes to this county, and county volume referred to for full text.

In Gloucestershire in 1086

EG 1 [1] **LAND OF THE KING** 162 d

34 Also in the manor of TEWKESBURY there belonged 4 hides not in lordship; they are in HANLEY (Castle). Before 1066 2 ploughs in lordship; 163 c

40 villagers and smallholders; 8 slaves, male and female.
A mill at 16d; woodland in which there is a hedged enclosure.
This land was Earl William's; now it is in the King's revenue in Hereford.
Value before 1066 £15; now £10.

EG 2	col. 163 d	1,40	ASHTON (under Hill)
EG 3	163 d	1,41	KEMERTON
EG 4	164 a, b	1,59	BECKFORD
EG 5	164 b	1,60	ASHTON (under Hill)
EG 6	165 c	10,7	HINTON (on the Green)
EG 7	165 d	11,10	(Cow) HONEYBOURNE
EG 8	166 a	12,6	WICKHAMFORD
EG 9	166 b	19,2	part of DEERHURST manor and Hundred.. KEMERTON
EG 10	166 b	20,1	KEMERTON
EG 11	167 b	34,1	PEBWORTH
EG 12	167 b	34,2	ULLLINGTON
EG 13	168 b	47,1	CHILDSWICKHAM
EG 14	169 b	62,1	PEBWORTH
EG 15	169 b	62,2·	(Broad) MARSTON
EG 16	169 c	66,4	ASTON (Somerville)
EG 17	170 c	78,7	BICKMARSH

In the Herefordshire folios in 1086

EH 1 [1] **LAND OF THE KING** 179 c

In GLOUCESTERSHIRE

42 The King holds HANLEY (Castle). Brictric held it. 4 hides. 180 d
In lordship 2 ploughs;
20 villagers, 17 smallholders and a reeve; between them they have 17½ ploughs. 9 slaves, male and female;
6 pigmen pay 60 pigs; they have 4 ploughs.
A mill at 2s; woodland 5 leagues in both length and width: it has been put outside the manor. A hawk's eyrie there.
A forester holds ½ virgate of land.
A villager of 'Baldenhall' pays 2 *ora* of pence to this manor.
[Value]

EH 2	col. 186 c	22,5	ROCHFORD
EH 3	186 c	23,1	ROCHFORD
EH 4	187 c	31,6	STOKE (Bliss)

In Staffordshire in 1086

ESt 1	247 d	7,2	(Upper) ARLEY

In Warwickshire in 1086

EW 1	244 a	37,6	IPSLEY
EW 2	244 b	43,2	BICKMARSH

Notes on the Text and Translation

Appendix I: The Hundreds, the County and the County Boundary

Appendix II: Tabulation of the details for the Borough of Worcester

Appendix III: Tabulation of the details for Droitwich including Witton and Salwarpe

Appendix IV: Worcestershire Domesday Material in Two Evesham Cartularies

Appendix V: Hemming's Cartulary of Worcester Church

Index of Persons

Index of Places

Maps and Map Keys

Systems of Reference

Technical Terms

NOTES ON THE TEXT AND TRANSLATION

BIBLIOGRAPHY and ABBREVIATIONS used in the Notes

AJ ... Antiquaries Journal.

Anderson ... O. S. Anderson *The English Hundred Names,* Lund 1934 (Lunds Universitets Årsskrift N.F. Avd. 1 Bd. 30 Nr. i).

Ann. Mon. ... *Annales Monastici*, Rolls Series No. 36, 6 vols., London 1864–69.

ASC ... *The Anglo-Saxon Chronicle* (translated G. N. Garmonsway), London 1960.

Atkins ... Sir Ivor Atkins *The Church of Worcester from the Eighth to the Twelfth Century*, part i, AJ xvii (1937) pp. 371-391; part ii, AJ xx (1940) pp. 1-38, 203-229.

Ballard ... Adolfus Ballard *The Domesday Boroughs*, Oxford 1904.

BCS ... W. de Gray Birch (ed.) *Cartularium Saxonicum*, 4 vols. with index, London 1885-1899, reprinted 1964.

Bigelow ... M. M. Bigelow *Placita Anglo-normannica: Law Cases from William I to Richard I preserved in Historical Records*, London 1879 (reprinted New York 1970).

Bosworth and Toller ... J. Bosworth and T. N. Toller *An Anglo-Saxon Dictionary*, 2 vols., Oxford.

Bridbury ... A. R. Bridbury *England and the Salt Trade in the Later Middle Ages*, Oxford 1955.

Brownrigg ... W. Brownrigg *The Art of Making Common Salt*, London 1748.

Cal Cl ... *Calendar of Close Rolls* (HMSO State Papers).

Cal Inq PM ... *Calendar of Inquisitions Post Mortem* (HMSO State Papers).

Chronicon ... W. D. Macray (ed.) *Chronicon Abbatiae de Evesham ad annum 1418*, Rolls Series No. 29, London 1863.

Clarke ... H. B. Clarke *The Early Surveys of Evesham Abbey: An Investigation into the Problem of Continuity in Anglo-Norman England*, Thesis (Ph.D.) Birmingham University, 1977.

Darlington AAE ... R. R. Darlington *Aethelwig, Abbot of Evesham* in EHR xlviii (1933) pp. 1-22; 177-198.

Darlington CWCP ... R. R. Darlington (ed.) *The Cartulary of Worcester Cathedral Priory (Register 1)*, Pipe Roll Society lxxvi (new series xxxviii), London 1968.

DB ... Domesday Book.

DB 1-4 ... Domesday Book, associated texts, introduction and indices published by the Record Commission, London 1783-1816.

DBH ... V. H. Galbraith and J. Tait (eds.) *Herefordshire Domesday*, Pipe Roll Society lxiii (new series xxv), London 1950.

DEPN ... E. Ekwall *The Concise Oxford Dictionary of English Placenames* 4th edition, Oxford 1960.

DG ... H. C. Darby and G. R. Versey *Domesday Gazetteer*, Cambridge 1975.

DGM ... H. C. Darby and I. B. Terrett *The Domesday Geography of Midland England*, 2nd edition, Cambridge 1971.

Douglas ... D. C. Douglas *William the Conqueror*, London 1964.

Ducange ... G. A. L. Henschel (ed.) *Glossarium Mediae et Infimae Latinitatis,* Niort and London 1884-7.

DS ... P. E. Dove (ed.) *Domesday Commemoration: Domesday Studies*, 2 vols., London 1888-1891.

EcHR ... Economic History Review.

ECWM ... H. P. R. Finberg (ed.) *The Early Charters of the West Midlands*, Leicester 1961.

EENS ... *Early English and Norse Studies presented to Hugh Smith*, ed. P. G. Foote and A. Brown, Methuen 1963.

EHR ... English Historical Review.

Ellis ... Sir H. Ellis *A General Introduction to Domesday Book*, 2 vols. 1833 (reprint 1971).

EPNS ... English Place-Name Society. References are to vol. iv *Worcestershire* (ed. A. Mawer, F. M. Stenton and F. T. S. Houghton, Cambridge 1927) unless otherwise stated.

ERN ... E. Ekwall *English River Names*, Oxford 1928.

Evesham A-Q ... See Appendix IV.

Exon ... *Liber Exoniensis* in DB4 (DB3 in certain bindings); see above.

FA ... *Inquisitions and Assessments relating to Feudal Aids with other analogous Documents preserved in the Public Records Office, AD 1284-1431*, HMSO 1899-1920, 6 vols.

Fees ... *Book of Fees (Testa de Nevill)*, 3 vols., HMSO 1920-31.

Finberg GS ... H. P. R. Finberg (ed.) *Gloucestershire Studies*, Leicester 1957.

Freeman ... E. A. Freeman *The History of the Norman Conquest of England*, 6 vols., Oxford 1867-79

Galbraith DB ... V. H. Galbraith *Domesday Book: its Place in Administrative History*, Oxford 1974.

Galbraith MDB ... V. H. Galbraith *The Making of Domesday Book*, Oxford 1961.

Gillan ... E. Gillan *The Borough of Droitwich and its Salt Industry 1215-1700* Thesis (M.A.) Birmingham University 1956.

GR ... Grid Reference.

Guéry ... C. Guéry *Histoire de L'Abbaye de Lyre*, Evreux 1917.

Habington ... Thomas Habington (ed. J. Amphlett) *A Survey of Worcestershire*, 2 vols., Worcestershire Historical Society 1898.

Harmer ... F. E. Harmer *Anglo-Saxon Writs*, Manchester 1952.

Harvey (1) ... S. Harvey *Royal Revenue and Domesday Terminology* in EcHR (2nd series) xx (1967) pp. 221-228.

Harvey (2) ... *Domesday Book and its Predecessors* in EHR lxxxvi (1971) pp. 753-773.

Hearne ... See Hemming.

Hemming ... Thomas Hearne (ed.) *Hemingi Chartularium Ecclesiae Wigorniensis*, 2 vols., Oxford 1723.

History of Abingdon ... J. Stevenson (ed.) *Chronicon Monasterii de Abingdon*, 2 vols., Rolls Series No. 2, London 1858.

ICC ... N. E. S. A. Hamilton (ed.) *Inquisitio Comitatus Cantabrigiensis*, London 1876.

John ... E. John *Land Tenure in England*, Leicester 1960.

KCD ... J. M. Kemble *Codex Diplomaticus Aevi Saxonici*, 6 vols., London 1839-48.

Ker ... N. R. Ker *Hemming's Cartulary: A Description of Two Worcester Cartularies in Cotton Tiberius A xiii*, in R. W. Hunt, W. A. Pantin and R. W. Southern (eds.) *Studies in Medieval History presented to Frederick Maurice Powicke*, pp. 49-75, Oxford 1948.

Kinvig ... R. Kinvig *The Birmingham District in Domesday Times*, British Association 1950.

KPN ... J. K. Wallenberg *Kentish Place-Names*, Uppsala 1931.

Leland ... John Leland (ed. L. Toulmin Smith) *Itinerary*, 5 vols., London 1906-10.

Little Domesday ... Essex, Norfolk and Suffolk in DB 2 (see above).

Maddocks ... P. G. Maddocks *The Salt Industry of Worcestershire*, Dissertation (B.A.) Birmingham University School of Geography, 1950.

Maitland DBB ... F. W. Maitland *Domesday Book and Beyond*, Cambridge 1897.

MCGB ... G. R. C. Davis *Medieval Cartularies of Great Britain*, London 1958.

ML ... Medieval Latin.

Mod. Fr. ... Modern French.

Mon. Ang. ... W. Dugdale *Monasticon Anglicanum*, 6 vols. in 8, London 1817-30, repr. 1846.

MS ... Manuscript.

Nash ... T. R. Nash *Collections for the History of Worcestershire*, 2 vols., London 1781-99.

ODan ... Old Danish.

OE ... Old English.

OEB ... G. Tengvik *Old English Bynames*, Uppsala 1938 (Nomina Germanica 4).

OED ... Oxford English Dictionary.

OFr ... Old French.

OG ... Old German.

OLD ... P. G. W. Glare (ed.) *Oxford Latin Dictionary*, Oxford 1968 on.

ON ... Old Norse.

Orderic Vitalis ... A. Le Prévost (ed.) *Historia Ecclesiastica*, 5 vols., Paris 1838-1855.

OS ... Ordnance Survey. 1st Edition Maps (early 19th century) were reprinted Newton Abbot 1969 on.

OScand ... Old Scandinavian.

Parkinson ... C. Parkinson *The Droitwich Brine-Springs and Saliferous Marls*, Geological Society Quarterly Journal, ii (1884).

Place-Name Elements ... A. H. Smith *English Place-Name Elements* parts I and II (EPNS vols. 25-26), Cambridge 1956.

PNDB ... O. von Feilitzen *Pre-Conquest Personal Names of Domesday Book*, Uppsala 1937 (Nomina Germanica 3).

PNK ... J. K. Wallenberg *The Place-Names of Kent*, Uppsala 1934.

Rastell ... Dr. Thomas Rastell *An Account of the Saltworks of Droitwich*, Philosophical Transactions xii (1678).

RBE ... H. Hall (ed.) *The Red Book of the Exchequer*, Rolls Series No. 99, 3 vols., London 1896.

RBW ... M. Hollings (ed.) *The Red Book of Worcester*, Worcs. Historical Society, 4 vols., 1934-50.

Reaney ... P. H. Reaney *Dictionary of British Surnames*, 2nd edition, London 1976.

Redin ... M. Redin *Studies on Uncompounded Personal Names in Old English*, Uppsala 1919.

Regesta ... H. W. C. Davis, C. Johnson and H. A. Cronne (eds.) *Regesta Regum Anglo-Normannorum* vol. i, Oxford 1913; vol. ii, Oxford 1956.

Register ... W. H. Hale (ed.) *Registrum sive Liber irrotularius et consuetudinarius Prioratus Beatae Mariae Wigorniensis*, Camden Society, London 1865.

RH ... *Rotuli Hundredorum*, Record Commission 1812-18, 2 vols.

RMLWL ... R. E. Latham *Revised Medieval Latin Wordlist*, London 1965.

Robertson ... A. J. Robertson *Anglo-Saxon Charters*, Cambridge 1939, 2nd edition, 1956.

Round CDF ... J. H. Round *Calendar of Documents preserved in France, vol. i 918-1206*, London 1899 (HMSO State Papers).

Round DS ... J. H. Round *An Early Reference to Domesday*, DS ii pp. 539-559.
Round FE ... J. H. Round *Feudal England*, London 1909.
Round VCH ... J. H. Round *Worcester, The Domesday Survey* in VCH (Worcs.) i pp. 235-340.
Sawyer (1) ... P. H. Sawyer *Evesham A, a Domesday Text*, Worcs. Historical Society, Miscellany I (1960) pp. 3-36.
Sawyer (2) ... P. H. Sawyer *Anglo-Saxon Charters: An Annotated List and Bibliography*, London 1968.
Sawyer (3) ... P. H. Sawyer *The 'Original Returns' and Domesday Book*, in EHR lxx (1955) pp. 177-197.
Taylor DSG ... C. S. Taylor *An Analysis of the Domesday Survey of Gloucestershire*, Bristol and Gloucester Archaeological Society, Bristol 1889.
Taylor GS ... C. S. Taylor *The Origin of the Mercian Shires* in Finberg GS pp. 17-51.
TE ... *Taxatio Ecclesiastica of Pope Nicholas IV*, London, Record Commission 1802.
VCH ... The Victoria History of the Counties of England. DB is translated with introduction by J. H. Round in Worcs. volume i (1901) pp. 235-340. References are to Worcestershire volumes unless otherwise stated.
VE ... J. Caley (ed.) *Valor Ecclesiasticus* Record Commission No. 9, London 1810-1834, 6 vols.
Vinogradoff ... P. Vinogradoff *English Society in the Eleventh Century*, Oxford 1908.
Worcester A-H ... Discussed in Appendix V.
Woulfe ... P. Woulfe *Irish Names and Surnames*, Dublin 1923.

The Editors are very grateful to Mr. G. C. Baugh, editor of the Victoria County History for Shropshire for help with *Caluestone* (E 8); to Mr. G. Bishop of the Ordnance Survey Cartography Division; to Dr. H. B. Clarke of University College, Dublin, for making material available for Appendix IV; to Mr. J. D. Foy for checking the translation and indices and for helpful suggestions; to Miss M. Henderson, senior assistant Archivist of the Worcester Record Office, for help with *Broc* (16,3); to Dr. D. R. Howlett, editor of the Dictionary of Medieval Latin from British Sources, for allowing consultation of the unpublished material relating to *hoccus* (1,3a); to Miss Dorothy McCull Librarian of the Local Studies Department of the City of Birmingham Public Libraries; to Dr. Alex Rumble for checking the translation of the Evesham and Worcester material (Apps. IV, V); to Mrs. B. Hopkinson for discussion about salt-extraction.

The Manuscript is written on leaves, or folios, of parchment (sheepskin), measuring about 15 by 11 i (38 by 28 cm.), on both sides. On each side, or page, are two columns, making four to each folio. Th folios were numbered in the 17th century and the four columns of each are here lettered a, b, c, d. T Manuscript emphasises words and usually distinguishes chapters and sections by the use of red ink. Underlining in the MS indicates deletion.

Like the other Midland shires, Worcester appears to have been the artificial creation of a unit of 120 hides, clustered around the county town, and coming into being in the first half of the eleventh century. It arose out of the Mercian province of the *Hwicce* which covered the area later occupied by Worcester, Gloucester and west Warwickshire. On its eastern and southern flanks, the County had in 1086 a number of outlying portions, within the Counties of Warwickshire and Gloucestershire and this interlacing of Counties continued until the major boundary changes of the nineteenth century which greatly altered the shape of the County on all sides (see App. I).

Even so, the Worcestershire folios do not reproduce the whole of the 1086 County. Hanley Castl well within the boundaries of Worcs., was counted as a part of Gloucestershire, and a number of othe Worcs. places, Feckenham, Hollow Court, Martley and Suckley, are briefly mentioned at the end of Worcs. as paying tax in Herefords. and duly appear in the folios of that County, along with several more (E 1-7).

Within the County in 1086 there were 12 Hundreds, five of them geographically compact; the other seven, scattered and much interwoven, belonged to Churches (see App. I).

The Hundred rubrication of the County is full and enables a much clearer idea of the 1086 arrang ment to be formed than is the case in many other Counties. This rubrication helps greatly with the identification of places; for although the County contains a number of places with the same basic name, such as Lench, Hampton and Churchill, it is usually possible to distinguish between them. A number of adjacent modern villagers, however, with the same basic name are now distinguished by affixes such as East and West, Walsh and Beauchamp. Many such villages are later creations, and othe if they existed in 1086, are rarely evidenced (Hill Croome and Ab Lench being exceptions). They are not here distinguished in text and index, and in such cases the Grid Reference refers to the larger village. Where these modern separate villages can be traced from individual DB holdings, this is recorded in the notes below.

In many Counties, the opening pages contain an account of the chief Boroughs. In Worcs. however, the details of Worcester and of Droitwich, centre of the salt industry, are scattered in the text: they are brought together in Apps. II-III.

Worcestershire Domesday is notable for the traces it records of the long-standing rivalry between Worcester Church and Evesham Abbey, especially fierce in regard to Hampton and Bengeworth (10, 11-12 note and Worcs. H in App. V). The County is also filled with the spoliations of the sheriff, Urso of Abetot, and of his brother Robert the Bursar, as well as of Odo, Bishop of Bayeux (see Ch. 26 note and Freeman V pp. 759-766). But these recent despoilers, especially of Church land, had followed others: Danes, Frenchmen, Richard Scrope and William Earl of Hereford.

The County is unusually rich in contemporary documentation. For the Abbey of Evesham, a series of surveys, antecedent to DB, or derived from it or illuminating it, has recently been edited by Dr. H. B. Clarke and is discussed in App. IV. Of them, Evesham A is a Domesday 'satellite', a document abbreviated from a stage of the Domesday enquiry earlier than DB itself. It is translated in full in App. IV and the corresponding section references, prefixed A, are given in the right-hand margin of the DB translation. The Abbey's domestic *Chronicon* published in 1863, the earlier part compiled by Thomas of Marlborough, Abbot 1229-36, also contains much to illustrate the DB text.

For the Church of Worcester, Hemming's Cartulary, the only printed edition published in 1723 and now very scarce, is a rich store. Besides containing an abstract of DB and a valuable later survey, it comprises documents related to the great dispute with Evesham Abbey about Bengeworth and Hampton, and a list by Hemming himself of lands alienated from the Church. Hemming also includes the Church's version of the privileges of Oswaldslow Hundred (DB 2,1) and as an addition to it the names of the Domesday Commissioners for the Shire: Bishop Remigius of Lincoln, Earl Walter Giffard, Henry of Ferrers and Adam, brother of Eudo the King's steward. The Register of Worcester priory, published in 1865 by the Camden Society, is also relevant to DB.

The Worcestershire Domesday was translated with valuable introduction and notes by J. H. Round in 1901 for the Victoria County History; he included selected translations of some early Worcester and Evesham documents. Succeeding volumes of VCH deal with the later history of the DB manors. The place-names are studied in an early volume of EPNS (1927) and the geography of the 1086 County by F. J. Monkhouse in DGM pp. 217-272.

References to other DB Counties are to the chapter and sections of volumes in the present series. Notes follow the correct order of the text, ignoring displacements; thus 12,2 follows 12,1 rather than 15,3.

WORCESTERSHIRE. *WIRECESTRESCIRE* written in red across both columns on folio 172 ab and abbreviated *Wirecscire* above columns 172 cd onwards. There is no heading on folio 178 a-d, most of which is blank.

C 1 THE CITY OF WORCESTER. Details of burgesses and buildings are tabulated in App. II.
THE COINAGE WAS CHANGED. Similar entries are found elsewhere, e.g. DB Sussex 12,1; Dorset B 1-4 (col. 75 a).
20s. DB uses the old English currency system which lasted for a thousand years until 1971. The pound contained 20 shillings, each of 12 pence, abbreviated £(ibrae), s(olidi) and d(enarii). DB often expresses sums above a shilling in pence (e.g. 40d in 2,4 instead of 3s 4d), and above a pound in shillings (e.g. 100s for £5 in C 2).
AT LONDON. Or 'to London', if they did not collect them. DB Herefords. C 9 (col. 179 a) implies a journey to London to fetch the dies.
15 HIDES. Counted as part of Fishborough Hundred (10,2 note). The hide is a unit of land measurement, either of productivity or of extent or of tax liability and contained 4 virgates. Administrations attempted to standardise the hide at 120 acres, but incomplete revision and special local reductions left hides of widely differing extents in different areas; see Dr. John Morris in DB Sussex Appendix.
EARL EDWIN. Earl of Mercia *c.* 1063-70; son of Algar who was also Earl of Mercia.

C 2 THE SHERIFF. Urso of Abetot, see Ch. 26 note.
THE KING'S LORDSHIP MANORS. Bromsgrove, Kidderminster and Droitwich, 1,1-3.
BY WEIGHT. In contrast to *ad numerum* 'at face value'; a simple means of avoiding financial

losses caused by clipping or alloying of coins.
AT 20 (PENCE) TO THE *ORA*. An *ora* was literally an ounce; a unit of currency still in use in Scandinavia. It was reckoned at either 16d or 20d. The 16d rate was the normal rate. The 20d rate was primarily a unit of account, found on estates in the King's hands, and was payment 'at face value'. For every 16d due in revenue, 20d was collected, the result being equivalent to a payment in 'blanched' or assayed money (see DB Glos. 1,58 *reddunt xl libras alborum nummorum de xx in ora*, 'they pay £40 of blanched money at 20 (pence) to the *ora*'). Assaying, testing by fire and 'blanching' were processes of melting a sample of coin to test for alloy or baser metal. See S. Harvey (1) and *Dialogus de Scaccario* (ed. C. Johnson 1950) p. 125.
A NORWEGIAN HAWK...A PACKHORSE. Similar payments are made to the King and Queen in DB Northants. B 36 col. 219 a, Warwicks. B 4 col. 238 a and Wilts. B 2 col. 64 c. Only here is the source of the revenue (the County and Hundred Courts) stated. The Norwegian hawk was probably a Gyr Falcon (or Gerfalcon), *falco rusticolus*, much prized by nobles and Kings in the middle ages; three varieties of falcon are recognised, the Iceland, the Greenland and the Norwegian.
£16 AT FACE VALUE. The sum is made up from
£10 of pence at 20 to the *ora*
100s at face value
20s at 20 (pence) to the *ora*.
PLEAS OF THE COUNTY AND FROM THE HUNDREDS. Revenue from the County and Hundred Courts.

C 3 12 HUNDREDS. That is, 7 ecclesiastical Hundreds (Oswaldslow a triple Hundred, 'Westminster' a double Hundred, 'Pershore' Hundred and Fishborough), with five other Hundreds (Came, Clent, Cresslau, Doddingtree and Esch). See App. I.
EXEMPT. *Quieti*, commonly in DB meaning 'immune from dues or service' (see E 4 below), 'free from tax'; or 'quit', 'settled', 'discharged'. See RMLWL s.v. *quietantia*, and 2,74 note. The exempt Hundreds are those of the Churches.

C 4 HIGHWAY ROBBERY. *Forestellum*, 'waylaying' or 'ambushing'.
HOUSE-BREAKING. *Heinfaram*, 'breaking into a house' or 'breach of the peace within a house'.
CORPORAL PUNISHMENT. Ordeal or mutilation, see Ellis i p. 281. But in DB Sussex 12,1 (Lewes) only a fine is involved.
EXCEPTION...WESTMINSTER...KING EDWARD. See Ch. 8 note and 8,1: 'King Edward held this manor and gave it to this church as exempt and freed from every claim . . .'
AS THE COUNTY STATES. The County Court.

C 5 FULL JURISDICTION. See Technical Terms and Maitland DBB pp. 80-107.
CAN GO WITH HIS LAND WHERE HE WOULD. He is free to choose any lord as his patron and protector of his lands. Many other lands were 'tied' to a particular manor or lord, as is seen in 1,1c. 2,1 etc.

L NOTES CONCERNING major landholders are to be found at the head of their individual chapters.

L 13 THE CLERGY OF WOLVERHAMPTON. *Clerici* here, *presbiteri* 'priests' in the chapter, which is numbered but has no heading.

L 22 HAROLD SON OF RALPH. 'Harold son of Earl Ralph' at the head of the chapter.

L 28 ALDEVA. The chapter is numbered on folio 178 a, but has no heading. See 28,1 note.

Ch. 1 THE MS, followed by Farley, does not give a number to Ch. 1, as happens in several DB Counties.

1,1a [IN CAME HUNDRED]. The Hundred heads are missed from the Land of the King; here supplied from Evesham A 162.
BROMSGROVE. The corresponding entries in Evesham A 162-167 are arranged differently. Grafton appears in A 163 as 5 hides. Woodcote Green is *Odenecote Roberti*, 3 hides in A 164. Cooksey (A 165), 2½ hides formerly held by Ernheit, now by William and Herbrand from Urso, is similar to 26,12, also held by the same men from Urso, but details of value, hidage and TRE holder differ: there were probably two estates there in 1086 (1,1c note). Details of the 2 hides 3 virgates of 'Willingwick' (1,1c) are given by Evesham A 166. The entry includes pigs and sheep, which feature in the Exon. and Little Domesdays, but were eliminated from the Exchequer version. Chadwick is given in A 167; Northwick in A 168. Discussion in Sawyer (1) pp. 20-21.
18 OUTLIERS. A number have been lost in the expansion of Birmingham. For 'LINDSWORTH', see EPNS p. 355, the name surviving in Lindsworth Road and Approach in the eastern part of Kings Norton parish. For WYTHALL, DB *Warthuil*, and WYTHWOOD see EPNS p. 358. For HOUNDSFIELD, see RH ii p. 283. 'TESSALL' survives now as Tessall Lane in Kings Norton; a Tessall Garage stands on the site of the former Tessall Farm. For REDNAL, see EPNS p. 356. LEA (Green) in Kings Norton, together with Houndsfield and Wythwood (parts of the ecclesiastical parish of Wythall), is still in Worcs., the rest of the parish of Kings Norton being

transferred to Birmingham in 1911 (see App. I). DG maps it in Warwicks., north east of Kings Norton. See DB Warwicks. EB W1 note and EPNS (Worcs.) pp. 334-354. For 'COMBLE', see EPNS p. 340; for 'TYNSALL', see EPNS p. 363 and VCH iii p. 24. The site can be traced approximately from the fact that it was lordship land of Bordesley Abbey in the manor of Hewell, VE iii p. 271. For 'SHURVENHILL', see EPNS p. 343.

A BEADLE. An under-bailiff, subordinate to a reeve, unpopular, with minor police functions; see Ellis i p. 247.

13 SALT-HOUSES. See 1,3a note.

300 MEASURES OF SALT. *Mittas salis*; a *mitta* was commonly reckoned as 8 bushels. See VCH i p. 270; VCH ii p. 257; Habington ii p. 297.

6 LEAD VATS. For boiling the brine, see 1,3a note.

,1b SUCKLEY. The abstraction is mentioned in X 3 where it is said to be in Doddingtree Hundred; see E 7.

EARL WILLIAM. William son of Osbern (William Fitz Osbern), brother of Bishop Osbern of Exeter. He was palatine earl of Hereford from 1067 to his death in battle in 1071. He was most probably also palatine earl of Gloucestershire and perhaps wielded extra powers in Worcestershire; see W. E. Wightman *The Palatine Earldom of William Fitz Osbern in Gloucestershire and Worcestershire (1066-1071)* in EHR vol. lxxvii (1962). William was joint 'regent' with Bishop Odo of Bayeux during King William's absence in 1067. He was also responsible, with Walter of Lacy and others, for defending the border of Herefords. and Glos. against the South Welsh. See DB Herefords. Introductory Note 2.

IN TOTAL. Referring to the whole manor of Bromsgrove.

URSO THE SHERIFF. Urso of Abetot, see Ch. 26 note.

BY WEIGHT. *Ad peis*, OFr. *peis*, Mod. Fr *poids*, derived from and corresponding to the Latin *ad pensum*; the Mod. Fr form is a mistaken humanist spelling as if from Latin *pondus*.

SO LONG AS HE HAD THE WOODLAND. For supplying the salt-houses at Droitwich with fuel.

,1c GRAFTON. DB *Grastone*, see EPNS p. 347.

COOKSEY (GREEN). Cooksey Parva coupled with Grafton in FA v p. 303, Cooksey Magna being the holding at 26,12. Evesham A 165 places this outlier in Came Hundred, with Bromsgrove, the rest (26,12) being in Clent. This corresponds to the later division, with one part in Bromsgrove and one in Upton Warren; VCH iii p. 24.

'WILLINGWICK'. Its approximate location can be known because it is associated with Chadwick here and in later records; see Fees p. 961, FA v p. 303, EPNS p. 345.

THEY COULD NOT WITHDRAW...MANOR. See C 5 note above.

1 RIDING-MAN. *Radchenistre* similar to *radman* (the latter translated here as 'rider' to maintain the Latin distinction). Of higher standing than a villager; originally a man who rode with messages or on escort duty, for the King or his lord (see 2,29); he also worked his lands and those of his lord, see 8,10a and DB Glos. 1,24. The term *radman* is common in north-west Mercia, up to the river Ribble. In the south-western Welsh marches and in Hampshire, *radchenist(re)* predominates. On two occasions in DB Glos. (1,15 and 19,2) *radchenistre* are glossed as *liberi homines*, although they were not apparently allowed to leave the manor (see DB Glos. 3,1 and Herefords. 1,4). In 8,9b *liberi homines* and in 8,10a *radmans* perform similar services. Discussion in VCH i pp. 250-1; Maitland DBB pp. 57, 66, 305-8; Vinogradoff pp. 69-71.

6 PLOUGHMEN. *Bovarii*, literally men who look after the oxen of which there were normally 8 to the plough. See DB Wilts. 28,10 note; VCH i p. 274; VCH (Shrops.) i pp. 302-4.

WOULD BE POSSIBLE. *Posset esse*; subjunctive, perhaps a different nuance from *potest esse* (translated 'possible', see 1,2). The two forms are about equally represented in Worcs.; see also 1,5 note below.

3 LEAGUES. DB *Leuga, leuua, leuuede*. A measure of length, usually of woodland, traditionally reckoned at a mile and a half. If so, some woodland will have been of enormous length (see DB Northants. 1,6 note). A sub-division of the league was the furlong, reckoned at 220 yards, an eighth of a mile. In Worcs. no figure is found higher than 4 for furlongs (2,33. 23,14). In view of the occasional use of 4 virgates for 1 hide, the Worcester league might consist of 4 furlongs, but such measures as '½ league long by 2 furlongs wide' (2,34. 18,3), where the two would be equivalent in a league of 4 furlongs, might suggest 5 or 6 furlongs to the league, that is nearer to 2/3 mile than to a mile and a half. Like the furlong (2,14 note), the league is sometimes used as a square measure (as here and in 1,2. 14,2. 19,14. 26,2; 5-6), though in some cases the other dimension has been omitted, as certainly at 23,1 *nemus i leuua longum*. Although *leuuede* is normally considered to be a form of *leuga, leuua,* it is used in Worcs. only as a square measure (1,1c. 2,84. 10,4;10. 19,12. 23,5;10-11. 24,1. 26,13).

THE FOREST. ML *Foresta* from *foris* 'outside', meaning land, not necessarily wooded, beyond the bounds of the manor or village. A number of entries in Worcs. state or imply the existence of a forest; those starred refer expressly to the King's Forest: *1,1d 'Willingwick' and Chadwick; *1,2 Kidderminster; 2,31 Ripple (Malvern Chase); 2,52 Hindlip and Offerton; 2,53 Warndon and White Ladies Aston; 2,54 Cudley; 2,56 Oddingley; 2,57 Huddington; 2,59 Churchill; *2,60 Bredicot; 2,61 Perry; 2,78 Crowle; *2,79 Hanbury; 2,81 Stoke Prior, Aston Fields, 'Baddington'; *2,84 Alvechurch; 18,3 Shell; *23,14 Bellington; *26,3 Cofton Hackett; *26,5 Woodcote Green; *E 2 Feckenham; E 3 Hollow Court; E 4 Bushley; E 5 Queenhill; E 6 Eldersfield. Plotted on a map, these 'forests' fall in the north centre and the south-west of the County, implying the existence of the great forests of Feckenham, Wyre and Malvern, which were all parts of the Forest of Dean, then extending as far north as the Teme; see VCH i p. 271; ii p. 197; DGM pp. 247-9.

1,1d WILLIAM SON OF ANSCULF. See Ch. 23 note.
'WILLINGWICK'. The entry is probably duplicated, though with differences of detail, at 23,4.
VALUE. *Valet* (*valebat, valuit* in the past tenses) normally means the sums due to lords from their lands; *reddit* (past *reddidit*) has a similar meaning (see 1,1b).

1,2 16 OUTLIERS. Of these Ribbesford was probably in Doddingtree Hundred, and some of the unidentified places may well have been in other Hundreds (see App. I).
ANOTHER FRANCHE...ANOTHER RIBBESFORD. Only one village is found at each place in later times, and it is likely that *alia* refers not to another village, but to another holding in the same village. Other examples are plentiful in DB, e.g. Seaborough in Somerset, Thistleton in Rutland.
WRIBBENHALL. Probably included the manor of Bewdley (GR SO 7875), VCH iv p. 308.
RIBBESFORD. One of the two may have included Rock (GR SO 7371), VCH iv p. 320; and one had been held by Worcester Church, Worcs. G 11 (in App. V).
MITTON. Lower Mitton, VCH iii p. 172; see 2,82 note.
SUDUUALE. Close to Sutton Common (GR SO 8175), VCH iii p. 167.
A MILL AT 5 *ORA*. For *ora* see C 2 note. The expression here is unusual. At 20d to the *ora* and 12 ounces or 240d to a pound, the mill is worth 100d or 8s 4d.
WHICH PAY. *redd'*, which could abbreviate *reddentes* (plural) or *reddens* ('which pays'), referring only to the house in Worcester.

1,3a DROITWICH. Details of the Borough and the salt industry are collected in Appendix III. The place-name DB *Wich* is OE *wic*, Latin *vicus* 'village' or 'settlement', there being no original connection with salt; see EPNS p. 286 and Place-name Elements s.v.
5 BRINE-PITS. Elsewhere in England, salt was normally gathered in pans on the coast or in tidal estuaries. With Nantwich, Middlewich and Northwich in Cheshire, Droitwich was the great centre of inland salt production. Rock salt is derived from the Keuper marls and Droitwich is situated in a trough where the upper Keuper marls fill a deep depression in the lower Trias or Permian rocks. The rock salt is dissolved in underground streams and can be extracted by sinking shafts to form brine-pits. At Droitwich the water was nearly saturated with salt, 25% of brine drawn from the former Upwich pit being salt.

Salt production was simple: brine was drawn from the pit and boiled in vats over a fire until the water had evaporated. Accordingly, DB mentions lead vats (1,1a;5), a lead works (2,50), salt-workers (1,1a), furnaces (8,13), many salt-houses where the production took place, and arrangements for the supply of timber (1,1a. 2,15;48. 8,12 and possibly 2,58). For another method, see note on *hocci* below.

Production, allocation and conveyance of salt would no doubt have been governed by an elaborate system of customs and dues as in Cheshire (DB section S, col. 268 a, b). Such an essential commodity was from earliest times under royal control, a series of grants and charters showing English Kings allotting rights to salt being conveniently summarised in ECWM. King William, and Edward before him, controlled the brine-pits and owned the largest single group of salt-houses.

The scattering of the Droitwich entries tends to make study of its resources difficult (see App. III), but there seem to have been about 250 salt-houses there in 1086, corresponding perhaps to the 300 shares of brine found in medieval documents. These belonged to landholders in Worcs. and adjacent Counties. In the Worcs. context, *salina* (here rendered by the inclusive term 'salt-house') will probably have been a building with a fire and vat (although *salinae* and *plumbi* are distinguished at 1,5; see also 8,13 note on *furni*). Salt would be conveyed to these houses, no doubt situated near the pits, boiled, stored and then carted to the manor owning the salt-house, on payment of the appropriate toll, probably along one of the saltways radiating from the Borough (EPNS pp. 4-9).

Further details will be found in the works by Parkinson, Maddocks, Gillan, Habington and Rastell cited in the Bibliography at the head of these notes, as well as in VCH vols. ii-iii and the HMSO 'Wells and Springs of Worcestershire' (1930).

'UPWICH'. The site was in Droitwich at St. Richard's Well on the north bank of the river Salwarpe, see VCH iii p. 73 and map facing p. 82. Later there were still five pits, named by Habington at 'Upwich', 'Middlewich' and 'Netherwich' (ii p. 296). This last, probably one of the unnamed pits in DB, was ¼ mile down river from 'Upwich'; 'Middlewich' will have lain between.

2 *HOCCI. Hoccus* is a word of uncertain origin and meaning, and occurs only four times in DB, thrice at Worcs. 1,3 and once at Herefords. 1,41 (E 3 below), always under Land of the King, and in connection with salt-making in Droitwich. In the Herefords. entry it appears in the unlatinized form *hoch.* A not dissimilar word *hoga* is later found in Norfolk and Lincolnshire in connection with salt-making, usually associated with the word *area. Hoga* is defined by RMLWL as 'how', 'mound', 'mound for drying salt': e.g. *tenent bovatam . . . et continet xl acras et unam hogam quae reddit iii busellos salis* (A Terrier of Fleet, Lincolnshire, ed. N. Neilson, in British Academy Records of Social and Economic History iv. 1920 p. 6); *medietas marisci maris quae vocatur Thrikynghammersch cum medietate unius domus ibidem, medietate unius bogae et medietate unius areae praefatae hogae pertinentis . . . item una salina cum hoga et area quae vocatur Alverscot apud Hathenesse* (Cal Cl 1321 14 Ed II m 3 d); *areae et hogae in manus domini: i acra are[ae] et hog[ae] vocat[a] Rodlandeshowe.* (Cal Cl 1338 12 Ed III ii m 8); *item est ibidem una salina cum una hoga et area quae reddit per annum x quart' salis* (Cal Inq PM Ed II 67 (4) m 5).

In a former Danish area of the country, derivation from OScand *haugr* 'heap', 'mound', 'hillock', 'hill', is likely. But *hoccus* can hardly represent *haugr* (*hoga*). The form *hoch*, latinized *hoccus*, might represent an unidentified OE noun **hoc(c)* perhaps 'a heap', 'a mound'. This would be cognate with ON *haugr* or modern German *Höcker* 'projection, protuberance; hump, hill' (the OE cognate **hocer* is inferred from place-names, see Place-Name Elements, s.v.), or with ON *hoka*, German *hocken* 'to crouch, squat, huddle', High German *Hock, Hocken* 'haycock, heap (of hay, etc.)', or even with the related Modern English *shock* 'a shock, a number of sheaves, a quantity of 60 (sheaves, objects)'; see OED s.v. and J. Pokorny, *Indogermanisches etymologisches Wörterbuch* I (Francke, Bern 1959) 589, for Germanic cognates and forms. The precise sense of this word in relation to the salt industry in Worcestershire, however, has not yet emerged. Mounds are found in connection with medieval salt extraction on the coast or in tidal estuaries and sea marshes. Such mounds were used for drying salt or leaching out impurities. Burning often took place on the mounds themselves which also had buildings on them. Sea-marsh, buildings and salt-houses are mentioned in the above examples. Such 'salt-mounds' have been excavated in Essex and Kent, see M. W. Thompson in *Archaeologia Cantiana* vol. lxx (1956) pp. 44-67. For the methods, see Bridbury Ch. 1; Brownrigg pp. 47-49 and Leland *Itinerary* iv 10. *Area* in connection with the Lincs. and Norfolk examples may be the Latin word 'threshing floor', 'court', 'enclosure', 'area', referring to the site of the salt-works which needed to be quite extensive, or from OScand *eyrr* 'gravelly bank', 'bank of a river', 'small tongue of land running out into the sea'. The relation of this to Droitwich needs further investigation.

HELPRIDGE. DB *Helperic*, identified in EPNS p. 282; nearby is Brinepits Farm, although some way from the known area of salt production.

AT A THIRD BRINE-PIT. *in iii puteo.* Having begun with a cardinal number (*in uno puteo*) the scribe probably omitted to interline *tio* to indicate that the *iii* stood for the ordinal *tertio* 'third', rather than *tres* 'three'. It is less likely that *puteo* is a scribal error for *puteis*, 'at three brine-pits' then being the correct reading, implying three brine-pits at 'Middlewich'.

AT 5 OTHER BRINE-PITS. The figure *v* may well be an error for 2(*ii*). 5 pits have been mentioned, 3 already named. One of these two may have been at 'Netherwich', see above.

FROM ALL THESE...£52. This probably refers to all the items in 1,3a, the payment from the *hocci* being mentioned separately.

b 51½ SALT-HOUSES. *li salinam 7 dimid'*. The singular occurs regularly in DB with the figures 21,31 etc.

-7 A MISCELLANEOUS GROUP OF ENTRIES, referring to other Counties, similar to X 2-3.

KINVER...IN STAFFORDSHIRE. KINGSWINFORD LIKEWISE. The details are in DB Staffs. 1,27 and 1,1. They are entered here because Tardebigge and Clent (1,5-6) pay revenue jointly with them.

TARDEBIGGE...AND CLENT. Their withdrawal from Worcs. is accounted for in Worcs. G 29 (in App. V). Both were subsequently taken entirely into Staffs., Tardebigge being transferred to Warwicks. in 1266; both places returned to Worcs. in 1844. See App. I.

THE SHERIFF. Of Staffordshire, see 1,5 below.

£15. The sum is in fact the revenues of the two manors, Tardebigge and Clent, not of three as stated. Kingswinford was separately valued at 70s.

1,5 ANOTHER POSSIBLE. *Fieri* here and in 2,85 for the more usual *esse*, omitted in translation; see 1,1c note above.

1,7 THE HALL OF GLOUCESTER. That is, the royal hall. See 7,1 note and DB Glos. G 1 (col. 162 a).
A GAP suitable for about 14 lines follows before Ch. 2. Some material such as people, value and customs may have been omitted from 1,7 (7,1 note), or the space left for additional lands of the King, such as appear in X 2-3. Similar gaps are found in the early folios of other DB Counties.

Ch. 2 FOR THE DISPUTE between Worcester and Evesham Churches over a number of lands, see 10,11-12 note and App. V (Worcs. H). Hemming (Worcs. G in App. V) lists a number of lands alienated from the Church. Some are found under other holders in DB, others appear correctly in Ch. 2 but were clearly *de facto* alienated when held by Urso or his brother Robert the Bursar.

2,1 ST. MARY'S CHURCH. Founded by Oswald, Bishop of Worcs. 961-992, also Archbishop of York from 972. It was completed in 983.
OSWALDSLOW...300 HIDES. The triple Hundred consisting of 16 of the Church's manors chosen to make a 300-hide unit, forms a compact area around Worcester with a number of detached parts lying to the south and east. It was formed in 964 by King Edgar and named after Bishop Oswald according to a charter many times reprinted, ECWM no. 109 pp. 56,112 = KCD vi 237-242 = Sawyer (2) 731. It begins grandly with *Altitonantis Dei largiflua clementia*, and arranges a number of privileges for Bishop and monks and that a number of lands are to be added to the 50 hides of Cropthorne to form the Hundred of *Cuthburgelawe* for the monks. This 'Hundred' is to be joined with the Bishop's Hundred of *Winburgetrowe* and the ancient episcopal Hundred of *Wulfereslaw* to form Oswaldslow.
The substance of this charter was accepted by Round and Maitland, though both were aware of its difficulties. Recently Darlington in CWCP has cast authoritative doubt on the document; it purports to allot privileges to the monks at a time before they existed at Worcester; it is a surprising omission from Hemming if it then existed, the earliest reference to it in fact being in 1136-9 in the confirmation charter of Stephen; it seems too clearly framed in the interest of the monks, giving them lands and privileges that are only in part supported by DB. For further discussion see Round in VCH i p. 246; Maitland DBB p. 268; John pp. 80-139; 162-166; Anderson pp. 140-1.
Only the Hundred of *Winburgetrowe* is evidenced later, but it is not unlikely that Oswaldslow (which may not take its name from Bishop Oswald, see Darlington CWCP p. xv and EPNS p. 89) was congealed from three separate Hundreds, of which the charter preserves the names if not the contents (see App. I). For the privileges and ownership of land within the Hundred, DB 2,1 is a safer guide (see also Worcs. H in App. V).
BY AN ARRANGEMENT OF ANCIENT TIMES. The detail spells out the sense of C 3 *uicecomes nichil habet in eis*. The privileges are similar to those enjoyed by the Bishop of Winchester in Taunton Hundred, (DB Somerset 2,1). Hemming reproduces this section with variants in Worcs. H (App. V), adding the procedure of the Domesday enquiry and the names of the Commissioners.
BISHOP OF THIS CHURCH. Bishop Wulfstan II 1062-95.
NOR IN ANY OTHER CASE. *Causa*, probably in the sense of 'lawsuit'; possibly in the diminished sense of 'matter', 'thing', as Mod. Fr *chose*.
TURN ELSEWHERE WITH THIS LAND. See C 5 note above.

2,2 THE BISHOP...HOLDS... His manors are listed first 2,2-61; those of the Church 2,62-79.
WHICH PAY TAX. *geld'*, assumed to be expanded to *geldantes* 'paying' (translated 'which pay' in this series) rather than to *geldant* 'pay'. *Geldantes* is written out in full in many identical phrases in DB Glos. (e.g. 11,9. 28,4. 31,2). Later abstracts of DB often use *geldabiles* 'taxable'.
5 HIDES ARE WASTE. Worcs. B 1 (in App. V) adds that the hides are in lordship.
IN LORDSHIP 13 HIDES. Normally entered before the people and resources, after the number of taxable hides.

2,3 WOLVERTON. Probably Over Wolverton, VCH iii p. 534; see 2,4.
THE SUPPLIES. To supply the needs of the Bishop and Church.
VALUE 100s. '£4' in Evesham A 85.

2,4 WOLVERTON. Probably Little Wolverton, VCH iii p. 534; see 2,3 note.
ALRIC HELD THEM ALSO IN KING WILLIAM'S TIME. Alric (Aethelric in E 5) was brother of Bishop Beorhtheah (Brictric) (1033-38); the story of the acquisition of this and other lands and their loss to Earl William is in Worcs. G 22 (in App. V).
ON THE TERMS HE COULD BEG. Latin *deprecari* means among other things 'to try to avert

by prayer', 'beg off', 'beg exemption or relief from' (see OLD s.v.). The suggestion here is of a bargain or plea to obtain relief from obligations. Similar phrases occur at 2,17;28;54;73. Round in VCH i p. 288 translates 'as it could be obtained from the reeve'.

2,5 WALTER PONTHER. *Ponther*; perhaps from ML *puntarius* 'sword-fighter' or *pontarius* 'bridge-builder'; OEB p. 265. This Walter also apparently appears with the surnames *Poer* in Evesham C and *Pubier* and *Puchier* in Worcs. B; both of which documents are Domesday abbreviations. See DB Glos. 19,2 note.

WHITTINGTON. Also 2,58, one of the two estates being perhaps at Battenhall (GR SO 8653), VCH iii p. 515.

AS THE ABOVE HIDES. That is, on the same terms as those in 2,4.

2,7 HOLT. Included the manor of Bentley, VCH iii p. 405 (GR SO 8162).

IN THE ABOVE MANNER. As he did the land in 2,4-5.

1 HEDGED ENCLOSURE. Frequent in the west midland shires. From OE *(ge)haeg* Latinized as *haia* 'hedge' (cf. Mod. Fr *haie*); a 'hay' or hedged enclosure into which game were driven for capture, see 18,4 *i haia in qua capiebantur ferae*. In Shropshire (4,8,10 and 6,15) 'hays' are 'for capturing roe-deer' *capreolis capiendis*. See Ellis i p. 114; Ducange s.v. *haga*; Place-Name Elements s.vv. *(ge)haeg, haga*.

[VALUE...]. The value clause is omitted. Evesham A 89 has 'Value now £6'.

2,8 URSO ALSO HOLDS. Repeated at the beginning of 2,8-12.

(LITTLE) WITLEY. The Oswaldslow Witley is Little Witley, VCH iii p. 405; Great Witley was in Doddingtree Hundred and probably surveyed as part of Redmarley (15,10. 20,2).

ARNWIN THE PRIEST. The acquisition is described in Worcs. G 12 (in App. V).

1 SESTER OF HONEY. The sester (Latin *sextarium*) is a measure, both liquid and dry (see E 13), of uncertain and probably variable size (see DB Glos. G 1 and 19,2); it was reckoned at 32 oz. for honey.

VALUE IS...10s. Evesham A 90 has 'Value 15s'.

2,9 TO THE REVENUE REEVE. *Praeposito firmae, firmae* being genitive or dative.

½ WIDE. In the MS *diimid'* in error. Farley corrects to *dimid'*.

NOW 15s. '12s' in Evesham A 94.

2,10 'CLOPTON'. A lost place in the southern part of St. Johns in Bedwardine parish, see EPNS p. 91. For its history, see Worcs. G 6 (in App. V).

BRICTMER. Probably the same man whom Urso succeeded at Powick and Broughton (8,10a-10b;24); see VCH i p. 289 note 1.

LIKE THOSE ABOVE. *ut supradicti*, masculine, referring to the holders of 2,3-5;8-9.

2,11 LAUGHERNE. *Laure* in DB, *Lawerne* in contemporary documents, see EPNS p. 93. The entry is split in Evesham A 92;95, the total value there being 7s. The *Register* p. 36a similarly refers to a ½ hide holding as *Lawerne Willielmi* and to a *Lawerne Albetot*, probably Urso's here.

URSO ALSO HAS...6s. This is written in the MS by the same scribe as the rest though in darker ink and cramped, presumably because added later.

1 VIRGATE. Evesham C 11 has '½ hide'.

2,12 GREENHILL. See EPNS p. 131; and for its acquisition by Urso, Worcs. G 13 (in App. V).

WHAT THOSE ABOVE (PAID). *quod supradicti*, masculine, referring to the holders of 2,3-5;8-9.

2,13 ROBERT THE BURSAR. Brother of Urso; see 2,73 note.

12 OAKS. Stands in place of an entry for woodland. Evesham C 13 has *xii cainas*, OFr *chesne*, Mod. Fr *chêne*, see Evesham C introduction in App. IV.

KENWARD. Perhaps the English Sheriff of Worcs., Urso's predecessor, see Worcs. H 2 (in App. V) and Round in VCH i p. 289 note 2. The monks of Worcester claimed that Robert seized this and other lands on Kenward's death, Worcs. G 5. See 2,19 and 2,73 for other lands of Kenward held by Robert.

2,14 COTHERIDGE. Lesser or Little Cotheridge, VCH iv p. 256 note 16.

WOODLAND, 3 FURLONGS. Used here as a square measure, see 1,1c note.

RICHARD HELD IT. Richard Scrope, father of Osbern, see Worcs. G 8 (in App. V). For the byname, see 19,1 note.

2,15 FLADBURY. A former possession of Evesham, see 10,11-12 note. It included land at Thorne and Throckmorton, VCH iii pp. 356,424.

20 STICKS OF EELS. A stick contained 25 eels.

2,16 BISHOP OF HEREFORD. Robert Losinga, bishop 1079-95.

INKBERROW. The Bishop holds 15½ hides there in chief (3,3 below). That holding, in Esch Hundred, was probably the later Greater Inkberrow, the present holding Little Inkberrow, VCH iii p. 420. The same division is found in Evesham A. In this edition the land is mapped in Esch Hundred. It included Shurnock (GR SP 0260), VCH iii p. 116.

BISHOP WALTER. Walter of Lorraine, chaplain to Queen Edith, and Bishop of Hereford, 1061-79.

2,17 AB LENCH. Long known by folk etymology as Abbots Lench as well as Hob and Habbe Lench; Ab derives from a personal name Aebba or Haebba (EPNS pp. 148-9).
MEADOW... . There is a gap of about 10 letters in the MS, presumably for a measurement.
ON THE TERMS HE COULD BEG. Round in VCH i p. 290 translates 'on such terms as he could obtain'; see 2,4 note.

2,18 (ROUS) LENCH. DB *Biscopsleng*, see EPNS p. 149; VCH i p. 290 note 3; VCH iii p. 498.
FRAN. *Franc* in Worcs. B (folio 137r (=138r), Hearne p. 301).

2,19 (WYRE) PIDDLE, MOOR AND HILL. All places would be difficult to identify but for their conjunction. For Piddle, see EPNS p. 155; for Moor and Hill, now a single parish, EPNS p. 135. *More* and *Pydele* are coupled in Fees p. 36, FA v p. 306, and Hill is *Hulle iuxta Fladebury* in Oswaldslow Hundred in FA v pp. 308-9.
THE OTHER ABOVE. *Aliā* abbreviating *aliam*, singular, and referring to 2,18.

2,20 BRADLEY (GREEN). Now the major settlement in the parish of Stock and Bradley; Bradley itself and its church lie just to the south at GR SO 9860.
ARCHBISHOP ALDRED. Bishop of Worcester 1047-1062; he held the see with that of Hereford 1056-60 and with York 1061-62. He was Archbishop of York until his death in 1069, and crowned William the Conqueror and his Queen Matilda.

2,21 CHURCH TAX. *circset*, OE *ciric-sceat*, an obscure tax, see Maitland DBB p. 321 ff. It was due in kind and payable at Martinmas; see 9,7 below.
BURIAL. Burial dues.
PLEAS TO THE SAID HUNDRED. Pleas to the Hundred Court.

2,22 FROM IT. From the woodland, as in 2,15.

2,23 TEDDINGTON. In the extreme south of the County, not to be confused with Teddington in Warwickshire; it probably included Alstone manor, VCH ii p. 471 (GR SO 9832).

2,24 BISHOP BRICTHEAH. A late 11th century form of Beorhtheah, PNDB p. 194; called Brictric in DB Herefords. 1,45 (= E 5 below). Bishop of Worcester 1033–1038.
ARCHBISHOP ALDRED. See 2,20 note.
PROVED HIS RIGHT TO. *Deratiocinauit* here, *diratiocinauit* at 9,6a, both active, but the deponent form occurs at 2,63. See DB Wilts. 24,14; 19; 42 for similar confusion.
HIS SON. Doda's son Brictric, see 2,63.

2,25 7 HIDES. Evesham A 105 accounts for 2 hides (worth £7) at Redmarley; 3 hides at Redmarley *Willelmi*.
REDMARLEY (D'ABITOT). The name is derived not from Urso, but from a junior branch of his family who were sub-tenants of the Beauchamps in the 12th and 13th centuries. This Redmarley is held from the Bishop of Worcester in Oswaldslow in FA v p. 307; see EPNS p. 156; Fees p. 36; VCH i p. 291 note 7; VCH iii p. 483. Worcester Church seems also to have held the other Redmarley at one time: Worcs. G 7 (in App. V) and 15,10 note.
2 HIDES. At Innerstone, VCH iii pp. 484-5; see 8,25 note.

2,26 PENDOCK. Divided in Evesham A 106 between Warner (value 20s) and Walter (6s), neither sub-tenant appearing in DB. The Church regarded Urso's land as alienated from it, Worcs. G 1 (in App. V).
AS ABOVE. That is, he gave service as in 2,25; *supradicta* is interlined, and the word is superfluous in view of *eadem* which Worcs. B (folio 137v (= 138v), Hearne p. 302) corrects to *easdem*, referring no doubt to the hides.

2,27 (LITTLE) WASHBOURNE. Great Washbourne has always been in Gloucestershire, to which Little Washbourne was transferred in 1844; see App. I.
SO THE BISHOP. *Episcopus vero. Vero* is here probably the consequence of his becoming a monk; elsewhere in DB it can have adversative force, 'but'.

2,28 ON THE TERMS HE COULD BEG. See 2,4 note above.

2,29 MEADOW, 6 ACRES. *Acras* is accusative after *habet*; contrast 2,32 where the meadow is not held by the tenant.
WAS A RIDER OF THE BISHOP FROM THERE. 'served for it as the Bishop's radman' in VCH i p. 292. It appears that some 'radmen' still performed the riding services that named them; but *inde* can have a temporal sense 'then' and a consecutive sense 'so' as well.

2,30 BRICTRIC SON OF ALGAR. A great English thane who held much land in the west. Many of his lands passed to Queen Matilda (see DB Cornwall 1,13 note) and, on her death in 1083, to King William. This land where he was a sub-tenant of Worcester Church probably became confused with lands where he was tenant-in-chief and so was lost to the Church on his death.
FROM THE BISHOP. *de ep̄o* is interlined. The MS has a faint hair-line after *tenuit* to show the correct position for the interlineation in the text; this is not shown in the facsimile nor by Farley.
IT IS IN KING WILLIAM'S HANDS. It appears in DB Herefords. 1,44 (E 4 below) with additional detail under the heading 'In Worcestershire'; cf. 2,36 note. In later times the

estate was in Pershore Hundred and known as the manor of Bushley Park; VCH iv p. 46.

2,31 RIPPLE. Included land at Ryall (GR SO 8640), VCH iii p. 490.
UPTON (ON SEVERN). Similarly coupled with Ripple in Worcs. C (folio 141r (= 142r), Hearne p. 314), it is *Upton super Sabrinam* Oswaldslow Hundred in FA v p. 309. Welland (GR SO 7939) was part of the grant, see Mon. Ang. i p. 609 (= ECWM no. 267 p. 106).
1 FEMALE. *et una ancilla* is interlined but with no hairline to show its correct position in the text.
IN MALVERN (CHASE). Part of the great northwards extension of Dean Forest, see 1,1c note.
FROM THIS...FROM IT. That is, from the woodland.
PASTURE DUES. DB *Pasnagium*, 'pannage', payment for pasturing pigs in the wood; see 3,3 note.
(TIMBER) FOR REPAIRING HOUSES. Cf. DB Wilts. 13,10, customary dues owing to the Church of Wilton's manor of South Newton '. . . 80 cartloads of timber and fodder for 80 pigs and what may be needed for repairing houses and fences (*ad domos et sepes reem(en)-dandos*)'.

2,32-34 CROOME. Of the three modern Croomes, DB distinguishes Hill Croome (*Hilcrūbe* 2,34). The hide at 2,32 was Earls Croome; the 5 hides at 2,33 Croome d'Abitot, see VCH i p. 292.

2,32 40[s]. In the MS *sol(idos)* is omitted in error, as happens several times. 'Value 40s' in Evesham A 112.

2,33 CROOME. *ad Crūbe* in DB, *ad aliā Crumbe* 'at another Croome' in Worcs. B (folio 138r (= 139r), Hearne p. 303). There are separate villages in later times, but *aliam* does not necessarily imply this, see 1,2 note.
SIGREF. DB *Sirof*, see PNDB p. 364.
(HER) MOTHER. Presumably Sigref's widow.

2,34 HILL CROOME. Included the manor of Baughton (GR SO 8741), VCH iii p. 321.

2,36 RALPH OF BERNAY. A supporter of Earl William of Hereford and Sheriff of Hereford under him. He is found in Worcs. G (in App. V) as a despoiler of Church land under Earl William. He was imprisoned by King William, and his lands, including those where he was a sub-tenant (cf. 2,30 note) fell to the crown. Bernay is in the département of Eure, France.
QUEENHILL. DB *Cūhille*, see EPNS p. 155.
ALRIC. Aethelric, brother of Bishop Beorhtheah (Brictheah, Brictric), E 5.
NOW IT IS IN THE KING'S HANDS. It is found in Herefords. 1,45 (E 5 below), with additional detail, under the heading 'In Worcestershire'.
VALUE WAS 40s. The current value is given as 40s in Evesham A 116.

2,37 BARLEY. DB *Burgelege*. See EPNS p. 141. It still survives as Barley House on OS 6 in. maps.
AS THAT ABOVE. That is, as in 2,36.
NOW IT IS IN THE KING'S HANDS. See 2,30 note above.

2,38 BLOCKLEY. The 38 hides are accounted for in Evesham A (117;120) as 33 at Blockley and 5 unnamed hides held by Hereward. This holder is only found in DB in 2,43 as holder of the 5 hides at Evenlode which are accounted for separately in Evesham A 122 but without a holder's name. The unnamed 5 hides of Evesham A 120 must be accounted for in the 25½ lordship hides of DB. They may have been at Dorn (GR SP 2034); Worcs. B 3 (in App. V) has a marginal note added *de hoc manerio tenet Urso v hidas in Dorne*, similarly in Evesham C 42. See VCH i p. 293 note 7. Urso's tenancy there may have been missed by the DB commissioners, or post-date DB. *Dorna* is held by the Bishop of Worcester in Fees p. 35. The manor of Blockley also included the hamlets of Aston Magna (GR SP 2035), Draycott (SP 1835), Upton Wold (SP 1434) and Paxford (SP 1837), VCH iii p. 267.

2,40 VALUE IS...15s. '£15' in Evesham A 119, probably in error.

2,41 (CHURCH) ICOMB. DB *Iacūbe*, see EPNS p. 143. This was the northern part of the modern parish, transferred to Glos. in 1844, the southern portion having been there in 1086. See VCH iii p. 412.
IT IS ASSESSED WITH THE HEAD OF THE MANOR. That is, at Blockley. The sentence replaces a value clause which should fall at the end of the entry, the entry for meadow having been omitted originally in error.

2,42-44 DAYLESFORD...EVENLODE...ABBEY OF EVESHAM. For the dispute between Worcester and Evesham about these lands see 10,11-12 note, Evesham D 7 and VCH iii pp. 336;348. According to Evesham N 1;5 they were 'acquired' by Odo of Bayeux from the Church of Evesham, see Ch. 11 note.

2,42 STEPHEN SON OF FULCRED. *Stephanus filius Wlwi* in Evesham C 41; D 7.

2,43 HEREWARD HELD. *Tenuit*, probably an error for *tenet*, which seems to be implied in Evesham C 41 and Evesham D 7; it may be an indication, however, that the land had not been returned to him after the Bishop of Bayeux had removed it (2,44).

2,44 ABBEY OF EVESHAM. DB *abb'* can abbreviate *abbas* 'Abbot', *abbatia* 'Abbey' and occasionally *abbatissa* 'Abbess'. *Abbatia* is clearly intended here, for the end of the sentence reads *de abbatia accepit.*

BISHOP OF BAYEUX. See Ch. 11 note. 'Received' is a polite way of saying 'seized' (*abstulit* in 11,2 and Evesham D 7, *per uiolentiam abstulit* in Evesham N 1). Until Odo's final downfall in England in 1088 it was not politic to be frank about his numerous thefts of church land.

2,45 TREDINGTON. See Worcs. B 4 (App. V). The manor included Talton (GR SP 2347), Newbold on Stour (SP 2446) and probably Armscote (SP 2444), VCH iii pp. 544-6.

SMALLHOLDERS. The MS *bord'* is partly obscured by an ink smudge, so that only the first and last letters are discernible.

£12 10s. '£15' in Evesham A 123.

2,46 BLACKWELL. For its earlier history, see Worcs. G 17 (App. V).

2,47 LONGDON. Near Shipston on Stour, now in Warwickshire, to be distinguished from the Longdon near Upton on Severn held by Westminster Abbey (8,9a).

2,48 NORTHWICK. Held by the Bishop of Worcester as *Norwyk iuxta Wygorniam*, in Oswaldsow Hundred in FA v p. 306.

25 HIDES. The detail amounts to only 23½, the omitted land being given as 1½ hides in Offerton, value 25s, in Evesham A 129 (see 2,52 note). Evesham C 46 has 26 hides. *hid'* is interlined with a hair-line in the MS to show its correct position in the text; this hair-line is not reproduced in Farley.

100 CARTLOADS OF TIMBER. As fuel to boil the water out of the brine, see 1,3a note.

2,49 90 HOUSES. The detail amounts to 89.

THE THIRD PENNY. A third of a Borough's total revenue, the remaining two-thirds going to the King; see J. H. Round *The 'Tertius Denarius' of the Borough* in EHR xxxiv (1919) pp. 62-4 and DB Glos. B1 note.

[VALUE]. *Valuit* or *valebat* is omitted, as sometimes elsewhere, the value being probably that of the third penny (see note below).

2,50 VALUE. Perhaps the value of those parts of Northwick manor mentioned in 2,48 and here, excluding the Borough revenue in 2,49.

£16 10s. '£16 3s' in Evesham A 125.

2,51 25 HOUSES. Perhaps the same as the 24 in 2,49; otherwise they are additional to the 90 there mentioned; see VCH i p. 242.

THEY PAY. Or perhaps 'he pays'; *redd't* could abbreviate *reddit* or *reddunt.*

2,52 HINDLIP AND OFFERTON. Evesham A assigns all 5 hides to Hindlip (A 126) and an additional 1½ hides to Offerton (A 129) *in terra de Lege*; see 2,48 note above.

FOREST. See 1,1c note.

EDRIC THE STEERSMAN. *Stirman*; the commander of a ship or fleet. Other Steersmen are Thorkell (8,1), Wulfheah (Beds. 53,15) and Stephen (Warwicks. B 2 col. 238 a), see OEB p. 271. Edric is probably the same man as Edric of *Hindelep* who witnessed the settlement of the dispute between Evesham and Worcester concerning Hampton and Bengeworth. He had been steersman of the Bishop of Worcester's boat in King Edward's time and leader of the Bishop's army in the King's service; see Worcs. H 2 (App. V).

2,53 WARNDON. In Evesham C 50 the original abbreviation of the DB entry has been replaced by '(Urso) holds 2 hides in Warndon and Trotshill' (GR SO 8855) and '½ hide in White Ladies Aston'; see 2,68 note.

(WHITE LADIES) ASTON. Or Aston Episcopi, EPNS p. 88.

2,54 AELFEVA. DB *Elfgiua*, elsewhere *Aelueua*, both from OE *Aelfgifu*, PNDB p. 173.

ON THE TERMS SHE COULD BEG. See 2,4 note above.

2,55 3 HIDES AND 1 VIRGATE. Evesham A 127 has 3½ hides.

(WHITE LADIES) ASTON. See 2,53 note above.

LORDSHIP OF THE HEAD MANOR. The head manor is probably Northwick 2,48. Grammatically *capitali* agrees with *dominio* 'chief lordship', but its position and similar phrases elsewhere in DB (e.g. Northants. 18,8 *cum capitali manerio appreciata est*) suggest that it is intended to describe *manerii*, the final *i* perhaps being a mistaken genitive, attracted by *manerii.*

2,56 ODDINGLEY. See Worcs. G 19 (in App. V).

SALT-HOUSE...MEADOW. Accusative after *habet.*

[VALUE...]. Omitted in DB; 'value 15s' in Evesham A 128.

2,57 SERVING AS A COUNTRYMAN. He rendered services such as a countryman did. A *rusticus* was probably a less prosperous villager; see VCH Wilts. ii p. 55 and 10,4 below. Cf. 2,4 *rustico opere.*

2,58 WHITTINGTON AND 'RADLEY'. Whittington was alienated from the Church by Earl William, Worcs. G 22 (in App. V); see 2,5 note. 'Radley', DB *Rodeleah*, was left unidentified by DG; it is mentioned in the bounds of Whittington in 989 and was probably on the northern border of the parish not far from Swinesherd, close to the present Red

Hill, VCH iii p. 516 note 51.
ONLY FOR FIRE-WOOD. That is, not for hunting or pasturing of pigs. The wood possibly went to the salt-houses at Droitwich, see 1,3a note. Cf. 2,48 and note.
LIKE THOSE ABOVE. That is, Thorkell and Wulfric (2,56-7).

59 CHURCHILL. Adjacent to Worcester, see FA v p. 308. To be distinguished from that near Kidderminster, 23,7.

60 BREDICOT. See Worcs. G 21 (in App. V).

61 'PERRY'. DB *Pirian*, now represented only by Perry Wood, see EPNS p. 161, which omits the DB reference.

62 OVERBURY. The survey of the monks' land now begins, see 2,2 note. Worcs. B 5 (in App. V) has the heading *de terra monachorum*. The holding at Overbury included Conderton (GR SO 9637) and that at Pendock included Berrow (GR SO 7934), see VCH iii pp. 470, 258. Berrow appears as a part of Pendock in Evesham A 135 (App. IV) in the form *Alaberge*. This represents *à la berge*, a fusion of a French preposition and article with OE *beorg* 'hill', 'hillock', 'mound', 'grave-mound'. This same Berrow and others in Worcestershire occur as *la Berwe* or *la Berge* in early documents.

63 DODA. DB *Doddus* may well be derived from a different form of the name, but he is clearly the same man who occurs in the dative as *Dodoni* in 2,24. See PNDB p. 263.
DODA HOLDS IT. From the parallel case in 2,24 it would appear that *tenet* here is a mistake for *tenuit*: Aldred has proved that the monks, not Doda's son, have the right to the land.
ARCHBISHOP ALDRED. See 2,20 note.
PROVED (THEIR)RIGHT TO. *diratiocinatus est*, deponent; see 2,24 note.

65 *WIBURGESTOKE*. Similarly associated with Harvington as *Wiburga Stoke* in Worcs. C (folio 141r (= 142r), Hearne p. 314).

66 ...STICKS OF EELS. There is a small gap in the MS after *redd'*, the number being omitted until ascertained.

67 MEADOW, 6 ACRES; WOODLAND. *acras* and *silvam* are accusative after *habet*.
THE SAID MANOR. Grimley 2,66.

68 HALLOW. The manor probably included Kenswick (GR SO 7958), VCH iii p. 368.
10 HOUSES. Cf. *Register* p. 52a.
2 RIDERS HOLD 2 HIDES. At Ravenshill (GR SO 9056) and Dunhampstead (SO 9160) in Worcs. B 5 (App. V). Worcs. G 24 records that Urso seized Ravenshill from the Church, perhaps this holding although it is not held by Urso in DB, perhaps a part of Warndon 2,53 which is adjacent and held by Urso in 1086.

69 WALTER OF 'BURGH'. *Burch* in Evesham C 65, *del Burc* in Evesham Q 29 (the survey of Droitwich) probably referring to the same man. DB *Burh*, from OE *Burg, Burh* 'fort', 'fortified place', 'manor', 'town', 'Borough'. The 'Burgh' here implied is not known, perhaps Eastbury itself, or the neighbouring *Burgh* of Worcester.
EASTBURY. DB *Eresbyrie*, see EPNS p. 129. For the dispute with Evesham Church involving this land, see 10,11-12 note. Land here was lost by the Church to Urso, see Worcs. G 13 (App. V).

70 ALRIC HELD THIS LAND. He obtained both these members of Hallow from his brother, Bishop Beorhtheah (1033-38), and lost them to Earl William, Worcs. G 22 (App. V).

71 HUGH OF GRANDMESNIL. Sheriff of Leicestershire, died 1094. Grandmesnil is in the département of Calvados, France.
LYPPARD. Earlier Leopard, DB *Lappewrte*, EPNS p. 161.
1 PLOUGH AND 6 OXEN. Normally there were 8 oxen to a plough-team; see 1,1c note above.
CHURCH TAX. See 2,21 note above.
ACKNOWLEDGEMENT OF THE LAND. Recognition that it was in the Bishop's jurisdiction. It had been given by Bishop Beorhtheah to a retainer, Worcs. G 23 (in App. V).

72 CROPTHORNE. The charter of Offa of Mercia (ECWM no. 227 p. 95 = BCS 235 = Sawyer (2) 118) allots the 50 hides as 7 at Cropthorne, 1 at Netherton, 2 at Elmley Castle, 1 at Kersoe, 14 at Charlton, 15 at Hampton and 10 at Bengeworth. Though spurious, the charter probably details the members of Cropthorne correctly. The detail of DB amounts to 40 hides, the 10 hides not accounted for being at Hampton, 2,74 note below. The 50 hides were said to have been part of the Hundred of *Cuthbergelawe*, see 2,1 note and App. I.

73 11 HIDES. They were at Charlton (GR SP 0045) and Elmley Castle (SO 9841). Robert's acquisition of Elmley Castle is described in Worcs. G 25 (App. V); the 7 hides he held of Charlton (Worcs. G 26) were formerly held by Godric, the other 7 hides being an unnamed part of Cropthorne. Robert died without issue, Elmley Castle passing to the Beauchamps, heirs of his brother Urso, and becoming *caput* of their barony. Evesham A 146 gives

'2 hides' in error, the value, '£7', being correct.
2 FEMALE SLAVES. In the MS and Farley *ancillę*; the facsimile does not reproduce the diphthong sign.
ON THE TERMS THEY COULD BEG. See 2,4 note above.

2,74 ABBOT. Or 'Abbey', see 2,44 note above.
5 HIDES. Hampton was a 15-hide member of Cropthorne (2,72 note above and Worcs. H in App. V). The disputed portion was probably Little Hampton, the remaining 10 hides being Great Hampton. They were later freed from tax, Worcs. C (folio 141r (= 142r), Hearne p. 315) stating: *v hidas apud Hamtun geldantes et x sunt quietae a geldo per breve regis*.
HAMPTON. Subject of the great dispute between Worcester and Evesham (10,11-12 note). Only the hidage is here given, the details appearing in 10,11. The compromise was reached before the Domesday Commissioners, see Worcs. H in App. V. The entry is omitted in Worcs. B (folio 138v (= 139v), Hearne p. 307).
THE OTHER (OBLIGATIONS) ARE FULLY DISCHARGED AT THE CHURCH OF EVESHAM. A difficult phrase. *Tota*, if not an error (*tota* for *cota* for *quota* 'share'), must agree with a feminine noun understood, probably *terra* 'land'. *Quieta* means 'exempt', 'immune', in DB before *de* or *ab* (C 3 note); here with *ad* it probably has the force of 'paid', 'obligation discharged'. Despite the change of tense from *habuit* to *ē* (abbreviating *est*), the phrase clearly explains the preceding sentence: that the Bishop of Worcester received before 1066 (and probably still) only the tax due to his Hundred (Oswaldslow), all other obligations being now (and probably then) discharged at Evesham; see 10,11-12 note and Worcs. H (App. V).

2,75 ABBOT. Or 'Abbey', see 2,44 note above.
BENGEWORTH. Like Hampton, it was involved in the great dispute with Evesham, see 10,11-12 note and Worcs. H in App. V.
4 HIDES...6 HIDES. The details of the 4 hides are given in 10,12; the remaining information here refers to the 6 hides held by Urso. In 1066 half of Bengeworth had been held by Arngrim and half by Azor (*Chronicon* p. 97; Worcs. G 27-28 in App. V). The Abbot of Evesham proved Arngrim's 5 hides to be his and was holding 4 of them in 1086, the 5th hide, mentioned in 10,12, being added to the 5 hides held by Azor that were held in 1086 by Urso. For a history of the estate, see VCH ii p. 397. The 6 hides are valued at £3 in Evesham A 147 and described as *pars Willelmi*, probably William de Beauchamp, heir of Urso.

2,76 IN ESCH HUNDRED. The 300 hides of Oswaldslow have been accounted for in 2,2-75. DB now lists the holdings of the Church in other Hundreds. In Worcs. C (App. V), these remaining lands are said to be *de Kinefolka*, that is, land of the 'King's people', referring to the north of the County, held by or subject to the Crown and contrasting with the south which was mainly church land; see App. I and Anderson p. 139.
CLEEVE (PRIOR). 'Prior' to distinguish it from Cleeve Bishops in Gloucester, see EPNS p. 314.
ATCH LENCH. Adjacent to Cleeve Prior. At 10,14, Atch Lench is 4½ hides, the odd ½ hide here making a 5 hide unit, see VCH i p. 297 note 5.
1 SESTER OF HONEY. An unusual render from a mill; see 2,8 note.
VALUE WAS £7. Evesham A 7 records this as the present value, no past value being given in Evesham A.

2,77 PHEPSON. DB *Fepsetenatun*, the fuller form surviving in Fepsinton Farm, see EPNS p. 137.
6 HIDES. The number is omitted in Worcs. B (folio 139v (= 140v), Hearne p. 308), but is given as 1 in Worcs. C (folio 141v (= 142v), Hearne p. 316).

2,78 CROWLE. *Croela Odonis* in Evesham A 10, where it has 6 hides.
IN DROITWICH A SALT-HOUSE. There is a gap, due to an erasure of about 2 letters, between *salina* and *Wich*, with the *in* written above.
SIGMUND. Holder of both Crowles (see 19,14) at one time, see Worcs. G 20 (in App. V).

2,79 HANBURY. DB *Hambyrie*; *Hambury iuxta Wycham* in FA v p. 306. The corresponding entry in Evesham A 8 gives 3 hides and a value of 100s. The holding probably included Temple Broughton (GR SO 9461), VCH iii p. 377.
URSO'S ½ HIDE is at *Estwde* (Astwood, GR SO 9365, in Dodderhill parish) in Evesham C 75, see EPNS p. 281.

2,80 SHIRE. *Vicecomitatus*. Since each County (*comitatus*) had its Sheriff (*vicecomes*) but few (including Worcs.) had an Earl (*comes*), the terms are interchangeable.
FREE. Free of tax, that is lordship land.
MARTINMAS. November 11th.
IN WORCS. B. (folio 139v (= 140v), Hearne p. 308) beside this entry is the marginal note *De Ciricsceate* 'On Church Tax', see 2,21 note above.

BUT IF...FORFEITURE...LAND. Cf. 9,7.

,81 'BADDINGTON'. Baddington mill is found on the first edition OS map; Bant Mill (6 in. OS) seems to stand on the site, see EPNS p. 359.

LORDSHIP. In the MS there is an ink blot over the last 2 letters of *dn̄io* and the *s* of *sunt.*

7 *ORA*. That is, 11s 8d at 20 pence to the *ora*, see C 2 note.

,82 6 OUTLIERS. One was at Waresley (GR SO 8470), 5 hides later held by Urso, its alienation described in Worcs. G 16 (App. V). It is mentioned also in Worcs. C (folio 141v (= 142v), Hearne p. 315). Another two outliers were probably Pepwell and Upper Mitton, see VCH iii pp. 384-5, and 1,2 note.

,83 WOLVERLEY. See Worcs. G 17. The holding included Horseley, Cookley and Burton, VCH iii p. 568.

,84-85 THESE ENTRIES are written in a cramped version of the same hand, probably inserted later.

,84 COFTON (HACKETT). A manor of ½ hide, later naming the parish, VCH iii p. 57; 26,3 note.

WAST HILLS. Also West Hill on the OS 6 in. map, see EPNS p. 335.

'TONGE'. In Alvechurch, EPNS p. 335. According to Habington, it lay between Alvechurch and Lea End.

HIS WOOD. That is, his Forest, see 1,1c note.

85 EARDISTON, KNIGHTON (ON TEME). Included in Worcs. B 6 (App. V) under the heading *de Linderyge* (Lindridge, GR SO 6769) which lies between them, see VCH iii pp. 444-445.

15 HIDES. There is a gap sufficient for about 7 letters following these words and in the left hand margin *rq̃* (for *require* 'enquire'). The scribe may have been unclear whether the 15 hides was a total or 15 hides each, and left a gap for a clarifying word.

A FURTHER 3 PLOUGHS. Exceptionally on an estate of the Church, see 2,80. For *fieri,* see 1,5 note above.

h. 3 THE BISHOP OF HEREFORD. Robert Losinga, Bishop 1079-1095.

2 KYRE. The three DB holdings (also 19,4;7) no doubt included the later Kyre Magna (Wyard) and Little Kyre, see EPNS pp. 55-56. See E 35 note.

BISHOP WALTER. Bishop of Hereford 1061-1079.

3 INKBERROW. Probably Great Inkberrow, see 2,16 note.

EARL HAROLD. Son of Earl Godwin and brother of Queen Edith; King of England Jan. 6th to Oct. 14th 1066. William the Conqueror did not recognise his title to the crown, hence the use of 'Earl' instead of 'King' in DB. He was Earl of East Anglia (1045), received half of Swein's earldom (1046), Earl of the West Saxons on his father's death in 1053, Earl of Hereford (1058). His holding of Inkberrow will have dated from before his accession, see VCH i p. 299 note 3. *Com̄* in the MS and Farley, but the abbreviation sign is not reproduced in the facsimile.

13 PLOUGHS. In Evesham A 6 the men have 12 ploughs.

100 PIGS. See 19,14 'woodland ½ league for 100 pigs'. The latter may simply mean that ½ league is sufficient wood for supporting 100 pigs; the present entry seems to be a payment for the right of pasture, see DB Middlesex 2,1; Surrey 1,2; Sussex 2,5 notes.

h. 4 ST. DENIS' (CHURCH). The Abbey of St. Dionysius in Paris. This single holding in Worcs. at Droitwich probably represents the provision of salt for the Church's land at Little Compton in Gloucestershire which had belonged to the Glos. Abbey of Deerhurst, DB Glos. 20,1.

,1 HIS PARK. The same is mentioned in 14,2 and survived into the 16th century, VCH iii p. 207. See E 3 note.

h. 6 CORMEILLES. Near Pont L'Evêque in the département of Eure, France; OEB p. 84. A Benedictine Abbey founded *c.* 1060 by William son of Osbern (see 1,1b note above).

1 ½ HIDE. Only the first letter of *dimidiam* is on the line, the rest being interlined, due to an erasure. Evesham C 86 has 1 hide. See E 35 note and Worcs. G 4 (in App. V).

EARL WILLIAM GAVE IT. William, Earl of Hereford 1067-1071. The confirmation charter of Henry II is in Mon. Ang. vi, p. 1077, see VCH i p. 240. Other gifts by him to the Church are mentioned in E 1;7.

,1 THE SAME CUSTOMARY DUES. The King's ½ hide is 1,7; no due or right is there mentioned (see 1,7 note), but it may have been a toll on the conveyance of salt, remitted under Stephen, see VCH iii p. 73 note 19. For such a toll, see DB Glos. 1,57.

Ch. 8 LAND OF ST. PETER'S, WESTMINSTER. The 200 hides of the Church's lands, together with the 100 hides of Pershore Church (Ch. 9) form a great triple Hundred akin to Oswaldslow (Ch. 2). The lands of Pershore and Westminster are inextricably intermingled, the Churches sometimes sharing a village. The Westminster lands had originally belonged to Pershore, which still retained some rights over all 300 hides (see 9,7), but were taken thence by King Edward the Confessor for Westminster Abbey, see EPNS p. 183 and VCH i pp. 257-259. The notification of William that St. Peter's, Westminster, should have Pershore and Deerhurst (DB Glos. 19,1-2) as given by King Edward with all the customs which pertained to them when in Edward's hands is in *Regesta* i no. 32. Another notification, possibly spurious, appears as no. 234 there. The original grant of 300 hides to Pershore is in a suspected charter of Edgar, BCS 1282 = ECWM 120 p. 116 = Sawyer (2) no. 786. Pershore at 200 hides seems to have been regarded as a single manor, with a number of outliers, see 8,22 note. In a number of entries in the chapter, a gap is left before the value clause (8,1-2;5;9a;9d;9e;10a;16-17).

8,1 200 HIDES. The detail amounts to 198, a further hide at Droitwich probably being in Clent Hundred, see App. I and 8,13 note below.

THORKELL, KING EDWARD'S STEERSMAN. See 2,52 note above.

8,2 WICK. Formerly Wick by Pershore, granted by King Edward to St. Peter's (notification dated 1076-82 in *Regesta* i no. 166; see also third note to 8,13).

6 HIDES. '6½ hides' in Evesham A 34 and in C 89 (App. IV), the ½ hide interlined in the latter.

URSO. His depredations included churches other than Worcester, see Ch. 26 note.

1 HIDE. Held by Robert in Evesham A 47. In Evesham B, Urso holds 3 hides at *Wicha Inardi*, the manor of Wick Piddle, VCH iv pp. 169-170. For *Inardus*, see 8,25 note.

GILBERT ½ HIDE. The manor of Wick Warren, VCH iv p. 170.

VALUE 25s. The ½ hide is worth 10s, the 1 hide 15s, in Evesham A 46-47.

8,6 BOTH WOOD AND OPEN LAND. *inter silvam et planum*, the same phrase being found at 9,2 and 10,10, and similar ones elsewhere in DB, e.g. Herts. 10,9; Cheshire 2,7; Glos. 1,57 and 10,11.

8,7 ECKINGTON. Evesham A 50 names an undertenant here as Hugh *de Wllavesella*, now Woollashill (GR SO 9440), holding 3 hides, probably those of Thurstan; see VCH iv p. 72.

2 COTTAGERS. *Cot'* for *cotarii*, apparently similar to *cotmanni, cotmani* (translated 'cottage-men', 20,6 note). For an allied group, *coscet* (singular), *coscez* and *cozets* (plural), in the south-western Counties, see DB Somerset 8,30 and Wilts. M 3 notes. *Cotarii* often occur in DB Wilts. in the same entry as *coscez*, suggesting a distinction; likewise *cotarii* are distinct from *cotmanni* in the *Register* p. 59b, though in each case the distinction is obscure. See Maitland DBB pp. 39-40. Cottagers (*cotarii*) are rare in Worcs., occurring in 8,16-17;21;24. 15,8. 19,14.

6 FREEDMEN. *Coliberti*, former slaves. A continental term, not otherwise found in England, used in DB to render a native term, stated on three occasions to be *(ge)bur* (8,10a and Hants. 1,10;23). The *coliberti* are found mainly in the Counties in Wessex and western Mercia, particularly in Wilts. and Somerset. Some of them at least seem to have held land and ploughs and paid various dues, as here and also in DB Herefords. 1,6. The only other occurrence of *coliberti* in Worcs. is 8,10a, see note. See also DB Oxon. 1,6 note.

MEADOW, 16 ACRES. In Urso's holding *acras* is accusative, no doubt a scribal error for *ac̄* (*acrae*).

8,8 WALTER PONTHER. See 2,5 note. His 1 hide is named in Evesham A 52 as *Bokindona* 'Bucknell Wood', lost in Besford; see EPNS p. 187.

IT IS...WASTE. Exceptionally it has a value; see also 9,6c and 21,1. Evesham A 52 has 'value 16s'. See DB Herefords. 6,1 note.

8,9a LONGDON. See 2,47 note. Evesham A 41;53-61 treats the holding differently. The 11 hides in lordship (8,9a) are at Longdon itself (A 41). Roger of Lacy's 5 hides (8,9g) are at Staunton (near Eldersfield, A 53, now in Glos. (GR SO 7829); see Sawyer (1) p. 14, VCH iv pp. 198-9). King William's 5 hides 3 virgates (8,9c) are divided between A 54 (5 hides at Eldersfield) and A 57 (3 virgates, see 8,9c note). Drogo's 1 hide (8,9d) is A 58, held by Alchere. William son of Baderon's 2½ hides (8,9f) are A 60 (the manor of Birtsmorton, VCH iv p. 30). The 5 hides held by Urso (8,9e) are represented by 2 hides at Chaceley (A 55; *Chaddesleia* in Evesham B, GR SO 8530, now in Glos.; see VCH iv p. 54); 1½ hides at Longdon A 56 (*Langeduna Osmundi* in Evesham B, now Chambers Court in Longdon, VCH iv p. 115); 1 hide held by Warengar (A 59) and ½ hide held by Robert (A 61). On this see Sawyer (1) p. 17.

30 HIDES. The 11 hides of lordship land and the 18 hides held TRE by 9 free men and

held in 1086 by Norman tenants total 29 hides. But the individual non-lordship holdings total 19 hides 1 virgate, in both DB and Evesham A. The 1 hide 1 virgate holding of Leofric (8,9g) seems to account for the excess.

,9b REINBALD. Reinbald *canceler* 'chancellor', see E 6 note below.
ALFWARD. Also *Eluuard, Aluuard* and *Eluuar* (8,9e note), OE *Aelfweard*.
AELFRIC. DB *Alfric*, PNDB p. 176; usually *Aluric* in DB, OE *Aelfric*.
GODRIC CLOCK. See OEB p. 304.

,9c KING WILLIAM HOLDS 5 HIDES AND 3 VIRGATES. The 5 hides are named at Eldersfield in Evesham A 54, and in C 104 (*Eadresfeld*); the remaining 3 virgates are probably at Pull Court in A 57. Both estates are named, but with different detail in DB Herefords. 1,44;46 (E 4;6 below).
[VALUE...]. The clause is omitted, perhaps because according to Evesham A 54 the 5 hides paid their dues in Hereford. See E 7 note below.

,9e URSO HOLDS 5 HIDES. Part was at Chaceley, part at Longdon, see 8,9a note above.
OF THE ABOVE. That is, of the 9 free men of 8,9b.
ALFWARD. DB *Eluuar* with the final *d* omitted, clearly the same man as *Eluuard* in 8,9b; see PNDB p. 181 and p. 410 (s.v. *-weard*).
8 MALE...SLAVES. *ii* interlined above *vi* as an addition.

,9g ROGER OF LACY HOLDS 5 HIDES. At Staunton, see 8,9a note above.

,10a POWICK. Evesham A 42;62-67;70 handle the details of the manor differently. Because neither Evesham A nor DB give full hidage details for subtenancies, it is difficult to make detailed comparisons. The 3 hides of A 42 correspond to 8,10a; Walter Ponther's estate (8,10d) is probably A 70 at Clevelode in Powick (GR SO 8247), see VCH iv pp. 186-7. Robert Parler's estate (A 63) was probably at Powick itself, the *Poiwica Inardi* of Evesham B (see 8,25 note). Urso's land (8,10b) is probably represented by A 62-66, individual parts being at Powick (A 62), Bransford (A 64), Madresfield (A 65, GR SO 8047, see VCH iv p. 119) and *Ad Bergam* (A 66). 1 hide of this land was at *Poiwicha Willelmi de Bello Campo*, in Evesham B, now Beauchamp Court in Powick, EPNS p. 224, VCH iv pp. 186-7. Gilbert son of Thorold's estate (8,10c) is probably A 67, Pixham (in Powick, GR SO 8348), although the values differ. The land of Arthur does not appear. *Ad Bergam* is probably 'Aggborough' a lost place in Madresfield, noted in EPNS p. 210 but without this reference. If derivation is from OE *ac* 'oak' and *beorg* 'hill', 'hillock', 'mound', 'grave-mound', the form found in Evesham A is an early confusion with the Latin preposition *ad*; see textual note to Evesham A 66.
3 HIDES. Also said to be 3 hides in Evesham A 42. But Urso's holding alone is said to be 5 hides in A 62. If Urso's land is 3 hides and the manor 5, the extra 2 hides would round up 'Westminster' Hundred to 200 hides, see App. I.
BOORS, FREEDMEN. Latin *Buri*, from OE *(ge)bur*, glossed in an interlineation as *coliberti*. The reverse occurs in Hants. (1,23), *vel bures* being interlined above *coliberti*; see 8,7 note above.
AETHELWARD. DB *Ageluuard*, clearly the same man as *Aeluuard* in 8,10b, despite the different spelling. From OE *Aethelweard*, PNDB p. 188.
KETELBERT. The occurrence of Ketelbern below (8,10c), clearly the same man, suggests alternative spellings of the same name, or perhaps a scribal error. For the latter entry, Evesham C 111 has *Ketelbertus*. Cf. *Osbertus* / *Osbernus* in Worcs. D (textual note 2 below) and Evesham C 14;46; also DB Devon Exon. Notes to Ch. 43.

,10b URSO HOLDS. See 8,10a note above.
AETHELWARD. See 8,10a note above.

,10c GILBERT SON OF THOROLD HOLDS. At Pixham, 8,10a note above.
KETELBERN. See 8,10a note above.

,10d WALTER PONTHER HOLDS. At Clevelode, see 8,10a note above.
½ PLOUGH. '2 ploughs' in lordship in Evesham A 70; no villagers' ploughs mentioned.

,10e 2 PLOUGHMEN. *bov'*, probably abbreviating *bovarios* 'ploughmen', see 1,1c note, rather than *boves* 'oxen', which VCH p. 301 has.

,11 (UPTON) SNODSBURY. DB *Snodęsbyrie*. Upton and Snodsbury were originally separate settlements, Upton here being included in the hidage of Snodsbury. The Abbot holds Upton *Stephani* in RBE p. 566 and Fees p. 139 and the Earl of Warwick (the Abbey's successor in some lands) holds the same Upton in FA v p. 305; see EPNS p. 230.
7 HIDES AND 1 VIRGATE...1 OF THESE HIDES... . *una virg'* and *hidis* have been interlined, the original text reading '7 hides, 1 of these has never paid tax'.
HAS NEVER PAID TAX. *nunq(uam) geld'* possibly 'never pays tax', since *geld'* can abbreviate *geldat* and *geldabat*; see 9,6a note below.
2 FRENCHMEN WHO SERVE. *Servientes* probably in the same sense as *faciebat*

servitium (e.g. 8,9b;14) rather than implying land held by serjeanty, on which see DB Leics. 13,63 note. There is, however, a possible equation between 1 Frenchman (10,16) and Evesham A 11's *quidam serviens*.
URSO HOLDS. The land was at Cowsden, GR SO 9453, (*Coulesduna*) in Evesham A 68, *Colleduma* in Evesham B; see VCH iv p. 210.

8,12 (MARTIN) HUSSINGTREE. Two separate villages merged in the 16th century, see EPNS p. 213. Edgar's charter of 972 (Ch. 8 note) grants 5 *mansae* at Martin and Hussingtree.
100 CARTLOADS OF TIMBER. See 2,48 note above.

8,13 DROITWICH. The 1 hide may have been in Clent Hundred with the rest of Droitwich, rather than regarded as an outlier of Pershore.
4 FURNACES. For boiling the water from the brine, perhaps not distinct from the *salinae*, see 1,3a note.
ST. PETER'S...TITHE AT DROITWICH. See *Regesta* i no. 166, a notification dated 1076-82 of various grants to St. Peter's, Westminster, including the 'tithe of all that the King holds in Droitwich'.

8,14 DORMSTON. Evesham A 69 and 71 seem to correspond in the number of ploughs and total value; the 2 hides of Albert were thus at *Pidelet*, North Piddle, see next note.

8,15 (NORTH) PIDDLE. *Piddle* is a river-name, Piddle Brook; see note 9,1a below, EPNS pp. 222, 155, 14 and DEPN s.n. Worcester, ERN s.n. Wyre for relevant discussion. The place 'Piddle' in 'Westminster' Hundred is North Piddle, FA v p. 305. DB *Pidelet* here and at 8,18 appears to contain the Norman-French diminutive *-et*, meaning 'Little' Piddle, presumably in contrast to Wyre Piddle (2,19 *Pidele*) in Oswaldslow Hundred, see EPNS p. 222. 'Little' must be supposed to refer not to the size of the holdings (*Pidelet* contains 9 hides and *Pidele* 5 hides), but to the size of the river. It may thus refer to an area rather than to a specific place. Dormston (8,14 and note) is some way from the modern North Piddle, but part of it was at *Pidelet*. Rivers often thus name holdings in Wilts. and Dorset DB and these are always difficult to locate precisely. The present land is said in Evesham A 72 and Evesham B to be at *Flavel* and *Pidelet* (Flyford Flavell and North Piddle); see VCH iv p. 83. In view of this, it must be asked whether the *-et* suffix form which appears in such instances (EPNS vol. 1 pt. 1 p. 94 and add *Barnjet* for Barming, Kent, PNK 133, KPN 8) and which has been identified with the French diminutive (R.E. Zachrissen 'Some English Place-Name Etymologies', *Studier i modern språkvetenskap* ix (1924) p. 127), should not rather be supposed the Norman French adoption of an OE collective suffix *-ett* (Place-Name Elements p. 160 s.v. *-et*). *Pidelet* would then more sensibly mean 'the Piddles, the places on, near or by Piddle, the Piddle district'.
5 HIDES. In the MS *ii hidę* was originally written, but corrected to *v hidę*. In Evesham A 72 these hides are held by Robert Parler, on whom see 8,25 note below.

8,16 ALFWARD, SAEWULF AND ALFWARD. In the Latin the names are added, apparently as an afterthought, after *TRE*, as in 8,9b and 8,26.
10 HIDES. *ibi x hide* is added in the left-hand margin.
3 HIDES AND 1 VIRGATE. '3 hides and 3 virgates' in Evesham A 73. Probably the manor of Sheriffs Naunton, VCH iv p. 145.

8,17 GRAFTON (FLYFORD). *Graftona Ebrandi* in Evesham B; see FA v p. 305; EPNS pp. 200-1.
2 HIDES, LESS 1 VIRGATE. '1 hide and 2 virgates' in Evesham A 74.
REAPED. *secabat* 'cut', which Evesham C 123 replaces by the more exact *falcabat* 'scythed'.
IN THE MEADOW. That is, in the meadow of his lord, *domini* being omitted; cf. 8,23.

8,18 (NORTH) PIDDLE. See 8,15 note.
4 HIDES. '3 hides' in Evesham A 75 and Evesham B (*Pidelet Radulfi*), the number of taxable hides.

8,19 6 HIDES. '6½ hides' in Evesham A 76.

8,20 GRAFTON (FLYFORD). See 8,17 note.

8,21 [VALUE...]. Apparently omitted in error.

8,22 IN THE SAME OUTLIER. That is, in Peopleton. In 8,21 Peopleton has not been said to be part of a manor; the implication is that all Ch. 8 lands are regarded as outliers of the manor of Pershore, see Ch. 8 note.
THE ½ HIDE HAS NEVER PAID TAX. In Evesham C 128, the 3½ hides did not pay tax, probably a careless misreading of DB.
THE OTHER ALFWY HELD 1 HIDE. In the MS a gap of about 7 letters follows, due to an erasure. Farley does not always print such gaps. The 'other Alfwy' may be Alfwy Black, 8,9b.

WULFRIC. There is no mention of who holds his land.
NOTHING THERE EXCEPT 2 ACRES OF MEADOW. The rest of the hide is presumably waste.
VALUE OF WHAT WALTER HOLDS 50s. Transposition signs direct the phrase to its proper place following the 'meadow, 10 acres'.

,23 COMBERTON. Included Little Comberton and a part of Great Comberton, VCH iv pp. 57;61; see 8,27.
ONE OUTLIER OF 10 HIDES. Named in Evesham A 80 as *Strenchesham* (Strensham GR SO 9039); VCH iv pp. 203-5.

,23-4 SERVED LIKE THE OTHERS. Like Alfwy and Wulfric of 8,22 and Edric of 8,23.

,24 BROUGHTON (HACKETT). *Brocton Inardi* in Evesham B; see next note.

,25 ROBERT PARLER. For the byname see OEB p. 263 and compare Reaney s.n. Parlour. Robert and his descendants held other church land of which Urso was legal or illegal tenant in 1086. A Robert Parler holds North Piddle in Evesham A 72 (= DB 8,15) and a part of Powick is called *pars Roberti Parlere* in Evesham A 63. A descendant of Robert was *Isnard* or *Inard* Parler who holds what is probably this same part of Powick in Evesham B (8,10a note). Hampton Lovett (26,17) is *Hamtun quam Inard Parler tenet* in Evesham D 1. Other places held by Urso in DB are named after Inard Parler in Evesham B: *Brocton Inardi* (Broughton Hackett 8,24) and *Wicha Inardi* (Wick 8,2). Innerstone (see EPNS p. 157 and 2,25 note), probably has the same origin. For a discussion of *Inard*, OG *Isenard*, see EENS p. 55.
A PIECE OF LAND. *Frustum terrae*, an unusual expression, probably indicating that it had not been, or was not known to have been, hidated.
APPEAR IN THE HUNDRED. *Pergit* means 'goes', 'proceeds', 'travels', implying that this land is not represented at meetings or courts of the Hundreds and that it pays no dues or services. RMLWL s.v. *pergo* suggests 'pay suit'; Round in VCH i p. 303 has 'nor owes services at the Hundred court'. In DB Herefords. 1,72 ('Newarne') 2½ hides are said to have 'met' or 'come to Hundred meetings' (*conveniebant*), and in Herefords. C 3 a horse owner went (*pergebat*) to hear pleas and to Hundred meetings.
WITHOUT...LIVESTOCK. *Pecunia* normally means 'cattle' (= *animalia*) in DB, its original Latin meaning (from *pecus* 'herd'), rather than 'money'. It possibly refers here to the plough oxen. Elsewhere in DB it sometimes has the sense 'resources'.

,26a ALFRED OF MARLBOROUGH. Lord of Ewyas Harold in Herefords. (Ch. 19; see note).
(SEVERN) STOKE. Clearly in 'Westminster' Hundred in DB, but 12 hides are included in Esch Hundred in Evesham A 17 (as *Stokes Roberti*); a further 3 hides are also listed in Esch Hundred but *de feudo Westmonasterii*. Boselin's land appears in Pershore Hundred in Evesham A 82.
ALFWARD AND WULFRIC. The names appear after *TRE*, apparently as an afterthought, see 8,16 note.

,26b AND PAY. Or 'it (the hide) pays': *redd't* abbreviates both *reddit* (singular) and *reddunt* (plural); see 2,51 note above.

,26c IN TOTAL, VALUE. That is, the total value of 8,26a,b,c.

,27 COMBERTON. The estate was later known as West Green, VCH iv p. 58.
AZOR. From ODan *Azur*, see OEB p. 172 s.n. *filius Azer*. Evesham C 138 has *Artur*, an interesting instance of rationalisation of a misunderstood reading (probably *Azzur*). An Arthur appears in 8,10e.
NOW 20s. Evesham A 83 has '10s'.

,28 £83. In the MS and facsimile $\overset{a}{q}t$; Farley omits the abbreviation sign over the *q*.

h. 9 ST. MARY'S OF PERSHORE. Pershore Abbey. Its 100 hides, with the 200 hides of Westminster Abbey (Ch. 8), form the triple Hundred of Pershore which had all belonged formerly to Pershore Abbey, see Ch. 8 note and App. I.

,1a PERSHORE. Evesham A 149-156 arranges the matter differently, detailing each outlier in turn and supplying additional information. The hidage it gives for the outliers is: Chivington 3 hides; Wick ½ hide; Abberton 6½ hides, value 25s; Drakes Broughton 3 hides (1 free); Wadborough 5 hides. Urso's 1½ hides (9,1b) held by *Acerus* were at Comberton (so also in Evesham B). They are said to be held from the King. See Sawyer (1) pp. 18-20.
(DRAKES) BROUGHTON. Apparently represented in Evesham B by the nearby Walcot (GR SO 9448) and Thorndon Farm (SO 9149), *Walecote* and *Torendune*.
AT (WYRE) PIDDLE. Or 'on the (River) Piddle'. DB *Pidele*, distinguished from North Piddle (*Pidelet*), see 2,19 and 8,15 notes. Wyre Piddle is adjacent to Pershore though held in DB by the Bishop of Worcester.

,1b IN ACKNOWLEDGEMENT. See 2,71 note.

ONE REVENUE OR 20s. *Firma* here is a fixed amount in kind, generally commuted to money. Cf. 'one night's revenue', DB Somerset 1,2 note.
A YEAR. *in anno* governs both the 'one revenue' and the '20s'.
ON THE DAY OF KING EDWARD'S DEATH. 5th January 1066.

9,1d ROBERT THE BURSAR. See 2,13 note.
A PARK. See E 3 note below.
LORDSHIP VILLAGERS. That is, those on the lordship land, 24 of them in 1086; see 9,1a.

9,1e WADBOROUGH. Evesham A 153 gives the same story.
COW PASTURAGE. *uaccaria*; see RMLWL s.v. *vacca*.
LIFE-SPAN OF THREE HEIRS. That is, of Godric and his two succeeding heirs; a common type of lease. Cf. 'lives of 3 men' in 23,1 below.
ONE REVENUE. See 9,1b note above.

9,2 OPEN LAND AND WOOD. See 8,6 note.

9,3 ALDERMINSTER. Now in Warwickshire, DB *Sture*; *stura* in Evesham A 158, but in the right-hand margin is *scilicet Aldremanestun' xx hide*. Alderminster is a 15th century corruption of Aldermanneston, EPNS p. 184. The early documents of the Worcestershire Churches consistently distinguish between *Sture in Ismere*, the river of Stourport, and *Sture* without suffix, the Warwickshire river. The use of a river name for a town is especially common in DB Wilts., Devon and Dorset.
11 PLOUGHS. '9 ploughs' in Evesham A 158.
1 MAN-AT-ARMS. Rare in Worcs. DB.
2 HIDES. Probably at Goldicote (GR SP 2451), VCH iv p. 8.
THIS LAND PAYS TAX. Farley's text does not show that this addition is almost entirely written in the right-hand margin of column 175b, sloping slightly downwards, the *h'* (*haec*) falling below the last stroke of the *xvii* (the value of the mills) two lines above. The scribe seems to be the same as for the main entry.

9,4 ABBOT EDMUND. Abbot of Pershore; died 1085.
CLAIMS BACK THIS LAND. Evesham A 160 says 'Urso claims these 4 hides mentioned above'. Besides the 2½ hides here, he is said in Evesham A 155 to claim land held by Leofwin the priest. The value in A 160 is that of the 2½ hides, however.
EXCHANGED. The land involved is unknown. Evesham A 160 says 'he exchanged them... for the land of which he has now been dispossessed'.

9,5a LEIGH. *Lega Ricardi* in Evesham B.
3 HIDES. The detail amounts to 3½ in 9,5a-c.

9,5b 1½ HIDES. Probably the manor of Braces Leigh (GR SO 7950), VCH iv p. 104.

9,5c BRANSFORD. According to Evesham N 2, Bransford and Acton Beauchamp (11,1) were given by Abbot Aethelwig of Evesham to Urso in exchange for Bengeworth (10,11-12 note).
THE COUNTY. That is, the County Court. The singular *dicit comitatus* slips naturally to the plural *nesciunt*.
ABBOT OF EVESHAM. *Abb'* can abbreviate *Abbas* or *Abbatia* 'Abbot' or 'Abbey'; if the former, it refers to Aethelwig who succeeded Manni in 1058 when the latter was seized by paralysis (*Chronicon* p. 87). Manni is said to have died on the same day as King Edward the Confessor, 5th January 1066 (*Chronicon* p. 88).
ON THE DAY OF KING EDWARD'S DEATH. See note above.

9,6a DOES NOT PAY TAX. *non geld'*, perhaps 'did not pay tax', since *geld'* can abbreviate both the present *geldat* and the past *geldabat*, see 8,11 note.
IN HEREFORDSHIRE. DB Herefords. 10,39 and 23,6 record parts of Mathon: ½ hide held by Roger of Lacy and ½ hide by Drogo son of Poyntz, both held before 1066 by thanes of Earl Oda. Mathon was for centuries a westward projection of Worcestershire. If 'Bagburrow' (DB Herefords. 2,28 = E 25) is correctly identified, Mathon will in 1086 have been divided from Worcestershire by a part of the Herefordshire Hundred of Winstree, thus forming a detached portion of the County. The Worcestershire part of the parish was transferred to Herefordshire in 1897. On Earl Oda see E 4 note.
THE COUNTY. See 9,5c note above.

9,6c WASTE. VALUE 5s. Waste land sometimes has a value, see 8,8 note above.

9,7 THE COUNTY STATES. The whole entry, preceded by a gallows sign, is written in a smaller version of the main hand: probably added later.
CHURCH TAX. See 2,21 note above.
ALL THE 300 HIDES. That is, the former possessions of the Church of Pershore, now divided with Westminster Church, see Ch. 8 note. Mathon (9,6), being in Doddingtree Hundred, is not included in the 300 hides.
DATE SHOULD BE MISSED. *dies fractus fuerit*, literally 'the day should be broken';

i.e. should he fail to pay corn on the day due. Cf. 2,80.
FIRST HE SHALL PAY WHAT HE OWES. The packload of corn first agreed.

Ch. 10 THE ABBEY OF EVESHAM had difficulty in retaining its lands under William I in the face of claims from Worcester Church and the depredations of Urso and Odo of Bayeux. Abbot Manni was crippled by paralysis in 1058 (see 9,5c note above) and was succeeded by the powerful Aethelwig (Alwin in DB), who acquired many lands for the Abbey (list in the *Chronicon* p. 95). He died in 1077 and his successor Walter found his authority and his ownership of lands under immediate attack, see 10,11-12 note and Worcs. H in App. V. A later survey of the Evesham manors taken *c.* 1104 is in Evesham J, App. IV.

10,1 [IN FISHBOROUGH HUNDRED]. The heading is implied in 10,2, all the places in 10,1-10 being in this Hundred.
3 FREE HIDES. The rest of the line is blank after this in the MS. The parchment is roughed up here, with a triangular mark after *liberę*; it is not possible to tell whether the scribe intended to fill the gap later.

10,2 FISHBOROUGH HUNDRED. An ecclesiastical Hundred consisting of 65 hides and 12 acres of the lands of Evesham Abbey, and forming, apart from Oldberrow and Ombersley, a compact area around Evesham. The total hidage given to Fishborough in Evesham A 18-32 (omitting A 30 Bengeworth which should be in Oswaldslow) is 65 hides 2 virgates; the two additional virgates are at Littleton, A 21. Evesham A has 1 hide more at Offenham, but 1 hide less at Badsey. DB notes that the Hundred is made up to 100 hides by additions that do not belong to Evesham; see App. I.
OF THESE, 12 HIDES ARE FREE. They are at Evesham (10,1) 3 hides; Lenchwick (10,3) 1 hide; Offenham (10,5) 1 hide; Aldington (10,5) 1 hide; Wickhamford (10,6) 3 hides; Ombersley (10,10) 3 hides.
20 HIDES OF DODDINGTREE. They are not detailed, see App. I.
15 HIDES OF WORCESTER. Cities and Boroughs are normally allotted a notional number of hides in DB, the figure being sometimes stated as for Droitwich (15,10 note), sometimes being necessary to make up the total for the Hundred.

10,3 LENCHWICK...NORTON. The context implies the parish of Norton near Evesham. Evesham A 20 treats Norton separately, but the entry for Lenchwick (A 19) includes the ploughs and value for both.
2,000 EELS. That is, 80 sticks.
VALUE BEFORE 1066 £7. The gap printed by Farley is caused by a tear in the parchment, with perhaps one or two letters erased before it; Farley does not print the gap caused by the same tear on the other side of the folio (9,4 after *xlii vill' cū*).

10,4 OLDBERROW...12 ACRES. A detached portion of Fishborough Hundred, now in Warwickshire. The modern parish, mapped in this edition, is considerably larger.
COUNTRYMEN, PIGMEN. *Rustici*, presumably a noun in apposition to *porcarii*, defining their status (see 2,57 note); as an adjective, 'rustic', 'rural', it would be otiose.

10,5 THE CHURCH ITSELF HOLDS. Repeated at the beginning of 10,5-16.
OFFENHAM...LITTLETON...BRETFORTON...ALDINGTON. Evesham A 21-24 arranges the details differently. For Offenham, A 22 gives 2 hides, one of them free, where DB lists only 1 free hide. From Evesham A 22 it is evident that the 3 ploughs in lordship and the 7 villagers' ploughs were at Offenham, and the 1086 value in DB is that for Offenham. DB omits ½ hide at Littleton (A 21), 2 lordship ploughs and the present value, 70s. Evesham A 21 has 8 men's ploughs at Littleton, DB has 4 ploughs at a place unspecified, held by 2 riders and 2 Frenchmen. Bretforton's 6 hides are said by Evesham A 24 to belong to Aldington, confirmed by later evidence; see Sawyer (1) pp. 16-17 and VCH ii p. 355.
LITTLETON. The foundation grant (ECWM p. 88 no. 10 = BCS 125 = Sawyer (2) 80) of 13 *mansae* is accounted for by this Littleton and the entry at 10,8. The grant was said to have contained 3 Littletons, *Chronicon* p. 71. The present entry is probably South Littleton, closest to Offerton; those at 10,8 were probably Middle and North Littleton; see VCH ii p. 409.
OXEN FOR 1 PLOUGH. Usually 8; see 1,1c note above.
THEY DRAW STONE TO THE CHURCH. An exceptional entry. The earliest parts of Offenham church seem to be 15th century; those of Bretforton and Littleton, 13th century (VCH ii pp. 423, 364, 410). While there may have been earlier churches on these sites, the stone was probably being taken to the nearby Abbey Church of Evesham. It had been largely rebuilt in 1044-58 by Abbot Manni, being consecrated in *c.* 1053 (ASC p. 184), but it was still being renewed and extended under Abbot Walter; see VCH ii p. 386 and the *Chronicon* p. 55. The latter (p. 97) records of Abbot Walter: *fecit etiam cryptas et*

ecclesiam superius usque ad navem, excepta turri, quam non perfecit nisi arcus et primas fenestras.

10,7 BADSEY. Evesham A 32, a later addition in a different hand, allots 5½ hides to the village and 4 ploughs to the villagers.
2 PLOUGHS. A gap of about 12 letters follows, before the villagers, due to an erasure.

10,8 LITTLETON. See 10,5 note.
VALUE...70s. Evesham A 27 has 'value 50s'.

10,10 THE CHARTERS OF THE CHURCH. See ECWM nos. 201 and 11, pp. 87, 89 (= BCS 116,130; Sawyer (2) 54,1250) for early grants of immunity in Ombersley.
BOTH WOOD AND OPEN LAND. See 8,6 note.
2,000 EELS. See 10,3 note.
VALUE...NOW £16. Evesham A 29 adds '*et Burgones xx solidos*'. *Burgones* is a difficult word; it is not found in RMLWL and only occurs in Ducange in the sense of 'sheepfold', a meaning unlikely here. It could originate in a badly written form of OE *burgmen* plural of *burgmann*, 'a burgher', 'a man who lives in a *burh* or town'. It could equally be a mistaken form of *burgenses*, 'burgesses' written *burgēses*: the nunnation mark would have been lost and a poorly written *e* read as an *o* and insular *s* as *n*. But this does not fully resolve the problem, since the DB entry has no mention of burgesses. It is possible, however, that they were in Droitwich, which is adjacent and is mentioned in the entry.

10,11-12 OSWALDSLOW HUNDRED...HAMPTON...BENGEWORTH. 2,74-5 (see notes above) record the Bishop of Worcester holding 5 hides at Hampton and 4 hides at Bengeworth as tenant in chief, with the Abbot as sub-tenant. Only the hidage is there given, the details being entered here. This compromise, affecting the disputed parts of the two lands, was finally arranged before the Domesday Commissioners (see Worcs. H in App. V) to the effect that the two lands belonged tenurially to Evesham, but fiscally and juridically to Worcester Church; for the latter reason they are counted in the Bishop's Hundred of Oswaldslow (see Bigelow p. 288). Evesham A 30-31 reflects the delicacy of the arrangement by apparently including the 4 hides of Bengeworth in Fishborough Hundred.

The immediate dispute had involved Hampton and Bengeworth and some houses in Worcester; but the rival claims were much older and involved more lands; see VCH ii p. 397f; *Chronicon* pp. 95-97; Hemming (126r (= 127r); Hearne p. 270ff.). Both the Abbey and the Church claimed rival foundation grants, and neither was above forgery. Evesham claimed a grant of Coenred, King of Mercia, of 708 (*Chronicon* p. 72) or of Coenred and Offa (King of the East Angles) of 709 (ECWM no. 10 p. 88 = BCS 125 = Sawyer (2) 80), giving them 9 *mansae* at Bengeworth and Hampton. Worcester, on the other hand maintained that the land was part of Cropthorne, granted by Offa of Mercia in 780 (2,72 note). A later group of doubtful charters (ECWM 340, 344, 354-5 pp. 127-129 = Harmer 48 = KCD 938, 911, 941 = Sawyer (2) 991, 1223, 1052, 1398) seem to give Evesham Abbey land and rights at Hampton and Bengeworth, two of them attested by Worcester Bishops.

The dispute lasted throughout William's reign. DB records an uneasy compromise in 1066, the 5 hides of Hampton paying only tax to the Bishop in Oswaldslow Hundred, all other services and dues being discharged at Evesham. The compromise reached in 1086 was preceded by a number of stages. On the death of Abbot Aethelwig (1077), according to the *Chronicon* his successor Walter was unwilling to accept the homage of a number of men who had held Evesham lands from Aethelwig, but hoped instead to secure their lands. These men turned to Odo, Bishop of Bayeux and half-brother of the King, and he, on the King's instruction, held a court at *Ildeberga* (see note below) to judge the case. Instead of awarding the lands to the Abbey, or to its tenants, he awarded them to himself and succeeded by this means in acquiring 28 villages. Of these, Walter succeeded in recovering Bengeworth and Hampton (and other lands mentioned below) and may briefly have enjoyed full possession and all rights. It is to this stage that Walter's proving of his right to 5 hides at Bengeworth recorded in DB 10,12 probably belongs (*Chronicon* p. 96; Bigelow p. 20).

It is unlikely that Odo can have awarded himself lands of Evesham Abbey at a judicial enquiry in the simple way that the aggrieved writer of the *Chronicon* suggests; it is more likely (as Hemming folio 127r (= 128r), Hearne p. 273 suggests) that Odo seized the lands on the death of Aethelwig and that the enquiry at *Ildeberga* was about their return. The *Chronicon* (p. 97) refers to the recovery in these terms: *de hiis [terris] vero, Walterus Abbas Westune, Hamptune et medietatem de Beningwrthe (quam Ernegrim tenuit) revocavit; medietatem vero, quam episcopus dedit Assere, occupavit Urso*. Arngrim's 5 hides were the 5 proved by Walter, *Assere* is the Azor of DB 2,75, the 1066 holder of 5 of the 6 hides held there by Urso in 1086.

British Library MS Cotton Vespasian B xxiv folio 28 contains two writs relating to these restorations (calendared in *Regesta* i 185-6, printed in the *Chronicon* p. xlviii). The first is from William to Archbishop Lanfranc and Odo and confirms on Evesham Abbey, Weston and Swell (in Glos.) and Bengeworth 'and other lands'. The second is from Odo himself to Wulfstan (Bishop of Worcester) and Urso, Durand and Walter, Sheriffs of Worcestershire, Gloucestershire and Warwickshire, explaining that William has confirmed on Evesham Abbey the lands that the Abbot proved before 7 shires (*sic*; '5 shires' in *Chronicon* p. 97, '4 shires' in DB 10,12): Weston, Swell, Bengeworth, Bevington, Wixford, Oldberrow, Kinwarton, Hillborough and Ragley. Hemming (folio 127r (= 128r), Hearne p. 273), telling the tale from the Worcester viewpoint, says that Odo sought from his half-brother King William all the lands which Aethelwig had held, apart from those that rightly belonged to the Abbey, and in the process acquired the lands Acton, Eastbury, Bengeworth etc. (see below) that Aethelwig had himself acquired from Worcester Church.

The outcome of this plea at *Ildeberga* did not please Bishop Wulfstan (see Worcs. G 28 in App. V) and further litigation ensued: (a) a hearing, probably in Worcester itself, before Geoffrey, Bishop of Coutances, at which the Abbot acknowledged a number of Worcester Church rights over the lands; (b) an attempt by the Bishop to persuade the Domesday Commissioners that Hampton and Bengeworth were of his lordship (these stages are discussed in Worcs. H, App. V below).

Earlier in William's reign, other lands had been involved in the dispute between Church and Abbey. Hemming (folio 126v (= 127v), Hearne p. 270ff.) contended that both Aethelwig and Wulfstan had enjoyed the King's support, but that while Wulfstan was interested in spiritual matters, Aethelwig had used his power to the disadvantage of the rival Church, acquiring Acton Beauchamp, Eastbury (2,69), Bengeworth, some houses in Worcester and Milcot and Weston in Warwickshire from the monks, as well as Evenlode and Daylesford (2,42-44) from the Bishop. The *Chronicon* (p. 95) admits that Evesham obtained these lands, but claims that Worcester Church had earlier seized them from the Abbey along with Stratford on Avon (DB Warwicks. 3,2) and Fladbury (2,15) which the Abbey never recovered. Bengeworth was acquired by Aethelwig from Urso in exchange for Acton Beauchamp and Bransford (see 11,1 note).

Some of these lands were among the 28 villages said to have been taken from the Abbey by Odo and which were never recovered. These are listed in Evesham N (in App. IV) and in the *Chronicon* (p. 97). The lists differ, the *Chronicon* adding Ragley, Temple Grafton, a second Chastleton, a second Salford and two Milcotes. In Evesham N, Lower Swell, Upper Slaughter and Childswickham seem to displace *Hudicote* (Hidcote Boyce), *Stoke* (Lark Stoke) and *Westun* (Weston on Avon) in the *Chronicon's* list. Two of these lands, Acton Beauchamp and Sheriffs Lench, are found in the Bishop of Bayeux's fief (11,1-2); others fell into other hands.

10,11 7 PLOUGHS. '6 ploughs' in Evesham A 31.
A YOUNG VINEYARD. *vinea novella*. The phrase is classical, *vineas novellas alligato crebro*, Cato *de Agricultura* 33,4.

10,12 ABBOT WALTER. Abbot of Evesham 1077-1104. The chronology of the Evesham Abbots is difficult; it is discussed in VCH i p. 264 by Round, and corrected in VCH ii p. 126. The dates quoted in older sources for Walter's death vary from 1084 to 1104. He is found as a witness to documents dating from the last years of the 11th century and the first years of the 12th. The earlier date for his death, found in the *Chronicon* and Round, is probably based on a misunderstanding of DB 26,16 'Abbot Walter...held it for more than 7 years', which records the length of Walter's tenure of Hampton Lovett prior to Urso's acquisition of it; not the time from his accession to his death.
ILDEBERGA. *Gildeneberga* in the *Chronicon* (p. 97); *Gildbeorh* in ECWM no. 118 (= BCS 1238 = KCD 1362 = Sawyer (2) 1325). In the Charter it appears in the bounds of Evenlode, on the road between Moreton in the Marsh and the four stones which preceded the present 4 shires stone and probably the 4 shires themselves (Dr. J. Morris in DB Warwicks. 3,14 note; EPNS (Worcs.) p. 124 and EPNS (Glos.) i p. 219; VCH (Worcs.) i p. 307 note 3). Until the 1931 boundary changes, the 4 shires which met here were Worcs., Warwicks., Glos., and Oxon. In DB Warwicks. 3,4 Bishop Wulfstan is reported as establishing his claim to part of Alveston before Queen Matilda (wife of King William, died 1083), in the presence of four sheriffdoms, probably on the same site.
THE BISHOP OF BAYEUX. See Ch. 11 note.

10,13 RANULF. Brother of Abbot Walter, Worcs. H 2 (in App. V) and VCH i p. 307.

10,14 ATCH LENCH. '3½ hides' in Evesham A 12, the current value being 20s. See Evesham P textual note 6a (in App. IV).

10,15 BEVINGTON. See 10,11-12 note. Wood Bevington and Cock Bevington are in Warwickshire, Bevington Waste partly in Warwicks., partly in Worcs., see EPNS (Worcs.) p. 331; (Warwicks.) pp. 220-1. The 1086 boundary may have been in a different place. Wood and

Cock Bevington, as members of Salford Priors, were held by Evesham Abbey (VCH Warwicks. iii p. 160) whose holdings thus spanned the County boundary.

10,16 CHURCH LENCH. Evesham D 5, J 10, P 17 and the *Chronicon* p. 97 record Urso as holding land here from Walter, a fact omitted by DB, unless the arrangement was made after 1086; see Evesham P introduction.
1 FRENCHMAN. Seemingly the *quidam serviens* of Evesham A 11.

10,17 DWELLINGS. Probably houses, but *masura, mansura* can include a group of buildings, see DB Wilts. M 1 col. 64c 'In...Malmesbury...25 dwellings (*masuras*) in which are houses (*domus*)'. *Masurae* also occur in 23,12. See DB Somerset 26,6 note, Ellis i p. 244 and RMLWL s.v. *mansa*.

Ch.11 BISHOP OF BAYEUX. Odo, half-brother of King William and elder brother of Robert, Count of Mortain. He was Earl of Kent from 1066/7-1082, then from 1087-88, and 'regent' during some of King William's absences abroad, notably in 1067 with Earl William of Hereford. At the time when DB was written he was in prison in Rouen, and many of his lands (as here and in Gloucestershire) were forfeited to the King. He was released by King William on his deathbed in 1087, returned to England, but rebelled against William Rufus, was defeated in 1088 and all his lands in England were confiscated. He fled to Normandy, dying in 1097. Bayeux is in the département of Calvados, France.
Both his lands in Worcestershire were obtained from Evesham Church. He had removed other lands from the Church, some of which he gave to Urso, see 10,11-12 note and Evesham D and N.

11,1 HELD. Odo's confiscated fief had not yet been granted afresh.
IN EXCHANGE. According to Evesham D 2, Abbot Aethelwig gave the land to Urso in exchange for land he had seized at Bengeworth, the latter being nearer to the Abbey. On the death of Aethelwig, Urso repossessed Bengeworth also. Evesham N 2 adds that the exchange included Bransford as well (9,5c). The *Chronicon* echoes this latter version, saying (p. 95) *has duas villas* [*Brainesford, Actune*] *dedit Ursoni pro Beningwrthe quam injuste occupavit, sicut medietatem iterum postea fecit et omnes tres iniuste detinet.* The monks of Worcester claimed that Aethelwig had first dispossessed them of Acton, before Urso seized it from the Abbot, Worcs. G 2 (in App. V).
The gap of about 2 letters after *excābitionē*, is due to an erasure.

11,2 (SHERIFFS) LENCH. So called from Urso the Sheriff, VCH i p. 290; EPNS p. 331; VCH iii p. 46. It is *Lenz Bernardi* in Evesham A 4 and D 4, the current value in the former being given as 40s.
CHURCH OF EVESHAM. DB records a grant of 2 hides by Gilbert son of Thorold; Evesham D 4 records this as a purchase by Aethelwig. The other 2 hides belonged to the Church before 1066. See also Evesham N 3.
EARL WILLIAM. See 1,1b note.
ABBOT ALFWY. The same man as Alwin, 26,15-16; *Ageluuius* in the *Chronicon*, and *Aethelwig* of ASC, the last form being the one preferred in these notes.
1 GOLD MARK. Usually reckoned at £6.
COLLECTED THE GOLD FOR THE KING'S USE. *recepit*, usually translated 'acquired' in this edition; the context however demands 'collected' or 'received'. See DB Somerset 1,14 note.

Ch.12 ST. GUTHLAC'S. The Priory of St. Guthlac's in Hereford.

12,1 NIGEL THE DOCTOR. One of King William's doctors and possibly also doctor to Earl Roger of Shrewsbury (Mon. Ang. vi p. 750, but see VCH Shrops. i p. 290). He also held land once belonging to St. Guthlac's in DB Herefords. Ch. 7.

12,2 THIS ENTRY is written later, below the marginal rulings, at the foot of column 176c exdented into the left-hand margin by about 3 letters. Transposition signs indicate its correct position.

Ch.13 THE CHAPTER HEADING IS OMITTED. The *presbiteri* of 13,1 are styled *clerici* in the list of landholders (col. 172a). A Hundred heading, Clent, needs to be understood from 12,1 in the absence of a chapter heading.

Ch.14 EARL ROGER. Roger of Montgomery, Earl of Shrewsbury from 1074 until his death in 1094.
IN BOTH ENTRIES FOR THIS CHAPTER there is a gap of about 13 letters after the number of hides, possibly for a fraction or for *geld(antes)*, see Worcs. D in App. V.

14,1 HALESOWEN. See 23,6 and E 8 notes.

1½ HIDES...FROM THE EARL. The ½ hide seems to have been an afterthought. This part of the manor was probably at Romsley (GR SO 9679), VCH iii p. 145.

14,2 SALWARPE. See E 8 note.
ALWIN YOUNG. *cilt*, from OE *cild*, 'childe', 'born to an inheritance', 'well-born', 'a young nobleman'. See OEB p. 244. He was son of Godwin and nephew of Earl Leofric; he repudiated his father's will restoring the estate to Worcester Church, see Worcs. G 14 in App. V.
PARK. See 5,1 note above.

Ch.15 RALPH OF TOSNY. Ralph III, also called Ralph of Conches (see 15,6 note). He was son of Roger I of Tosny and brother-in-law of William son of Osbern (Douglas p. 86). He was lord of Clifford Castle in Hereford, his chief seat being at Flamstead in Hertfordshire (DB Herts. 22,1). He died some time before March 1102. Tosny and Conches are in the département of Eure, France. Placenames in Toney, e.g. Newton Toney in Wilts., are named after his descendants.

15,1 WORSLEY. Identified by VCH iv p. 234 as Wordley in Astley, but see EPNS p. 37 note 1.

15,2 'LINDON'. DB *Linde*. In Rock. It lay to the north-east of the parish, but has not been precisely located; see EPNS pp. 57,63; VCH iv p. 323.
EARL ALGAR. Earl of East Anglia 1051-52 and 1053-57, then Earl of Mercia 1057-62. He was outlawed in 1055 and again in 1058, but won back his position on each occasion with the help of Gruffydd ap Llywelyn, King of Gwynedd and Powys. Algar was the son of Earl Leofric and the Lady (Countess) Godiva; father of Earls Edwin and Morcar; died *c.* 1062.

15,3 *HALAC*. Probably in Rock parish, see VCH iv p. 320.
2 PLOUGHS POSSIBLE. The transposition sign for 12,2 is next to this line, not, as Farley prints it, on the line below; but though displaced from its normal position in the manorial details, this addition belongs with 15,3 rather than with 12,1.

15,4 RALPH ALSO HOLDS. Repeated at the beginning of 15,4-9;11-14.
ALTON. Acquired from Worcester Church, see Worcs. G 9 in App. V.

15,5;7 ROCKMOOR. DB *More*, formerly Moor in Rock, held as *Mora Hugonis* by Roger *de Toeney* in Evesham B. This land is later known as the manor of Cheney's More, VCH iv p. 322.

15,6 BAYTON. Included the manors of Shakenhurst (GR SO 6773) and 'Tymberlake', VCH iv p. 238. A 'hay' (see 2,7 note above) is mentioned in Bayton in the grant of Alton (15,4) 'with its church and all his forest of Wyre and all he had therein save his hedged enclosure (*haia*) at *Beitone*' by 'Ralph *de Conchis* son of Roger of Tosny' to the Abbey of St. Evroul; Round CDF no. 625 p. 219.

15,7 ROCKMOOR. See 15,5 note.

15,9 ASTLEY. Taken from Worcester Church, Worcs. G 10 (in App. V). In 1210-12 William of Beauchamp held Shrawley (GR SO 8064) from Ralph *de Toeni* (RBE p. 567), possibly a part of this holding of Astley, to which it is adjacent.
ST. TAURIN'S CHURCH. In Evreux, département of Eure, France. For the grant see Round CDF no. 316 p. 106.
WOODLAND, 1 LEAGUE...WIDE. Entered in the right-hand margin; probably, but not certainly, the same woodland as that which pays nothing.

15,10 REDMARLEY. See 2,25 note. This is probably the later manor of Redmarley Oliver, VCH iv p. 373; see 20,2 note. Land at this Redmarley (*iuxta Duddantreo sita*) seems to have been held by Worcester Church, Worcs. G 7 (in App. V), in addition to its other land at Redmarley d'Abitot in the south of the County. The Doddingtree Hundred Redmarley was later seized by Urso, but DB records no holding of his there, though he held 1 hide of the adjacent Astley.
VALUE BEFORE 1066, 30s. In the MS an 7 has been added, later and in error, between *valb'* and *xxx*.

15,11 RALPH ALSO HOLDS. See 15,4 note above.
SHELSLEY. Shelsley Beauchamp, the entry at 19,6 being Shelsley Walsh, see VCH iv p. 332. A third Shelsley, Shelsley Kings, was part of the royal manor of Martley, see X 3, E 1 and EPNS p. 77.
13 SMALLHOLDERS. Followed by a gap of about 11 letters, due to an erasure; a line has been drawn to link the smallholders with their ploughs.

15,12 EASTHAM AND 'BASTWOOD'. Formerly Worcester Church land, Worcs. G 4 (in App. V).
'BASTWOOD'. DB *Bestewde* lay in the part of Eastham parish that is to the east of Piper's Brook, the site of the manor being that of the present Eastham Grange; VCH iv p. 270, EPNS p. 48.
3 HIDES. Followed by a gap of about 7 letters, see Ch. 14 note and Worcs. D in App. V.

15,13 QUEEN EDITH. Wife of King Edward the Confessor, daughter of Earl Godwin (19,12 note). She died in 1075.

15,14 OR LAND. *vel terra* is entered below the marginal rulings.
THE 10 HIDES WHICH PAY TAX. Boroughs are often notionally assessed in hides to complete the hundredal organisation of a County, see 10,2 note and App. III. The 10 hides of Droitwich are represented by the entries at 1,7. 4,1. 5,1. 7,1. 8,13. 12,1. 15,14. 18,6. 22,1. 24,1. 26,16. The 1 hide of Westminster Abbey (8,13) is, however, said not to pay tax. The 10 hides reappear in a later survey of Droitwich discussed as Evesham Q in App. IV below.

Ch.16 RALPH OF MORTIMER. Son of Roger of Mortimer, he received a number of estates forfeited by Roger son of William (son of Osbern) in 1074, including Wigmore Castle in Hereford (DB Herefords. 9,1) which became his seat. Mortemer is in the département of Seine-Maritime, France; see OEB pp. 101-2.

16,1 SODINGTON. DB *Sudtune*, in Fees pp. 140,527 it is *Suthinton*; see VCH i p. 311 note 3, EPNS p. 60.
1 HIDE. A gap of about 7 letters follows, see Ch. 14 note.

16,3 *BROC*. A lost place, possibly part of Sodington (16,1) with which it is associated in RBE p. 567 and Fees p. 140, *Suthinton* and *Brok* there being held by Roger *de Mortuo Mari*. If this is OE *Broc*, 'marsh', 'brook' (usually the latter in place-names) it possibly refers to a tributary of the Teme or Severn, the ½ fishery showing that it is on a stream or river. There is still a Brook Farm (EPNS p. 70) on the north-east border of Rock parish adjacent to Ribbesford wood (GR SO 777720), on the Gladder Brook, but at the far end of the parish from Sodington.
FECHE. From Old Irish *Fiacha*, Modern Irish *Feagh*, Latinized as *Fiachus*. The reservations expressed in PNDB p. 250 are not well-founded; many Irish had come to north-west England in the 10th century with the Norwegians and scattered Irish names (such as Duncan in DB Somerset 19,86) would be expected. See Redin and Woulfe s.n.

16,4 CONNINGSWICK. DB *Colinguic*, see EPNS p. 71.

Ch.17 ROBERT OF STAFFORD. In the Chapter heading of the MS *Robeti* is an error for *Roberti*.

17,1 MORTON (? UNDERHILL). Identified with Abbots Morton by VCH and EPNS, but the latter was clearly an ecclesiastical holding in DB (10,13). See Sawyer (1) on Evesham A 3. The burgess and salt-house may well have been at Droitwich, see App. III.

Ch.18 ROGER OF LACY. Son of Walter of Lacy (died 1085) and Ermelina (Emma), see W. E. Wightman *The Lacy Family in England and Normandy, 1066-1194*, Oxford 1966. He rebelled in 1088 and 1094, was banished and his lands given to his brother Hugh. Roger also held lands in Berkshire, Herefordshire, Gloucestershire and elsewhere. He died some time after 1106 in Normandy where he had attained high office under Duke Robert. Lacy is now Lassy in the département of Calvados, France.

18,3 SHELL. DB *Scelves*, EPNS p. 138. The Evesham A entry for *Heisse* (A 15) appears to correspond to *Scelves* (see Sawyer (1) *ad loc.*); the Hundred name, Esch, Ash, its site otherwise unknown, is thus perhaps a part of Shell; see VCH iii p. 1.
SLAVES...SALT-HOUSES. The reason for these being in the accusative is not apparent.
4 SALT-HOUSES WITH WOODLAND...60 MEASURES. The render of the salt-houses (60 measures) has been added as an afterthought, sandwiching the wood which has nothing to do with salt.
VALUE...NOW 15s. In Evesham A 15 the value, *cum tota silva*, is 40s; *sine silva*, 15s.
IN AN ENCLOSURE. Similar phrases in DB Oxon. 1,5 (*silva est in defen' regis*) and Warwicks. 27,3 (*silva...sed in defenso regis*) suggest that the woodland has been put into the King's Forest, see 1,1c note above. Herefordshire entries show the forms *defenso*, *defensu* and *defensione* (DB Herefords. 1,43. 2,2;9;24;56).

18,4 1 HEDGED ENCLOSURE. *Haia*, see 2,7 note above.
WHERE. In the MS *in qud́*, with the oblique line over the *a* to indicate the ablative; Farley does not print this oblique line, though it is usually his practice to do so, see 23,1. 26,17 etc.
2 PLOUGHS. '5' in Evesham A 16.

18,5 MARTLEY. In Doddingtree Hundred, see X 3, the Hundred head being here omitted. The entry appears to be incomplete and was probably an afterthought.

18,6 THE ENTRY is added at the foot of column 176c, below the marginal rulings, in the middle of 19,2, both lines beginning 8 letters into the left-hand margin. Transposition signs indicate the correct position.
AELFRIC MAPSON. *Mapesone* in the MS; Farley misprints *Mapes ne*; for the byname see OEB p. 160.

THEY PAY. *Redd(un)t*, apparently referring to the burgesses and the salt-houses, as the figure 1½ in Latin is normally followed by a singular verb. Cf. 22,1.
3½ MEASURES. Presumably of salt.
HIS MANOR OF HEREFORD. Roger holds a number of lands in Herefordshire (DB Ch. 10) but no manor of Hereford itself is mentioned. He holds some houses in the Borough (10,7) but his principal Herefordshire manor was probably Weobley (10,48), later *caput* of the Lacy barony.

Ch.19 OSBERN SON OF RICHARD. Son of Richard Scrope. Lord of Richard's Castle in Herefordshire. In the Book of Fees a number of his lands are held from the honour of *Castrum Ricardi* (Richard's Castle) by William *de Stutevill'*, which assists in the identification of some places.

19,1 IN DODDINGTREE HUNDRED. Written in the MS midway between the Ch. 19 heading and the first line of 19,1; not as Farley prints it.
RICHARD SCROPE. He appears to be a Norman who settled in Herefordshire at the time of the Confessor, continued a landholder after the Conquest, and was succeeded by his son Osbern (Ch. 19 note above), see OEB p. 224, DEPN s.v. Shrewsbury, PNDB p. 349 note 1. The surname, despite OEB's hesitations and DEPN's accidental complication (this family's surname is not the origin of *Shrewsbury*), is obviously an Anglo-Scandinavian nickname, the Old Norse by-name *Skrōpi*, presumably anglicized **Scrōp(e)* which would produce Anglo-Norman *Scrupe, Escrob, Scrob*; see E. Björkman, *Zur Englischen Namenkunde* (Halle, 1912), 76, and E. H. Lind, *Norsk-Isländska Personbinamn från Medeltiden* (Uppsala 1920-1921), 333. It looks as if a pre-Conquest Norman settler has been given an Anglo-Scandinavian surname.
22 PACKLOADS. See E 15 note.

19,2 TENBURY (WELLS). Formerly Worcester Church land, Worcs. G 4 (in App. V). It included the manor of Sutton Sturmy (GR SO 6165), VCH iv p. 367.
14 VILLAGERS AND SMALLHOLDERS. *xiiii inter villanos et bordarios*, i.e. together the villagers and smallholders totalled 14.

19,3 OSBERN ALSO HOLDS. Repeated at the beginning of 19,3-14.
CLIFTON (ON TEME). An outlier of the Gloucestershire manor of Westbury on Severn, see E 35 note, but also formerly Worcester Church land, Worcs. G 4 (App. V).
ROBERT D'OILLY. Sheriff of Warwickshire from the early to late 1080s, of Oxford and perhaps Berkshire. He was Castellan of Oxford Castle under King William and is called the Constable of Oxford; *History of Abingdon* ii 7 and 12. He was probably married to one of the daughters of Wigot of Wallingford, see Freeman iv App. Note C. For Oilly, see OEB p. 103.

19,4 KYRE. DB *Chure* (*Cuer* at 19,7). One of the holdings was the later Kyre Wyard, held as *Cure Wyard* from William *de Stutevill'* in Fees p. 959; see VCH iv p. 282. Both lands had been outliers of the Gloucestershire manor of Westbury on Severn, see E 35 note; one had belonged to Worcester Church, Worcs. G 4 (App. V).
GRAIN. *Frumentum*, a term covering all cereal plants, corn, wheat, barley etc.; the render here is probably the same as the *annona* of 19,1;19.

19,5 STANFORD (ON TEME). See E 35 note. It is held as *Stanford Esturmi* from William *de Stuttevill'* in Fees p. 960.

19,6 SHELSLEY. See E 35 note. Shelsley Walsh, held as *Seldesley le Waleys* from William *de Stutevill'* in Fees p. 960; see 15,11 note and VCH iv p. 335.
SIGMUND. A Danish thane of Earl Leofric; he held it from Worcester Church, Worcs. G 3 (App. V). Edwin (C 1 note) was Leofric's grandson.

19,7 KYRE. See 19,4 note.

19,8 HOMME (CASTLE). DB *Hāme*, though the form is not given in EPNS. Long known as Ham Castle, but recent owners of what is now a private house have restored the form found in Hemming (Worcs. G 4 in App. V), first recorded by the Ordnance Survey in 1965. Ham Bridge at GR SO 7361 preserves the more normal modern form. The land formerly belonged to Worcester Church, see Worcs. G 4 (App. V); E 35 note.

19,9 (LOWER) SAPEY. Held as *Sapi Pichard* from William *de Stutevill'* in Fees p. 959; see VCH i p. 313 note 6 and EPNS p. 75. It was formerly held by Worcester Church, Worcs. G 9 (in App. V); see E 35 note. Upper Sapey lay to the north, just over the border in Herefords., and was possibly part of the Bishop of Hereford's manor of Bromyard (DB Herefords. 2,49) in 1086, it being held from him in FA ii p. 378.
ONLY 9 CATTLE. *Animalia*, commonly called *animalia otiosa* 'idle animals' elsewhere, that is beef or dairy cattle in contrast to the ploughing oxen, though occasionally, as perhaps here, they seem to take the place of the plough-team statement. However, there are several occurrences of *animalia* in ploughs (where one would expect *boves* 'oxen') in the Exon additions to DB Devon (17,26; 28; 38 etc.). Cattle and other animals were counted in

the surviving circuit returns (the Exon. and Little Domesdays) but normally omitted from the Exchequer version, except to make a particular point.

19,11 EDVIN (LOACH). See E 35 note.

19,12-13 A CLENT HUNDRED heading seems to be omitted.

19,12 WYCHBOLD. Including Crutch (GR SO 9066) and Dodderhill (SO 8964), VCH iii pp. 57, 59. The land had been seized from Worcester Church by Edwin, brother of Earl Leofric, see Worcs. G 30 in App. V.
EARL GODWIN. Earl of the West Saxons; father of Earl (King) Harold and Edith (wife of King Edward the Confessor). Died in 1053. The rest of this line has been left blank, perhaps for some additional information.

19,13 ALDGEAT. DB *Aeldiet*, perhaps Aldith (OE Ealdgyth); PNDB pp. 240-1. Possibly Aldith wife of King Gruffydd (and later of Earl Harold) who was Osbern's predecessor in DB Warwicks. 6,5.

19,14 CROWLE. DB *Croelai*; *Croela Gualteri* in Evesham A 9, later known as the manor of Froxmere Court or Crowle Hackett, VCH iii p. 331. The land had been held by Sigmund (2,78), probably the same man who held Shelsley (19,6). See Worcs. G 20 in App. V.
THE REMAINING TWO LINES of this entry are written at the foot of column 176d below the marginal rulings, in the middle of 20,3. They extend about 4 letters into the central margin, not shown by Farley, and are separated from the 18,6 entry by a gallows sign. Transposition signs indicate the correct position in the text. It would seem that the whole entry was written later as the first two lines are cramped.
WOODLAND...FOR 100 PIGS. See 3,3 note.
40[s]. *Sol(idos)* omitted in error, probably because of lack of space at the end of the column; *xl solidos* in Evesham A 9.

Ch.20 GILBERT SON OF THOROLD. Probably the same man as Gilbert of Bouillé, see DB Warwicks. B 2 note, and 11,2 here.

20,1 DODDENHAM. It included the manor of Ankerdine (GR SO 7356), VCH iv p. 261.
CEOLMER. PNDB p. 214.

20,2 REDMARLEY. In Great Witley parish; the holding probably became the later manor of Redmarley Adam, VCH iv p. 374; see 2,25 and 15,10 notes.
1½ HIDES... A gap of about 4 letters follows, due to an imperfection in the parchment; but see Ch. 14 note.

20,3-4 HANLEY. The two holdings no doubt represent between them the villages of Hanley Child and Hanley William. In Evesham Q 18 (App. V) the second village is called *alia Hanleg*, see 1,2 note. A further ½ hide, making a 5-hide unit, may have lain just over the border in Herefordshire: ½ hide at *Hanlei* is held by Roger of Lacy in Plealey Hundred in DB Herefords. 10,75.

20,4 KENWARD. See 2,13 note.

20,6 HADZOR. Formerly held by Worcester Church, Worcs. G 18 (App. V).
COTTAGE-MEN. *Cotmanni*, like *cotarii*, see 8,7 note. They are infrequent in Worcs. DB, others being at 23,2. 26,3;6.

Ch.21 DROGO SON OF POYNTZ. On Poyntz, see OEB p. 194.

21,1 WASTE...VALUE. Or perhaps 'it is waste and was waste before 1066. The value was 5s'. The *TRE* falls between the two clauses.

21,2 LAND FOR 2 PLOUGHS. The estimated number of ploughlands is rarely recorded in DB Worcs.; see 23,14 and DGM p. 232. They are regularly entered in the adjacent Warwicks. and Staffs., but only rarely in Glos. or Herefordshire.

21,3 GLASSHAMPTON. DB *Glese*, see EPNS p. 34.

21,4 MARTLEY. See E 1. X 3. The virgate is named as *Pudiford*, now Pudford Farm (GR SO 7461), in Evesham Q 24.

Ch.22 HAROLD SON OF EARL RALPH. Ralph the Timid, son of Countess Goda (King Edward's sister) and Count Drogo. He came to England in 1041 and was Earl of Hereford from 1053 or earlier to 1057. He may have inherited part of the earldom of Swein, see Harmer p. 570. In 1066 Harold was presumably a minor because in DB Middx. 9,1 he is said to have been then in the charge of Queen Edith, his aunt. In 1086 he held land in Worcs. and Warwicks.; Ewyas Harold in Herefords. (19,1) is named after him.

22,1 7 SALT-HOUSES...SALT. Cf. DB Glos. 61,2 where the same Harold has 50 measures of salt from a salt-house.

Ch.23 WILLIAM SON OF ANSCULF. William of *Pinkeni* (Picquigny near Amiens in the département of Somme, France), so named in DB Wilts. 24,19. 68,22-23. Ansculf is Ansculf of *Pinchengi* in DB Bucks. 17,2. He was lord of Dudley castle (23,10) and an

important figure in the midland counties.
AFTER THE NUMBER OF HIDES gaps of varying size are found in the entries at 23,1-4; 6-8;10-13. See Ch. 14 note and Worcs. D in App. V.

23,1 WOOD. *Nemus*, a rare substitute for *silva* in DB (see also 26,2 below). It is the usual word in Exon. DB, rendered by *silva* in the Exchequer version. The width is omitted, see 1,1c note.
BISHOP OF CHESTER. Peter, but the title is an anachronism. Until 1075/6 the Bishop's seat was at Lichfield. Other transfers to larger towns were made at about the same time, including the move from Dorchester on Thames to Lincoln (1072). In 1102 Chester was replaced by Coventry.
LIVES OF THREE MEN. A lease, in this case for Wulfwin, his widow and his son. Cf. 9,1e.
BISHOP (OF) LI(CHFIELD?). Probably Lichfield. The MS leaves room for 3 or 4 letters after *Li*... Since the land was to revert to Chester (Lichfield, see note above), Wulfwin's son was probably Leofwin, Bishop of Lichfield (1053-1067). But since DB names the new see of Chester, *Li*... could also stand for a new contemporary see, Lincoln, in which case the son was Wulfwy, Bishop of Dorchester on Thames, also 1053-1067. Space may have been left in the MS because Winchester did not know which see was meant. The purpose of the oral will was to deter claims by lay heirs; it failed, for William succeeded to Selly Oak as to other holdings of Wulfwin.

23,2 WILLIAM ALSO HOLDS. Repeated at the beginning of 23,2-14.

23,4 'WILLINGWICK'. See 1,1d note.

23,6 [IN CLENT HUNDRED]. The heading inserted in the margin at 23,8 should certainly have included 23,7 Churchill which is on the far side of Clent from its boundary with Came, and probably 23,6 Warley which is, however, adjacent to the Clent-Came boundary.
WARLEY. Formerly Warley Wigorn, VCH iii p. 145, to distinguish it from the other part of the parish Warley Salop, part of Earl Roger's manor of Halesowen (14,1); see App. I.

23,7 2 HIDES... In the MS there is an erasure here of about 11 letters, and it was probably not written over as it normally would have been (see 26,1 note), for the same reasons as other gaps were left in this chapter (see Ch. 23 note above).

23,8 BELL (HALL). DB *Bellem*, see 26,13 note.
2 *ORA*. That is 3s 4d at 20 pence to the *ora*, see C 2 note above.
WILLIAM SON OF OSBERN. Earl William of Hereford, see 1,1b note above. As he died in 1071, he can only just have taken the land from Hubert if the latter had held it for more than 5 years after 1066; see VCH i p. 316.

23,12 ACARD. A French name. There is an Acard of Ivry in DB Beds. 23,17.
2 DWELLINGS. See 10,17 note above.
A LITTLE WOOD. *Siluula*, referring to the size of the trees, not the extent of the wood; elsewhere *parva silva, nemusculum, silva minuta*.

23,14 BELLINGTON. Later part of Chaddesley Corbett parish and thus in Cresslau Hundred, EPNS p. 235. It is possible that a Cresslau Hundred head should be supplied, though in other chapters Cresslau lands occur before those in Clent Hundred. As a border place and part of the castlery of Dudley, it could well have been in Clent Hundred in 1086.
IN HIS CASTLERY. Subject to the jurisdiction of his castle at Dudley (23,10 above). Bellington is 9 miles south-west of Dudley. There are a number of examples in DB Herefords. of lands subject to a castle; see DB Herefords. Introductory note 3.
HOLLAND. See PNDB p. 291.
LAND FOR 5 PLOUGHS. See 21,2 note.

Ch.24 WILLIAM SON OF CORBUCION. Appointed Sheriff of Warwickshire soon after 1086.

24,1 WITTON IN DROITWICH. DB unusually specifies the locality for Witton; see also 26,16.
TUINI. An unparalleled personal name, possibly a miscopying of *Tumi* which has the same number of minim strokes. PNDB p. 388 note 4 says that Farley has misprinted *Tuini* for *Tumi*, but the former is the clear reading of the MS.
3 SALT-HOUSES. This and the following details refer to Witton, not to Worcester.
PART OF 1 SALT-HOUSE. *Partem*, accusative in error, probably influenced by *reddunt*.

Ch.25 WILLIAM GOIZENBODED. His main holdings were in Glos. (DB Ch. 34). He was son of Richard 'a young man' (25,1), see DB Glos. 34,8 note. The byname is left unexplained in OEB p. 390. The ending is *-boded*, past participle of OE *bodian* 'to announce'.

Goizen- is perhaps *Guizen-* a French form of OE *wiccan* 'witch', where *w* has become *gu* (as in French *guerre* 'war' from OG **werra*), a common feature of Central French, sometimes found in Anglo-Norman, and *z* represents the sounds [ts] or [tʃ] a French rendering of OE *-cc-*. The name may thus be OE **wiccanboded*, 'foretold by a witch' or 'cursed by a witch'. Other forms of this byname in related texts are *Guezenboeth* in Worcs. D and *Cunteboiz'* in Evesham N 14 (see DB Glos. Appendix).

25,1 CHAWSON. See VCH i p. 317 note 5 and p. 329 note 1.
RICHARD A YOUNG MAN. The interlined *iuvenis* probably represents OE *geonga* 'young' or *geongran* 'younger', the latter used often to distinguish an older and younger person of the same name. It is common from the late 10th century, and distinct in sense from *cilt* (14,2 note), see OEB p. 314. This Richard also appears in DB Glos. 34,8 apparently as William's father; that entry states that King William gave the widow of Alwin the Sheriff in marriage to *Ricardo cuidam juveni*. It is not clear whether *iuvenis* had become a byname by 1086
1 PLOUGH. A gap of about 9 letters follows, perhaps merely to mark off the value clause, usually entered on a separate line on folio 177 c,d; but possibly for the later addition of woodland, pasture etc.

Ch.26 URSO OF ABETOT. Brother of Robert the Bursar, he was Sheriff of Worcs. and called Urso of Worcester in DB Glos. 65,1. He helped to crush the revolt of Earl Roger of Hereford in 1075; his heirs through a daughter are the Beauchamps. His holdings as tenant or subtenant in the County total nearly 200 hides, or a sixth of the County, including important holdings at Droitwich, centre of the salt industry. He rapaciously seized much Church land, and in 1086 held all the land that the Bishop of Bayeux held and had 'acquired' from Evesham Abbey (Ch. 11 note). Worcs. DB is silent about his injustices, which nonetheless appear between its lines (see however E 14 Old Sodbury); but his depredations are evident even in his own chapter where 26,15-17 consist of land formerly held by Evesham Church. In 9,4 he is found claiming part of the 30-hide manor of Broadway; see Round in VCH i p. 262 ff. and Freeman v App. pp. 759-766. Abetot is in the département of Seine-Maritime, France.

26,1 COOKHILL. DB *Cochehi*, said to be in Doddingtree Hundred, where no place of the name has been identified. The corresponding entry in Evesham appears to be A 5 *Cokehelle*, Cook Hill now in Inkberrow parish, in Esch Hundred (the reference omitted in EPNS). With this estate Esch Hundred totals exactly 100 hides; see App. I.
IN LORDSHIP 1 PLOUGH; ...2 MORE PLOUGHS POSSIBLE. In Evesham A 5 '1 plough between the men (i.e. villagers)'.
(HE HAS) 1 BURGESS...4 MEASURES OF SALT. *unum burgensem . . . iiii mittas salis*. The accusative does not follow naturally from the nominative *ii servi*; some such verb as *habet* 'he has' must be understood.
70s. In the MS it is written over an erasure and is very blurred.

26,2 URSO ALSO HOLDS. Repeated at the beginning of 26,2-17.
'OSMERLEY'. See VCH iii pp. 254-5, EPNS p. 334.
WOOD. *Nemus*, see 23,1 note above.

26,3 COFTON (HACKETT). The manor of Cofton Richard, VCH iii p. 56.

26,4 BENTLEY. The parish name Bentley Pauncefote preserves the name of an early holder from the Beauchamps, see Fees p. 961 and RBE p. 567.

26,5 WOODCOTE (GREEN). *Wdecot' Stephani* in Evesham Q 8. See 1,1a note.

26,6 HUNWULF. OE *Hunwulf*, OG *Hunulf*, OScand. *Hundulf*.
5 *ORA*. That is, 8s 4d at 20 pence to the *ora*, C 2 note.

26,7 ALFKELL. DB *Euchil*, PNDB p. 144.
3 *ORA*. That is, 5s (see 26,6 note above).

26,8 DOVERDALE. DB *Lunvredele*, see EPNS p. 239. It is held from the barony of William *de Bello Campo* in Fees p. 961.

26,9 ALFGEAT. *Eliet*, other forms in DB being *Aelget, Aliet, Aluiet, Aluied,* from OE *Athelgeat* or *Aelfgeat*, PNDB p. 146.
HELD. In the MS, the singular *tenuit* has been changed to *tenuer̄* (= *tenuerunt*, plural), no doubt when *7 Eliet* was interlined.
WHO HAS NOTHING. Smallholders normally have ploughs in DB. It is unusual for smallholders to succeed the 'resources' paragraph.

26,10 HAMPTON (LOVETT). Another part is 26,17. One part was formerly owned by Worcester Church (Worcs. G 15 in App. V), together with 'Thickenappletree' (27,1); probably this portion, as both have the same *TRE* holder.
14 *ORA*. 280 pence or £1 3s 4d at 20 pence to the *ora* (C 2 note).

26,11 A SMALL WOOD. *parva silva*, no doubt the same as *siluula* (23,12 note).

26,12 COOKSEY (GREEN). See 1,1c note.
ATILIC. See PNDB p. 169. The name is an *-ic* derivative of a poorly recorded Scandinavian personal name *Atli*.
2 HIDES. In the MS *hide*; Farley prints *hidae* as though there were a diphthong mark under the *e*.

26,13 BELBROUGHTON. DB *Brocton*. The modern name represents a fusing of DB *Bellem* (now represented by Bell (Hall) 23,8) and *Brocton*, see EPNS pp. 274-5. Worcs. G 17 (App. V) records how Broughton, Bell Hall, Chaddesley Corbett and Fairfield were all originally held by Worcs. Church, then by Godiva, wife of Earl Leofric, and were seized from her by Earls Edwin and Morcar (her sons). It is possible that the 2 hides included parts of Bell Hall (23,8), Chaddesley Corbett (28,1) and Fairfield (GR SO 9475). The original grant to Worcester Church included Salwarpe and Hampton Lovett, as well as Bell Hall, Belbroughton and Fairfield, ECWM no. 243 p. 100 (= BCS 360 = Sawyer (2) 181); see VCH iii p. 14.
COUNTESS GODIVA. 'Lady' Godiva, wife of Earl Leofric and mother of Earls Edwin and Morcar; she died between 1066 and 1086.
5 *ORA*. 8s 4d, see 26,10 note above.

26,14 CUSTOMARY DUE. In the MS a blot obliterates the final *e* of *c̄suetudine*.
3 SMALLHOLDERS WHO HAVE NOTHING. See 26,9 note above.

26,15-17 UPTON (WARREN), WITTON, HAMPTON (LOVETT). Evesham D 1;3 record that these lands were held by some of Urso's men-at-arms from the Abbey of Evesham until the death of Abbot Aethelwig, whereupon Urso seized the lands; see *Chronicon* p. 97. In Evesham N 1;3 they were said to have been taken from the Abbey by Odo of Bayeux (Ch. 11 note); see 10,11-12 note.

26,15 ABBOT ALWIN OF EVESHAM. Aethelwig, see 11,2 note.
3 HIDES... There follows a gap of about 3 letters, possibly caused by the long tail of the 7 in the line above; but see Ch. 14 note.

26,16 FIFTH YEAR OF KING EDWARD'S REIGN. June 1046-June 1047.
HAROLD'S WAR AGAINST THE NORSE. Harold met and defeated the invading Norse army led by Harold Hardrada and also his outlawed brother Tosti at Stamford Bridge on 25th September 1066, 3 weeks before the Battle of Hastings.
AS LONG AS HE LIVED. That is, until 1077.
ABBOT WALTER. See 10,12 note.

26,17 HAMPTON (LOVETT). Left unidentified by VCH and DG. In Evesham D 1, however, it is *Hamtun quam Inardus Parler tenet*, that is Hampton Lovett. Urso had added the Evesham portion of the vill to his own (26,10). For *Inardus Parler* see 8,25 note.
3 *ORA*. 5s at 20d to the *ora* (C 2 note).
THROUGH A DOCUMENT. *Textum*, probably his grant to the Church (cf. 26,16), rather than a sacred text or the Bible; see VCH i p. 319; RMLWL s.v. *textum*.

Ch.27 HUGH DONKEY. *Lasne*, correctly L'Asne from OFr *Asne*, Mod.Fr *âne*, Latin *asinus*, 'ass', 'donkey'. He probably came to England with William son of Osbern and served under him in defending the English border against the Welsh.

27,1 'THICKENAPPLETREE'. DB *Tichenapletreu*, EPNS p. 305. Probably in the eastern part of Hampton Lovett parish, and partly in St. Peter and St. Augustine, Dodderhill, see Worcs. G 15 (in App. V); Habington i p. 242; VCH iii p. 155. The Came Hundred head seems to be an error for Clent.
3 HIDES... There is a gap of about 3 letters in the MS; see Ch. 14 note.

Ch.28 THE CHAPTER IS NUMBERED but not headed in the text. It is *xxviii Eldeue* in the List of Landholders, col. 172a. One of the names is in error. *Eldeue* represents OE **Ealdgifu*, whereas *Eddeue* here is OE *Eadgifu*.

28,1 CHADDESLEY (CORBETT). So called to distinguish it from Chaceley (part of Longdon 8,9), formerly *Chaddeslega*; see EPNS p. 193. Part had belonged to Worcester Church; see Worcs. G 17 (in App. V) and 26,13 note.

X THE REMAINING ENTRIES appear as an addendum, marked off from Ch. 28 by a small gap in the MS. Both the hand and the colour of the ink of the MS are the same as for the preceding entries.

X 1 WULFMER. Probably the same man who preceded Ralph of Tosny and Drogo son of Poyntz in other estates in the County (15,3;8;10-11. 21,1-3). Hillhampton would naturally be associated with Redmarley (15,10) held before 1066 by Wulfmer and Ulfketel. In Evesham Q 27, the name is *Almarus*, perhaps a scribal error for *Ulmarus* 'Wulfmer'.

X 2 FECKENHAM, HOLLOW (COURT). Details are in DB Herefords. 1,40-41 (E 2-3 below).
HOLLOW (COURT). With Hollowfields Farm in Hanbury the name represents 'Holloway', DB *Holewei, Haloede*, EPNS p. 323, VCH i p. 321 note 6 and VCH iii p. 376. It is *Holeweya* in Fees p. 1290.
RETURN. *Breve*, usually in DB meaning a 'writ': *breve regis*, the King's writ, putting a man in possession of land. But here and in X 3 it clearly refers to the return for the *Terra Regis* in Herefordshire DB. See VCH i p. 280 and p. 320 notes 3-4.

X 3 MARTLEY, SUCKLEY. See DB Herefords. 1,39;47 (E 1;7 here) and 1,1b.
PAY TAX HERE. That is, in Doddingtree Hundred.

PLACES ELSEWHERE. Because of the complex changes in the County boundary since the 11th century, summarised in Appendix I, a distinction is here made between places that were in the County in 1086, but entered in the folios of adjacent Counties (prefixed E), and those in adjacent Counties in 1086, but later transferred to Worcestershire (EG for Gloucestershire etc.). The latter are listed after the 'E' entries, cross-referenced to the Counties concerned.

E 1-7 ALL THESE LANDS are entered in the Herefordshire folios but under Worcestershire Hundred heads, or said to be in Worcestershire in 1086. These manors' lands and revenue were unjustly taken from Worcestershire and placed in Herefords. by William son of Osbern (Earl of Hereford 1067-71, see 1,1b note). When his son, Roger, forfeited his lands in 1075 after his rebellion, they fell to the crown. Martley, Feckenham, Hollow Court and Suckley are cross-referenced in Worcester X 2-3 and 1,1b. Their *TRE* holders show that they were royal land. The other lands found in the Herefordshire folios are portions of church lands accounted for in the text of Worcestershire under their ecclesiastical holders, but said there to be *in manu regis*.

E 1 MARTLEY. In X 3 the hidage is given as 13. The bounds probably included Areley Kings (GR SO 8070), VCH iv p. 288. See ESt 1 note below and Mon. Ang. vi pp. 1075-76.
2 WEIRS. For trapping fish in a pool. See Worcs. G 11 (in App. V) and VCH i p. 272.
2,500 EELS AND 5 STICKS. That is, 2,625 eels.
A BEADLE. See 1,1a note.
GIFTS. Usually to the Queen. OE *gaersuma, gaersum(e)* 'treasure, profit of office'; ME *gersum* 'a premium, a fine'. A gift-payment or fine, usually to gain liberty from some other obligation. The word occurs in the same connection in DB Oxfords. 1,12 and Warwicks. B 4 (col. 238a). In Kent 3,18 there is a payment of 100s to the Archbishop of Canterbury *de garsūnne*. In Northants. B 36 (col. 219a) in a similar context, Latin *donum* 'gift' is used. See Ellis i p. 174; *gersum* in OED.
RALPH OF BERNAY. See 2,36 note above.

E 2 FECKENHAM. Noted above at Worcs. X 2.
ST. MARY'S CHURCH. The Abbey of Lyre, from later evidence, see Guéry p. 159 and Mon. Ang. vi 1092. It was founded in 1046 by (Earl) William son of Osbern. Lyre is La Vieille-Lyre in the département of Eure, France.
WALTER OF LACY. Died 1085. Father of Roger of Lacy (see Ch. 18 note above) who also gave land to this Church in Glos. (DB Glos. 17,1).

E 3 HOLLOW (COURT). See X 2 note above and Mon. Ang. vi pp. 1075-76.
A PARK FOR WILD ANIMALS. For hunting. *Parcus* is usually an area of woodland for hunting within the manor, contrasting with *foresta* (1,1c note), land outside. In this case, the park has been included in the Forest.
1 *HOCH*. Latinised as *hoccus* in Worcs. See 1,3a note.
1 HOUSE...2 PLOUGH-SHARES. A burgess in Gloucester similarly pays 4 plough-shares (*soccos*), DB Glos. 39,12; see also Herefords. 1,7.
THESE TWO MANORS. That is, Feckenham and Hollow Court.

E 4 BUSHLEY. The land belonged to Worcester Church and is said at 2,30 to be *in manu regis*. The value is there given as 40s. In Fees p. 139 Hugh *de Colcumba* holds ½ virgate in Bushley for looking after the hedged enclosure (*haya*) there; see also RBE p. 568.
BRICTRIC. Son of Algar in 2,30.
LEOFING. Lyfing, Bishop of Worcester 1038-40, then 1041 to his death in 1046.
3 GOLD MARKS...A SILVER MARK. The gold mark was worth £6, the silver, 13s 4d.
HE BOUGHT THE WHOLE. The detail of the arrangements in 2,30 is different.
A DAIRYMAID. Or 'dairyman', Latin *daia*, either masculine or feminine. See RMLWL s.v. *daya*.
PULL (COURT). *La Pulle* in Fees p. 139; see VCH i p. 322 note 3 and EPNS p. 105. The house that marks the site is now Bredon School. In Fees the place is likewise associated with Bushley to which Earl William had joined it. Bushley, as part of the lands of

Worcester Church, was in Oswaldslow Hundred, but Pull Court had been part of Longdon (8,9), a manor of Westminster Church. It is here mapped in Oswaldslow. The 3 virgates of Pull Court probably represent the unnamed 3 virgates of the 5 hides 3 virgates held by Reinbald and Aelfric before 1066 in 8,9c, the 5 hides being Eldersfield, E 6 below.
EARL ODA. Became Earl of Somerset, Devon and Dorset and 'the Wealas' in 1051 on the banishment of Earls Godwin and Harold, but lost the earldom on their return and was compensated with the earldom of the Hwiccas. He was a benefactor of Deerhurst and Pershore Churches; he became a monk at the latter, being buried there after his death in 1056. See VCH i pp. 257-60 and Robertson pp. 456-58.
MONKS OF LYRE...1 VIRGATE. Recorded in Bushley in Fees p. 140.
OUTSIDE HIS MANORS. *extra suos* $\overline{M}$, *suos* being an error for *sua*, *manerium* being neuter.
TO GUARD THE WOODLANDS. Cf. DB Glos. 37,3. In RBE p. 568 and Fees p. 139 Pull Court is held *pro custodienda haya de Bisseleg*.

E 5 QUEENHILL. DB *Chonhelme* and *Cūhille*, see VCH i p. 322 note 8 and EPNS p. 155. The entry is a duplicate, with different detail, of 2,36, said to be *in manu regis*.
BISHOP BRICTRIC. The same as Bishop Brictheah 2,24, that is Beorhtheah, Bishop of Worcester 1033-38.
DAIRYMAID. See E 4 note above.
ST. MARY'S OF LYRE...½ VIRGATE. Held by the Prior of Lyre in Fees p. 140. See E 2 note above.

E 6 ELDERSFIELD. Formed part of the original grant by King Edgar to Pershore Church (Ch. 8 note), but alienated by Earl William. These 5 hides are part of the unnamed 5 hides 3 virgates of Longdon (8,9c), the other 3 virgates being at Pull Court, E 4 note above.
REINBALD THE CHANCELLOR. Also called Reinbald the Priest, and Reinbald of Cirencester (DB Berks. Ch. 61), of which church he was dean or provost. He was the first chancellor of England and held land in Berks., Dorset, Herefords., Glos., Bucks., Somerset etc. See Round in FE p. 421 ff.; *Regesta* i pp. xiii, xv; W. H. Stevenson in EHR vol. xi (1896) p. 731 note.
ST. MARY'S. Of Lyre. The Prior held 1 virgate in Hardwick in Eldersfield (GR SO 8132) in Fees p. 140. See VCH i p. 322 note 11; VCH iv p. 79; Mon. Ang. vi p. 1092; TE 217a.
1 VIRGATE OF LAND. There is an erasure after this in the MS; the scribe may have intended to add more details later when available.

E 7 SUCKLEY. See X 3.
10 IMPOVERISHED SMALLHOLDERS. That is, without ploughs; see 26,9 note.
A KEEPER OF 12 BEEHIVES. Literally 'a keeper of the bees of 12 hives'.
ST. MARY'S. Of Cormeilles; VCH i p. 323 note 1, Mon. Ang. vi pp. 1075-76.
EARL ROGER. Earl of Hereford from 1071 until his rebellion in 1075 (see E 1-7 note above); son of William son of Osbern, his predecessor as Earl of Hereford.
THESE SIX MANORS. DB Herefords. 1,42-47, the four Worcs. manors of Bushley (with Pull Court), Queenhill, Eldersfield and Suckley (E 4-7 above) together with Hanley Castle (see EH 1) and Forthampton, both in Gloucestershire in 1086. This implies that the entry for Pull Court is part of that for Bushley.

E 8 EARL ROGER. Of Shrewsbury, see Ch. 14 note above.
CHAWSON. Formerly Chauson, DB *Caluestone*, probably a variant form of *Celvestune* 25,1 which re-appears as *Chalvestona* in Evesham B (see Appendix IV). Although remote from the Shropshire border, this outlier of Morville may have been drawn out of Worcs. by Earl Roger's reorganisation of his manors in the same way as Halesowen (14,1 see Appendix I) was later and more permanently; see VCH Shropshire iii p. 43 (correcting i p. 286). The hide would be adjacent to Salwarpe (Roger's other Worcester holding 14,2) and would possibly provide salt-rights for Morville.

E 10 M. Marginal abbreviation for *manerium*, 'manor'.
...PACKLOADS OF SALT. *summas salis*; the figure is omitted. The size of the packload is unknown, but in the case of salt in Cheshire (S1,4 col. 268b) it contained 15 *bulliones* 'boilings'. It is used of corn several times in Worcs. (e.g. 2,57;80;82).

E 15 MEASURES OF SALT. *mensurae salis*; of uncertain size, used once of corn in DB Shrops. 4,3,45.

E 20 FROM THESE. From these 22s.

E 25 'BAGBURROW'. Now represented by Bagburrow Wood just south-east of Mathon (GR SO 7445). The place was in Winstree Hundred in 1086 and cannot have been Backbury (near Dormington in Greytree Hundred) preferred by VCH and DG; see 9,6a note.

E 30-32 THE LAND OF EARL ROGER, of Shrewsbury, DB Shrops. Ch. 4, is arranged by subtenants because of its size, hence the references contain three figures (as Ch. 5, the Count of Mortain, in DB Cornwall). 4,1 is Roger's lordship holding.

E 35 6 HIDES...IN KYRE. 2 hides were held by the Bishop of Hereford (3,2), and 4 by Osbern son of Richard (19,4;7).

CLIFTON ON TEME 10 HIDES. Composed of 9½ hides held by Osbern son of Richard in Clifton on Teme, Stanford on Teme, Shelsley, Homme Castle and Lower Sapey (19,3; 5-6;8-9) and ½ hide held at Tenbury Wells by the Abbot of Cormeilles (6,1).

IN EDVIN LOACH 1 HIDE. Held by Osbern son of Richard (19,11). Newent was in Gloucestershire and Kingstone in Herefordshire. William son of Richard does not recur in DB holding any of these lands.

ABBOT OF CORMEILLES. Or 'Abbey', see 2,44 note above.

SONS. *f.* with no abbreviation sign, perhaps singular *filius*, referring to William, though maybe plural *filii* as Osbern was also son of Richard (Scrope); see 19,1. The equally ambiguous abbreviation *f'* is repeated in Evesham K 10 (see Glos. Appendix).

FIR-WOOD. Perhaps the Forest of Dean. However, *Sapina* might result from an earlier mistranscription of *Sapian* (Lower Sapey); see BCS 240, EPNS p. 75.

EG 1 HANLEY (CASTLE). Geographically within Worcestershire, but regarded as a part of Gloucestershire both in DB Glos. and Herefords., Brictric son of Algar having withdrawn it from Worcs. and attached it to his great manor of Tewkesbury. It is duplicated in Herefords. (EH 1 below) because Earl William had withdrawn its revenues there, as in E 1-7 above. The Glos. and Herefords. entries originate from different returns and there are many differences:

DB Glos. 1,34	DB Herefords. 1,42
4 hides outside the lordship	4 hides
2 lordship ploughs before 1066	2 lordship ploughs
40 villagers and smallholders	20 villagers, 17 smallholders
— — —	21½ villagers' ploughs
8 male and female slaves	9 male and female slaves
a mill at 16d	a mill at 2s
woodland containing a hedged enclosure	woodland 5 leagues long and wide, put outside the manor and containing a hawk's eyrie
— — —	a forester holds ½ virgate
— — —	a villager of 'Baldenhall' pays 2 *ora* of pence
value before 1066 £15; now £10	(see E 7 note above)

EG 8 WICKHAMFORD. Formerly identified with Childswickham, but the 1 hide here added to the 9 of Wickhamford and Bretforton makes a 10-hide manor. See DB Glos. 12,6 note.

EG 9 DEERHURST. See Ch. 8 note.

EG 10 KEMERTON. All the other places mentioned remain in Gloucestershire.

EG 17 BICKMARSH. Partly in Glos. in 1086 and partly in Warwicks (EW 2 below). Until recent times it was a hamlet in that part of the Gloucestershire parish of Welford that lay in Warwickshire. In 1931 the major part of Bickmarsh was joined with Pebworth (transferred into Worcs. at the same time), a part remaining in the Warwicks. parish of Dorsington; (see App. I).

EH 1 HANLEY(CASTLE). See EG 1 note.

'BALDENHALL'. EPNS p. 210. Lost in Great Malvern parish, and probably corresponding roughly in area to the ecclesiastical parish of Guarlford. 1 virgate here was granted to the Priory of Great Malvern by Edward the Confessor as of the fee of Hanley, suggesting that the village lay within the bounds of Hanley Castle in the 11th century. It was merged with Great Malvern manor in the mid-16th century and in the time of Edward VI was stated to fall between Great Malvern and Guarlford, though it no longer existed; see VCH (Worcs.) iv p. 125.

ESt 1 (UPPER) ARLEY. See EPNS p. 30, VCH (Worcs.) iii p. 5. So called to distinguish it from Areley Kings or Nether Areley, adjacent to Stourport, part of the royal manor of Martley in 1086 (X 3, E 1). It was transferred from Staffs. in 1895. For the grant to Wolverhampton Church see ECWM no. 331, p. 124.

EW 2 BICKMARSH. Transferred from Warwickshire in 1931, another part (EG 17) being in Glos. until then. Three Shires Elms (GR SP 100489) marked the meeting point of the County boundaries of Worcs., Warwicks. and Glos. until 1931.

APPENDIX I
The Hundreds, the County and the County Boundary

The Hundreds

The text of DB says more about the Worcestershire Hundreds than is the case in many other Counties: 'In the County itself there are 12 Hundreds; 7 of them are exempt, as the Shire states, so the Sheriff has nothing in them...' (C 3). It is apparent that these 12 Hundreds consisted of 5 geographically compact Hundreds, each containing a number of lords (Came, Clent, Cresslau, Doddingtree and Esch), and 7 ecclesiastical Hundreds, geographically scattered and consisting of the triple Hundred of Oswaldslow, the artificial Hundred of Fishborough, the double Hundred of Pershore containing the lands of Westminster Church, and the single Hundred of Pershore containing Pershore Church lands. The last two Hundreds are nowhere named in the text of DB, though they are both called Pershore in Evesham A and B and in later times. They arose from a division of the 300 hides originally granted to Pershore Church (Ch. 8 note), and are here named 'Westminster' and 'Pershore' Hundreds for clarity.

The text also gives the hidage of these ecclesiastical Hundreds: there are 300 hides in Oswaldslow (2,1); in 'Westminster' 200 hides (8,1); that 'Pershore' Hundred contained 100 hides is clear from 9,7. Fishborough Hundred, held by the Church of Evesham, consisted of 65 hides to which were added 15 hides for the city of Worcester and 20 hides of Doddingtree: 'they make up the Hundred' (10,2). The taxable hidage for Droitwich Borough (10 hides) is also given (15,14; see Appendix III).

In Worcestershire a reasonable reconstruction of the 1086 Hundreds can be made, because the Hundred headings are fuller than in many Counties, those of the 5 'territorial' Hundreds being entered in each chapter in the same order: Doddingtree, Esch, Came, Cresslau, Clent.

There are a few difficulties: as in other Counties, headings are omitted from the land of the King, and occasionally at the end of chapters. They need to be supplied at 19,12-13 and 23,6-7. Moreover, Cookhill (26,1) is given in Doddingtree by the text of DB and in Esch, correctly, in Evesham A. 'Thickenappletree' (27,1) is said to be in Came Hundred, but as part of Hampton Lovett it was probably in Clent. Hampton and Bengeworth (10,11-12) are correctly placed in Oswaldslow in DB, but Bengeworth is in Fishborough in Evesham A (30), maybe in error, perhaps in an attempt to win the dispute for Evesham Abbey. In Evesham A 31 Hampton is included in Fishborough Hundred, but said to be in Oswaldslow Hundred.

A few places were divided between Hundreds: thus Inkberrow was partly in Oswaldslow (2,16), partly in Esch (3,3). Cooksey Green, a border land, seems to have been partly in Came Hundred, as an outlier of Bromsgrove (1,1c), and partly in Clent (26,12). Severn Stoke, wholly in 'Westminster' Hundred in DB (8,26), is divided between 'Westminster' and Esch in Evesham A 82;17. Part of Mathon (9,6a) was in Herefordshire.

The origin of the Hundreds, which in the Mercian area preceded the formation of the shires, is obscure and in the case of Worcestershire it is especially difficult to perceive the original pattern, if any, behind the 1086 arrangement (see Anderson pp. 138-9). The whole may have consisted of geographically compact Hundreds like those that remained in 1086 in the north of the County. But in the south, any earlier disposition was erased by the reorganisation of the ecclesiastical Hundreds. The foundation charter for Oswaldslow (2,1 note) records how the triple Hundred was reconstituted from the Hundreds of *Wulfereslaw, Winburgetrowe* and *Cuthburgelawe*. Though the charter as a whole is not to be trusted, its information about the Hundreds may be substantially correct. Only 'Winburntree' is found later (RH ii p. 283B, EPNS p. 87. See *Register* p. 68a). *Cuthburgelawe* is said to have belonged to the monks and to have contained the 50 hides of Cropthorne and other manors which add a further 70 hides (VCH i p. 247). 'Winburntree' included Blockley and Tredington. Even though these three Hundreds preceded Oswaldslow, they also seem to have been scattered ecclesiastical Hundreds, and if they were themselves ever re-arranged from compact Hundreds with a number of different lords, the re-organisation will necessarily have involved 'Pershore', 'Westminster' and Fishborough Hundreds as well, since they are all much intermingled in the south of the County.

The artificiality of the 1086 arrangement is apparent in the interlacing of parts of the different ecclesiastical Hundreds and in the detached portions of them lying well within the adjacent Counties of Warwickshire and Gloucestershire.

Such dispersed ecclesiastical Hundreds are found in other Counties; in Somerset for example, the Hundred of Bishop Giso of Wells is scattered in different parts of the County and was even in the process of formation at the time of the Domesday survey (see DB Somerset Places Notes Ch. 6 and Appendix I).

The object in creating these ecclesiastical Hundreds seems to have been to give the churches special privileges within their Hundreds. But not all church land was in church Hundreds (e.g. 2,76 ff. 9,6 ff. 10,13 ff). It is noteworthy that lands held by the churches in 1066 but alienated from them before 1086 were in non-ecclesiastical Hundreds, where they were more vulnerable to rapacious men like Urso or Odo. In part, however, this reflects the arrangement of DB which records all Oswaldslow land in Ch. 2, even though Urso and others held much of it, and the Church of Worcester appears from Hemming (Worcs. G in Appendix V) to have regarded it as lost.

The County

Whereas the shires in the south and south-east of the country were formed at a quite early date (all those south of the Thames being mentioned in the Parker MS of the Anglo-Saxon Chronicle before 892), the Mercian shires were of later formation. Taylor (GS) has shown how the Mercian shires are not recorded before early in the 11th century, mostly before 1016, although Worcs. itself is not referred to before 1038. It is likely that the mapping into shires was for the provision of men and ships for the expulsion of the Danes, and that the re-organisation was the work of Edric *Streona*, ealdorman of Mercia. Of him Hemming in Worcs. G (folio 130r = new folio 131r, Hearne p. 280) says: 'He behaved like an under king, to such an extent that he joined village to town and shire to shire at his will, for he joined the County of Winchcombe, which then existed on its own, to the County of Gloucester' (*et quasi sub-regulus dominabatur, in tantum ut villulas vilis et provincias provinciis pro libito adiungeret nam vicecomitatum de Wincelcumb, que per se tunc erat, vicecomitatui Gloeceastre adiunxit*).

The result of this re-organisation was the division of the land between the Thames and the Humber into blocks of 1200 or 2400 hides, a pattern that stands out clearly in the 'County Hidage' discussed by Maitland (DBB p. 456).

Because of the need to fit a County into 1200 hides, or multiples of it, the resulting county boundaries often ignore natural geographical divisions as well as ecclesiastical dioceses. In the case of Worcester, the conflict between the desire not to exceed 1200 hides, and the wish to keep the scattered ecclesiastical Hundreds within one County produced the strange county border with its many detachments that survived virtually unchanged into the 19th century.

The 'County Hidage' allots 1200 hides to Worcester, and any quick sum of the lands listed in DB produces a figure close to that. Maitland, who studied the question in detail (DBB pp. 451-455), concluded that the County in 1086 contained 1204 hides. His total consisted of Oswaldslow (300), 'Westminster' (200), 'Pershore' (100), Fishborough (65) and 5 'territorial' Hundreds of 539 hides in all. In fact his true total is 1203, the discrepancy being due to his counting 'Westminster' as a perfect 200 hides, whereas the sum of its individual parts, according to his reckoning, is 199 hides.

But Maitland's figures need further adjustment. He wrongly includes all 10 hides of Droitwich at 15,14, when only one is really accounted for there, the remaining 9 hides being recorded elsewhere in the schedule (see Appendix III). He thus counts 9 hides twice. He also included 1 virgate of Martley at 21,4, which is duplicated in the account of Martley in E 1; and 3 virgates of 'Willingwick' (23,4) are almost certainly a repeat of those in 1,1d. His figure should thus read 1193.

To this, however, should be added the 1 hide at Chawson mentioned in the Shropshire folios (E 8), and probably the 4 hides of Hanley Castle which had evidently been drawn out of Worcestershire, where they rightly belonged, and placed in Gloucestershire (EG 1, EH 1 notes). These adjustments produce a figure of 1198 hides. The difference between this and the ideal 1200 is probably accounted for by an error in the schedule for 'Westminster' Hundred. It is said to contain 200 hides (8,1), but Maitland counted only 199. Of these, the 1 hide of Droitwich (8,13) should no doubt be counted in Clent Hundred. This leaves 2 hides to be found. There are grounds for thinking that the hidage of Powick is wrong (8,10a note), or it may be that Nafford (8,25), described as a *frustum terrae*, counts as something. The Evesham A entries for this Hundred add 1 virgate at Longdon, ½ hide at Wick, ½ hide at Pirton, but give 1 hide less at North Piddle. Whatever may be the reasons for the discrepancies, if this Hundred is counted as a perfect 200 hides, the total for the County appears to be an exact 1200 hides.

It should be noted in this count that the only entries drawn from other Counties are Chawson and Hanley Castle, a total of 5 hides. Those Worcestershire places listed in the Herefordshire folios (1,39-41; 44-47 = E 1-7) are already included in the County total, either by being referred to in X 2-3, or, as alienated portions of large church manors, they have already been counted in the total of their head manor in Worcestershire. The 12 acres of Oldberrow are disregarded (10,4) and Martley is counted as 13 hides, not as 10 hides 1 virgate as given in Herefords. (1,39 = E 1). The notional 15 hides of Worcester city are included (10,2). Round (in VCH i p. 323) thought that Forthampton had been part of Worcestershire, by whose boundary it is almost completely surrounded. He suggested that it had been drawn into Gloucestershire as an outlier of Tewkesbury. But if the above figures are correct, there is no room in the total hidage of Worcestershire for its 9 hides.

It is more difficult to arrive at the exact composition of each of the 'territorial' Hundreds, a task which Maitland did not attempt. If a count is made of each Hundred according to the heads in the text of DB, supplemented or adjusted where necessary, the hidages for each Hundred seem to be: Doddingtree 121 hides 3 virgates; Cresslau 98 hides; Clent 104 hides; Esch 100 hides; Came 92 hides 1 virgate.

The exact composition of these Hundreds may never be recovered. In the case of Esch Hundred, the chance survival of the whole of Evesham A shows that Cookhill (under a Doddingtree Hundred head in DB) was in Esch, thus making exactly 100 hides. Were Evesham A complete for other Hundreds, further adjustments might be made. Bellington (23,14) was, for example, geographically within Cresslau Hundred, and counted there in later times, but it falls at the end of a group of Clent Hundred places in DB, and it has been counted there in the above figures, as a part of Dudley's castlery, even though a Cresslau Hundred head could easily have been omitted from the text of DB. If a border land is wrongly placed in a Hundred, it can easily upset the hidage count. Moreover, large manors such as Kidderminster in Cresslau and Bromsgrove in Came, with a number of scattered outliers, some of which have still to be identified, clearly fell into several Hundreds. Hundred heads must sometimes be supplied, increasing the uncertainty. Nonetheless, 3 out of the 5 Hundreds, Esch, Cresslau and Clent, are surprisingly close to the ideal figure of 100 hides.

Doddingtree Hundred has 121 hides 3 virgates, and the fact that it is oversize explains the addition of 20 of its hides to Fishborough (10,2), making both Hundreds nearly 100 hides each. It may be no coincidence that Doddingtree and Came Hundreds, on opposite sides of the County are not of regular size. The process of arranging 1200 hides around Worcester may have left part of Came in Warwickshire and thrust Doddingtree into an area that was naturally Herefordshire. Doddingtree's westward extension is nearly severed by Rochford and Stoke Bliss which long remained in Herefordshire, and it is interesting to note that the Worcestershire lands in this western peninsula of the County, Berrington, Bockleton, Kyre and Tenbury, total 20 hides 2 virgates, nearly the amount of Doddingtree's excess.

The Domesday Hundreds were by no means the same as those that survived into the 19th century. A number of important changes were made later in the middle ages. While Doddingtree Hundred survived almost intact (though losing Eardiston and Knighton to Oswaldslow, Mathon to Pershore, and Wychbold and Elmbridge to Halfshire, VCH iv p. 218), Pershore Hundred acquired Bushley, Hanley Castle, Mathon and Upton on Severn. To the 300 hides of Oswaldslow were added Alvechurch, Stoke Prior and 'Osmerley' from Came, and Cleeve Prior, Crowle, Hanbury and Inkberrow from Esch, as well as Wolverley and Hartlebury from Cresslau, and Eardiston and Knighton from Doddingtree (VCH iii pp. 246-248). To Fishborough were added Bengeworth and Hampton, Abbots Morton, Atch and Sheriffs Lench and parts of Church Lench and Bevington to form Blackenhurst Hundred (VCH ii p. 347). From Cresslau, Esch, Came and Clent (less the transfers to other Hundreds) was formed a single major Northern Hundred, Halfshire (VCH iii p. 1).

The County Boundary

The 1086 County boundary, with its island detachments within neighbouring Counties survived nearly intact until the 19th century. Since then, a number of Boundary Orders have transferred parishes from and into the County, eliminating all detachments, and altering its shape. In the north-east, parts of Worcestershire have been taken into Birmingham by the major city expansions of 1911 and 1931. These complex changes are summarised below:

SHROPSHIRE BORDER

Halesowen (14,1) was in Worcestershire in 1086, but subsequently abstracted by Earl Roger, together with the part of Warley known as Warley Salop, in the early 12th century, and only returned to Worcestershire from Shropshire in 1832 and 1844 (see 23,6 and E 8 notes).

TRANSFERRED FROM STAFFORDSHIRE

Upper Arley was transferred in 1895. Clent was counted as part of Worcestershire in 1086, though its revenue was in Staffordshire (1,5); it was then in Staffordshire until 1844 before being returned to Worcestershire. Tardebigge was in Worcestershire in 1086, but paid tax in Staffordshire (1,6); then in Staffordshire until 1266, thereafter in Warwickshire until 1844 before returning to Worcestershire. Amblecote was counted as a part of Staffordshire in 1086 and is still in that County, although a part of the Worcestershire parish of Old Swinford.

TRANSFERRED INTO BIRMINGHAM

Northfield parish, including Bartley Green and Selly Oak (1911); Kings Norton parish (1911), including most of Rednal, 'Lindsworth', Moseley and 'Tessall', but excluding (a) the ecclesiastical district of Wythall (the DB places of Wythall, Wythwood, Lea Green and Houndsfield); (b) Cofton Hackett and part of Rednal. Yardley was transferred in 1911.

TRANSFERRED FROM WARWICKSHIRE

Ipsley (1931)
Bickmarsh (1931) (see below)

TRANSFERRED TO WARWICKSHIRE

Alderminster (1931)
Tredington parish, including Blackwell and Longdon (1931)
Tidmington (1931)
Oldberrow (1894)
Shipston on Stour (1931)
for Bevington, see 10,15 note

TRANSFERRED FROM GLOUCESTERSHIRE

Ashton under Hill (1931)
Kemerton (1931)
Beckford (part) (1931)
Hinton on the Green (1931)
Cow Honeybourne (1931)
Childswickham (1931)

TRANSFERRED TO GLOUCESTERSHIRE

Blockley parish, including Dorn (2,38 note) and Ditchford (1931)
Cutsdean (1931)
Daylesford (1931)
Evenlode, including the site of *Ildeberga* (1931)

Pebworth parish, including Broad Marston and Ullington (1931)
Aston Somerville (1931)
Bickmarsh (1931), see EG 17 note
(Also transferred in 1931 was part of Forthampton.
For Hanley Castle, in Glos. in 1086, see EG 1 note)

TRANSFERRED FROM HEREFORDSHIRE

Rockford (1832; 1844)
Stoke Bliss (1897)

Church Icomb (part 1844); the rest of the parish was always in Glos.
Redmarley d'Abitot (1931)
Teddington (1931)
Little Washbourne (1844)
The parish of Alstone (not named in DB) was transferred in 1844; those of Chaceley and Staunton in 1931, see 8,9 notes

TRANSFERRED TO HEREFORDSHIRE

Acton Beauchamp (1897)
Edvin Loach (1893)
Mathon (1897). A part of Mathon was in Herefords. in 1086 (9,6a note)

APPENDIX II

Tabulation of the details for the Borough of Worcester

DB ref.	Manor	*Domus*	*Mansurae*[1]	Burgesses	Pay
1,2	KIDDERMINSTER	1[2]			
2,49	NORTHWICK	90[3]			
2,51	WORCESTER	25[4]			100s
10,17	WORCESTER		5 *wastae*		
			23		20s
14,1	HALESOWEN	1			12d
15,9	ASTLEY			2	2s
23,12	PEDMORE		2		2s
24,1	WITTON			1	2s
26,2	'OSMERLEY'	1			16d
26,15	UPTON WARREN			1	2s
28,1	CHADDESLEY CORBETT			2	12d
E 1	MARTLEY	3			12d
E 3	HOLLOW COURT	1			2 plough-shares
		2[5]			nothing
E 4	BUSHLEY	1			1 silver mark
E 7	SUCKLEY			1	nothing
E 9	CODDINGTON		3		30d

Notes:
1. Probably the same as *domus*, see 10,17 note.
2. This house and another at Droitwich pay 10d; see 1,2 note.
3. The Bishop holds 45, Urso 24, Osbern son of Richard 8, Walter Ponther 11, Robert the Bursar 1; see 2,49 note.
4. In Worcester market-place, possibly a duplication of the 24 above (note 3).
5. They belong to Feckenham.

APPENDIX III

Tabulation of the details for Droitwich including Witton and Salwarpe

DB ref.	Manor	Hides	*Domus*	Burgesses	SALT *Salinae*	SALT Other	Payment from	Payment to Droitwich
1,1a	BROMSGROVE				13		300m	300c[7]
						3 *salinarii*		
						6 *plumbi*		
1,1c	BROMSGROVE				1		10s	
1,2	KIDDERMINSTER		1[1]					
1,3a	DROITWICH[2]		11[3]					
	'UPWICH'				54	1 pit;2 *hocci*	6s 8d	
	HELPRIDGE				17	1 pit	–	
	'MIDDLEWICH'				12	1 pit;2 parts		
						of 1 *hoccus*	6s 8d	
	–				15	5 pits[4]	–	
1,5	TARDEBIGGE				7	2 *plumbi*	20s +	
							100m	
1,7	DROITWICH	½h						
2,7	HOLT				1		13d	
2,15	FLADBURY							Timber[5]
2,48	NORTHWICK				1		100m	100c
2,50	NORTHWICK		3				3m	
						(1) *fabrica*		
						plumbi	2s	
2,68	HALLOW +							
	BROADWAS		10				5s	
					1		50m	
2,77	PHEPSON				?[5]		10s	
2,78	CROWLE				1		3s	
2,79	HANBURY				?[5]		105m	
2,82	HARTLEBURY		5				5m	
2,84	ALVECHURCH				1		50m	
					7		70m	
4,1	DROITWICH	1h		18			4s 6d	
					1		20d	
5,1	SALWARPE	1h		4[6]	6		–	
7,1	DROITWICH	½h						
8,12	MARTIN HUSS-							
	INGTREE							100c
8,13	DROITWICH	1h				4 *furni*	60s +	
							100m[7]	
					1		10s	
				31			15s 8d	
9,1a	PERSHORE				1		30m	
10,10	OMBERSLEY				1		–	
12,1	DROITWICH	1h		9	?[5]		30s[8]	
14,1	HALESOWEN				1[9]		4s	
14,2	SALWARPE				5[6]		60s	
15,9	ASTLEY				1		64d +	
							18m	
15,13	ELMLEY LOVETT		5				20d	
					4[10]		70s	
15,14	DROITWICH	1h						

DB ref.	Manor	Hides	*Domus*	Burgesses	SALT *Salinae*	SALT Other	Payment from	Payment to Droitwich
18,6	DROITWICH	½h		11	1½		32½m[8]	
19,12	WYCHBOLD				26		£4 12s	
				13[11]			—	
22,1	DROITWICH	1h		20	7		50m[8]	
24,1	WITTON	2h			3		60m	
					part of 1		10m	
26,2	'OSMERLEY'				1		12m	
26,8	DOVERDALE				1		4s	
26,13	BELBROUGHTON				5		100m + 5 *ora*	
26,15	UPTON WARREN				3		40m	
26,16	WITTON	½h		7[12]			—	
					1½		30d	
27,1	'THICKEN-APPLETREE'				1		30m	
28,1	CHADDESLEY CORBETT				5		21s 4d	
E2	FECKENHAM[13]				4		—	
E3	HOLLOW COURT				4	1 *hoch*	—	
(BUCKINGHAMSHIRE)								
E10	PRINCES RISBOROUGH					1 *salinarius*	?pk[5]	
(GLOUCESTERSHIRE)								
E11	TEWKESBURY				2		—	
E12	STANWAY				1		—	
E13	THORNBURY						40st or 20d	
E14	OLD SODBURY	1v					25st[7]	
E15	MICKLETON						24mn	
E16	ROCKHAMPTON				1		4pk	
(HEREFORDSHIRE)								
E17	MARDEN				?[5]		9pk or 9d	
E18	MUCH MARCLE						60m	5s from woodland
E19	CLEEVE						25m[7]	
E20	LEOMINSTER						30m	5s for woodland
E21	ULLINGSWICK				part of 1		—	
E22	MORETON JEFFRIES				1		—	
E23	LEDBURY				part of 1		—	
E24	EASTNOR				part of 1		—	
E25	'BAGBURROW'				part of 1		—	
E26	TUPSLEY				1		16m	

DB ref.	Manor	Hides	*Domus*	Burgesses	SALT *Salinae*	SALT Other	Payment from	Payment to Droitwich
E27	WELLINGTON						17 m at 30d	
(OXFORDSHIRE)								
E28	BAMPTON				?[5]		£9 13s[14]	
E29	GREAT ROLLRIGHT						3pk	
(SHROPSHIRE)								
E30	DONNINGTON				5		20s	
E31	DITTON PRIORS				1		2s	
E32	CAYNHAM						4pk	
(WARWICKSHIRE)								
E33	BINTON						3pk	
E34	HILLBOROUGH				1		3s	

Abbreviations:

- c. cartloads of timber (*caretedes*)
- h. hides (*hidae*)
- m. measures of salt (*mittae*)
- mn. measures of salt (*mensurae*)
- pk. packloads of salt (*summae*)
- st. sesters (*sextaria*)
- v. virgates (*virgatae*)

Notes: Witton and Salwarpe are counted as parts of Droitwich since their hides make up the 10 taxable hides of which the Borough consisted in 1086 (15,14 note). It is assumed that *Wich* throughout refers to Droitwich rather than to Nantwich, Middlewich or Northwich in Cheshire, the other area of inland salt production.

1. This house and one in Worcester pay 10d; see 1,2 note.
2. At 1,3b it is recorded that Earl Edwin had 51½ *salinae* and 6s 8d from the *hocci*.
3. King Edward had 11 houses.
4. See penultimate note to 1,3a.
5. No figure is given.
6. Not said to be in Droitwich, but probably there, since the rest of Witton is, 26,16.
7. Before 1066.
8. The payment of the *salinae* and the burgesses is counted together.
9. Not necessarily still in existence in 1086. The text reads *Olwin habuit*.
10. Only the houses are said to belong to Droitwich.
11. Only the burgesses are said to belong to Droitwich. They reap and serve.
12. Only the burgesses are said to belong to Droitwich.
13. For the Chapter and section references of these places in the relevant County volumes, see the Elsewhere section.
14. The sum is from the *salinae* and from customary dues.

Burgesses and salt-houses are also mentioned in the following Worcestershire entries, and one or other or both may well refer to Droitwich. (sal. = *salina*; burg. = burgers).

1,2	KIDDERMINSTER	2 sal. at 30s
2,56	ODDINGLEY	1 sal. at 4s
3,3	INKBERROW	1 sal. which pays 15m
17,1	MORTON ?UNDERHILL	1 burg. who pays 10s; 1 sal. which pays 2s and 8
18,3	SHELL	4 sal. with woodland....pay 60m
19,13	ELMBRIDGE	1 sal. at 4s
19,14	CROWLE	1 burg. at 2s; 2 sal. at 6s
20,6	HADZOR	7 sal. pay 111m
23,8	BELL HALL	1 sal. at 2 *ora*
26,1	COOKHILL	1 burg. at 16d and 4m
26,6	RUSHOCK	1 sal. at 5 *ora*
26,10	HAMPTON LOVETT	7 sal. pay 14 *ora*
26,11	HORTON	1 sal. at 40d
26,17	HAMPTON LOVETT	1 sal. which pays 3 *ora*

References to salt in neighbouring Counties may also pertain to Droitwich:

GLOUCESTERSHIRE

1,13	AWRE	1 sal. at 30 pk (on the Severn estuary)
34,8	GUITING POWER	5 sal. pay 20pk
39,6	TEMPLE GUITING	1 sal. at 20s and 12 pk
61,2	TODDINGTON	from 1 sal. 50m

A salt-toll is mentioned under 1,57 Chedworth.

WARWICKSHIRE

1,1	BRAILES	Value now £55 and 20 pk
6,18	WASPERTON	A mill at 20s, 4 pk and 1000 eels
28,16	STUDLEY	1 sal. which pays 19 pk
40,2	HASELOR	1 sal. which pays 4s and 2 pk

All references to salt in Herefordshire and Shropshire specify Droitwich. There is none in Staffordshire.

APPENDIX IV

Worcestershire Domesday Material in Two Evesham Cartularies

Two cartularies of Evesham Abbey, British Library MS Cotton Vespasian B xxiv and Harleian MS 3763, contain, amongst miscellaneous other documents, a number of surveys dating from between 1086 and 1192 and closely related to Domesday Book. These surveys either derive from earlier stages of the Domesday Inquest itself, or are later abbreviations of the Exchequer Book, or Domesday-style surveys of the same lands and they often supplement or illustrate the statements of Domesday Book itself. Although they were known to Round and the first two were named Evesham A and B and used by the compilers of the EPNS volume for Worcestershire in 1927, serious study has long been hampered by the lack of a published text and scholarly discussion of these chaotic cartularies. This need has now been handsomely supplied by Dr. H. B. Clarke in his Birmingham Ph.D thesis which is to be revised and published in due course by the Worcestershire Historical Society.

The editors are most grateful to Dr. Clarke, now of University College, Dublin, for his great generosity in making parts of his thesis available to help preparation of the Worcestershire volume, as for the Gloucestershire one in the same series. Readers are referred to the thesis (cited in the Bibliography at the head of the Notes) or its published version for a masterly discussion of the manuscripts, an impeccable text and a sound and full consideration of the many problems.

In all, 16 surveys are found in the two MSS, ten in the first, four in the second, with two (E and G) being duplicated in each. Dr. Clarke has allotted a letter to each survey and numbered each section within. The details of the relevant 'satellites' and surveys are as follows:

(a) British Library MS Cotton Vespasian B xxiv:

A	(folios 6r-7v)	A fragmentary list of Worcestershire manors arranged by Hundreds and derived from a Domesday 'satellite', 1086.
B	(folio 8r)	A hidage schedule of the Worcestershire manors of William de Beauchamp and Roger de Tony, 1136.
C	(folios 8v-10v)	A Worcestershire hidage schedule probably derived from DB and revised to 1108.
D	(folios 10v-11r)	A list of lands obtained by Urso of Abetot from Evesham Church, compiled *c.*1108.
E	(folio 11r,v)	A list of manors subinfeudated by the Abbots of Evesham, compiled *c.*1130.
F	(folio 11r)	A hidage schedule of Evesham Abbey's holding in Gloucestershire, probably derived from a 'satellite'.
G	(folio 12r,v)	A list of Evesham manors subinfeudated, compiled *c.*1192.
H	(folio 12v)	A summary of county assessment totals for Evesham Abbey manors, *c.*1088.
J	(folios 49v,53r)	A Survey of Evesham manors in Worcestershire and Northamptonshire, *c.*1104, independent of DB.
K	(folios 57r-62r)	A hidage schedule of all Gloucestershire holdings in 1086, derived from a pre-Domesday 'satellite', but including two surveys of the Boroughs of Gloucester and Winchcombe, partly updated to *c.*1100.
L	(folio 57v)	A detailed survey of the Gloucestershire manors of Beckford and Ashton under Hill, *c.*1126.
M	(folios 62r-63v)	A partial hidage schedule for Gloucestershire in 1086, derived from a pre-DB satellite, excluding Chapters 1 and 51-78.

(b) British Library Harleian MS 3763:

N	(folios 60v-61r)	A list of manors removed from Evesham Church *c.*1078 by Odo of Bayeux, probably compiled *c.*1097.

O	(folio 61r,v)	A list of Evesham manors subinfeudated, compiled *c.*1130.
P	(folio 71v)	A hidage schedule for the Worcestershire manors of Evesham Church and Odo of Bayeux (Chs. 10-11), *c.*1104.
Q	(folio 82r)	An incomplete hidage schedule for Worcestershire derived from DB, but in a different order, with a *c.*1126 survey of Droitwich.

Translated below with Dr. Clarke's numbering is the whole of Evesham A, D and P and those parts of Evesham C, N and Q which in any way supplement or differ from the information given in Domesday. Only textual notes are given below each text discussion of other problems being found in the note to the corresponding DB entry: the reference numbers of these are given in the left-hand margin. Translation has been from the MSS, cross-checked with Dr. Clarke's text (and Professor Sawyer's in the case of Evesham A). The parts of the surveys relating to Gloucestershire are fully discussed in the Glos. volume of this series.

EVESHAM A Introduction

MS: British Library MS Cotton Vespasian B xxiv folios 6r-7v. Edition and Discussion i H. B. Clarke; P. H. Sawyer (1). Discussion in Galbraith (DB pp. 84-88).

The close relation of this text to Domesday Book has been observed since at least the late 18th century. But although it was referred to by Round and its place-name forms cited in the Worcestershire EPNS volume (1927), its true nature was not recogni until Sawyer's edition of 1960. Where previously it had been thought to be an abstract of Domesday Book, with added material, Sawyer convincingly showed that the document was a true Domesday satellite: an abbreviation of material gathered in the course of the complex stages of enquiry that produced Domesday Book.

Evesham A is a 12th-century abbreviation of a survey of Worcestershire estates, normally giving the place-name, the value at the time the original survey was made, the number of ploughs and the hidage, sometimes with the name of the holder. Most figur agree with DB, but even if allowance is made for scribal errors, a significant number, especially statements of value, differ. A number of personal names are not found in DE While Domesday usually names the major landholder and his immediate tenant (where all the land is not in lordship), it does not normally name further subtenants. In Evesham A the additional personal names seem usually to be those of such subtenants.

Evesham A is fragmentary, containing the Hundreds of Esch, Fishborough, Pershore (including the lands of Westminster and Pershore Churches) entire, but breaking off at the beginning of Came Hundred. It or its original was no doubt a complete account of the shire, Hundred by Hundred, thus contrasting with Domesday which is arranged by tenants-in-chief. In the case of those Hundreds, all ecclesiastical, held by a single tenan in-chief, the order of the individual estates in Evesham A and in DB is close but not identical. The accounts of Fishborough and Oswaldslow Hundreds and of the Pershore Abbey holdings in Pershore Hundred are parallel, but in the case of the Westminster Abbey lands in Pershore Hundred, the villages containing lordship land are first listed, then those that are partially subinfeudated, then those wholly so. In this way parts of the same villages are separated, while DB mainly recombines the information.

In the case of the only complete 'territorial' Hundred, Esch, the order is entirely different. In Domesday Book, the constituent parts of the Hundred are scattered in th chapters of the relevant tenants-in-chief, church and lay. In Evesham A, the Hundred i listed as a whole, and with one exception (Crowle where both holdings in the village ar entered together) the lands of each holder are entered in groups within the account of the Hundred. Moreover, the order of the landholders in Evesham A is quite different from that of the DB chapters.

There are further discrepancies: for example, some large manors with a number of members, such as Longdon, Pershore, Powick and Bromsgrove, are treated in quite different ways by the two documents.

The surviving portion of Evesham A omits about 15 estates, some of which, such as Phepson, may have been accidentally missed in copying. To the information contained in DB, on the other hand, it adds a number of tenants' names, especially on estates held by Urso the Sheriff. A number of place-names have explanatory additions such as *Croela Odonis, Croela Gualteri*, which distinguish villages of the same basic name. Some of these additional names may have been added in the late 12th century by the abstractor, rather then being part of the original. Such is A 147, Bengeworth, where the *pars Willelmi* must refer either to the first or the second William de Beauchamp (1131-70 or 1170-1197). The place-name forms themselves are frequently closer to the original English form of the name: in any place-name study, the DB forms often stand out as a deformation of the original name, probably as a result of mis-handling by Norman scribes. Moreover, a Latin first declension termination in *-a* is often preferred, as in Exon. DB, to the English terminations of Exchequer DB. Whereas DB rarely names the constituent villages of a large manor, Evesham A does in a number of cases (A 52-55;64-68;70-72; 146;154;163). *Villici* is regularly found in place of DB *villani* for 'villagers'.

On the basis of such differences, Sawyer shows that neither Evesham A nor DB can have been abstracts of each other, but that they must have had a common source. Although Evesham A is an abstract which selects hidage and value, it no doubt reproduces the order of its source, and the latter was probably a set of returns arranged by Hundreds and derived from an early stage of the Domesday enquiry. The most likely stage was that before the material was presented to the juries of each Hundred for checking. On this hypothesis, the differences between DB itself and the source of Evesham A would be explained on the one hand by the elimination from the source of Evesham A of details such as animals, sub-tenancies, distinctive additions to place-names that were considered unnecessary for the finished Exchequer DB; and on the other by additional material brought to light at the Hundred courts and subsequently, that is after the compilation of the source of Evesham A but before the drafting of the Exchequer text. A late change probably involved Bengeworth. Evesham A 30 includes it in Fishborough Hundred, which is probably where the Abbot of Evesham claimed it to be in a transparent attempt to resolve thus the long dispute with the Church of Worcester (10,11-12 note above and Worcs. H below). In Evesham A 31 Hampton is similarly included in Fishborough Hundred, though said to be in Oswaldslow. DB correctly notes the two estates in the Church of Worcester's fief, but details them among the Evesham lands, though beneath an Oswaldslow Hundred heading.

What immediately preceded and followed the composition of the source of Evesham A is a matter for speculation. Sawyer may well be right in thinking that the 'original returns' were those of tenants-in-chief who produced individual schedules for their fiefs, covering more than one Hundred, and probably more than one County. These were then rearranged in hundredal form in preparation for scrutiny by the Hundred juries. This notion of a double return, by fief and by Hundred can be read into the *Inquisitio Comitatus Cantabrigiensis* which also appears to set out the procedure of the Domesday enquiry which was: *per sacramentum vicecomitis scirae et omnium baronum et eorum Francigenarum et totius centuriatus, presbiteri, praepositi vi villanorum uniuscuiusque villae* (ICC p. 97). But none of these original returns survives. The *Inquisitio* and Bath A, a fragment from a Bath cartulary (discussed by R. Lennard in EHR (1943) pp. 32-41, in Galbraith (DB pp. 88-91) and in Appendix II of the Somerset volume in this series), both seem to represent the same stage of the Domesday enquiry and are similarly arranged by hundreds.

The amount of detail supplied by Evesham A varies, information for the lands of Pershore Abbey being consistently fuller. The fact that no lordship or tenant ploughs are mentioned in the whole of Oswaldslow Hundred, held by the Church of Worcester, nor on that Church's lands in Esch Hundred, suggests that tenants-in-chief furnished the 'original returns' and that the degree of detail varied. Some of the differences may be due to the abbreviation that produced Evesham A. If the original survived, entry A 166 for 'Willingwick' which includes livestock (as in the Exon. Domesday book) might seem less exceptional. For further discussion of the 'original returns' the reader is referred to the articles by P. H. Sawyer (3) and S. Harvey (2) cited in the Bibliography at the head of the Notes.

What followed the stage represented by Evesham A, at least for the three eastern and five south-western counties was the compilation of enormous volumes, circuit returns, in which the material was rearranged in fiefs, though still largely in Hundred order within them. The Little Domesday was never abbreviated, but Exon. Domesday was condensed into Exchequer Domesday, by the omission of such detail as animals, many bynames and the hidage of villagers' land, and by the adoption of more concise Latin formulae. No circuit return survives for the midland shires, and it is not clear whether one existed, or whether the original of Evesham A, supplemented by the Hundred enquiries, was re-arranged and abstracted in one operation.

EVESHAM A: Translation folio

DB ref.	Place-name		
			In the Lord's name, Amen[1]
ESCH HUNDRED			
X 2 (E 2)	FECKENHAM	(1)	In *Eisse* Hundred. *Feckeham*[2] has 10 hides.
X 2 (E 3)	HOLLOW (COURT)	(2)	*Holoweie*, 3 hides.
17,1	MORTON (?UNDERHILL)	(3)	*Mortuna*, 4 hides. 2 ploughs in lordshi and 4 ploughs among the men. Value £4.
11,2	(SHERIFFS) LENCH	(4)	*Lenz Bernardi*, 4 hides. 2 ploughs in lordship and 2 among the men. Value 40s.
26,1	COOKHILL	(5)	*Cokehelle*, 2½ hides. 1 plough among the men. Value 50s.
3,3	INKBERROW	(6)	*Inteberga*, 15½ hides. 4 ploughs in lordship and 12 among the men. Valu now £12.
2,76	CLEEVE (PRIOR)	(7)	*Cliua*, 10½ hides. Value £7.
2,79	HANBURY	(8)	*Hamburga*, 3 hides. Value 100s.
19,14	CROWLE	(9)	*Croela Gualteri*, 5 hides. 1½ ploughs i lordship and ½ plough among the me Value 40s.
2,78	CROWLE	(10)	*Croela Odonis*, 6 hides. Value 70s.
10,16	CHURCH LENCH	(11)	*Chirchlenz*, 4 hides. 2 ploughs in lordship; among the men, 2 ploughs and 1 plough of a serving man. Value 30s.
10,14	ATCH LENCH	(12)	*Hecheslenz*, 3½ hides. 1 plough in lordship and 1 plough among the men Value now 20s.
10,13	(ABBOTS) MORTON	(13)	*Mortona*, 5 hides. 1 plough in lordship and 4 ploughs among the men. Value 30s.
10,15	BEVINGTON	(14)	*Biuintona*, 1 hide. 1 plough in lordshi Value 10s.
18,3	SHELL	(15)	*Heisse*, 2 hides. 1 plough in lordship. Value now with the whole wood, 40s; value without the wood, 15s.
18,4	KINGTON	(16)	*Kintona* has 5 hides and 2 ploughs in lordship and 5 among the men. Value 50s.

DB ref.	Place-name		
8,26a	(SEVERN) STOKE	(17)	*Stokes Roberti*, 12 hides of the King's Holding and 3 hides of the Westminster Holding.[3] In the vale of Evesham.[4]
FISHBOROUGH HUNDRED			
10,1	EVESHAM	(18)	In *Fischberge* Hundred. *Evesham* has 3 hides which do not pay tax and 3 ploughs in lordship and 4 among the men. Value now 110s.
10,3	LENCHWICK	(19)	*Lenchwic*, 1 hide. 5 ploughs in lordship and 11 ploughs among the men. Value now £7.
10,3	NORTON	(20)	*Nortona*,[5] 7 hides.
10,5	LITTLETON	(21)	*Liteltuna*, 6½ hides. 2 ploughs in lordship and 8 ploughs among the men. Value now 70s.
10,5	OFFENHAM	(22)	*Offeham*, 2 hides; one of these does not pay tax. 3 ploughs in lordship and 7 among the men. Value now £6 10s.
10,5	ALDINGTON	(23)	*Aldintona*, 1 hide which does not pay tax. 2 ploughs in lordship and 1 plough among the men. Value now 40s.
10,6	BRETFORTON	(24)	*Brotfortona*, 6 hides, which belong to *Aldinton'* (Aldington).
10,6	WICKHAMFORD	(25)	*Wichwana*, 3 exempt[6] hides. 4 ploughs in lordship and 10 ploughs among the men.
10,6	BRETFORTON	(26)	*Brotfortona*, 6 hides which perform service at *Wichwana* (Wickhamford). Value now £6.
10,8	LITTLETON	(27)	*Liteltona*, 7 hides. 2 ploughs in lordship and 7 among the men. Value now 50s.
10,9	(CHURCH) HONEYBOURNE	(28)	*Huniburna*,[7] 2½ hides. 4 ploughs in lordship[8] and 4 among the villagers. Value now £4.
10,10	OMBERSLEY	(29)	*Hambreslega*, 15 hides; 3 of these are exempt. 5 ploughs in lordship and 20 among the men. Value now £16; the burgesses (*Burgones*) 20s.
10,12	BENGEWORTH	(30)	*Benninchwrtha*, 4 hides. Value 60s.
10,11	HAMPTON	(31)	*Hamtona*, 5 hides which lie in *Oswaldeslowe* (Oswaldslow Hundred). 3 ploughs in lordship and 6 among the villagers. Value now £6.
10,7	BADSEY	(32)	*Badeseia*, 5½ hides. 2 ploughs in lordship and 4 among the villagers.[9]
PERSHORE HUNDRED			folio 6v
8,1	PERSHORE	(33)	In *Persor'* Hundred are 2 hides which never paid tax. Value £14.

DB ref.	Place-name		
8,2	WICK	(34)	*Wicha*, 6½ hides. Value 60s.
8,3	PENSHAM	(35)	*Pennesham*, 2 hides. Value now 60s.
8,4	BIRLINGHAM	(36)	*Burlingeham*, 1 hide. Value 50s.
8,5	BRICKLEHAMPTON	(37)	*Brichthelmentona*, 10 hides.
8,6	DEFFORD	(38)	*Depford*, 10 hides. Value 50s.
8,7	ECKINGTON	(39)	*Hekintona*, 9 hides. Value 100s.
8,8	BESFORD	(40)	*Bezford*, 4 hides. Value 20s.
8,9	LONGDON	(41)	*Langentona*, 11 hides. Value £9.
8,10	POWICK	(42)	*Poiwicha*, 3 hides. Value £20.
8,11	(UPTON) SNODSBURY	(43)	*Snodesbery*, 11 hides. Value £7 10s.
8,12	(MARTIN) HUSSINGTREE	(44)	*Husintre*, 6 hides. Value 30s.
8,13	DROITWICH	(45)	At *Wich*, 1 hide (belonging) to the Abbot. Value including salt[10] and everything 112s; value of the tithe £8.
8,2	WICK	(46)	Gilbert of[11] *Wich* holds ½ hide. Value 10s.
		(47)	Robert holds 1 hide. Its value is 15s.
8,4	BIRLINGHAM	(48)	Robert has 2 hides and 1 virgate at *Burlingeham*. Value 40s.
8,7	ECKINGTON	(49)	In *Hekintona* he has 4 hides, less 1 virgate. Value now 40s.
		(50)	Hugh of *Wllauesella*[12] (Woollashill) has 3 hides in the same village. Value 60s.
8,8	BESFORD	(51)	*Bezforda*, 5 hides. Value 30s.
8,8	BESFORD	(52)	*Bokindona* ('Bucknell'), 1 hide.[13] Value 16s.
8,9	LONGDON	(53)	In *Stantona* (Staunton), 5 hides. Value 20s.
		(54)	In *Heldresfelde* (Eldersfield), 5 hides, which pay their dues at Hereford.
		(55)	*Chaddeslege* (Chaceley), 2 hides. Value 20s.
		(56)	*Langentona* (Longdon), 1½ hides. Value 20s.
		(57)	The King has 3 virgates.
		(58)	Alchere has 1 hide. Value 15s.
		(59)	Warengar has 1 hide. Value 20s.
		(60)	William son of Baderon has 2½ hides. Value 40s.
		(61)	Robert has ½ hide. Value 10s.
8,10	POWICK	(62)	In *Poiwicha*[14] ... the Sheriff has 5 hides 2 ploughs in lordship. Value 21s.
		(63)	Value of Robert Parler's part, 20s.
		(64)	*Branesford* (Bransford). 2 ploughs in lordship. Value 2 hides.[15]
		(65)	*Madresfeld* (Madresfield) has 1 virgate of Powick. 2 ploughs in lordship. Value 20s.

DB ref.	Place-name		
8,10	POWICK	**(66)**	*Ad Bergam* ('Aggborough')[16] has 1 plough in lordship from the same land. Value 35s.
		(67)	*Picresham* (Pixham)[16] has 3 ploughs in lordship. Value 23s.
8,11	(UPTON) SNODSBURY	**(68)**	In *Coulesduna* (Cowsden), 3 hides and 3 virgates. 3 ploughs in lordship and among the men. Value 50s.[17]
8,14	DORMSTON	(69)	In *Dormestona*, 3 hides. 2 ploughs in lordship and 3 ploughs among the men. Value 60s.
8,10	POWICK	(70)	*Cliuelade* (Clevelode)[16] has 2 ploughs in lordship. Value 25s.
8,14	DORMSTON	(71)	In *Pidelet* (North Piddle), 2 hides. 1 plough in lordship and ½ plough among the men. Value now 30s.
8,15	(NORTH) PIDDLE	(72)	In *Flavel* (Flyford Flavel) and *Pidelet* (North Piddle) Robert Parler has 5 hides and 5 ploughs. Value 60s.
8,16	NAUNTON (BEAUCHAMP)	(73)	In *Neuuintona*,[18] 10 hides. Of these Herbrand holds 3 hides and 3 virgates. Value of the Sheriff's part, £4; of Herbrand's part, 40s.
8,17	GRAFTON (FLYFORD)	(74)	In *Graftona*, 1 hide and 2 virgates. Value 30s.
8,18	(NORTH) PIDDLE	(75)	In *Pidelet*, 3 hides. Value 60s.
8,19	PIRTON	(76)	*Perintona*, 6½ hides. Value 50s.
8,20	GRAFTON (FLYFORD)	(77)	In *Graftona*, 7 hides. Value 69s.
8,21	PEOPLETON	(78)	In *Piplintona*, 1 hide. Value 8s 4d.
8,23	COMBERTON	(79)	*Cumbrintona*, 9 hides. Value 70s.
		(80)	*Strenchesham* (Strensham), 10 hides. Value 5s.
8,24	BROUGHTON (HACKETT)	**(81)**	*Brochtona*, 3 hides. Value 30s.
8,26	(SEVERN) STOKE	**(82)**	Value of Boselin's land, 20s.
8,27	COMBERTON	**(83)**	*Cumbrintona*, 2 hides. Value 10s.[19]

folio 7r

OSWALDSLOW HUNDRED

2,2	KEMPSEY	**(84)**	In *Oswaldeslawe* Hundred. In *Camesi*, 24 hides. Value £8.
2,3	MUCKNELL	**(85)**	Of these hides, Urso the Sheriff has *Mucheulla*, 7 hides. Value £4.
2,4	WOLVERTON	**(86)**	*Wlfrintona*, 2 hides of the above hides. Value 40s.
2,5	WHITTINGTON	(87)	*Witintona*, 2 hides. Value 40s.
2,6	WICK (EPISCOPI)	(88)	*Wike*, 15 hides. Value £8.
2,7	HOLT	(89)	Of these hides, Urso the Sheriff has 5 hides at *Holt*. Value now £6.
2,8	(LITTLE) WITLEY	(90)	*Witerlega*, 1 hide. Value 15s.
2,10	'CLOPTON'	(91)	*Cloptune*, 1 hide. Value 15s.
2,11	LAUGHERNE	(92)	*Lawerne*,[20] ½ hide. Value[21] 6s.

DB ref.	Place-name		
2,13	LAUGHERNE	(93)	*Lawerne,*[20] ½ hide. Value 20s.
2,9	KENSWICK	(94)	*Chechinwich*, 1 hide. Value 12s.
2,11	LAUGHERNE	(95)	*Lawerne,*[20] 1 virgate. Value 12d.
2,12	GREENHILL	(96)	*Grimhelle*, 1 hide. Value 6s.
2,15	FLADBURY	(97)	*Fladebury*, 40 hides. Value £9.
2,17	AB LENCH	(98)	*Hebbelenz*, 5 hides of these 40 hides. Value £4.
2,16	INKBERROW	(99)	*Inteberge*, 5 hides. Value 30s.
2,18	(ROUS) LENCH	(100)	*Lenz*, 7 hides. Value £7.
2,20	BRADLEY (GREEN)	(101)	*Bradelega*, 1 hide. Value 20s.
2,21	BISHAMPTON	(102)	*Bishantune,*[22] 10 hides. Value £10.
2,22	BREDON	(103)	*Bridona*, 35 hides. Value £9 10s.
2,23	TEDDINGTON and MITTON	(104)	*Tetintona* and[23] *Muttona*, 4 hides. Value £4.
2,25	REDMARLEY (D'ABITOT)	(105)	*Rudmerlege*, 2 hides. Value of these two, £7. In *Rudmelege Willelmi*, 3 hides.
2,26	PENDOCK	(106)	*Penedoch,* 2 hides. Value of Warner's part, 20s; of Walter's part, 6s.
2,27	(LITTLE) WASHBOURNE	(107)	*Wasseburna,* 3 hides. Value 40s.
2,29	(BREDONS) NORTON	(108)	*Nortona,* 2 hides. Value 20s.
2,28	WESTMANCOTE	(109)	*Westmenecote,* 4 hides. Value 60s.
2,30	BUSHLEY	(110)	*Bisselega,* 1 hide. Value 40s.
2,31	RIPPLE	(111)	*Rippele,* 25 hides. Value £10.
2,32	CROOME	(112)	*Crumbe,* 1 hide. Value 40s.
2,34	HILL CROOME	(113)	*Hulcrumba,* 3 hides. Value £4.
2,33	CROOME	(114)	*Crumbe,* 5 hides. Value 40s.
2,35	HOLDFAST	(115)	At *Holeuest,*[24] 1 hide. Value 20s.
2,36	QUEENHILL	(116)	*Cuinhulle,* 1 hide. Value 40s.
2,38	BLOCKLEY	(117)	*Blocchelai,* 33 hides. Value £20.
2,39	DITCHFORD	(118)	Richard holds 2 hides. Value 30s.
2,40	—	(119)	Asgot (*Astgot*) holds 1½ hides. Value £15.
?2,38	BLOCKLEY	(120)	Hereward [holds] 5 hides. Value 40s.
2,42	DAYLESFORD	(121)	*Dailesford,*[25] 3 hides. Value 60s.
2,43	EVENLODE	(122)	*Eunelate,* 5 hides. Value 60s.
2,45	TREDINGTON	(123)	*Tredintona,* 23 hides. Value £15.
2,47	LONGDON	(124)	Gilbert son of Thorold [holds] 4 hid Value 60s.
2,48	NORTHWICK	(125)	*Norwiche,* 25 hides. Value £16 3s.
2,52	HINDLIP	(126)	*Hindelep,* 5 hides. Value 20s.
2,55	(WHITE LADIES) ASTON	(127)	Ordric (*Ordrich*) holds 3½ hides. Value 40s.
2,56	ODDINGLEY	(128)	In *Odingelega,* 1 hide. Value 15s.
2,52	OFFERTON	(129)	*Alchrintona,*[26] 1½ hides in the land o *Lege* ('Leigh'). Value 25s.
2,59	CHURCHILL	(130)	*Chirchhulle,* 3 hides. Value 20s.
2,60	BREDICOT	(131)	*Bradicote,* 3 hides. Value 20s.

DB ref.	Place-name		
2,61	'PERRY'	(132)	*Pyrya,* 1 hide. Value 20s.
2,53	WARNDON	(133)	*Warmindone,* 1 hide and 3 virgates. Value 16s.
2,54	CUDLEY	(134)	At *Cudelege,* 1 hide. Value 10s.
2,62	OVERBURY with PENDOCK	(135)	In *Ouerberga,* 6 hides, and in the same land *Alaberga* (Berrow) has 1 hide and *Penedoch.* Value of the whole, £6.
2,63	SEDGEBERROW	(136)	*Sechesberga,* 4 hides. Value 60s.
2,64	SHIPSTON (ON STOUR)	(137)	*Schepwastona,*[27] 2 hides. Value 50s.
2,66	GRIMLEY	(138)	*Grimelega,* 3 hides. Value £3.
2,65	HARVINGTON	(139)	*Heruertona,* 3 hides. Value 50s.
2,67	KNIGHTWICK	(140)	*Chechinwick,* 1 hide. Value 20s.
2,68	HALLOW	(141)	*Hamlega,* 7 hides. Value 100s.
2,69	EASTBURY	(142)	*Alesberga,* ½ hide. Value 5s.
2,70	HIMBLETON and SPETCHLEY	(143)	*Aelmeltone* and *Spechlege,* 3½ hides. Value 50s.
2,71	LYPPARD	(144)	*Lappewrtha,* ½ hide. Value 20s.
			folio 7v
2,72	CROPTHORNE	(145)	*Croptorna,*[28] 50 hides. Value £6.
2,73	—	(146)	*Halmelega* (Elmley Castle), 2 hides. Value £7.
2,75	BENGEWORTH	(147)	*Benninchwrth'.* William's part, 6 hides. Value £3.
PERSHORE HUNDRED			
9,1	PERSHORE	(148)	In *Persore*[29] Hundred. In *Persora,*[30] 26 hides which pay tax.[31]
	CHIVINGTON	(149)	In *Chiuintona,* 3 hides.
	WICK	(150)	*Wick,* ½ hide.
	ABBERTON	(151)	*Eadbrichtona,* 6½ hides. Value 25s.
	(DRAKES) BROUGHTON	(152)	In *Broctuna,* 3 hides. One of these 3 is free (*franca*), so it is explained, for Urso's use, by the judgement of the County (Court).
	WADBOROUGH	(153)	In *Wadberga,* 5 hides. Godric, a thane, bought one of these before 1066[32] for the life of 3 heirs and afterwards it was to revert to the lordship supplies from which it had been sold. In acknowledgement he owed from it each year a revenue to the Abbot and to his household for as long as it pleased the man who gave the revenue. The (land) which Godric bought, Urso holds for life. He has there 2 ploughs in lordship. Value 40s.
	COMBERTON	(154)	Acer held 1½ hides of the above hides from *Cumbrintona.* Now U(rso) the Sheriff has it from the King.

DB ref.	Place-name		
9,1	COMBERTON	(155)	Now it has 5 ploughs in the Abbot's lordship; 22 ploughs among the men. Of the above land, Urso claims the land that Leofwin the priest holds. Value of all this, £12.
		(156)	In the same *Cumbrintona,* 2 ploughs in lordship. Value 50s.
9,2	BEOLEY and YARDLEY	(157)	*Bielege,* 21[33] hides with one member, *Gardelegia.* Value £5. 1 plough in lordship and 9 among the men.
9,3	ALDERMINSTER	(158)	In *Stura* ('Stour'), that is *Aldremanestu* 20 hides,[34] ... hides and 4 ploughs in lor ship and 9 ploughs among the men. Value £9.
9,4	BROADWAY	(159)	*Bradewege,* 30 hides. Value £14 10s.
		(160)	Of these there are 2½ hides of free (*franca*) land, as the Sheriff has explained, with the County (Court) as witness. Urso the Sheriff claims these 4 hides mentioned above as the King's gift and he has exchanged them with Abbot Edmund for that land of which he has now been dispossessed. Value now 30s.
9,5	LEIGH and BRANSFORD	(161)	*Lega,* 3 hides. The Abbot has 1 hide of these in lordship and 1 hide at *Berneford*; value £4. Rainer has 1 hide; value 40s.[35]
CAME HUNDRED			
1,1	BROMSGROVE	(162)	In *Cammel* Hundred. 30 hides at *Bremesgraue.*
	GRAFTON	(163)	*Grastone,*[36] 5 hides.
	WOODCOTE (GREEN)	(164)	*Odenecote Roberti,* 3 hides which pay tax. It has not been assessed, because it is (part) of the 30 hides of *Bremes-graue* (Bromsgrove).
	COOKSEY (GREEN)	(165)	Ernheit had *Chocheseia.* William has 2 hides from the Sheriff's[37] Holdings.[38] Value before 1066, 10s; value now 10s. Herbrand has ½ hide.
	'WILLINGWICK'	(166)	Brictwy (*Brichthveit*) had 3 hides, less 1 virgate, in *Walingewica* before 1066. He could not leave the lord, who had *Bremesgraue* (Bromsgrove), without his permission. Value before 1066, 20s. Walter holds this (land) from the Sheriff, and when the Sheriff acquired it he found no resources there. But now he has 1 plough, 2 slaves, 61 pigs, 2 sheep, 5 smallholders. They have

DB ref.	Place-name		
			1 plough. The King has taken the wood and placed it in (his) Forest. Value now 10s.
1,1	CHADWICK	**(167)**	Frewin and Alnoth had 3 hides in *Chaldeswic*. Value before 1066, 60s. Alfred now holds them from the Sheriff.
23,2	NORTHFIELD	**(168)**	*Northfeld,* 6 hides.[39]

EVESHAM A. Textual Notes

1. This heading is written in the top margin, probably marking the beginning of the document, possibly of the cartulary.
2. (A 1). Before *Feckeham* is written an *a*, probably in error, since Feckenham appears to be the subject of *habet* 'has'.
3. A 17 is a later addition in another hand.
4. This heading is written in the right-hand margin in a large late medieval hand.
5. (A 20). *Nortona* has been altered from *Mortona*.
6. (A 25). *quietas* ('exempt') in the MS is a scribal error for the nominative plural *quietae* to agree with *hide*.
7. (A 28). *Huniburna* has been altered from *Huniburga*, the *g* being marked for deletion and an *n* written above.
8. (A 28). *in dominio* is interlined, with a mark after *car̄* ('ploughs') to show its correct position.
9. A 32 is a later addition in another hand.
10. (A 45). The MS has *sal'* with an abbreviation line through the *l*, followed by a letter written then altered, wrongly reproduced by Sawyer as *salt'*.
11. (A 46). The MS has *del* possibly with an abbreviation line through the *l*. *Del* is found occasionally for *de* in MSS of the period (see Evesham A 1 and Evesham Q 29), the *l* being derived from the French definite article.
12. (A 50). *Wllauesella* has been altered from *holouesella, holo* being lined through for deletion and *Wlla* (or *Wlta*) written above.
13. (A 52). After *i hida, et* and possibly a *u* (for *ualet*?) have been erased, though still visible, and *ual xvi sol* interlined.
14. (A 62). After *Poiwicha* there is a *v*, originally *.v.* (for *v hid'* or perhaps for *Vrso* as in A 154), written then erased, though still visible.
15. (A 64). *Valent ii hidas* ('Value 2 hides') is either a MS error for *Valent ii solidos* (or some such phrase) or the scribe omitted the value of the 2 hides.
16. (A 66;67;70). The syntax is unclear. *Ad Bergam habet..., Ad Picresham habet..., In Cliuelade habet...* should mean 'At *Berga*, At Pixham, In Clevelode, he or she or it has ...' but it is not clear what the subject is. *Ad Bergam* (see 8,10a note) is probably a corruption of *Acberge* 'Oak-hill', wrongly assimilated to Latin *Ad*; and this may have led the scribe to begin the next entry with *Ad*, when Pixham should be the subject of *habet*. Similarly *In Cliuelade habet...* seems to confuse phrases such as *Madresfeld habet i virgatam...* 'Madresfield has or contains 1 virgate...', with *In Coulesduna iii hidae*, 'In Cowsden (are) 3 hides...' in which *sunt* is understood. In the translation the place-names are assumed to be the subject of *habet*.
17. (A 68). The figure *l* '50' is written above an erasure of apparently 2 letters, the first being an *l*; probably a figure error.
18. (A 73). *Neuuintona*. The *i* is fatter than usual and in darker ink and is probably an early correction from an *e*.
19. A 83 is written in the lower margin on the right-hand side of the page.
20. (A 92;93;95). *Lawerne* has been altered from *Laure*, the *ure* being both lined through and underlined and *werne* interlined above.
21. (A 92). After *ualent* (a scribal error for *ualet*), *et* is erased.
22. (A 102). *Bishantune* has been altered from *Bissantune*, a deletion mark being written under the second *s* and an *h* interlined above.
23. (A 104). At the end of the line in the MS, after *et*, the letters *Mu* (probably the beginning of *Muttona*) have been written and then erased (though still visible), presumably through lack of space for the rest of the place-name.
24. (A 115). *Holeuest* has been changed from *Houestre*, the *re* being lined through and marked for deletion and *le* interlined with a mark to show its correct position.

25. (A 121). *Dailesford* has been substituted in the margin, with transposition signs beside it, for *Aleford* which is lined through for deletion.
26. (A 129). The MS reads *Alrichehtona*, the *r*, *i* and *e* being marked for deletion.
27. (A 137). The *h* in *Schepwastona* is interlined.
28. (A 145). The *r* in *Croptorna* is interlined.
29. (A 148). *Persore* has been altered from *Persone*, the *ne* being marked for deletion and the *re* interlined.
30. (A 148). *Persora* has been altered from *Persona*, but although only *r* is interlined there are deletion dots under both the *n* and the *a*, the second probably in error.
31. (A 148). *geld'* is interlined.
32. (A 153). *tempore* of *tempore Regis Eadwardi* is an interlineation.
33. (A 157). After *Bielege*, *i* is erased and *xxi* interlined above with a mark to show its correct position.
34. (A 158). 'That is *Aldremanestun'*, 20 hides' is entered in the left-hand margin in a different hand, with a mark corresponding to one above and between *Stura* and *hid'*.
35. (A 161). After *ualet*, *xl* is erased, this having apparently been first altered from *xv*.
36. (A 163). *Grastone*, standing for Grafton, a Domesday outlier of Kidderminster, not *Ginstone* (an unidentified place) read by Sawyer.
37. (A 165). *vicecomitis* is interlined.
38. (A 165). After *feudo* 'Holding', *mortemer* is deleted.
39. (A 168). The text breaks off here, at the bottom of folio 7v.

EVESHAM B Note

MS: British Library MS Cotton Vespasian B xxiv folio 8r. Edited by H. B. Clarke; translated and discussed by Round in VCH (Worcs.) i pp. 327-330; see also FE p. 178.

Dated by Dr. Clarke to *c.* 1136, this is a fragmentary survey, only the latter part survivin of the lands of two important Worcestershire barons, William de Beauchamp and Roger de To(s)ny. Although similar to abbreviations of DB, in that it includes place-names and hidage, it is independent. It is not reproduced below, because of this independence, but it is helpful in identifying more precisely a number of Domesday holdings, and is cited occasionally in the Notes. William de Beauchamp is found holding the lands held ir 1086 by Urso, and by his brother, Robert the Bursar, together with lands seized by Ursc after 1086. In the surviving portion of the text they are listed in the Hundred order Cresslau, Came, Pershore, Esch, Clent, Doddingtree; Pershore Hundred here, as in Evesham A, includes the lands of Pershore and Westminster Churches. The lands of Roge of Tosny are, without exception, those held by Ralph of Tosny in Domesday (Ch. 15).

EVESHAM C Introduction

MS: British Library MS Cotton Vespasian B xxiv folios 8v-10v. Discussion in H. B. Clark

Evesham C is an abbreviation of Domesday Chs. 2-8, written in three hands of the late 12th century. It may originally have been intended as an abstract of the whole of Worcester Domesday apart from Ch. 1, but was never completed, perhaps because it was too great a labour. The next text in the cartulary begins on the same page as the last par of Evesham C. Urso appears still to have been alive when Evesham C was completed: the document must date from before his death in 1108.

The text is in the same order as the Domesday survey and normally contains the plac name, the name of the holder, the hidage and states whether the hides are taxed. Similar abbreviations of DB are Bath B (Appendix II in the Somerset volume of this series); the Breviate (Public Record Office E36/284) which was probably based on a lost original an of which there are two copies (Public Record Office E164/1 and British Library MS Arundel 153); the survey of the lands of Worcester Church in Worcestershire, Gloucester shire, Warwickshire and Oxfordshire, discussed as Worcs. B below; and the 12th century survey of Kent (British Library MS Cotton Vitellius C8). In both matter and manner, Evesham C is close to Worcs. B, but with sufficient differences of substance to prove that it was not derived from it. Such abbreviations, though not useful for tax collection, which continued to be by Hundreds, would have been helpful to the King's agents in individual shires, who would in the centuries following 1086 continue to need to know who held which lands and what their value was. An abstract held in each County would save the inconvenience of referring to the larger and remoter original.

Evesham C supplies some additional information: for example it names Urso's land at Dorn (C 42), part of the Bishop of Worcester's large manor of Blockley, which had been omitted from DB, though implied in Evesham A 120 and found in the Domesday abbreviation Worcs. B 3. It further names subdivisions of Domesday manors at Astwood (C 75) and Eldersfield (C 104), and corrects or expands the DB entry for Warndon and White Ladies Aston by the addition of Trotshill (C 50), possibly a post-1086 change.

Such changes were no doubt the product of local knowledge, and corrections to DB, but the bulk of Evesham C must have been abbreviated directly from DB. Had it been abstracted from a west-midland 'circuit return', similar to the Exon. or Little Domesdays, much greater differences of order, phrasing and detail would have been expected. Apart from the additions noted above, a few mistakes due to carelessness, and the normal free treatment of personal and place names, the only differences between Evesham C and DB are of phrasing, and these could be expected if the scribe was not abstracting mechanically, but summarising in his own words.

Evesham C 13 is a good example. Overall, the entry is a copy and slight abbreviation of Worcs. 2,13, the information being given in the same order and presented in the same way. The differences are in the spellings of place and personal names, which scribes change at will, and in details: *in Lawerne* for DB *ad Laure*, where *in* is more normal in DB and the Evesham scribe has perhaps missed the nuance of *ad* in standardising; *de prato* for *prati* is probably the scribe's own more medieval way with the genitive; *cainas* (OFr *chesne*, Mod. Fr *chêne*, see Ducange s.v. *chesnus*, *casnus*) is probably the scribe's word for the more classical and literary *quercus* of DB. Elsewhere the scribe simplifies DB, occasionally disentangling syntax as in C 122 *qui has terras tenent, serviebant sicut alii liberi homines*, where DB (8,16) has *serviebant* in its classical position at the end of the sentence. Figures are invariably reproduced in the same form, e.g. 2 hides less 1 virgate, even where alternatives (1 hide and 3 virgates) exist.

EVESHAM C: Translation

Only changes or additions to DB are given

DB ref.	Place-name		(In Oswaldslow Hundred) folio 8v
2,11	LAUGHERNE	(11)	(Urso) also holds 3 virgates in *Lawerne*. Urso also has ½ hide there from the Bishop's lordship. Value 6s.
2,13	LAUGHERNE	(13)	Also of this manor Robert the Bursar holds ½ hide in *Lawerne*. He has 1 plough there, with 1 smallholder and a mill at 5s; meadow, 6 acres; 12 oaks (*cainas*). Kenward (*Kynewardus*) holds it. Value 20s.
			folio 9r
2,42-44	DAYLESFORD and EVENLODE	(41)	Stephen son of Wulfwy [holds] 3 hides in *Dailesford*; Hereward [holds] 5 hides in *Eunelade*. The Abbot of Evesham held these two lands, *Dailesford* and *Eunelade*, from the Bishop of Worcester, until the Bishop of Bayeux received them from the Abbey. These lands were for the monks' supplies.
2,38-44	BLOCKLEY and members	(42)	Of this manor Urso holds 5 hides in *Dorna* (Dorn).[1]
2,48	NORTHWICK with TIBERTON	(46)	In the same Hundred, the Bishop holds *Norwic'* with one member at *Tibertonia*. 26 hides which pay tax ...

DB ref.	Place-name		
2,53	WARNDON and (WHITE LADIES) ASTON	(50)	He also holds 2 hides in *Warmendona* and *Trotteswella* (Trotshill). Similarly Urso holds ½ hide in *Estona.*[2]
			folio 9v
2,69	EASTBURY	(65)	Of this manor Walter *de Burch* holds ½ hide in *Heresbyrya*.
2,79	HANBURY	(75)	Similarly the Bishop holds[3] *Hambyry*. 14 hides. Urso holds ½ hide of this (land) in *Estwde* (Astwood).
6,1	TENBURY (WELLS)	(86)	The Church of Cormeilles [holds] 1 hide in *Tametebyri* in *Dudintr'* (Doddingtree) Hundred.
8,2	WICK	(89)	In *Wica* are 6½ of those hides.
			folio 10r
8,9c	part of LONGDON	(104)	Of this land King William held 5 hides and 3 virgates in *Eadresfeld* (Eldersfield Reinbald and Aelfric hold them.
8,10c	part of POWICK	(111)	Gilbert son of Thorold holds what Alfwy and Ketelbert held. 2 ploughs in lordship and 1 plough belonging to 7 smallholders.
8,17	GRAFTON (FLYFORD)	(123)	Urso also holds *Grafton'*. 2 hides, less 1 virgate. The man who holds this (land) scythed (*falcabat*) for 1 day in the meadow and performed other services.
8,22	PEOPLETON	(128)	In the same outlier, Godric holds 3½ hides which have never paid tax. Alfwy (*Halewi*) holds 1 hide and 1 virgate. This virgate has never paid tax. The other Alfwy (*Alewi*) holds 1 hide and Wulfric (*Wlfrich*) holds 3 virgates. One of these (hides) did not pay tax before 1066. They served like other free men.
			folio 10v
8,27	COMBERTON	(138)	Urso holds *Cumbrinton'*. 2 hides. Arthur held it.

Textual Notes

1. C 42 is written in the right-hand margin of the MS in a different hand, with transposition signs to show its correct position in the text.
2. C 50 is written in the right-hand margin of the MS in a different hand and is a substitute for *Idem tenet i hidam et iii uirgatas in Warmendona et Estona* ('He also holds 1 hide and 3 virgates in *Warmendona* and *Estona*'), which has been crossed out.
3. (C 75). After *tenet* 'holds' in the MS the place-name *hertleberie* has been crossed out before *Hambyr*
4. (C 104) *in Eadresfeld* is written in the left-hand margin of the MS in a different hand, with transposition signs to show its correct position in the text.

EVESHAM D Introduction

MS: British Library MS Cotton Vespasian B xxiv folios 10v-11r. Discussion in H. B. Clarke and R. R. Darlington AAE, pp. 187-191.

This document consists of notes concerning manors formerly held by Evesham Church and obtained from it by Urso the Sheriff after the death of Abbot Aethelwig. Evesham N, a close parallel, makes it plain that Urso acquired the lands with the connivance of Odo, Bishop of Bayeux. The original document was perhaps compiled *c.* 1078 after the death of Aethelwig, when the principal spoliations took place, probably at the time of Odo's judicial enquiry (see Worcs. H and 10,11-12 note), but it has been updated to *c.* 1108 or after, for it records the death of Urso. Moreover, William I is referred to as William *senior*; Hampton Lovett is in the hands of Isnard Parler, probably son of the Domesday tenant, and at Church Lench (D 5) is recorded a subtenancy apparently later than 1086 and a return of the estate to the Church under Henry I. The notes may well have attained their present form at the death of Urso as a timely record of his 'acquisitions' which the Church then hoped to recover.

The record appears to have been intended as a list of the alienation of only those manors acquired by the Church before 1066; those obtained after the Conquest are not mentioned, nor are further losses, alluded to in D 6. The final entry (D 7) is preceded by one blank line, apparently to mark off lands that were tenancies in chief from Daylesford and Evenlode (2,42-44) where the Abbey was a sub-tenant of Worcester Church. This entry seems also to have had a different source, perhaps DB itself or Evesham C 41 to which it is virtually identical apart from strengthening *accepit* to *abstulit*.

The opening statement, D 1, is amplified in the two following entries; thereafter D 3-6 continue the notes with the mention of further manors, D 6 rounding off the original notes.

EVESHAM D Translation

folio 10v

DB ref.	Place-name		
		(1)	Urso the Sheriff and some of his men-at-arms had these lands from Evesham Abbey in the time of Abbot Aethelwig: *Actun* (Acton Beauchamp), *Hamtun* which Inard Parler holds (Hampton Lovett), *Uptun* (Upton Warren), *Wittun* (Witton) ½ hide.
11,1	ACTON (BEAUCHAMP)	(2)	*Actun* was (part) of the Church's lordship before 1066, likewise for 12 years after 1066. After that, Abbot Aethelwig gave the said land *Actun* to Urso in exchange for another land called *Benningwrthe* (Bengeworth), since it was situated close to the Church. The Church had this *Benningwrthe* in lordship for as long as the said Abbot lived. But after this Abbot's death, Urso violently encroached on both lands, that is *Benninchwrthe* and *Actun*, and kept them. The Church has lost them entirely unjustly.
26,17 26,15 26,16	HAMPTON (LOVETT) UPTON (WARREN) WITTON	(3)	Some of Urso's men-at-arms held *Heamtun* and *Vptun* and *Wittun* from the Church in return for service. But after the Abbot's death, with Urso encroaching on these lands, (the Church) was unable to have service.
11,2	(SHERIFFS) LENCH	(4)	*Leinch Bernardi*[1] is the name of a village situated close to the Abbey. 4 hides there.

The Church had 2 hides of these in lordship before 1066. Then in the time of the elder King William, Abbot Aethelwig bought another 2 hides of the same village with the Church's money from Gilbert son of Thorold with the consent of the same King William. For many years, during the life of the same Abbot, the Church had all of them together in lordship.

folio 11r

But when the same Abbot died, Urso violently seized all these 4 hides, with the support of Bishop Odo, and the Church has unjustly lost them.

10,16 CHURCH LENCH (5) Abbot Walter granted another lordship village called *Chyrchlench* to him on these terms that during his lifetime he should hold the said land in return for service, and that after his death it should return to the Church. After Abbot Walter's death with no (new) Abbot yet here, King Henry granted him the service of Ranulf, the Abbot's brother. But before his death, because he had encroached on it unjustly, he returned it to the Church in the presence of many witnesses.

(6) There was a larger number of other villages which the Church had in the times of Abbot Aethelwig and of the other Abbots that preceded him. But the Abbey was wrongfully despoiled through the actions of Bishop Odo. Now very many of the King's barons have them and the Church lacks them.[2]

2,42-44 DAYLESFORD, EVENLODE (7) Stephen son of Wulfwy [holds] 3 hides in *Dailesford*. Hereward [holds] 5 hides in *Eunelade*. The Abbot of Evesham held these 2 lands, *Dailesford* and *Eunelade*, from the Bishop of Worcester, until the Bishop of Bayeux took them away from the Abbey. These lands were for the monks' supplies.

Textual Notes

1. (D 4). *Bernardi* is interlined.
2. (D 6). A blank line in the MS follows this entry.

EVESHAM J Note

MS British Library Cotton Vespasian B xxiv folios 49v, 53r. Discussion in H. B. Clarke and R. R. Darlington AAE pp. 192-5, 197-8.

Attention should be drawn to this document although it is not reproduced below. Dated by Professor Darlington to *c.* 1104 it is independent of Domesday Book, but noteworthy as a rare early example of a Domesday-type survey of manors and their taxation. Apart from Badby and Newnham in Northamptonshire, it is concerned with the Worcs. manors held by Evesham Church in DB, with the exception of Oldberrow and Ombersley (detached parts of Fishborough Hundred in 1086), and Abbots Morton and Bevington (Esch Hundred in 1086). The remaining manors are entered in a different order, with Domesday Hundreds intermingled, but taken as a whole they probably represent the new Hundred of Blackenhurst which was certainly in existence by 1107 according to a royal charter (British Library MS Harley 3763 folios 82v, 119r (2 copies), calendared in *Regesta* ii, 69 no. 831; see VCH (Worcs.) ii p. 347).

The particular interest of the document for students of Domesday lies in the close comparison that can be made between the state of the 11 manors for which details are given in DB and Evesham J. Evesham J has less detailed manorial information than DB, but the details that are parallel in both point to a remarkable stability in the period from 1086 to *c.* 1104. For instance the 252 persons forming the main classes of population in 1086 are 244 in *c.* 1104 and there have been only slight changes in the number of ploughs. Evesham J throughout substitutes *rustici* for DB *villani* and *bovarii* for *servi* (on this latter see 1,1c note). It further provides details of personal names and the hidage of subtenancies. If the hidage of the omitted Oldberrow and Ombersley is assumed to be the same in *c.* 1104 as in 1086, the total hidage for Fishborough Hundred is the same (65 hides, 12 acres) in both documents, although individual hidages are discrepant. The implication seems to be that the Abbot was free to alter the assessments of individual manors within the overall hidage of his 'Hundred'.

EVESHAM N Introduction

MS: British Library Harleian MS 3763 folios 60v-61r. Discussion in H. B. Clarke and R. R. Darlington AAE pp. 19-21, 186-7, 188-90.

This list of manors removed from Evesham Church *c.* 1078 by Odo, Bishop of Bayeux, is not derived from DB, but adds a number of details to it.

Although it relates to spoliations effected by Odo *c.* 1078, following the death of Aethelwig and the appointment of Walter, it often records the names of the land-holders, and where these can be dated, they were alive at the very end of the eleventh century and at the beginning of the twelfth. The document was dated by Professor Darlington to *c.* 1100 and may, as Dr. Clarke suggests, have been compiled following the death of Bishop Odo early in 1097, perhaps in the hope that the Church's lands might then be recovered.

The inventory is similar to Evesham D (which concerns only Worcestershire) and to that in the Evesham *Chronicon* pp. 96-7, though with differences of detail (see 10,11-12 note). It concerns 29 manors, 122 hides in all in Worcestershire, Warwickshire, Oxfordshire and Gloucestershire, those shires that formerly met at the four-shires stone (10,12 note). The manors in other Counties in 1086, not reproduced below are:

Warwickshire		*Oxfordshire*	*Gloucestershire*
Arrow	Broom	Salford	Quinton
Exhall	Bidford on Avon	Cornwell	Upper Slaughter
Wivleshale	Binton	Chastleton	Lower Swell
Atherstone on Stour	Salford Priors	Dornford	Childswickham
Little Dorsington	(Temple Grafton)	Shipton-on-Cherwell	Pebworth

EVESHAM N Translation

DB ref. Place-name folio 60v

(1) Bishop Odo.[1] Noted here are the lands which Bishop Odo of Bayeux violently took away from the Church of Mary, Holy Mother of God, at Evesham in the time of Abbot Walter.

11,1 9,5c 10,12	ACTON (BEAUCHAMP) BRANSFORD BENGEWORTH	(2)	In Worcestershire: *Acton'*, 5 hides; in *Branesford'*, 1 hide. These were in lordship, for the supplies of God's servants of this Church. In the course of time, Abbot Aethelwig gave these lands to Urso (*Hurso*) the Sheriff in exchange for 6 hides in *Benigwrth'*. But the Sheriff now has all these lands and the Church lacks them.
11,2 26,17 26,15 26,16	(SHERIFFS) LENCH HAMPTON (LOVETT) UPTON (WARREN) WITTON	(3)	Similarly, *Lench*, 4 hides of lordship (land). Likewise *Hamton'*, 4 hides, and *Hupton'*, 3 hides and *Withon'*, 1 hide. These (hides) were free.
		(4)	The Sheriff has these 7 villages by gift of Odo and the Church lacks them.
2,42-44	EVENLODE, DAYLESFORD	(5)	*Eunelad'*, 7 hides of lordship (land). Now a man-at-arms called Brian has them. *Deilesford*, 3 hides of lordship (land). William Hastings has them. ...
		(10)	Abbot Aethelwig (*Eilwius*) held all these lands noted here, with great freedom for many years before 1066 and later, during the reign of the elder King William. Also after the said Abbot's death so long as the Church of Evesham was in the King's hands, it had them for many days, without challenge. But afterwards, when Abbot Walter succeeded, in the same year as he undertook the abbacy, because he was less endowed with worldly[2] wisdom than he should have been, Bishop Odo violently took away the lands by great ingenuity. He transferred them to the men-at-arms he wished and until this day this holy Church has remained despoiled of these lands. . . . . . .

Textual Notes

1. (N 1). *Odo Ep(is)c(opus)* is a rubric in the left-hand margin of the MS.
2. (N 10). In the MS deletion dots have been written under *scl'ari*, the normal abbreviation for *seculari* 'worldly', which is then written in full.

EVESHAM P Introduction

MS: British Library Harleian MS 3763 folio 71v. Discussion in H. B. Clarke.

According to a marginal heading, this is an account of free and taxable hides in Fishborough Hundred according to the 'roll of Winchester' (*rotulum de Winton'*). The heading is not quite accurate, for in fact the document is an abbreviated list of all the entries in Chs. 10 (Evesham Church) and 11 (Bishop of Bayeux) of Domesday, thus including other Hundreds as well. The list has been updated to *c.* 1104.

The order of entries (except for one of the parts of Bretforton, probably omitted in error) is identical to that of Domesday, and the phrasing so close, apart from those changes inevitable in an abbreviation, that the document seems to have been derived directly from Exchequer Domesday, or from a breviate then existing.

Even so, there are a few discrepancies: the hidage given for Fishborough Hundred in P 3 (65 hides with apparently 90 from Doddingtree and 15 of Worcestershire 'making up the Hundred') appears to be a confusion since the hides given in the text (with an adjustment for Bretforton) are the DB total of 65 (see P 3 textual note). Moreover some individual hidages vary: Littleton has 6 hides in DB 10,5 and 4½ in P 6. Another part of Littleton has 7 hides in DB 10,8 and 5 in P 9. Abbots Morton has 5 hides in DB 10,13 and 3 in P 14. Atch Lench has 4½ hides in DB 10,14 and 2 in P 15.

The figures involving half hides cannot be the result of faulty transcription and this suggests that the information contained in DB has been updated to take account of new tax assessments. Evesham A and J seem to show that the taxability of individual manors within a Hundred could be adjusted provided that the total for the Hundred was maintained. An alternative hypothesis that Evesham P is derived from a pre-Domesday hidage summary is difficult to sustain in view of the extreme closeness of order and phrasing in Evesham P and Exchequer DB.

Entry P 13 'Urso holds one of them' is perhaps a misunderstanding of Domesday's 'Urso holds a fifth hide'. In another entry (P 17 Church Lench) there is added information that Urso holds the 4 hides. This subtenancy is not found in DB but is given in Evesham D 5 and J 10. Moreover, the *Chronicon* concludes its list of Odo's spoliations (similar to Evesham N) with *Leinch quam Ursini tenent contra Rotulum Winton'* (p. 97). This *Leinch* is probably Church Lench, but the 'roll of Winchester' in the *Chronicon* and in P 1 is mysterious. It could well refer to DB itself which does not record this subtenancy of Urso (see 10,16 note). Although Domesday is not in the form of a roll, *Rotulum* may here be used in the loose sense of 'book' (see the example quoted in DBH p. xxx; see Ellis i pp. 1-2; VCH i p. 265); or some other document could be meant, for as Galbraith points out (MDB p. 212) the more usual terms for DB itself in the later 11th century were *breve, descriptio* and *liber*. In the latter case the most likely document would be a now lost abstract or breviate of DB in roll form, rather than some pre-Domesday geld document to which the term 'roll of Winchester' seems also to have been applied (see S. Harvey (2) p. 767, referring to RBW pp. 442-3).

EVESHAM P Translation

folio 71v

DB ref.	Place-name		
	FISHBOROUGH HUNDRED	(1)	The number of free hides, the number that pay tax and are assessed for military service (*de Forinseco*; literally 'from outside'), in *Fisseberga* Hundred, according to the Roll of Winchester.[1]
10,1	EVESHAM	(2)	In Evesham, where the Abbey is situated, are 3 free hides.
10,2	–	(3)	The same Church has 65 hides in *Fissesberges* Hundred. 12 hides of these are free. 90 hides[2] of *Dudutore* (Doddingtree) lie in that Hundred and 15 hides of Worcestershire make up the Hundred.
10,3	LENCHWICK, NORTON	(4)	The Church itself holds *Lenchwick.* There is 1 free hide. In *Nortona,* 7 hides; they pay tax.
10,4	OLDBERROW	(5)	In *Vlleberga* there are 12 acres of land.
10,5	OFFENHAM, LITTLETON, BRETFORTON, ALDINGTON	(6)	In *Huffeham* there is 1 free hide. In *Litletona,* 4½ hides;[3] they pay tax. *Bretfertona,* 6 hides; they pay tax. 1 outlier, *Aldint',* belongs to this manor. 1 free hide there.
10,6	WICKHAMFORD	(7)	The Church itself holds *Wikewan'*. There are 3 free hides.

DB ref.	Place-name		
10,7	BADSEY	(8)	In *Baddeseia* 6½ hides.
10,8	LITTLETON	(9)	Similarly, *Litleton'*, 5 hides; they pay tax.[4]
10,9	(CHURCH) HONEYBOURNE	(10)	In *Huniburn'* 2½ hides; they pay tax.
10,10	OMBERSLEY	(11)	In *Ambreleg'* there are 15 hides, both wood and open land. 3 of these[5] are free.
10,11	HAMPTON	(12)	In *Hampt'* there are 5 hides which pay tax and lie in *Oswaldeslawe* (Oswaldslow) Hundred.
10,12	BENGEWORTH	(13)	In *Benigwrth'*,[6] 4 hides which pay tax. Urso holds one of these.
10,13	(ABBOTS) MORTON	(14)	In *Morton'*, 3 hides which pay tax.
10,14	ATCH LENCH	(15)	In *Accheslench'* 2½ hides[6a] which pay tax.
10,15	BEVINGTON	(16)	In *Biuinton'* 1 hide which pays tax.
10,16	CHURCH LENCH	(17)	In *Chirchelench'*,[7] 4 hides which pay tax. Urso holds them.
11,1	ACTON (BEAUCHAMP)	(18)	The Bishop of Bayeux holds *Acton'*, and Urso from him, in *Dudintroe* (Doddingtree) Hundred. It belonged to the Church of Evesham before 1066. But later, Urso acquired it from the Abbot in exchange for another land. Now he holds it from the Holding of the Bishop of Bayeux.[8] 6 hides there. 3 of these do not pay tax.
11,2	(SHERIFFS) LENCH	(19)	The Bishop also holds *Lench'*, and Urso from him. 4 hides there which pay tax. The Church held these 4 hides for many years until the Bishop of Bayeux took them away from the Church and gave them to Urso.[9]

Textual Notes

1. (P 1). This entry is written in 2 short lines on the right-hand half of the folio in the space between the ending of the previous document and the beginning of Evesham P proper, possibly written after the folio was completed.
2. (P 3). '90 hides' is *quater xx*^ti *et x hide*; as DB has *xx hidę* it may be that the scribe of P mistook the *xx* as *xc* (90) and then copied out the misread figure in the form, more common at that time, of '4 x 20 + 10'.
3. (P 6). *et dimidia* of *iiii hide et dimidia* '4½ hides' is interlined.
4. (P 9). *et geldant* '(and) they pay tax' is interlined.
5. (P 11). *Et hiis* in the MS is a scribal error for *ex hiis* 'of these'.
6. (P 13). The *r* of *Benigwrth'* is interlined.

6a (P 15). Before *ii hide 7 dim̄*. there is an erasure of either *i* or *ii*, the scribe having originally written either *iii hide* or *iiii hide*. It is interesting that the hidage given in DB is 4½, but in Evesham A 12 it is 3½ hides.

7. (P 17). In the MS the second *c* of *Chirchelench'* has been substituted for another letter.
8. (P 18). In the MS *Baiocn̄sis* 'of Bayeux' has probably been corrected from *Baion̄sis*.
9. (P 19). The *r* of *Ursoni* 'to Urso' is interlined.

EVESHAM Q Introduction

MS: British Library Harleian MS 3763 folio 82r. Discussion in H. B. Clarke, Round FE p. 146 and in VCH (Worcs.) i pp. 330-1.

This is a one-page fragment written in two columns with no interlining or marginalia, containing a composite document which consists of:

(a) a hidage schedule of Worcestershire fiefs, closely related to DB (Q 1-28);
(b) an account of the 10 hides of Droitwich dating from *c.* 1126 (Q 29);
(c) the tax assessments of some places for which the Sheriff of Worcester was responsible (Q 30-35).

Only Q 1-28 are reproduced below. They represent the fragment of what was probably a longer hidage list, containing tenants-in-chief, names of manors, their tax assessments, with some references to subtenants.

The chief holders are those of Domesday, except for Roger son of Poyntz (Q 21). This is perhaps an error for Drogo, the careless scribe having missed the large initial letter of the original, as would seem to be the case in DB Somerset 20,2-3 (Exon. *Rogo*, for DB's *Drogo*; see Exon. Notes). The phrasing throughout is so close to that of Exchequer DB that Evesham Q was probably derived from it or from an abbreviation. All surviving examples of 'circuit' or earlier returns, another possible source of the document, show marked differences in style and arrangement within chapters. The only major discrepancy between Evesham Q and DB is in the order of chapters. The surviving list begins with Urso's chapter (the order of entries being 26,17;11-16;5); then follow entries from Chs. 1 and 12 (manors held by Urso), then an abbreviation of all the entries in Chs. 16, 20, 21, 27, 28 and X1. The list concludes with Ch. 22,1. This divergence of order from DB recalls Evesham K. Within Urso's chapter, however, the discrepancy is not as great as appears. The entry Q 1 should correspond to 26,10 (Hampton Lovett) but the detail shows that the scribe is here abbreviating 26,17, the other part of Hampton Lovett, perhaps having placed the two parts of the village together. The entry for 26,5 displaced at the end (Q 8) could have been missed. Apart from this and the single entry Q 28 (DB 22,1) the chapters are abstracted internally in DB order. But the principle of selection is elusive.

Important differences from DB are the place-name *Wdecote Stephani* for DB *Wdecote* (Q 8), also found in Evesham B; the location of Roger son of Poyntz's virgate of Martley at Pudford, and the information that Chaddesley Corbett is held by the Earl of Gloucester. This last dates the document to 1122 or after when the first earl of Gloucester was created. There are also differences in the hidage of 'Willingwick' (2 hides in Q 9; 2 hides 3 virgates in DB) and Dunclent (2 hides in Q 10; 3 hides in DB).

Evesham Q 29, not reproduced below, is a hidage account of Droitwich, dated *c.* 1126, and discussed fully by Dr. Clarke and by Round (FE p. 177; VCH (Worcs.) i pp. 330-1). The 10 hides of Domesday Droitwich (15,14 note) are mostly identifiable, in the hands of their later holders.

EVESHAM Q Translation

DB ref.	Place-name		folio 82r
26,17	HAMPTON (LOVETT)	(1)	(The Abbot of Evesham)...[1] held them before 1066 and bought them from a thane who could rightly sell (his land). Robert holds this manor from Urso.
26,11	HORTON	(2)	Similarly Urso holds 2 hides in *Horton'*.
26,12	COOKSEY (GREEN)	(3)	In *Kokeseia*, 2 hides.
26,13	BELBROUGHTON	(4)	In *Brocton'*, 2 hides.
26,14	–	(5)	Urso also holds 1 hide exempt from tax and from every customary due. Robert holds it. Aelfric held it before 1066.
26,15	UPTON (WARREN)	(6)	Similarly Urso holds *Vpton'*, and Erlebald (*Hereboldus*) from him. 3 hides there.

DB ref.	Place-name		
26,16	WITTON	(7)	Urso also holds *Witton' Gunfrei.* ½ hide.
26,5	WOODCOTE (GREEN)	(8)	Similarly *Wdecot' Stephani.* 1½ hides.
1,1c	'WILLINGWICK', CHADWICK	(9)	In *Willingwik'*, 2 hides. In *Chadeleswik'*, 3 hides.
12,2	DUNCLENT	(10)	In *Dunclent*, 2 hides.
16,1	SODINGTON	(11)	Ranulf (*Randulfus*) of Mortimer holds *Suthinton'* in *Dudintr'* (Doddingtree). 1 hide there.
16,2	MAMBLE	(12)	In *Mameleg'*, ½ hide.
16,3	*BROC*	(13)	In *Broc*, ½ hide.
16,4	CONNINGSWICK	(14)	In *Cullingwik'*, 1 hide.
20,1	DODDENHAM	(15)	Gilbert son of Thorold holds *Dodeham* in *Duddintre* (Doddingtree) Hundred. 1 hide
20,2	REDMARLEY	(16)	In *Rudmerleg'*, 1½ hides.
20,3	HANLEY	(17)	In *Hanleg'*, 1½ hides, and Roger (holds) from him.
20,4	HANLEY	(18)	In another *Hanleg'*, 3 hides, and Hugh (holds) from him.
20,5	ORLETON	(19)	In *Alreton'*, 1½ hides.
20,6	HADZOR	(20)	In *Haddesour'*, 2 hides.
21,1	HOLLIN	(21)	Roger[2] son of Poyntz holds *Holma.* 1 hid
21,2	STILDON	(22)	In *Stilledon'*, ½ hide.
21,3	GLASSHAMPTON	(23)	In *Glesene*, 1 hide.
21,4	MARTLEY	(24)	In *Pudiford* (Pudford), 1 virgate. Entirely in *Dutdintre* (Doddingtree) Hundred.
27,1	'THICKENAPLETREE'	(25)	Hugh Donkey holds *Tikenapetre*, 3 hides. In *Camel* (Came) Hundred.
28,1	CHADDESLEY (CORBETT)	(26)	Edeva holds *Chadeslega.* 25 hides there, but 10 are free. Now the Earl of Gloucester holds (them).
X 1	HILLHAMPTON	(27)	Aelmer holds *Hulhamton'*, 1 virgate there
22,1	DROITWICH	(28)	Harold son of Ralph held 1 hide in *Wich'*. . . .

Textual Notes

1. This one-page document, written in 2 columns, begins in the middle of a sentence.
2. (Q 21). In the MS after *Rogerus* is written R̤ , the two dots denoting deletion.

APPENDIX V

Hemming's Cartulary of Worcester Church

British Library MS Cotton Tiberius A xiii is a Worcester Cartulary containing a large number of charters, deeds, bounds and surveys of the lands belonging to the Bishop or the monks of Worcester. Its only printed edition, by Thomas Hearne, was published in Oxford in 1723 in two volumes from a copy of the Cotton MS made for Richard Graves of Mickleton, Gloucestershire, this latter MS surviving in the Bodleian Library, Oxford, as Rawlinson MS B 445. The Cotton MS was damaged in the fire of 1733, but although charring at the edges has destroyed some of the marginalia, most of the body of the MS is still legible (but see the textual notes to Worcs. B and D below). It is briefly described in MCGB pp. 123-4 and there is a full palaeographic study in Ker. The Anglo-Saxon texts are mostly in BCS and have been calendared by Finberg in ECWM and in Sawyer (2), but the Cartulary as a whole badly needs a modern critical edition and discussion.

Hearne appears to have believed that the whole cartulary was the work of Hemming, a monk of the monastery of St. Mary's, Worcester, but it has long been appreciated that it falls into two distinct halves: part I (folios 1-118), called Tiberius I by Ker, dates from the early 11th century, probably from the time of Bishop Wulfstan I (1002-1023) and consists mainly of charters and deeds arranged by Counties; part II ('Tiberius II') folios 119-142,144-152,154-200, to which should be added 3 folios (110,143,153) written on smaller pieces of parchment, is Hemming's Cartulary proper, assembled and largely written by him in the last decade of the 11th century, its compilation being described by him in the *Enucleatio Libelli* (see Worcs. G below).

This simple division is complicated in two ways: firstly Hearne did not include folios 110,143,153 in his numbering, and in consequence the foliation given in the margin of his edition is sometimes between 1 and 3 folios different from the latest foliation of the MS used by Ker (in this edition the old foliation is given first, the most recent foliation second, where it differs).

Secondly, 'Tiberius I' originally contained a number of blank spaces that have been filled, in hands of the 12th and late 11th centuries with material more closely related to Hemming.

It is some of this inserted material and much of Tiberius II that is akin to Domesday. Although Hearne's edition is rare and scholarly consultation difficult, it is impossible within the limits of this County volume to reproduce all the material that is related in any way to DB. Instead, the major divisions of relevant material are briefly described below (Ker's lettered divisions given in the left-hand column) and the most important texts are discussed in greater detail, and summarised or translated in the following pages. Hearne's text has been checked against the Cotton MS (but see the textual notes to Worcs. B and D). The letter allotted to each text is an extension of the system adopted by Mr. J. Moore for the Gloucestershire volume in this series. Worcester A–E are also discussed by him there.

LATER MATERIAL INSERTED INTO TIBERIUS I

Ker A iii	folio 21v (Hearne pp. 49-50). An extract of DB detailing the Church tax payable to the Churches of Westminster and Pershore at Martinmas.
Ker C iii	folio 33v (Hearne p. 72). The privileges of Oswaldslow Hundred, abstracted from DB (2,1) and duplicated in Ker I(2) below. (Discussed as Worcs. F.)
Ker C v-vi	folios 35v-37r (Hearne pp. 75-79). Documents related to the dispute between Worcester and Evesham about Hampton and Bengeworth; the first, the agreement between Wulfstan II and Walter is also in Tiberius II, folio 135v (= 136v). Discussed below as Worcs. H.
Ker C vii	folio 37r (Hearne pp. 79-80). A writ of William Rufus demanding payment from the honour of Worcester on the death of Wulfstan II (1095). Discussed in Round FE pp. 308-313, and in Atkins ii p. 209.

Ker C viii folios 37v-38r (Hearne pp. 80-83). Record of the great plea between Evesha and Worcester concerning Hampton and Bengeworth. Discussed as Worcs. H

Ker D iii folio 39r (Hearne pp. 83-84). An incomplete hidage schedule of lands held l Worcester Church in Gloucestershire, antedating DB. Discussed as Worcs. A in the Gloucestershire volume of this series.

TIBERIUS II (HEMMING)

Ker H folios 118r-132v (= 119r-133v), Hearne pp. 248-288. The *Codicellus Possessionum*, the core of Hemming's work, detailing property alienated fro Worcester Church. At its end is an explanation of the genesis of his work an an elaborated version of DB 2,1 giving the procedure of the Inquest and the names of the Commissioners. The *Codicellus* is discussed as Worcs. G belov the Oswaldslow paragraph as Worcs. F.

Ker H i folio 133r (= 134r), Hearne pp. 289-291. A survey of houses in Worcester held by the monks and Church, including Hemming's name and dating from about 1100 (see Round DS p. 545, Atkins ii pp. 210-211).

Ker I folios 133v-140v (= 134v-141v), Hearne pp. 291-313. A series of documents relating to Oswaldslow and to the DB survey:
(1) the agreement between Wulfstan II and Walter about Hampton and Bengeworth (also on folio 35v, see above). Discussed as Worcs. H.
(2) an abstract of Worcs. DB Ch. 2 together with a similar list of the Church land in Gloucestershire and Warwickshire. (See Worcs. B below, and the Gloucestershire volume.)
(3) two documents relating to Oswaldslow, but not to DB: the first a list of those who swore, in the time of Bishop John (1151-7), see Round DS p. 54 the second a letter of Bishop Oswald (961-992) to King Edgar (957-975) concerning the liberty of Oswaldslow Hundred. Discussed in Darlington CWCP p. xvi.

Ker I ii folio 141r,v (= 142r,v), Hearne pp. 313-316. A list of the holdings of the Bishop and monks probably dating from 1115. Discussed as Worcs. C below.

Ker L folios 175r-186r (= 178r-189r), Hearne pp. 395-425. A miscellaneous collection of documents relating to estates granted to the Church or regaine for it by Bishops Aldred (see 2,20 note) and Wulfstan II (1062-95).

Ker N ii folio 174r (= 177r), Hearne p. 393. A list, in Old English, of taxes levied by William on the valuables of the Church.

Ker N iii folio 174v (= 177v), Hearne pp. 393-5. A list of the holders of the 999 tax-paying hides in Worcestershire, apparently based on DB. Discussed as Worcs. D below.

Another Worcester document of different provenance (RBW pp. 442-3), a hidage schedu of Worcester Church lands in lordship in Gloucestershire had been thought to antedate DB, but has been shown by Professor Darlington (CWCP pp. xlvi-xlvii) and J. Moore (in the Glos. volume of this series) to date from the middle of the 12th century.

In the translations below, square brackets enclose MS omissions; round brackets editorial additions or explanations.

WORCESTER B Introduction

Text: folios 136v-140v (= 137v-141v), Hearne pp. 298-313.
Discussion in DBH pp. xxviii-xxx and Galbraith DB pp. 109-111.

This document is headed *Descriptio Terrae Episcopatus Wigornensis Ecclesiae secundum Cartam Regis quae est in Thesauro Regali* and is an abstract of DB (here referred to as *Carta Regis*), based on the Exchequer text. It includes lands of Worcester Church from DB Worcs. (Ch. 2), Glos. (Ch. 3) and Warwicks. (Ch. 3), and is written in the main cartulary hand, being no later than the beginning of the 12th century. The abstract begi with a faithful copy of Worcs. 2,1, no doubt included in full because of its importance i detailing the Church's privileges (see Worcs. F below). There follows an abbreviation of DB which concentrates on hidage and holders and omits manorial details such as villagers, wood, ploughs and value. In format it is like the official Breviate and other similar documents (see Evesham C in Appendix IV) and was no doubt intended as a convenient hand-list of manors and their continuing tax liability. But there are sufficient differences to suggest that both documents had DB as their common source while being independent of one another. Their close similarity is best explained by their having both been abstracted for the same purpose. The Breviate itself was written in about the second quarter of the 13th century but it may well have been copied from an earlier original.

A few divergences from DB are worthy of note. For a number of entries Worcs. B adds the hides in lordship. As often happens, place and personal names are not copied directly from DB, but are generally given in a more recognisably English form e.g. *Codrige* for DB *Codrie* (2,14); *Huntintune* for DB *Hudintune* (2,57); *Radeleag* for DB *Rodeleah* (2,58). *Mittes (salis)* is preferred to DB's first declension Latinization *mittas*. The entry for Hampton (2,74) is omitted entirely.

Finally, the text names a few subtenancies, including Urso's land at Dorn which is omitted from (or later than) DB, although included in Evesham C (2,38 note). Such additions and differences may derive from partial revision of DB material, from local knowledge or from satellite documents such as 'circuit-returns' related to earlier stages of the DB enquiry. Nonetheless, the document as a whole, like Evesham C, is so heavily influenced by DB order and phrasing that it must have been an abbreviation made directly from it.

Only entries that differ from or add to DB are given below. The extracts are numbered in order; numbers have not been allocated to the paragraphs not reproduced from Hemming. B 3 below is B 7 in the Gloucestershire volume.

WORCESTER B Translation

DB ref.	Place-name			
2,2	KEMPSEY	(1)	*KEMESHEGE* In this Hundred (Oswaldslow), the Bishop of this Church holds *Chemeshege*. 24 hides which pay tax. 5 of these hides are waste. The hides are in lordship[1] ...	136v (= 137v) Hearne p. 299
2,31	RIPPLE, UPTON (ON SEVERN)	(2)	*RIPPEL* In the said Hundred, the Bishop also holds *Rippel*, with one member *Vpton*. 25 hides which pay tax. The hides are in lordship[2] ...	138 r (= 139r) Hearne p. 303
2,38	BLOCKLEY	(3)	*BLOKELAI* In the same Hundred, the Bishop also holds *Blokelai*. 38 hides which pay tax. In lordship 25½ hides[3] ... . Urso holds 5 hides of this manor in *Dorne* (Dorn).[4]	
2,45	TREDINGTON, TIDMINGTON	(4)	*TREDINTONE*[5] In the same Hundred, the Bishop also holds *Tredintun*, with 1 member *Tidelminton*. 23 hides which pay tax. 1 of these is waste. The hides are in lordship.[6] ...	

DB ref.	Place-name			
2,62	OVERBURY, PENDOCK	(5)	LAND OF THE MONKS,[6a] (at) *VFERABIRI* (Overbury), *SECGESBEARVE* (Sedgeberrow) etc. In the same Hundred, the Church itself holds *Oureberia* with *Penedoc*. 6 hides which pay tax. ...	138v (= 139v) Hearne p. 306
2,68	HALLOW, BROADWAS		The Church itself holds *Halhegan* with *Bradeuuesham*. 7 hides which pay tax. To this manor belong 10 houses in *Wic* (Droitwich) at 5s and a salt-house which pays 50 measures (*mittes*) of salt. 2 riders hold[7] 2 hides of this land at *Raeueneshyll* (Ravenshill) [and] *dunhamstyde* (Dunhampstead).[8]	139r (= 140r)
2,85	EARDISTON, KNIGHTON (ON TEME)	(6)	*LINDERYGE* (LINDRIDGE) St. Mary's holds in *Dodintret* (Doddingtree) Hundred *Ardoluestone*[9] and *Cnistetone* for the monks' supplies. The two manors are of 15 hides.	139v (= 140v) Hearne p. 309

Textual Notes

The folios containing Worcs. B have been considerably damaged and discoloured by fire, particularly at the edges; it has not proved possible to check Hearne's text throughout.

1. (B 1). 'The hides are in lordship' is written in the left-hand margin of the MS with transposition signs to show its correct position in the text.
2. (B 2). 'The hides are in lordship' is written in the right-hand margin of the MS with transposition signs to show its correct position in the text.
3. (B 3). 'In lordship 25½ hides' is written in the right-hand margin of the MS with transposition signs to show its correct position in the text.
4. (B 3). 'Urso holds ... *Dorne*' is written in the right-hand margin of the MS.
5. (B 4). In the MS *TREDINTONE* in red (like the other headings in Worcs. B); Hearne omits the final *E* in error.
6. (B 4). 'The hides are in lordship' is written in the right-hand margin of the MS with transposition signs to show its correct position in the text.

6a. (B 5). The heading *DE TERRA MONACHORUM* is written in red ink above the entry, with *VFERABIRI* and *SECGESBEARVE* (not *SECGESBARVE* as in Hearne) preceded by gallows signs and in red ink in the left-hand margin.

7. (B 5). 'hold' is *teñ* in the MS; Hearne wrongly extends to *tenet,* singular; (*teñ* can abbreviate both singular and plural).
8. (B 5). 'at *Raeueneshyll* [and] *dunhamstyde*': *ad Raeuenshyll* is written in the right-hand margin of the MS with *dunhamstyde* squashed into the beginning of the next line.
9. (B 6). *Ardoluestone*; Hearne misreads *Ardouelstone*.

WORCESTER C Note

Text: folios 141r-141v (= 142r-142v), Hearne pp. 313-316.
Discussion by Round in FE pp. 169-80 and VCH i pp. 324-327.

This document is a brief survey of the lands of Worcester Church in Worcestershire and lists the hidage of each head manor together with the hides held by certain named sub-tenants. It is similar in form to abstracts of DB, but like Evesham B and the 12th century Northamptonshire survey (Round in FE pp. 215-224 and VCH Northants. i pp. 357-389) it is independent of DB and later in date. The schedule appears to have been drawn up early in the 12th century and is dated by Round to 1108-1118, that is after the death of Urso and before that of the Count of Meulan. Closer dating is possible, since Robert

Marmion and Walter de Beauchamp both succeeded to their estates in 1114-1115 and Dr. Clarke suggests that the document was a product of the vacancy of the Worcester see between 1112 and 1115. The document is thus likely to be no later and no earlier than 1115.

It is cited occasionally in the notes to this volume, so a brief discussion is called for. While in no sense an abstract of DB, the arrangement of DB seems to have influenced its compiler. For the Hundred of Oswaldslow, the chief manors are listed in DB order, and the total hidage of each is normally the same as in DB. But many DB subtenancies have been re-assigned, amalgamated or sub-divided. Those lands that were not in Oswaldslow, corresponding to DB 2,76-85, are given in a different Hundred order (Cresslau, Came, Esch, Doddingtree) and are grouped together under the general heading *in Kinefolka* (see 2,76 note). Occasional details illuminate the text of DB: the sub-division of Cropthorne (2,72 note) and the fact that Hartlebury (2,82) contained Waresley. Phepson (2,77) is said to contain only 1 hide compared to 6 hides in DB, but this discrepancy is neatly explained by a writ of Henry I (Worcester *Register* p. 58b, see Round in VCH i p. 326 note 7). It is clear from the survey that Urso had continued to expand his lands at others' expense after 1086. His lands and those of his brother Robert the Bursar are found divided between Walter de Beauchamp and Robert Marmion.

WORCESTER D Introduction

Text: folio 174v (= 177v), Hearne pp. 393-395.

Worcester D is a list of Worcestershire landholders in chief with the numbers of their tax-paying hides, said to be 999 in all, though the actual total appears to be 1003 hides. It is clearly related to DB and probably not much later than it, the landholders named being those of DB Chs. 2-28 with Wulfmer (X 1) and they are given in exact DB order. But the compiler also had access to information other than that contained in DB, since DB does not always distinguish carefully between tax-paying hides (*hidae geldantes*) and free hides (*liberae*). For many entries DB merely states the number of hides and in some chapters (see Ch. 14 and 23 notes) a gap is left after the number of hides, possibly for the insertion of their taxability. For most chapters of DB, the number of hides said to pay tax added to those about which nothing is said, produces the exact figure of Worcester D. For Chs. 8, 10,15 and 23 however, the figures do not agree. In every case, the DB total exceeds the total of Worcs. D, suggesting that DB has omitted to note a number of free hides or that their exemption dates from after 1086.

WORCESTER D Translation

DB Chapter	IN WORCESTERSHIRE	174v (= 177v)
2	The Bishop of Worcester holds 388½ hides which pay tax, apart from the land of the Abbot of Evesham.	
3	The Bishop of Hereford holds 20 hides which pay tax.	
4	The Church of St. Denis, 1 hide which pays tax.	
5	The Church of Coventry, 1 hide which pays tax.	
6	The Church of St. Mary of Cormeilles, ½ hide which pays tax.	
7	The Church of St. Peter of Gloucester, ½ hide which pays tax.	
8	The Church of St. Peter of Westminster, 188 hides and 1 virgate which pay tax.	
9	The Church of Pershore, 103 hides which pay tax.	
10	The Church of Evesham, 73 hides which pay tax.	
11	The Bishop of Bayeux, 7 hides of land that belonged to the Church of Evesham. They pay tax.[1]	
12	The Church of St. Guthlac, 4 hides which pay tax.	
13	The Priests of Wolverhampton, 2 hides which pay tax.	
14	Earl Roger, 15 hides which pay tax.	

15 Ralph of Tosny, 34 hides and 3 virgates which pay tax.
16 Ralph of Mortimer, 3 hides which pay tax.
17 Robert of Stafford, 4 hides which pay tax.
18 Roger of Lacy, 12 hides which pay tax.
19 Osbert son of Richard,[2] 37 hides and 3 virgates which pay tax.
20 Gilbert son of Thorold, 10½ hides which pay tax.
21 Drogo son of Poyntz, 2 hides and 3 virgates which pay tax.
22 Harold son of Earl Ralph, 1 hide which pays tax.
23 William son of Ansculf (*Hasculfi*), 31 hides[3] and 3 virgates which pay tax.
24 William son of Corbucion, 2 hides which pay tax.
25 William Goizenboded (*Guezenboeth*), 1 hide which pays tax.
26 Urso of Abetot, 40½ hides which pay tax.
27 Hugh Donkey, 3 hides which pay tax.
28 Edeva, a woman, 15 hides which pay tax.
X 1 Wulfmer holds 1 virgate of land which pays tax.[4]

Sum in total 999 hides which pay tax.

Textual Notes

The folio containing Worcs. D has been much charred and discoloured by fire and it has not proved possible to check Hearne's text throughout.

1. '7 hides of land that belonged to the Church of Evesham. They pay tax': *vii hidas geld' de terra quę fuit ęcclesia de Eouesham: ęcclesia* is a scribal error for the genitive *ęcclesię* 'of the Church'.
2. 'Osbert son of Richard': *Osbertus* in the MS, probably a scribal error for *Osbernus* (as DB and elsewhere; but see Evesham C 14;46 where the form *Osbertus* is used). Cf. *Ketelbertus/Ketelbernus* in 8,10a note.
3. '31 hides': *xxxi 7 hidas* in the MS, the *7* being included in error.
4. A gap of about 7 lines follows this entry. The 'sum total', preceded by a gallows sign, is written at the foot of the folio.

WORCESTER F Introduction

Text: folio 132r,v (= 133r,v), Hearne pp. 287-288, also in Ellis i pp. 20-21.
Discussion in Round, VCH i pp. 245-6; DS ii pp. 546-7.

DB 2,1 sets out the privileges enjoyed by the Church and the Bishop of Worcester in the 300-hide 'Hundred' of Oswaldslow. That these were of crucial importance to the Church is shown by a number of documents relating to the Hundred including the forged charter *'Altitonantis'* (2,1 note), the letter of Oswald to King Edgar (see Ker I(3) above) and three versions of Worcester DB 2,1: I in folio 33v (Hearne p. 72); II the text cited above; III in folio 136v (= 137v), Hearne p. 298.

Version III stands at the head of the abbreviation of DB (Worcester B) and is a faithful copy of DB 2,1. The versions I and II merit further discussion.

Version II reproduced below is, according to its heading, 'Evidence of the Liberty of Oswaldslow Hundred, confirmed by the sworn oath of the whole Shire of Worcester in the reign of the elder William'. It seems to have been intended by Hemming to conclude his *Codicellus* (Worcester G): a version of DB 2,1 is followed by a statement of the procedure by which it was sworn and the names of the Domesday Commissioners. Furthermore, it adds that the Commissioners had it set down in a document (*cartula*) which is kept in the royal treasury with Domesday book (*cum totius angliae descriptionibus*). The Commissioners' job was to enquire into and record the possessions and customs of the King and his barons in this County and several others, and they are named as Bishop Remigius of Lincoln, Earl Walter Giffard, Henry of Ferrers and Adam, brother of Eudo the King's Steward. *Comes* (Earl) as a title of Walter Giffard may be an anachronism, since it is usually said that he was created Earl of Buckingham in 1100, though Orderic Vitalis (vol. ii p. 221) states that the appointment was due to William I.

It happens that none of the Commissioners held land in Worcester and might have been expected to do their duty impartially.

The document (*cartula*) may be distinct from DB itself. Strictly read, the Latin means that the *cartula* was kept with the 'Descriptions of the whole of England', in which case it may well have been a copy of the Church's original submission, or a royal confirmation of it. On the other hand, *cum* is often used loosely, and the meaning could be that the document was in Domesday itself (as section 2,1), as Galbraith (DB pp. 110-11) seems to think.

The exact nature of the document reproduced by Hemming is unclear. There are a number of small differences from DB, and three substantial ones. For DB *ita ut nullus vicecomes ullam ibi habere possit querelam*, Hemming has *ita ut nec uicecomes nec aliquis regalis seruitii exactor possit ibi habere ullam querelam*. Secondly, for DB *et si quid de ipsis cuicunque homini quolibet modo attributum vel prestitum fuisset...*, Hemming has *et quocunque modo prestitae fuissent et cuicumque prestitae fuissent...* . Thirdly, whereas the DB entry ends at *se vertere poterat*, the Worcester text adds a statement dealing with hereditary rights and fees.

The question is whether Hemming's text is the sworn original of which DB 2,1 is a version, or whether Hemming's text was copied and expanded on the basis of DB. In the first and third cases of difference noted above, there are clear advantages to the Church in the added phrases. In the first case, although *nec aliquis... exactor* is marginal, the first *nec* before *uicecomes* anticipates it and it seems to have been an integral part of Hemming's original, whatever that was. The third case about hereditary rights is an attempt to avoid church property being alienated by the heirs of the man to whom it was first leased, a common cause of the loss of land in Worcester G. The second example appears to be an attempt to clarify a rather dense sentence in DB. On balance it seems likely that Hemming 'improved' DB 2,1 for incorporation in his *Codicellus*.

Version I of DB 2,1 is mainly a direct copy of the Domesday text, but it is notable that the scribe has not hesitated to incorporate in it phrases from Version II: thus he has *neque in placitis* for DB *nec in aliquo placito*, and the phrase *quocumque modo prestitae...* as in Version II. In one case Version II leads him into error, for he includes the first *nec* instead of the DB *nullus* before *vicecomes*, but omits the marginal *nec* clause that alone makes the first *nec* explicable.

WORCESTER F Text (English translation follows)

Abbreviated forms are only extended where there is no reasonable doubt.

Text: folio 132r,v (= 133r,v), Hearne pp. 287-288. 132r (= 133r)

INDICULUM LIBERTATIS DE OSVVALDES LAVVES HUNDRED, QUAE A TOTO uice comitatu uireceastrae sacramento iuris iurandi firmata est Willelmo seniore regnante.[1]

In uicecomitatu uuireceastre habet sancta maria de uuireceastre unum hundred, quod uocatur Oswaldes lau, in quo iacent ccc hidae, de quibus episcopus ipsius aecclesiae a constitutione antiquorum temporum, habet omnes redditiones socarum, et omnes consuetudines inibi pertinentes ad dominicum victum et regis seruitium et suum ita ut nec uicecomes nec aliquis regalis seruitii exactor[2] possit ibi habere ullam querelam, neque in placitis, neque in aliqua re, teste uicecomitatu. Et hae predictae ccc hidae fuerunt de ipsius dominio aecclesiae et quocunque modo prestitae fuissent et cuicumque prestitae fuissent ad seruiendum inde episcopo, ille, qui eam prestitam 132v
terram tenebat, nullam omnino consuetudinem sibimet retinere poterat nisi per (= 133v)
episcopum; neque terram retinere, nisi usque ad impletum tempus quod ipsi inter se constituerunt et nusquam cum hac se uertere poterat nec iure hereditario eam usurpando retinere, aut feudam suam eam clamare poterat nisi secundum uoluntatem episcopi et secundum conuentionem quam cum illo fecerat. Hoc testimonium totus uicecomitatus uuireceastre dato sacramento iuris iurandi firmauit, exhortante et adlaborante piisimo et prudentissimo patre, domino Wulstano episcopo, tempore regis Willelmi senioris coram principibus eiusdem regis, Remigio scilicet Lincolniensi episcopo, et comite Walterio giffardo, et henrico de fereris, et Adam fratre Eudoni dapiferi regis, qui ad inquirendas et describendas possessiones et consuetudines, tam regis quam principum suorum, in hac prouincia et in pluribus aliis ab ipso rege destinati sunt eo tempore quo totam Angliam idem rex describi fecit. Vnde super hac re facta ab ipsis inquisitione, et

testimonio totius uicecomitatus sacramento firmato, in autentica regis cartula hoc testimonium scribi fecerunt, et regali suaque auctoritate stabilitum deinceps absque querela et calumnia eandem libertatem firmam episcopo de ipso hundred, et terris ad eum pertinentibus permanere rege annuente iudicauerunt. Ad huius rei confirmationem exemplar eius in autentica regis cartula, ut predixi, scriptum est, quae in thesauro regali cum totius angliae descriptionibus conseruatur.

WORCESTER F Translation

Evidence of the Liberty of Oswaldslow Hundred, confirmed by the sworn oath of the whole Shire of Worcester in the reign of the elder William[1] 132r (= 133r)

In the County of Worcester, St. Mary's of Worcester has one Hundred which is called Oswaldslow, in which lie 300 hides. By an arrangement of ancient times, the Bishop of this Church has from them all the payments of the jurisdictions, all customary dues there which belong to the supplies of the household, both the King's service and his own, so that neither the Sheriff nor anyone who compels service to the King[2] can have any suit there neither in the pleas nor in anything. The Shire confirms this. The said 300 hides were (part) of the lordship of the Church itself and in whatever manner they had been leased and to whomever they had been leased to serve the Bishop therefrom, the man who 132v
held this leased land could not keep back any customary due at all for himself, (= 133v)
except through the Bishop, nor keep the land except until the completion of the time which they had arranged between them; nor could he ever turn elsewhere with this (land); nor keep it by usurping hereditary rights over it nor could he claim it as (part of) his Holding, except in accordance with the will of the Bishop, and in accordance with the agreement that he had made with him. The whole Shire of Worcester confirmed this evidence through a sworn oath, with the exhortation and encouragement of the most holy and wise father, lord Bishop Wulfstan, in the time of the elder King William, before the same king's leading men, that is Bishop Remigius of Lincoln, Earl Walter Giffard, Henry of Ferrers and Adam, brother of Eudo the King's steward. They had been sent by the King himself to seek out and set down in writing the possessions and customs, both of the King and of his leading men, in this province and in several others, at the time when the same king had (details of) the whole of England set down in writing. In addition, when they had completed their enquiry and the evidence had been confirmed by an oath of the whole Shire they had this evidence written down in an authentic royal document, then confirmed by royal authority and their own without dispute or challenge. With the King's agreement, they judged that the Liberty of that Hundred and of the lands belonging to it should remain confirmed on the Bishop. As confirmation of this fact, a copy was, as I said above, written down in an authentic royal document which is kept in the royal exchequer with the written descriptions of the whole of England.

Textual Notes

1. The heading is in red, the last three words (*Willelmo seniore regnante*) extending at right angles down the right-hand margin. It was obviously written after the marginal addition noted below, because the latter interrupts these last 3 words.
2. 'Nor anyone who compels service to the King' is an addition in paler ink in the right-hand margin, the first word *nec* being written in a space at the end of the line after *uicecomes* 'Sheriff'.

WORCESTER G Introduction

Text: folios 118r-132r (= 119r-133r), Hearne pp. 248-286.

The core of Hemming is the *Codicellus possessionum*, a list of the former possessions of Worcester Church stolen from it by force or fraud beginning in the reigns of Aethelred (978-1016) and Canute (Cnut) (1016-1035), especially at the hands of the Danish king Swein and Canute's son Harthacnut. At the end of the *Codicellus*, in summing up his little book (*enucleatio libelli*), he explains how the work was begun at the instigation of Bishop Wulfstan II (1062-1095). He, anxious to record documentary proof as well as memories of the Church's former possessions, ordered the muniments' chest to be opened to see what documents had decayed or been removed. Having repaired or recovered them, he had them bound into two volumes which contained (1) the first grants, privileges and charters of the Church; (2) the chirographs of lands recovered by Bishop Oswald (961-992) with the assistance of King Edgar (959-975) and leased for the lives of two or three men. Wulfstan also asked for the lands of the monks, specifically those *ad victum monachorum*, 'for the monks' supplies', to be gathered separately and divided in the same way. This Hemming claims to have done, but of his work, only a part survives. There are no chirographs in his part of the Cartulary, but folios 144-52 and 154-7 (new foliation) contain a number of charter copies.

Hemming's concern is with the monks' lands which he hopes will be restored to the monastery when peace and justice have returned to England. Hence he deals in detail with the lands taken from the monks, but only in passing with those alienated from the Bishop. His work is of primary importance for the early history of so many Domesday holdings that it is unfortunate that documents that would enable his accuracy to be checked have rarely survived. He seems to have been concerned for the main body of texts he was copying, but less accurate in copying e.g. lists of witnesses. Ker (p. 65) concludes that "it is safer to trust to the main facts than to the details of his stories".

His plan, as he explains it, is to describe Worcestershire lands geographically beginning with those lying to the west of the river Teme (118v = 119v), then discussing a group that lies between the Teme and Severn (119v = 120v), finally proceeding to those that lie east of the Severn (122r = 123r).

The majority of these lands were either seized from the Church in times of invasion by the Danes or Normans, or were first leased out by the Church for one or more lives, but not thereafter returned by heirs, or they were seized by third parties.

Many of the TRE tenants are the same as in Domesday, and many of the lands are found, as expected, under other landholders in DB. But a number are still counted among Church lands in Ch. 2. Where this is so, they are frequently found tenanted by Urso or his brother Robert, and must have been *de facto* alienated.

The list of Worcestershire lands is concluded by Bengeworth (no. 28 below), after which Hemming describes the conflict between Wulfstan II and Aethelwig (discussed below in Worcs. H). A description of the small number of Church lands lost in Herefordshire, Shropshire, Staffordshire, Warwickshire and Gloucestershire follows, and the *Libellus* ends with the *enucleatio* in which Hemming tells how he came to write it.

His narrative adds much to DB, but is interspersed with reflections and proofs that despoilers of the Church are punished. It is too long to be reproduced here, but it is summarised below, the numbering being that of the present editors.

LANDS BEYOND THE RIVERS SEVERN AND TEME — Hearne pp. 249-52, 118v (= 119v)

1 *PEONEDOC* (Pendock 2,26)
Given to the monastery by Northman, his son becoming a monk at the same time, when Wulfstan was deacon. It was removed from the monastery with other lands by Ralph the Sheriff (Ralph of Bernay) aided by William (son of Osbern) Earl of Hereford (1067-1071).

2 *ACTUNE* (Acton Beauchamp 11,1)
Held by Ordwy from the Church, but taken from it, on his death, by Aethelwig (Abbot of Evesham) and later from him by Urso who gave it to his daughter as her dowry.

3 *SCELDESLAEHGE* (Shelsley 19,6) 119r (= 120r
Held by Sigmund until he was deprived of it on the arrival of the Normans.

4 *CLIFTUNE* and *EASTHAM* (Clifton on Teme 19,3 and Eastham 15,12)
During the reign of Aethelred (978-1016) the Church lost to the Danes *Cliftun* (Clifton on Teme 19,3), *Homme* (Homme Castle 19,8), *Eastham* (Eastham 15,12), *Bufawuda* ('Bastwood' 15,12), *Temedebyrig* (Tenbury Wells 6,1 and 19,2) and *Cyr* (Kyre 19,4 or 19,7).

LANDS BETWEEN THE RIVERS SEVERN AND TEME Hearne pp. 252-58

5 *LAWERNA* (Laugherne 2,13) 119v (= 120v
'Situated not far beyond the River Severn'. Held from the monastery by the parents of Kenward, and then by him and returned to the monastery on his death. Soon afterwards it was seized by Robert (the Bursar) brother of Urso.

6 *CLOPTUN* ('Clopton' 2,10) 120r (= 121r)
Held from the monastery by Alfward (*Aelfgeardus*) husband to Matilda, a Lady of Queen Edith's chamber. Later acquired by Urso who ceased all service from it.

7 *RYDMERLEGE* (Redmarley, see 15,10 note)
Situated close to *Duddantreo* (Doddingtree). Leased to Urso on condition that he rendered service, which he failed to do.

8 *CODDARYCGE* (Cotheridge 2,14)
Held by Ernwy and his brother *Spiritus* (Spirtes the Priest) favourite of Harold Harefoot (1037-40) and Harthacnut (*c.* 1040-1042). After the expulsion of Spirtes from England it was seized by Richard Scrope.

9 *AELFINTUN* and *SAPIAN* (Alton 15,4 and Lower Sapey 19,9) 120v (= 121v)
Granted by Bishop Beorhtheah (1033-38) (*Brihtegus*) to his brother-in-law. On their deaths, Richard son of Scrope (i.e. Richard Scrope) seized Lower Sapey and left it to his son (Osbern son of Richard). Alton was acquired by Aethelric brother of Bishop Beorhtheah, and given to his son Godric. It was subsequently acquired by Ralph of Bernay supported by his lord, Earl William (of Hereford 1067-71). It was later granted by King William to Ralph of Tosny who gave it to the Church of Saint Evroul. (Lower Sapey is in fact beyond the Teme.)

10 *AESTLEGE* (Astley 15,9)
Held by a Dane, *Ocea*, and taken from him by Ralph (of Bernay), supported by Earl William (of Hereford).

11 *RIBETFORDE* (Ribbesford 1,2) 121r (= 122r)
Its villagers were responsible to the monastery for maintaining fish-traps and other snares for game (*captatorias sepes piscium et alias uenatorias*). It was seized by the Danes, then by Thurstan of Flanders and not restored on his exile.

12 *WITLAEGE* (Little Witley 2,8)
Leased by Bishop Aldred (1047-62) and Wulfstan, at that time prior, to Ernwy (*Earnwius*; DB *Arnuinus*) a priest of Edric *Siluaticus* (Edric the Wild). Taken from him by Ralph of Bernay and not returned to the monastery on his imprisonment.

13 *GRIMMANHYLLE* and *EARESBYRIG* (Greenhill 2,12 and Eastbury 2,69)
At first seized by Urso, but later granted to him by the monastery through fear of his power. At first he rendered all services, but later failed to do so.

LANDS LYING TO THE EAST OF THE RIVER SEVERN Hearne pp. 259-69

14 *SALAWARPE* (Salwarpe 14,2) 122r (= 123r)
Held from the monastery by Godwin, brother of Earl Leofric (of Mercia, died 1057), and restored by his will. But Godwin's son, Aethelwin (*Agelwinus*; *Aeluuinus cilt* in DB), aided by his uncle Leofric, removed it from the monastery.

15 *HEAMTVNE* (Hampton Lovett 26,10) 122v (= 123v)
A possession of the monastery, but Wulfstan was unable to recover it from Erngeat son of Grim who was supported by Earl Leofric. Wulfstan made it a condition of Erngeat's son becoming a monk that the monastery should recover Hampton, or at least that part called *Thiccan apeltreo* ('Thickenappletree' 27,1), but he refused, and after his death the land fell into other hands.

16 *WARESLEAGE* (Waresley, unnamed part of Hartlebury 2,82) 123r (= 124r)
Belonged to the monastery when Alstan was prior and Witheric provost (*prepositus*). Later, under Wulfstan, it was leased to Alwin son of Brictmer. After his death all his lands were seized by Urso.

17 *CEADDESLAEGE* and *BROCTVNE* (Chaddesley Corbett (26,13 note) and Belbroughton 26,13)
Earl Leofric son of Leofwin held a number of lands from the monastery. He returned *Wulfardilea* (Wolverley 2,83) and *Blarewaelle* (Blackwell 2,46) which he had long held illegally, and at the end of his life promised to return others: *Caedeslaeh*, *Beolne*, *Broctun*, and *Forfeld* (Chaddesley Corbett, Bell Hall, Belbroughton and Fairfield 26,13 note). His wife (Countess) Godiva made various gifts to the monastery and arranged for annual payment from his lands, but they were seized from her by Earls Edwin and Morcar. (For Leofric's grant of Wolverley and Blackwell, see A. J. Robertson p. 210 no. cxiii = ECWM p. 130 no. 359 = Sawyer (2) 1232.)

18 *HEADDESOFRE* (Hadzor 20,6) 123v (= 124v)
'Lying to the east of Droitwich'. Offered by Brictwin to the monastery at the same time as he made his grandson Edwin a monk. Brictwin's son, Brictmer, gave it to the monastery. After the Norman invasion, it was taken by Earl William (of Hereford 1067-71) and given to one of his supporters, Gilbert (son of Thorold).

19 *ODDUNCGALEA* (Oddingley 2,56) 124r (= 125r)
'Land of one hide (*cassati*)', leased by Godwin, deacon of the Church, to Kinethegan a noble clerk (*clericus*), in return for 5s a year. The agreement was not honoured by his heirs who withdrew the land from the monastery.

20 *CROHLEA* (Crowle 2,78)
Removed from the monastery during Danish rule. Sigmund a Dane and soldier of Leofric (Earl of Mercia) already held the other Crowle (DB 19,14) and set about impoverishing the monastery's portion. Later, Aethelwin, prior of the monastery, granted the land to him for his lifetime on condition that he served the monastery on naval and military expeditions.

21 *BRADICOTE* (Bredicot 2,60) 124v (= 125v)
Leased by Bishop Oswald (961-992) to Goding a priest, in exchange for writing duties. He produced many books for the monastery. It was held by him and his heirs until the Normans seized it.

22 *HYMELTVNE, SPAECLEA* and *WLFRINTVNE* (Himbleton and Spetchley 2,70; Wolverton 2,3-4)
Bishop Beorhtheah (1033-38) coming from Berkshire had little land in Worcestershire, but granted certain members of *Halhega* (Hallow 2,68), namely *Hymeltun* (Himbleton 2,70), *Spaeclea* (Spetchley 2,70) and *Wlfrintun* (Wolverton 2,3-4, part of Kempsey in DB) and 1 hide in *Hwitintun* (Whittington 2,58) to Aethelric, his brother. William (Earl of Hereford 1067-71) seized them from him.

23 *LAPPA WYRTHIN* (Lyppard 2,71) 125r (= 126r)
Bishop Beorhtheah granted to a retainer Herlwin, who had accompanied him and Gunhilda daughter of King Cnut (Canute) to Saxony to marry the Emperor Conrad (*Cono*; actually Henry—later Henry III son of Conrad II, in 1036), ½ hide in Lyppard on condition that he gave 1s to the Church on the feast of the Assumption. The Church thus lacks the land.

24 *RAEFNESHYLLE* (Ravenshill, see 2,68 note)
Granted by Bishop Beorhtheah to Brictwin a kinsman, and later seized by Urso.

25 *ELMLAEGE* (Elmley Castle, part of Netherton and Cropthorne 2,72)
Granted by Bishop Beorhtheah to an assistant, then recovered for the monastery by Bishop Leofing (*Liuingus*: Bishop Lyfing 1038-46). Granted by the latter to a man-at-arms Aethelric *Kiu*. Returned to the monastery after his death then held by Witheric the provost (*prepositus*), but seized by Robert (the Bursar), brother of Urso. (For Leofing's grant, see KCD 764 = ECWM p. 128 no. 347 = Sawyer (2) 1396.)

26 *CEORLATVNA* (Charlton, part of Cropthorne and Netherton 2,72) 125v (= 126v)
Half belongs to the monastery, the other half, 7 hides, is now alienated. The latter was acquired by a certain wealthy man for the lives of three men. It was held by him and his son, then by a certain Godric *Finc*. It was recovered by Wulfstan, claimed by the French invaders, but Wulfstan obtained a writ (*breve*) from the King, putting him in possession. Later, Robert (the Bursar) brother of Urso, supported by the Queen, seized it.

27 *BENNINGWURTHE* (Bengeworth 2,75)
5 hides, granted by Bishop Beorhtheah (1033-38) to *Atsere* (DB *Azor*), a kinsman who was the Bishop's chamberlain. Thence it was acquired by Urso.

28 *BENNINGWYRTHE* (Bengeworth 10,12) 126r (= 127r)
Another part of Bengeworth was held by Arngrim who transferred service to Aethelwig, Abbot of Evesham, who encouraged him to do so. He was subsequently expelled from the land which then passed fully to Evesham. (Hemming then relates the conflict between Wulfstan and Aethelwig over Bengeworth, not summarised; see 10, 11-12 note and Worcs. H.)

29 STAFFORDSHIRE Hearne pp. 276-77
SWINFORD (Kings Swinford 1,4) in Staffordshire, and *CLENT* 128r (= 129r)
(Clent 1,6) and *TERDEBIGGAN* (Tardebigge 1,5) in Worcestershire, formerly belonged to Worcester Church. Purchased by the deacon Aethelsige (*Aegelsius*), one of the King's counsellors, from Aethelred (978-1016). Aethelsige died during the turbulent period following the death of Aethelred, and *Aeuic*, Sheriff of Staffordshire, seized the lands, with the result that they are still in the hands of the Sheriff of Staffordshire, though situated in Worcestershire.

30 WARWICKSHIRE Hearne pp. 277-80
Hemming records among the losses of the Church's lands in Warwickshire that of *Wicbald* (Wychbold 19,12) in Worcestershire, seized by Edwin, brother of Earl Leofric. 128v (= 129v)

WORCESTER H Introduction

Text: folios 35v-38r (Hearne pp. 75-83).
Discussion in Round, VCH i pp. 255-256; DS ii pp. 542-544; Bigelow pp. 16-19, 287-90.

Bengeworth and Hampton near Evesham and some houses in Worcester together with a number of other lands were long a source of dispute between Worcester Church and Evesham Abbey. Both could produce charters, genuine or forged, granting the lands to them and as a result, the early history of the estates is difficult to disentangle (see 2,74-75 and 10,11-12 notes).

On the death of Abbot Aethelwig (1077) these two estates, together with all the other Evesham lands, seem to have been the subject of a judicial enquiry conducted at *Ildeberga* by Bishop Odo of Bayeux. Odo may have used the hearing to 'acquire' many of the Abbey's estates, but Hampton and Bengeworth were restored to the Abbey. DB 10,12 records that the Abbot of Evesham proved his right to 5 hides at Bengeworth before Odo at *Ildeberga*. At this stage, Evesham Church probably recovered total possession of the land, that is lordship and all services and dues. But in DB, Hampton and Bengeworth are regarded both in 1066 and 1086 as members of Worcester Church's manor of Cropthorne (2,74-75), lying in Oswaldslow Hundred, but with the Church of Evesham as subtenant (10,11-12). This arrangement whereby the Abbot holds from the Bishop seems to have been reached only after a second hearing, this time under Geoffrey, Bishop of Coutances, at which the Bishop of Worcester attempted to have restored most of his rights over the land. A number of documents related to this hearing and its sequel are included in Hemming and reproduced and translated below. They are:

1 A writ of William I from Normandy to Archbishop Lanfranc and Geoffrey, Bishop of Coutances (folio 36v, Hearne p. 77-78); calendared in *Regesta* i 184). Geoffrey is to settle the matter of jurisdiction (*sac* and *soc*) between Wulfstan and Walter and restore the position as it was before 1066 when the tax was last taken for ships. William implies that the case should involve restoring rights to Wulfstan. He is to have the houses in Worcester and all his tenants must be prepared to serve both him and the King.

2 An unofficial Worcester record of the ensuing trial (folios 37v-38r, Hearne pp. 80-83), compiled in the late 11th century. This seems to have taken place in Worcester and involved a preliminary hearing leading to a full trial at which the Bishop produced witnesses and the Abbot, unable to prove his case, recognised the Bishop's claim.

3 The confirming writ of William, addressed to Urso and Osbern son of Richard (folio 36v-37r, Hearne pp. 78-79, calendared in *Regesta* i 230; Hemming gives a duplicate on folio 38r,v (Hearne p. 82) as the final paragraph of (2) above). By it the Bishop is granted *sac* and *soc* and service and all customary dues relating to Oswaldslow, as he had them before 1066. He is to have service from the 4 hides of Bengeworth and the houses in Worcester. From the 15 hides of Hampton, he proved his right to *soc* and tax and *expeditio* (military and naval service), church tax and burial dues.

4 A writ from Geoffrey, Bishop of Coutances, to the Domesday Commissioners (on whom see Worcs. F above), (folio 36r,v, Hearne p. 77; calendared in *Regesta* i 221). Geoffrey records the outcome of the trial in much the same terms as the King's writ, (3) above.

5 The record of a further agreement between Wulfstan and Walter, this time in front of the Domesday Commissioners (folios 35v-36r, Hearne pp. 75-76, repeated on folio 135v (= 136v), Hearne p. 296). It repeats much of 3 and 4 above, and represents the compromise recorded in Domesday. It seems to have arisen from a further claim by the Bishop that the land should be in his lordship.

Throughout, 15 hides of Hampton are said to be in dispute, but DB makes it clear that only 5 hides were involved. Hampton was a 15-hide member of Cropthorne, see 2,74 note.

The documents clearly refer to the period between 1077 (the accession of Abbot Walter) and 1086, but they are difficult to date more precisely. William was in Normandy in the summer and autumn of 1082, at Easter 1083 and in the summer of 1084, and his first writ must date from one of these absences.

The documents form two groups, the first (nos. 1-3) relating to the plea, the others (nos. 4-5) to the Domesday enquiry. There may have been a gap of months or years between the two. Wulfstan seems to have seized the chance afforded by the Domesday enquiry to have Hampton and Bengeworth declared as part of his lordship (*sed episcopus ibi plus calumniabatur quia reclamabat totam ipsam terram ad suum dominium*). The Commissioners may have asked Geoffrey to clarify the position, and then proceeded to arrange their own compromise.

WORCESTER H Texts (English translations follow)

Abbreviated forms are only extended where there is no reasonable doubt.

1 *Writ of King William from Normandy to Archbishop Lanfranc and Geoffrey, Bishop of Coutances* (folio 36v = Hearne pp. 77-78).

W[illelmus], rex anglorum Lanfranco archiepiscopo et Gosfrido episcopo 36v
Constantiensi salutem. Facite ita esse socam et sacam inter episcopum Wlstanum et Walterum abbatem de Euesham sicut erant die qua nouissime, tempore regis Eduuardi, geldum acceptum fuit ad nauigium faciendum, et ad istud deplacitandum sis, Gosfride presul, in meo loco, et ut plene episcopus Wlstanus suam rectitudinem habeat stude, et domos, quas episcopus contra abbatem reclamat in Wireceastra, facite sibi iuste habere. Et ut omnes illi, qui terras eius tenent, parati sint semper in meo seruitio et suo. Teste Rogero de iuerio.

2 *A Worcester reminiscence of the great plea between Wulfstan and Walter* (folios 37v-38r = Hearne pp. 80-83)

[H]aec commemoratio placiti quod fuit inter W[lstanum] episcopum et 37v
Walterum abbatem de eouesham, hoc est quod ipse episcopus reclamabat super ipsum abbatem sacam et socam et sepulturam et circsceat[1] et requisitiones et omnes consuetudines faciendas ecclesiae Wigornensi in hundredo de oswaldeslawe[2] et geldum regis et seruitium et expeditiones in terra et in mari de xv hidis de hantona et de $\overset{\text{or}}{\text{iiii}}$ hidis de Benningewrde[3] quas debebat abbas tenere de episcopo, sicut alii feudati ecclesiae ad omne debitum seruitium regis et episcopi libere tenent. De hac re fuit magna contentio inter episcopum et abbatem; qui abbas diu resistens iniuste hoc defendebat. Ad ultimum tamen haec causa uentilata et discussa fuit per iustitiam et breue et preceptum regis Willelmi senioris quod misit de normannia in presentia Gosfridi Constantiensis episcopi, cui rex mandauerat ut interesset predicto placito et faceret discernere ueritatem inter episcopum et abbatem et fieri plenam rectitudinem. Uentum est in causam. Conuentus magnus factus est in Wirecestra vicinorum comitatuum et baronum ante Gosfridum episcopum. Discussa est res, facta est supradicta reclamatio W[lstani] episcopi super abbatem. Abbas hanc defendit; episcopus legitimos testes inde reclamauit qui tempore regis Edwardi hoc uiderant et predicta seruitia ad opus episcopi susceperant. Tandem ex precepto iustitiae regis et decreto baronum itum est ad iuditium; et quia abbas dixit se testes contra episcopum non habere, iudicatum est ab optimatibus quod episcopus testes suos nominaret et die constituta adduceret et per sacramentum dicta episcopi probarent, et abbas quascumque uellet relliquias afferret. Concessum est ab

utraque parte. Venit dies statuta. Venit episcopus W[lstanus] et abbas
Walterus et ex precepto Gosfridi episcopi affuerunt barones qui interfuerant
priori placito et iuditio. Attulit abbas relliquias, scilicet corpus sancti Ecguuini.
Ibi affuerunt ex parte episcopi probabiles personae, paratae facere predictum 38r
sacramentum. Quarum unus fuit Edricus, qui fuit tempore regis Edwardi
stermannus navis episcopi, et ductor exercitus eiusdem episcopi ad seruitium
regis; et hic erat homo[4] Rodberti Herefordensis episcopi, ea die qua sacramentum
optulit et nichil de episcopo W[lstano] tenebat. Affuit etiam Kinewardus qui
fuit uicecomes Wirecestrescire, qui hoc uidit et hoc[4a] testabatur. Affuit etiam
Siwardus diues homo de Seropscyre et Osbernus filius Ricardi et Turchil de
WareWicscyre et multi alii seniores et nobiles quorum maior pars iam dormiunt.
Multi autem adhuc superstites sunt qui illos audierunt et adhuc multi de tempore
regis Willelmi idem testificantes. Abbas autem uidens sacramentum et probationem
totam paratam esse, et nullo modo remanere si uellet recipere,[5] accepto ab amicis
consilio, episcopo demisit sacramentum et totam querelam recognouit et omnem
rem sicut episcopus reclamauerat et inde concordiam se facturum cum episcopo,
conuentionem fecit. Et inde sunt legitimi testes apud nos, milites (homines)[6]
sanctae Mariae et episcopi qui hoc uiderunt et audierunt, parati hoc probare per
sacramentum et bellum contra Rannulfum fratrem eiusdem Walteri abbatis quem
ibi uiderunt qui cum fratre suo tenebat illud placitum contra episcopum, si hanc
conuentionem negare uoluerit, factam inter episcopum et abbatem. Habemus
etiam sacri ordinis uiros, sacerdotes et diaconos, paratos illud affirmare iuditio
Dei.

*Confirmation of the outcome of the Hearing by William to Urso the Sheriff and
Osbern son of Richard Scrope* (folio 36v-37r = Hearne pp. 78-79).
W[illelmus] rex anglorum Ursoni uicecomiti et Osberno filio escrob et omnibus 36v
francis et anglis de Wireceastre scire, salutem. Volo et precipio ut episcopus
Wlstanus ita pleniter habeat socam et sacam et seruitia et omnes consuetudines
ad suum hundred et ad terras suas pertinentes sicut melius habuit tempore regis
Eduuardi et de terris quas ipse diraciocinauit abbatem de euesham de suo feudo
tenere scilicet iiii hidis ad Bennincuuyrthe et domos in ciuitate; precipio ut si
abbas illas uult habere, sibi inde seruiat sicut alii sui feudati. Et de xv hidis de
hamtona unde episcopus diraciocinauit socam et geldum et expeditionem et
cetera mea seruitia ad suum Hundred et ciricescot et sepulturam ad suam uillam
pertinere, precipio ne ullus ei contra teneat sed sic habeat omnia de illis ad meum 37r
opus et suum sicut coram Goisfrido episcopo et coram uobis secundum meum
preceptum, testante uicecomitatu, diraciocinatum et iuratum est. Teste ipso
Goisfrido episcopo et Rogero de iuerio.

Testimony of the Bishop of Coutances to the Domesday Commissioners (folio
36r,v = Hearne p. 77)
Gosfridus Constantiensis episcopus Remigio episcopo et Walterio Giffardo et 36r
Henrico de ferer' et Adam[7] ceterisque baronibus regis, salutem. Sciatis quod ego
testimonium fero quia dum ex precepto regis placitum tenui inter eipscopum
Wlstanum et abbatem de ueshand[8] quod episcopus diraciocinauit iiii hidas ad
bennincuuyrthe et domos in ciuitate de suo feudo esse ita quod abbas sibi debet
inde seruire sicut alii sui feudati. Et deraciocinauit socam et sacam de hantona
ad suum hundred Osuualdeslauue quod ibi debent placitare et geldum et
expeditionem et cetera ḷegis[10] seruitia de illis xv hidis secum debet persoluere[9]
et ciricsceat et sepulturam ad suam uillam croppethorn debent reddere. Hoc fuit
deratiocinatum et iuratum coram me et Vrs de abetot et Osberno filio escrob et 36v
ceteris baronibus regis, iudicante et testificante omni uicecomitatu.

Compromise reached before the Domesday Commissioners (folios 35v-36r =
Hearne pp. 75-76)
CONVENTIO INTER WLSTANUM EPISCOPUM ET WALTERIUM ABBATEM 35v
Haec est confirmatio conuentionis factae inter episcopum Wlstanum et Walterium
abbatem de eouesham de xv hidis in heamtone et iiii in benincuuyrthe; hoc est

quod ipse abbas recognouit, teste omni conuentu uuigornensis aecclesiae et multis fratribus de eouesham et Remigio episcopo et henrico de fereris et Waltero giffardo et Adam regis principibus qui uenerant ad inquirendas terras comitatus, quod illae xv hidae iuste pertinent ad Osuualdes lauue hundredum episcopi et debent cum ipso episcopo censum regis soluere et omnia alia seruitia ad regem pertinentia et inde idem requirere ad placitandum;[11] et de iiii hidis predictis in benninscuuyrthe 36r
similiter. Sed episcopus ibi plus calumniabatur quia reclamabat totam ipsam terram ad suum dominium. Sed quia ipse abbas hoc humiliter recognouit, rogatu ipsorum qui affuerunt, ipse episcopus permisit illam terram ipsi abbati et fratribus tali pacto ut ipse abbas faciat inde tam honorabilem recognitionem et seruitium sicut ipse ab ipso episcopo et quamdiu requirere poterit. Huius conuentionis testes sunt prenominati barones regis et alii quorum nomina hic habentur.

✠ Serlo abbas de gloecestre	✠ Nigellus clericus remigii episcopi
✠ Vlf monachus remigii episcopi	✠ Wlsi presbiter
✠ Rannulfus monachus eiusdem	✠ Edric de hindelep
✠ Alfuuinus monachus de sancto remigio	✠ Godric de piria
✠ Ailricus archidiaconus	✠ Ordric niger
✠ Frithericus clericus	✠ Alfuuinus filius brihtm̃

WORCESTER H Translation

1 (Writ of King William sent from Normandy to Archbishop Lanfranc and Geoffrey, Bishop of Coutances)
Folio 36v, Hearne pp. 77-78
W[illiam], King of the English, greets Archbishop Lanfranc and Geoffrey, Bishop of 36v
Coutances. Bring it about that full jurisdiction is arranged between Bishop Wulfstan and Abbot Walter of Evesham as it was before 1066 on the day when tax was last received for ship-building. In settling this claim, Bishop Geoffrey, be in my place, and ensure that Bishop Wulfstan has his full rights, and let the Bishop justly have the houses in Worcester which he claims against the Abbot; and let all those who hold his lands be always ready in my service and his.
Witnessed by Roger of Ivry.

2 (A Worcester Reminiscence of the Great Plea between Bishop Wulfstan and Abbot Walter)
Folios 37v-38r, Hearne pp. 80-83
This is a record of the plea that took place between Bishop W[ulfstan] and Abbot 37v
Walter of Evesham, to the effect that the Bishop claimed of the Abbot that full jurisdiction, burial dues, Church tax,[1] suits and all customary dues should be made to Worcester Church in the Hundred of Oswaldslow,[2] together with the King's tax, service and military service on land and sea, from the 15 hides of Hampton (2,74. 10,11) and from 4 hides of Bengeworth[3] (2,75. 10,12), which the Abbot ought to hold from the Bishop in the same way as other tenants of the Church hold freely for every service due to King and Bishop.

There was a great dispute on this subject between Bishop and Abbot; the Abbot long resisted and wrongfully denied the case. In the end this case was aired and heard in accordance with the justice, writ and command of the elder King William, which he sent from Normandy, in the presence of Geoffrey, Bishop of Coutances, whom the King had commanded to preside over the said plea and make evident the truth between Bishop and Abbot and cause full justice to be done.

They assembled for the case. There was a great gathering before Bishop Geoffrey in Worcester of men of neighbouring Counties and barons. The matter was investigated. Bishop W[ulfstan] made the said claim against the Abbot. The Abbot denied it. The Bishop then claimed (to have) genuine witnesses who before 1066 had seen this and had undertaken the said services for the Bishop's benefit. Finally in accordance with the command of the King's justice and the decree of the barons, the matter came to trial; and since the Abbot said he had no witnesses against the

Bishop, it was decided by the nobles that the Bishop should name his witnesses and produce them on the day appointed and that they should support the Bishop's words on oath. The Abbot was to bring whatever relics he wished. Both sides agreed. The appointed day arrived. Bishop W[ulfstan] came and Abbot Walter, and, in accordance with the command of Bishop Geoffrey, there were present the barons who had been at the previous plea and trial. The Abbot brought relics: the body of
Saint Egwin. Present there on the Bishop's side were trustworthy people, prepared 38r
to make the said oath. One of them was Edric who had been, before 1066, the steersman of the Bishop's boat, and leader of the same Bishop's army in the King's service: he was the man[4] of Robert, Bishop of Hereford, on the day that he gave his oath and he held nothing from Bishop W[ulfstan]. Present also was Kenward who was Sheriff of Worcestershire and who saw and bore witness to this.[4a] Present also was Siward, a wealthy man from Shropshire, and Osbern son of Richard, and Thorkell of Warwickshire and many other elders and nobles, the majority of them now dead. But many who heard these men are still alive, and many still of King William's time who bear witness to the same.

Now the Abbot, seeing the complete readiness to take the oath and try the case, and that no way was left if he wished to prove (his case),[5] took the advice of his friends and left the oath to the Bishop, accepted the whole plaint and agreed that the whole matter was as the Bishop had claimed and that he would thus make a settlement with the Bishop. There are among our number genuine witnesses of this, men-at-arms, men[6] of St. Mary's and of the Bishop, who saw and heard this, ready to prove this on oath and by judicial combat against Ranulf, brother of the same Abbot Walter. They saw him there, with his brother, upholding that plea against the Bishop, should he wish to deny this settlement made between Bishop and Abbot. We also have men of the holy order, priests and deacons, ready to affirm the same before God's judgement.

3 (Confirmation of the Outcome of the Hearing by King William to Urso the Sheriff and Osbern son of Richard Scrope)
Folios 36v-37r, Hearne pp. 78-79

W[illiam], King of the English, greets Urso the Sheriff and Osbern son of Scrope 36v
and all the French and English men of Worcestershire. I wish and command that Bishop Wulfstan should have full and complete jurisdiction, services and all customary dues that belong to his Hundred and his lands, just as fully as he had them before 1066. And concerning the lands which he proved that the Abbot of Evesham held from his Holding, that is the 4 hides at Bengeworth and the houses in the city (of Worcester), I command that if the Abbot wishes to have them, he should give him service from them as do his other tenants. And concerning the 15 hides of Hampton, for which the Bishop proved that jurisdiction, tax, military service and the rest of the services due to me belonged to his Hundred and that Church tax and burial dues belonged to his village (Cropthorne 2,72), I command
that no-one should hold them in defiance of him, but that he should have every- 37r
thing from them for my benefit and his, as was proved and sworn before Bishop Geoffrey and before you in accordance with my command, with the Shire as witness.
Witnessed by the same Bishop Geoffrey and Roger of Ivry.

4 (Testimony of the Bishop of Coutances to the Domesday Commissioners)
Folio 36r,v, Hearne p. 77

Geoffrey, Bishop of Coutances, greets Bishop Remigius, Walter Giffard, Henry of 36r
Ferrers, Adam[7] and the rest of the King's barons. You should know that I bear witness that, in the course of my hearing a plea between Bishop Wulfstan and the Abbot of Evesham[8] in accordance with the King's command, the Bishop proved that 4 hides at Bengeworth and houses in the city (of Worcester) belonged to his Holding so that the Abbot must give him service from them just as his other tenants do. And he proved that full jurisdiction from Hampton (belonged) to his Hundred of Oswaldslow; that they should hold pleas there; and that with him they should render[9] tax, military service and the other legal[10] services from those 15

hides and they should pay Church tax and burial dues to his village of Cropthorne.
This was proved and sworn before me, Urso of Abetot, Osbern son of Scrope and 36v
the rest of the King's barons, with the whole Shire hearing and witnessing it.

5 (Compromise reached before the Domesday Commissioners)
Folios 35v-36r, Hearne pp. 75-76
AGREEMENT BETWEEN BISHOP WULFSTAN AND ABBOT WALTER 35v
This is a confirmation of the agreement made between Bishop Wulfstan and Abbot
Walter of Evesham, concerning 15 hides in Hampton and 4 in Bengeworth, to the
effect that the Abbot, witnessed by the whole congregation of the Church of
Worcester and by many brothers from Evesham and Bishop Remigius, Henry of
Ferrers, Walter Giffard and Adam, nobles of the King who had come to survey
the land in the County, acknowledged that those 15 hides rightly belong to
Oswaldslow, the Bishop's Hundred, and should with the Bishop pay the King's
dues and all other services belonging to the King and ask him to hold pleas there;[11]
likewise for the said 4 hides in Bengeworth. But the Bishop was claiming more 36r
there since he demanded all that land as his lordship. But because the Abbot
humbly acknowledged this, at the request of those present the Bishop himself
granted that land to the Abbot and the brothers on the condition that the Abbot
should give as honourable an acknowledgement and service as is required by the
Bishop and for as long as he requires it.

The witnesses of this agreement are the King's barons named above and others, whose names are put here:

+ Serlo, Abbot of Gloucester
+ Ulf, a monk of Bishop Remigius
+ Ranulf, a monk of the same man
+ Alwin, a monk of St. Rémy
+ Archdeacon Alric
+ Frederic the Clerk
+ Nigel, the Clerk of Bishop Remigius
+ Wulfsi the priest
+ Edric of Hindlip
+ Godric of 'Perry'
+ Ordric Black
+ Alwin son of Brictmer

Textual Notes

1. (H 2). The third *c* in *circsceat* is interlined.
2. (H 2). The second *s* in *oswaldeslawe* is interlined.
3. (H 2). The *ge* in *Benningewrde* is interlined.
4. (H 2). *et hic erat homo...* might also possibly be translated as "and here was a man...", a different witness, not Edric the Steersman.

4a. (H 2). 'this'; in the MS *h̄* which can abbreviate both singular *hoc* and plural *haec*. Hearne extends to *hec* and *hoc* in this sentence; this edition has extended *h̄* to *hoc*.

5. (H 2). 'no way was left if he wished to prove (his case)': *nullo modo remanere si uellet recipere*. An obscure phrase, probably best explained by the scribe having confused *nullum modum* (the accusative of an accusative and infinitive clause after *uidens* 'seeing') with the much commoner phrase *nullo modo* 'in no way'. *Recipere* probably has the rare legal sense of 'authenticate' or 'prove'.
6. (H 2). *Homines* 'men' is interlined above *sanctae Mariae* with a mark after *milites* to show its correct position. A contrast is intended between the *milites*, the Bishop's men-at-arms, who are prepared to settle the dispute by judicial combat, and the men of the holy order (*sacri ordinis uiros*) etc. who will affirm before God's judgement.
7. (H 4). The names *Remigio, Wualterio, henrico* and *Adam* are interlined above *R. W. H.* and *A.* respectively in the text.
8. (H 4). Evesham: *ueshand* in the Ms, no doubt a scribal error.
9. (H 4). 'they should render': *debet persoluere*; the singular, *debet* is probably a scribal error for *debent* which would be in sequence with the other plurals.
10. (H 4). 'Legal': *legis* is probably a mistake for *regis* (see H 3 'the rest of the services due to me', referring to the King, and H 5 'all other services belonging to the King'), though the meaning could be 'services that were due by law'. In the MS there is a dot, most probably a deletion mark, under the *l* of *legis*, but nothing is interlined in correction. Hearne does not print the dot.
11. (H 5). 'ask him to hold pleas there': *inde idem requirere ad placitandum. Idem* is probably a scribal error for the accusative *eundem*, referring to the Bishop, *requirere* being dependent on *debent* earlier, of which the 15 hides are the subject.

INDEX OF PERSONS

Familiar modern spellings are given when they exist. Unfamiliar names are usually given in an approximate late 11th century form, avoiding variants that were already obsolescent or pedantic. Spellings that mislead the modern eye are avoided where possible. Two, however, cannot be avoided: they are combined in the name of 'Leofgeat', pronounced 'Leffyet' or 'Levyet'. The definite article is omitted before bynames, except where there is reason to suppose that they described the individual's occupation. The chapter numbers of listed landholders are printed in italics. It should be emphasised that this is essentially an index of personal names, not of persons. It is probable that in the case of some entries of single names more than one person bearing the same name has been included. Likewise, a person who elsewhere bears a title or byname may be represented under the simple name (e.g. in Worcs. plain Urso may well refer to Urso of Abetot).

CHURCHES AND CLERGY

SECULAR TITLES AND OCCUPATIONAL NAMES

INDEX OF PLACES

The name of each place is followed by (i) the number of its Hundred and its numbered location on the maps in this volume; (ii) its National Grid Reference; (iii) chapter and section references in DB. Bracketed figures here denote mention in sections dealing with a different place. Unless otherwise stated, the identifications of DG and VCH and the spellings of the Ordnance Survey are followed for places in England, of OEB for places abroad. Inverted commas mark lost places with known modern spelling; unidentifiable places are given in DB spelling in italics. Places with bracketed Grid References do not appear on modern 1 : 50,000 Ordnance Survey maps. The National Grid Reference system is explained on all Ordnance Survey maps, and in the Automobile Association Handbooks; the figures reading from left to right are given before those reading from bottom to top of the map. In Worcester all Grid References are in 100 kilometre grid square SO except those prefixed by P which are in square SP. Some places which were in Worcester in 1086 are now in adjacent counties: their modern county is given after the place-name. The Worcester Hundreds are Came (1); Clent (2); Cresslau (3); Doddingtree (4); Esch (5); Fishborough (6); Oswaldslow (7) and 'Pershore and Westminster' (8). The letters a, b, c etc. following the Hundred number refer to separated portions of the Hundred on the maps. Within each Hundred, or portion of a Hundred, places are numbered alphabetically. Places in other adjacent counties in 1086 but subsequently transferred to Worcester are distinguished by letters in the Hundreds column: G here stands for Gloucester, H for Hereford, ST for Stafford and W for Warwickshire. A name in brackets following a place-name is that of the parish or an adjacent major settlement, given to distinguish one place from others of the same name.

	Map	Grid	Text
Clifton on Teme	4-10	71 61	19,3. E 35
'Clopton'	7a-—	— —	2,10
Cofton Hackett	1-10	P00 75	2,84. 26,3
Comberton	8d-9	95 42	8,23;27.9,1a
'Comble'	1-—	— —	1,1a
Conningswick	4-11	(73 71)	16,4
Cookhill	5-3	P05 58	26,1
Cooksey Green	2-7	90 69	1,1c. 26,12
Cotheridge	7a-6	78 54	2,14
Cradley	2-8	94 85	23,13
Earls Croome	7b-3	86 41	2,32-33
Croome d'Abitot	7b-5	(88 44)	2,32-33
Hill Croome	7b-4	88 40	2,34
Cropthorne	7d-3	99 44	2,72
Crowle	5-4	92 55	2,78. 19,14
Cudley	7a-7	89 54	2,54
Cutsdean (Glos.)	7f-3	P08 30	2,24
Daylesford (Glos.)	7f-4	P24 25	2,42;44
Defford	8d-10	91 43	8,6
Ditchford (Glos.)	7f-5	21 36	2,39
Doddenham	4-12	75 56	20,1
Dormston	8d-11	98 57	8,14
Doverdale	3-2	86 66	26,8
Droitwich	2-9	89 63	1,(1a;1c;2); 3a; (5); 7. (2,7;15;48; 50;68;77-79;82;84). 4,1. (5,1). 7,1. 8,(12); 13. (9,1a. 10,10). 12,1. (14,1. 15,9; 13).14. 18,6. (19,12). 22,1. (24,1. 26,2;8;13; 15-16. 27,1. 28,1. E 2-3; 10-34)
Dudley	2-10	94 90	23,10
Dunclent	3-3	86 75	12,2
Eardiston	4-13	69 68	2,85
Eastbury	7a-8	82 57	2,69
Eastham	4-14	65 68	15,12
Eckington	8d-12	92 41	8,7
Edvin Loach (Herefords.)	4-15	66 58	19,11. E 35
Eldersfield	8h-1	80 31	E 6
Elmbridge	2-11	90 67	19,13
Elmley Lovett	3-4	86 69	15,13
Evenlode (Glos.)	7f-6	P22 29	2,43-44
Evesham	6c-4	P03 43	10,1. (26, 15-17)
Fastochesfelde	3-—	— —	1,2
Feckenham	5-5	P00 61	X 2. E 2;(3)
'Fickenappletree', see 'Thickenappletree'			
Fladbury	7d-4	99 46	2,15
Fockbury	1-11	94 72	1,1a

	Map	Grid	Text
Franche	3-5	82 78	1,2
Frankley	1-12	99 80	23,3
Glasshampton	4-16	78 66	21,3
Grafton (nr. Bromsgrove)	1-13	94 69	1,1c
Grafton Flyford	8d-13	96 56	8,17;20
Greenhill	7a-9	(82 58)	2,12
Grimley	7a-10	83 60	2,66
Habberley	3-6	80 77	1,2
Hadzor	2-12	91 62	20,6
Hagley	2-13	91 80	23,9
Halac	4-—	— —	15,3
Halesowen	2-14	96 83	14,1
Hallow	7a-11	82 58	2,68
Ham Castle, see Homme Castle			
Hampton (nr. Evesham)	7d-5	P02 43	2,74. 10,11
Hampton Lovett	2-15	88 65	26,10;17
Hanbury	5-6	94 63	2,79
Hanley (nr. Stockton on Teme)	4-17	67 65	20,3-4
Hanley Castle	G-5	83 41	(E 4). EG 1. EH 1
Hartlebury	3-7	84 70	2,82
Harvington	7d-6	P05 48	2,65
Hatete	3-—	— —	26,9
Helpridge	2-16	(91 66)	1,3a
Hereford (Herefords.)	—-—	— —	(1,16. 18,6. X 2-3. E 1; 3;7. EG 1)
Cook Hill, see Cookhill			
Hill	7d-7	98 49	2,19
Hillhampton	4-18	77 65	X 1
Himbleton	7a-12	94 58	2,70
Hindlip	7a-13	87 58	2,52
Hinton on the Green	G-6	P02 40	EG 6
Holdfast	7b-6	85 37	2,35
Hollin	4-19	72 70	21,1
Hollow Court	5-7	97 58	X 2. E 3
Holt	7a-14	82 62	2,7
Homme Castle	4-20	73 61	19,8
Church Honeybourne	6c-5	(P11 44)	10,9
Cow Honeybourne	G-7	(P11 43)	EG 7
Horton	2-17	87 66	26,11
Houndsfield	1-14	(P08 76)	1,1a
Huddington	7a-15	94 57	2,57
Hurcott	3-8	85 77	1,2
Martin Hussingtree	8c-1	88 60	8,12
Church Icomb (Glos.)	7f-7	P21 22	2,41
Ildeberga (Glos.)	7f-8	(P23 32)	(10,12)
Inkberrow	5-8	P01 57	2,16. 3,3
Ipsley	W-2	P06 65	EW 1
Kemerton	G-8	94 37	EG 3;9-10
Kempsey	7a-16	85 49	2,2
Kenswick	7a-17	79 58	2,9
Kidderminster	3-9	83 76	1,2

	Map	Grid	Text
Kingswinford (Staffs.)	ST-2	88 88	1,4;(5-6)
Kington	5-9	99 55	18,4
Kinver (Staffs.)	ST-3	84 83	1,4
Knighton on Teme	4-21	63 69	2,85
Knightwick	7a-18	73 55	2,67
Kyre	4-22	62 63	3,2. 19,4; 7. E 35
Laugherne	7a-19	82 56	2,11;13
Lea Green	1-15	(P09 75)	1,1a
Leigh	8d-14	78 53	9,5a-5b
Ab Lench	7d-8	P01 51	2,17
Atch Lench	5-10	P03 50	2,76. 10,14
Church Lench	5-11	P02 51	10,16
Rous Lench	7d-9	P01 53	2,18
Sheriffs Lench	5-12	P01 49	11,2
Lenchwick	6c-6	P03 47	10,3
Leopard, see Lyppard			
'Lindon'	4-23	(75 71)	15,2
'Lindsworth' (Warks.)	1-16	(P06 79)	1,1a
Littleton	6c-7	P07 46	10,5;8
Longdon (Warks.)	7f-9	P22 41	2,47
Longdon (nr. Upton on Severn)	8f-1	83 36	8,9. (E 4)
Lutley	2-18	94 83	13,1
Lyppard	7a-20	87 55	2,71
Malvern Chase	7b-7	77 40	(2,31)
Mamble	4-24	68 71	16,2
Broad Marston	G-9	P14 46	EG 15
Martin Hussingtree, see Hussingtree			
Martley	4-25	75 59	18,5. 21,4. X 3. E 1
Mathon (Herefords.)	4-26	73 45	9,6
'Middlewich'	2-19	(89 63)	1,3a
Mitton (in Bredon)	7c-2	90 34	2,23
Mitton (in Stourport on Severn)	3-10	81 72	1,2
Moor (near Pershore)	7d-10	97 47	2,19
Moor (in Rock), see Rockmoor			
Abbots Morton	5-13	P02 55	10,13
Morton Underhill	5-14	P01 59	17,1
Moseley (Warks.)	1-17	P07 83	1,1a
Mucknell	7a-21	90 51	2,3
Nafford	8d-15	94 41	8,25
Naunton Beauchamp	8d-16	96 52	8,16
Netherton	7d-11	99 41	2,72
Northfield (Warks.)	1-18	P02 79	23,2
Northwick	7a-22	85 57	2,48
Norton (near Evesham)	6c-8	P04 47	10,3
Bredons Norton	7c-3	93 39	2,29
Kings Norton (Warks.)	1-19	P05 78	1,1a
Oddingley	7a-23	90 59	2,56

	Map	Grid	Text
Offenham	6c-9	P05 46	10,5
Offerton	7a-24	89 58	2,52
Oldberrow (Warks.)	6b-1	P12 66	10,4
Oldington	3-11	81 73	1,2
Ombersley	6a-1	84 63	10,10
Orleton	4-27	69 67	20,5
'Osmerley'	1-—	— —	26,2
Overbury	7d-12	95 37	2,62
Ovretone	1-—	— —	2,84
Pebworth	G-10	P12 46	EG 11;14
Pedmore	2-20	91 82	23,12
Pendock	7e-1	78 32	2,26;62
Pensham	8d-17	94 44	8,3
Peopleton	8d-18	93 50	8,21-22
'Perry'	7a-25	(86 54)	2,61
Pershore	8d-19	94 45	8,1;28. 9,1a
Phepson	5-15	94 59	2,77
North Piddle	8d-20	96 54	8,15;18
Wyre Piddle	7d-13	96 47	2,19. (9,1a)
Pirton	8d-21	88 47	8,19
Powick	8d-22	83 51	8,10
Pull Court	7b-8	(86 36)	E 4
Queenhill	7b-9	86 36	2,36. E 5
'Radley'	7a-26	(85 53)	2,58
Redmarley (in Great Witley)	4-28	75 66	15,10. 20,2
Redmarley d'Abitot (Glos.)	7e-2	75 31	2,25
Rednal (Warks.)	1-20	P00 76	1,1a
Ribbesford	4-29	78 74	1,2
Ripple	7b-10	87 37	2,31
Rochford	H-1	62 68	EH 2-3
Rockmoor	4-30	72 71	15,5;7
Rushock	3-12	88 71	26,6
Salwarpe	2-21	87 62	5,1. 14,2
Lower Sapey	4-31	69 60	19,9
Sedgeberrow	7d-14	P02 38	2,63
Selly Oak (Warks.)	1-21	P03 82	23,1;5
Shell	5-16	95 59	18,3
Shelsley	4-32	72 63	15,11. 19,6
Shipston on Stour (Warks.)	7f-10	P25 40	2,64
'Shurvenhill'	1-22	(93 73)	1,1a
Upton Snodsbury	8d-23	94 54	8,11
Sodington	4-33	69 71	16,1
Spetchley	7a-27	89 53	2,70
Stanford on Teme	4-34	70 65	18,2. 19,5
Stildon	4-35	71 69	21,2
Stockton on Teme	4-36	71 67	18,1
Stoke Bliss	H-2	65 62	EH 4
Stoke Prior	1-23	94 67	2,81
Severn Stoke	8d-24	85 44	8,26
Stone	3-13	85 75	26,7
Stoulton	7a-28	90 49	2,3
Suckley	4-37	72 51	1,1b. X 3 E 7

Places not named (main entries only are included, not subdivisions of a named holding).

Holdings or Sub-Holdings not named in DB but named in Evesham or Worcester material in Appendices IV and V (References are to the notes). For other parts of starred places, see Index of Places above.

MAPS AND MAP KEYS

Places are mapped in their 1086 Hundreds as evidenced in the text. On the maps and in the map keys separated parts of Hundreds are distinguished by letters (a, b, c etc.) after the Hundred figure. Where possible, single detached places are directed by an arrow to the main body of their Hundred and numbered with it. Such detachments are starred in the map keys. Apart from dots, the following symbols indicate places on the map:

⊕ a place in Oswaldslow Hundred (Church of Worcester);

□ a place belonging to Pershore Church in the combined Hundred of 'Pershore and Westminster';

■ a place belonging to Westminster Church in the same combined Hundred;

◪ a place divided between Pershore and Westminster Churches;

○ a place in another County in 1086, later transferred to Worcestershire.

County names in brackets after a place-name in the map keys are those of the modern (pre-April 1974) county to which places in the Domesday county of Worcester were later transferred.

Hundred boundaries and the County boundary are based on the EPNS map with minor alterations.

The County boundary is marked on the map by thick lines, continuous for 1086, broken where uncertain, dotted for the pre-1974 modern boundary; Hundred boundaries are marked by thin lines, broken where uncertain. All detachments of Worcestershire, except Dudley in the extreme north of the County, had been absorbed into neighbouring counties by 1974.

National Grid 10-kilometre squares are shown on the map borders. Each four-figure square covers one square kilometre, or 247 acres, approximately 2 hides, at 120 acres to the hide.

In the Hundred of 'Pershore and Westminster' places marked (P) were held by Pershore Church; those marked (W) by Westminster Church. Villages marked (WP) were divided between the two Churches.

WORCESTERSHIRE NORTH WESTERN HUNDREDS

3 Cresslau Hundred
1 Chaddesley Corbett
2 Doverdale
3 Dunclent
4 Elmley Lovett
5 Franche
6 Habberley
7 Hartlebury
8 Hurcott
9 Kidderminster
10 Mitton
11 Oldington
12 Rushock
13 Stone
14 Sutton
15 Trimpley
16 Wannerton
17 Wolverley
18 Wribbenhall
Unmapped
Bristitune
Fastochesfelde
Hatete
Suduuale
Teulesberge

4 Doddingtree Hundred
1 Abberley
2 Acton Beauchamp (Herefords.)
3 Alton
4 Astley
5 'Bastwood'
6 Bayton
7 Berrington
8 Bockleton
9 Carton
10 Clifton on Teme
11 Conningswick
12 Doddenham
13 Eardiston
14 Eastham
15 *Edvin Loach (Herefords.)
16 Glasshampton
17 Hanley
18 Hillhampton
19 Hollin
20 Homme Castle
21 Knighton on Teme
22 Kyre
23 'Lindon'
24 Mamble
25 Martley
26 *Mathon (Herefords.)
27 Orleton
28 Redmarley
29 Ribbesford
30 Rockmoor
31 Lower Sapey
32 Shelsley
33 Sodington
34 Stanford on Teme
35 Stildon
36 Stockton on Teme
37 Suckley
38 Tenbury Wells
39 Worsley
Unmapped
Broc
Halac

6 Fishborough Hundred
6a
1 Ombersley
2 *Worcester

Places later in Worcestershire †
H In Herefordshire in 1086
1 +Rochford
2 +Stoke Bliss

St In Staffordshire in 1086
1 Upper Arley
2 Kingswinford (Staffs.)
3 Kinver (Staffs.)

* Detachments

† *Except St 2-3. See 1,4 note.*
\+ *Detachments of another County within Worcestershire in 1086*

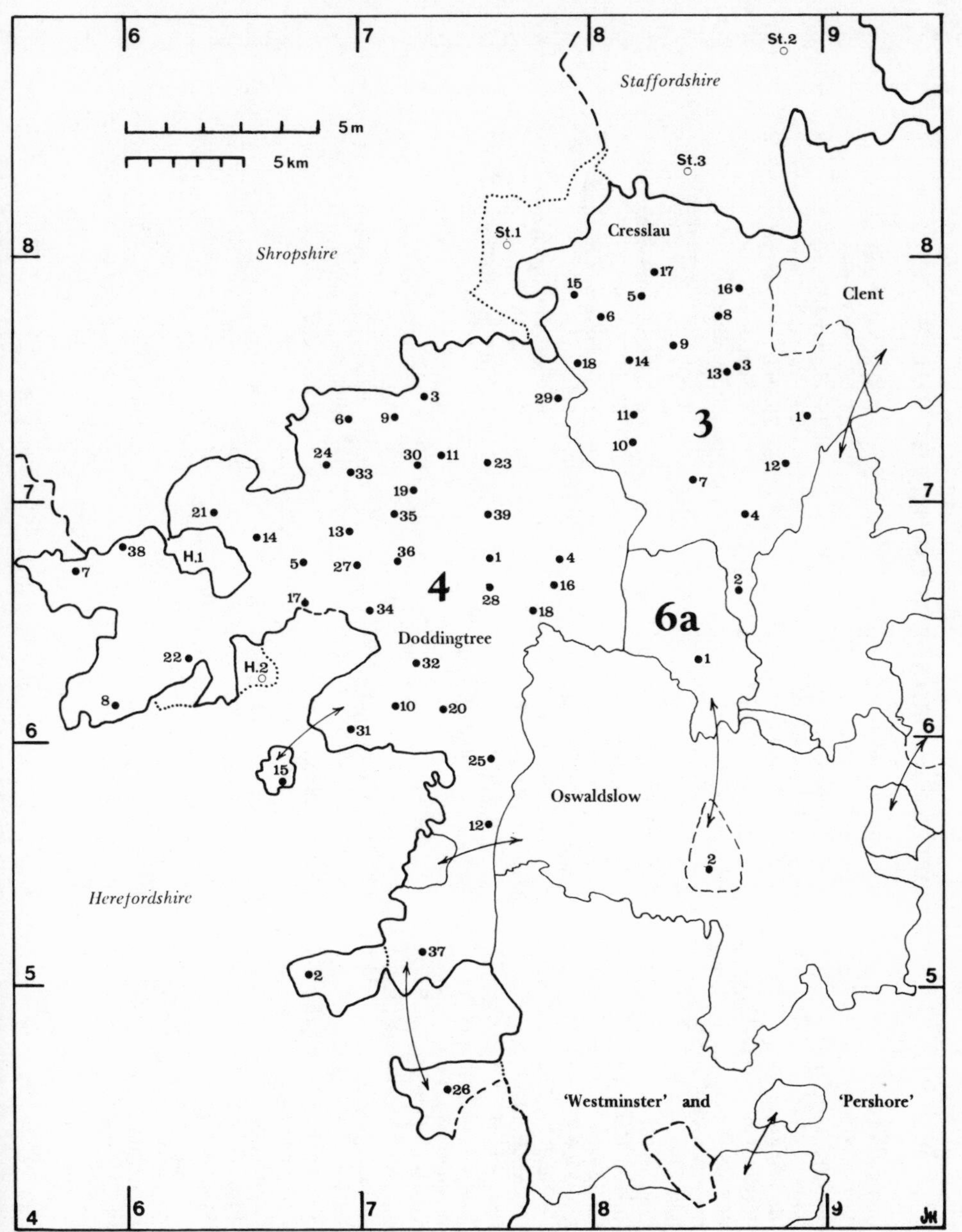
Staffordshire
Shropshire
Herefordshire
5 m
5 km
St.1
St.2
St.3
H.1
H.2
Cresslau
Clent
Doddingtree
Oswaldslow
'Westminster' and
'Pershore'
3
4
6a
JH

WORCESTERSHIRE NORTH EASTERN HUNDREDS

1 Came Hundred
1 Alvechurch
2 Ashborough
3 Aston Fields
4 'Baddington'
5 Bartley Green (Warks.)
6 Bentley
7 Bromsgrove
8 Burcot
9 Chadwick
10 Cofton Hackett
11 Fockbury
12 Frankley
13 Grafton
14 Houndsfield
15 Lea Green
16 'Lindsworth' (Warks.)
17 Moseley (Warks.)
18 Northfield (Warks.)
19 Kings Norton (Warks.)
20 Rednal (Warks.)
21 Selly Oak (Warks.)
22 'Shurvenhill'
23 Stoke Prior
24 Tardebigge
25 'Tessall' (Warks.)
26 Timberhanger
27 Tutnall
28 'Tynsall'
29 Wast Hills
30 'Willingwick'
31 Woodcote Green
32 Wythall
33 Wythwood
Unmapped
'Comble'
'Osmerley'
Ovretone
'Tonge'

2 Clent Hundred
1 Belbroughton
2 Bell Hall
3 Bellington
4 Chawson
5 Churchill
6 Clent
7 Cooksey Green
8 Cradley
9 Droitwich
10 *Dudley
11 Elmbridge
12 Hadzor
13 Hagley
14 Halesowen
15 Hampton Lovett
16 Helpridge
17 Horton
18 Lutley
19 'Middlewich'
20 Pedmore
21 Salwarpe
22 Old Swinford
23 Upton Warren
24 'Upwich'
25 Warley
26 Witton in Droitwich
27 Wychbold
Unmapped
'Thickenappletree'

6 Fishborough Hundred
6b
1 Oldberrow (Warks.)

8 Pershore and Westminster Hundred
8a
1 Yardley (Warks.) (P)

8b
1 Beoley (P)

Places later in Worcestershire
W In Warwickshire in 1086
2 Ipsley

* Detachments

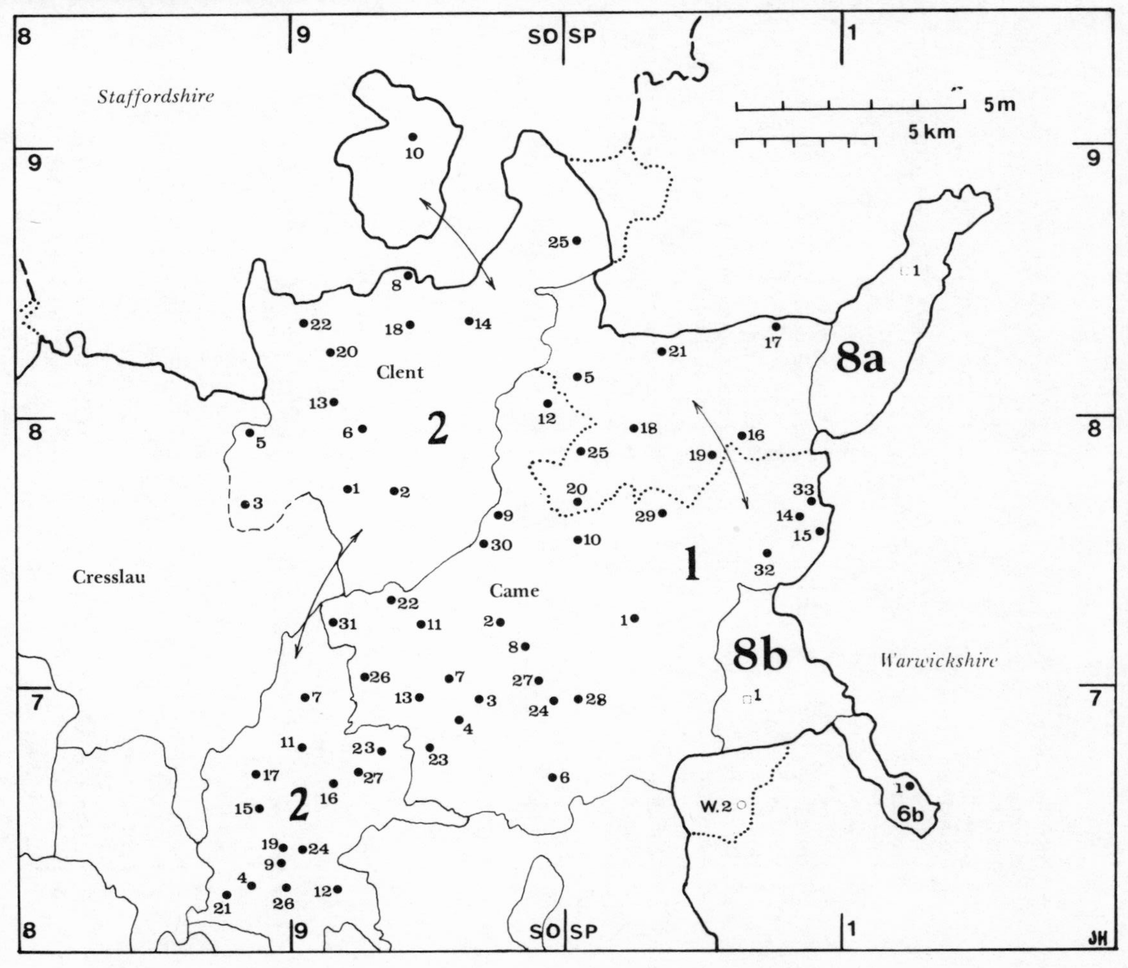

Staffordshire
Warwickshire
Clent
Came
Cresslau
2
1
8a
8b
6b
W.2
SO SP
5 m
5 km
JH

WORCESTERSHIRE SOUTH WESTERN HUNDREDS

7 **Oswaldslow Hundred**
7a
1 White Ladies Aston
2 *Bradley Green
3 Bredicot
4 Broadwas
5 Churchill
6 Cotheridge
7 Cudley
8 Eastbury
9 Greenhill
10 Grimley
11 Hallow
12 Himbleton
13 Hindlip
14 Holt
15 Huddington
16 Kempsey
17 Kenswick
18 *Knightwick
19 Laugherne
20 Lyppard
21 Mucknell
22 Northwick
23 Oddingley
24 Offerton
25 'Perry'
26 'Radley'
27 Spetchley
28 Stoulton
29 Tibberton
30 Warndon
31 Whittington
32 Wick Episcopi
33 Little Witley
34 Wolverton
Unmapped
'Clopton'
7b
1 Barley
2 Bushley
3 Earls Croome
4 Hill Croome
5 *Croome d'Abitot
6 Holdfast
7 Malvern Chase

* Detachments

8 Pull Court
9 Queenhill
10 Ripple
11 Upton on Severn
7e
1 Pendock
2 Redmarley d'Abitot (Glos.)

8 **Pershore and Westminster Hundred**
8c
1 Martin Hussingtree (W)
8d
1 Abberton (P)
2 Besford (W)
3 Birlingham (W)
4 Bransford (P)
5 Bricklehampton (W)
6 Drakes Broughton (P)
7 Broughton Hackett (W)
8 Chivington (P)
9 Comberton (WP)
10 Defford (W)
11 *Dormston (W)
12 Eckington (W)
13 Grafton Flyford (W)
14 Leigh (P)
15 Nafford (W)
16 Naunton Beauchamp (W)
17 Pensham (W)
18 Peopleton (W)
19 Pershore (WP)
20 North Piddle (W)
21 Pirton (W)
22 Powick (W)
23 Upton Snodsbury (W)
24 Severn Stoke (W)
25 Wadborough (P)
26 Wick (WP)
8f
1 Longdon (W)
8h
1 Eldersfield (W)

Places later in Worcestershire
G In Gloucestershire in 1086
5 +Hanley Castle
Unmapped
'Baldenhall'

\+ *Detachments of another County within Worcestershire in 1086*

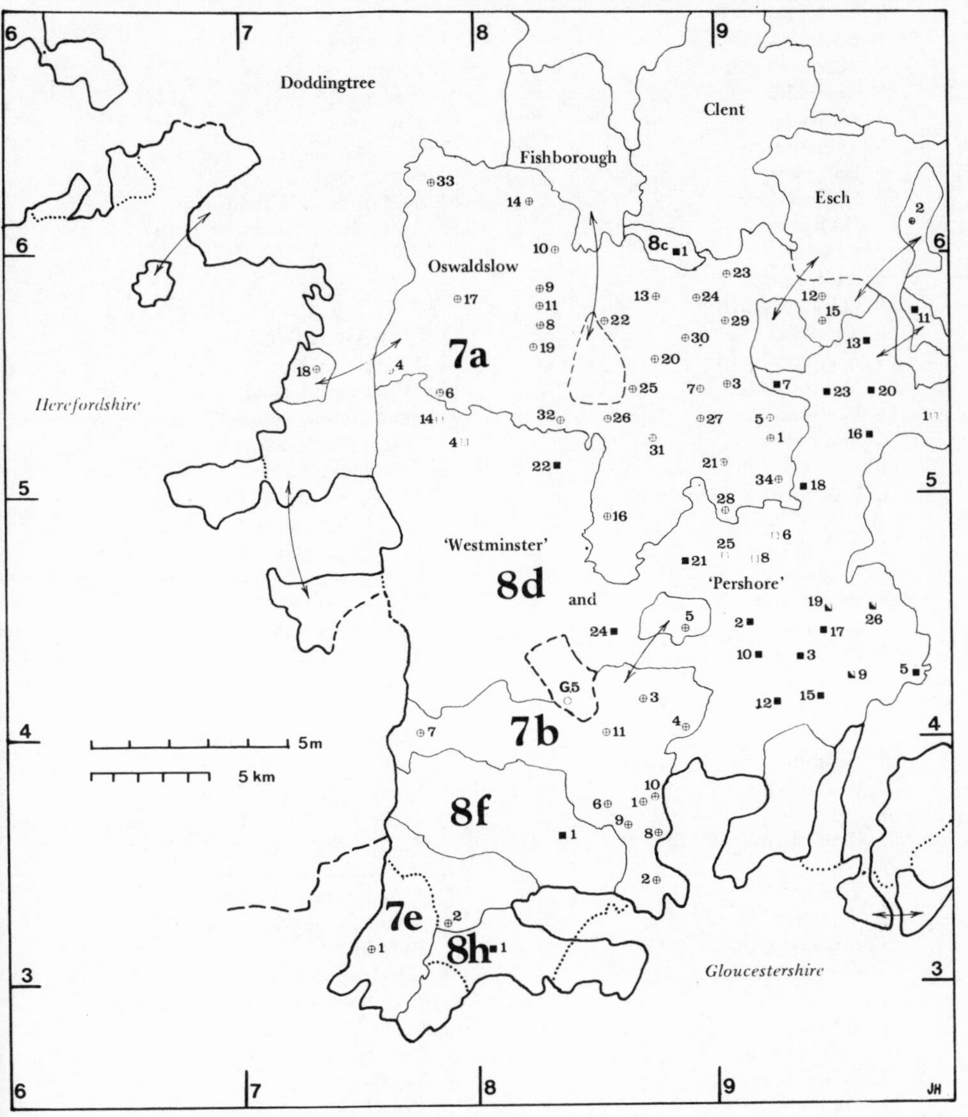
Doddingtree
Clent
Fishborough
Esch
Oswaldslow
7a
Herefordshire
'Westminster'
8d
and
'Pershore'
8c
7b
8f
7e
8h
Gloucestershire
5m
5 km
JH

WORCESTERSHIRE SOUTH EASTERN HUNDREDS

5 Esch Hundred
1 Bevington (Warks.)
2 *Cleeve Prior
3 Cookhill
4 *Crowle
5 Feckenham
6 Hanbury
7 Hollow Court
8 Inkberrow
9 Kington
10 Atch Lench
11 Church Lench
12 Sheriffs Lench
13 Abbots Morton
14 Morton Underhill
15 Phepson
16 Shell

6 Fishborough Hundred
6c
1 Aldington
2 Badsey
3 Bretforton
4 Evesham
5 Church Honeybourne
6 Lenchwick
7 Littleton
8 Norton
9 Offenham
10 Wickhamford

7 Oswaldslow Hundred
7c
1 Bredon
2 Mitton
3 Bredons Norton
4 Westmancote
7d
1 Bengeworth
2 Bishampton
3 Cropthorne
4 Fladbury
5 Hampton
6 *Harvington
7 Hill
8 Ab Lench
9 Rous Lench
10 Moor
11 Netherton
12 Overbury
13 Wyre Piddle
14 Sedgeberrow
15 Teddington (Glos.)
16 Little Washbourne (Glos.)
Unmapped
Wiburgestoke
7f
1 *Blackwell (Warks.)
2 Blockley (Glos.)
3 *Cutsdean (Glos.)
4 *Daylesford (Glos.)
5 Ditchford (Glos.)
6 *Evenlode (Glos.)
7 *Church Icomb (Glos.)
8 **Ildeberga* (Glos.)
9 *Longdon (Warks.)
10 *Shipston on Stour (Warks.)
11 *Tidmington (Warks.)
12 *Tredington (Warks.)

8 Pershore and Westminster Hundred
8e
1 Alderminster (Warks.) (P)
8g
1 Broadway (P)

Places later in Worcestershire
G In Gloucestershire in 1086
1 Ashton under Hill
2 Aston Somerville
3 Beckford
4 Childswickham
[5 +Hanley Castle] (see SW map)
6 Hinton on the Green
7 Cow Honeybourne
8 Kemerton
9 Broad Marston
10 Pebworth
11 Ullington

W In Warwickshire in 1086
1 Bickmarsh

* Detachments
\+ *Detachments of another County within Worcestershire in 1086*

Esch
5
Warwickshire
Oswaldslow
Fishborough
6c
'Pershore'
7d
7c
8e
8g
7f
Oswaldslow
Gloucestershire
5 m
5 km
SO SP
JM

SYSTEMS OF REFERENCE TO DOMESDAY BOOK

The manuscript is divided into numbered chapters, and the chapters into sections, usually marked by large initials and red ink. Farley, however, did not number the sections. References have therefore been inexact, by folio numbers, which cannot be closer than an entire page or column. Moreover, half a dozen different ways of referring to the same column have been devised. In 1816 Ellis used three separate systems in his indices; (i) on pages i-cvii; 435-518; 537-570; (ii) on pages 1-144; (iii) on pages 145-433 and 519-535. Other systems have since come into use, notably that used by Vinogradoff, here followed. This edition numbers the sections, the normal practicable form of close reference; but since all discussion of Domesday for three hundred years has been obliged to refer to page or column, a comparative table will help to locate references given. The five columns below give Vinogradoff's notation, Ellis' three systems, and that employed by Welldon Finn and others. Maitland, Stenton, Darby and others have usually followed Ellis (i).

Vinogradoff	*Ellis (i)*	*Ellis (ii)*	*Ellis (iii)*	*Finn*
152 a	152	152a	152	152ai
152 b	152	152 a	152.2	152a2
152 c	152 b	152 b	152 b	152bi
152 d	152 b	152 b	152 b2	152b2

In Worcestershire, the relation between the Vinogradoff column notation, here followed, and the chapters and sections is:

172	a	C 1-5.		Landholders
	b	1,1	-	1,3a
	c	1,3b	-	2,1
	d	2,2	-	2,15
173	a	2,15	-	2,28
	b	2,29	-	2,45
	c	2,45	-	2,59
	d	2,60	-	2,70
174	a	2,71	-	2,80
	b	2,81	-	7,1
	c	8,1	-	8,9b
	d	8,9c	-	8,14
175	a	8,15	-	8,25
	b	8,26	-	9,4
	c	9,4	-	10,4
	d	10,5	-	10,17
176	a	11,1	-	15,3. 12,2
	b	15,4	-	15,14
	c	16,1	-	19,2. 18,6
	d	19,2	-	20,3. 19,14
177	a	20,3	-	23,1
	b	23,2	-	23,14
	c	24,1	-	26,8
	d	26,9	-	27,1
178a	a	28,1	-	X 3
	b	blank column		
	c	blank column		
	d	blank column		

TECHNICAL TERMS

Many words meaning measurements have to be transliterated. But translation may not dodge other problems by the use of obsolete or made-up words which do not exist in modern English. The translations here used are given in italics. They cannot be exact; they aim at the nearest modern equivalent.

BEREWIC. An outlying place, attached to a manor. *outlier*
BORDARIUS. Cultivator of inferior status, usually with a little land. *smallholder*
BOVARIUS. A man who looked after the plough-oxen (1,1c note). *ploughman*
CARUCA. A plough, with the oxen that pulled it, usually reckoned as 8. *plough*
COLIBERTUS. A continental term rendering Old English *(ge)bur*, (8,7 note), a freedman, sometimes holding land and ploughs. *freedman*
COTARIUS, COTMANNUS. Inhabitant of a *cote*, 'cottage'; often without land, distinct from one another (see 8,7 note). Respectively *cottager, cottage-man*
DOMINICUS. Belonging to a lord or lordship. *the lord's* or *lordship*
DOMINIUM. The mastery or dominion of a lord (*dominus*); including ploughs, land, men, villages, etc., reserved for the lord's use; often concentrated in a *home farm* or *demesne*, a 'Manor Farm' or 'Lordship Farm'. *lordship*
FEUDUM. Continental variant of *feuum*, not used in England before 1066; either a landholder's holding, or land held by special grant. *Holding*
FIRMA. Old English *feorm*, provisions due to the King or lord; a fixed sum paid in place of these and of other miscellaneous dues. *revenue*
GELDUM. The principal royal tax, originally levied during the Danish wars, normally at an equal number of pence on each *hide* of land. *tax*
HIDA. A unit of land measurement, generally reckoned at 120 acres, but often different in practice; a measure of tax liability, often differing in number from the hides actually cultivated; see note C 1. *hide*
HUNDRED. A district within a Shire, whose assembly of notables and village representatives usually met about once a month. *Hundred*
LEUGA, LEUUA, LEUUEDE. A measure of length, usually of woodland, generally reckoned at a mile and a half, possibly shorter (see 1,1c note). *league*
M. Marginal abbreviation for *manerium*, 'manor'. *M*
MITTA. A 'mit' or measure, usually of salt, generally reckoned at 8 bushels (1,1a note). *measure*
PRAEPOSITUS, PRAEFECTUS. Old English *gerefa*, a royal officer. *reeve*
QUARENTINA. A quarter of a virgate (see 1,1c note). *furlong*
RADMAN, RADCHENISTRE. A sub-group of the *liberi homines* 'free men', of higher status than a villager; originally a man who rode with messages or on escort-duty (see 1,1c note). Respectively *rider, riding man*
rq. Marginal abbreviation for *require*, 'enquire', occurring when the scribe has omitted some information.
RUSTICUS. Probably a less prosperous villager (2,57 note). *countryman*
SACA German *Sache*, English *sake*, Latin *causa*, 'affair', 'lawsuit'; the fullest authority normally exercised by a lord. *full jurisdiction*
SEXTARIUM. A liquid or dry measure of uncertain size, reckoned at 32 oz. for honey (see 2,8 note). *sester*
SOCA. 'Soke', from Old English *socn*, 'seeking', comparable with Latin *quaestio*. Jurisdiction, with the right to receive fines and other dues; also the district in which such *soca* was exercised. *jurisdiction*
STICHA. A measure, usually of eels, at 25 to the *sticha*. *stick*
SUMMA. A dry measure, mainly of salt, corn and fish (E 10 note). *packload*
TAINUS, TEGNUS. Person holding land from the King by special grant; formerly used of the King's ministers and military companions. *thane*
T.R.E. *tempore regis Edwardi*, in King Edward's time. *before 1066*
VILLA. Translating Old English *tun*, 'town'. The later distinction between a small *village* and a large *town* was not yet in use in 1066. *village* or *town*
VILLANUS. Member of a *villa*, usually with more land than a *bordarius*. *villager*
VIRGATA. A fraction of a hide, usually a quarter, notionally 30 acres. *virgate*

ADDITIONS AND CORRECTIONS

which have been noted in earlier volumes by County Editors as the series has progressed, and by readers. References are to chapter, section and line.

BERKSHIRE

Notes: 1,31 BOOR. *for* on two occasions, both in Hampshire, where *vel coliberti* is interlined *read* on three occasions (Hants. 1,10;23 and Worcs. 8,10a). 1,39 VALUE ... *for* Farler *read* Farley. Systems of Reference: line 2 *for* Ferley *read* Farley.

CORNWALL

Exon. Introduction left-hand page *add* (The King holds) above BLISLAND. Left margin *for* 01.*b*. *read* 101.*b*. Exon. Introduction right-hand page third paragraph penultimate line *for* working *read* wording. 5,4,19 line 1 *Clunewic/Gluinawit* Mr. W. M. M. Picken points out that this is certainly to be equated with Kilminworth (SX 23 53), also in Westwivelshire Hundred ('F'). *Delete* ?Clinnick. OJP. Technical Terms: DOMINIUM *for* mastery or dominium *read* mastery or dominion.

OXFORDSHIRE

B 3 *for* 20 pence *read* 20 (pence). 1,7b line 6 *for* R. d'Oilly *read* R(obert) d'Oilly. 7,3 line 5 *for* pasture as much *read* pasture, as many. Notes: Abbreviations: *add* Davis *Regesta* . . . H. W. C. Davis (ed.) *Regesta Regum Anglo-Normannorum* vol. i (1913). Dugdale MA . . . W. Dugdale *Monasticon Anglicanum*, 6 vols. in 8, London 1817-30. Notes: B 8 TAYNTON *for* 'I, Baldwin *read* 'I, Baldwin. 1,6 BOOR *for* on two occasions, both in Hampshire, where *vel coliberti* is interlined *read* on three occasions (Hants. 1,10;23 and Worcs. 8,10a). 1,7 R(OBERT) D'OILLY *for* Sherrif *read* Sheriff. 6,1 REVENUE *for* emphasis *read* emphasises. 6,6 COLUMBAN *for* has been *read* had been. 59 EARL WILLIAM *for* B 5 note *read* B 7 note. B 9 Jernio *read* Jeruius. 58,16 Gernio *read* Geruius. Notes: B 9 JERNIO, also GERNIO 58,16, both indexed GERNIO. There is no such pers. n. as *Gernio*. The spellings probably represent *n* by mistake for *u* or *v*, and *o* by mistake for the *-us* abbreviation; thus *Jeruius*, *Geruius*, for OG *Gerwig*, Forssner 111, cf. notes to Glos. 76,1, Hants. 1,37. Notes: 58,16 GERNIO, see B 9 JERNIO. Persons Index: *for* Goderun *read* Godrun. Places Index: to *Elsewhere in Britain* should be added all places in Berks., Bucks. and Worcs. listed in main index. Wiltshire *delete* Winchcombe. Gloucestershire *add* Winchcombe.

SOMERSET

5,24 line 2 *add* Land for 6,17 line 3 the figure is 6½ hides. 9,4 line 1 *for* it paid for 5 *read* it paid tax for 5. 19,64 line 6 *read* 25 goats. 19,73 line 1 *delete* it 40,1 line 5 *read* woodland 1 league. Bibliography and Abbreviations: (p. 291) under *Regesta for* Davies *read* Davis. Notes: p. 298 5,43 HE COULD GO ... *for* protecter *read* protector. p. 300 for 8,36 41 read 8,36-41. Appendix 1 p. 373 line 3 *insert* stop after (25). p. 378 Note 25 *for* 8,34 note *read* 8,35 note. Technical terms: DOMINIUM *for* mastery or dominium *read* mastery or dominion.

WARWICKSHIRE

11,3 line 1 *read* In lordship 1; B 2 line 9 *for* Gilbert [of] Bouille *read* Gilbert [of] Bouillé. Textual notes: 16,5-6 *add* Farley does not print these figures. They are here supplied from the MS. Notes: B 2 *for* GILBERT OF BOUILLE *read* GILBERT OF BOUILLÉ. 3,4 ALDRED *for* 1016-1061 *read* 1047-1061. Persons Index: *for* Gilbert of Bouille *read* Gilbert of Bouillé. Harold son of Earl Ralph *delete* B 2 reference *add* new entry Harold B 2. *Places outside Britain for* Bouille *read* Bouillé. Map and Places Index: Fillongley C 38 *delete* southernmost dot and number. Lindsworth *read* 'Lindsworth' Grid ref. 0*6* 79. Northfield Grid ref. read 0*2* 79. Tessall read 'Tessall' Grid ref. 0*0* 78.

WILTSHIRE

1,1 *indent* line 10. 7,2 line 1 *add* stop after Abbot. 8,7 line 10 *add* stop after 6 slaves. 13,8 line 1 *add* stop after 10 hides. Abbreviations: PNDB *for* Uppdala *read* Uppsala. Notes: 1,3 THANELANDS line 3 *read* See Finn pp. 28-9; 138-9. *for* 1,18 TITHE *read* 1,19 TITHE. 12,6 *for* elswhere *read* elsewhere. 13,3 6 OXEN *for* 28,20 note below *read* 28,10 note below. *Add* 18,2 LATTON and EYSEY. For the grant by King William of these lands to Reinbald, see C. D. Ross (ed.) *The Cartulary of Cirencester Abbey* no. 26. 24,13 *for* entry. *read* entry, 45,2 ON LEASE FROM *for* p'restū *read* p'prestū. 51 THIS CHAPTER *delete* second sentence. Places Notes: *add* at 18,2 LATTON and EYSEY. A further hide, forming with these 9 hides a 10-hide manor, was probably in Gloucestershire, see DB Gloucs. 71,1 note. *Add* at 45,2 1 HIDE, LESS ½ VIRGATE ... CHIPPENHAM. This land was possibly at Kingswood near Wotton under Edge which remained a detached outlier of Wiltshire in Gloucestershire until 1844, see DB Gloucs. E 16 note. Technical terms: TRE *insert* gap between *before* and *1066*. DOMINIUM *for* mastery or dominium *read* mastery or dominion.